Gail Sheehy's
#1
Bestseller
PASSAGES

Men and women continue growing up adult from 18 to 50. There are predictable crises at each step. The steps are the same for both sexes but the developmental rhythms are not. Understanding this, we can use each crisis to stretch to our full potential, instead of holding ourselves or our partners to blame.

"*Passages* shakes you up, shakes you out, and leaves you shaking hands with yourself."
—Shana Alexander

"A lively, passionate and readable message to the present generation in middle life. *Passages* shows that there is a pattern in our lives, a pattern of adult developmental stages, which once recognized can be managed."
—Margaret Mead

"A book about how not to waste the only life you have . . . It has lit a fire under me . . . It's dynamite."
—Mary Ellin Barrett

PASSAGES
IS YOUR LIFE STORY.
You'll recognize yourself, your friends, and your lovers.

"Provokes the same recognition that we experience in a good novel . . . Her research is thorough and imaginative . . . irresistibly invites the reader to join in."

—The New York Times Book Review

NEW INSIGHTS ON THE TWENTIES, THE THIRTIES, THE FORTIES, AND BEYOND.
Mid-Life Crisis: Best Chance for Couples to Grow Up
The Sexual Diamond: Facing the Facts of the Male and Female Sexual Life Cycles

AMERICA'S #1 BESTSELLER BY GAIL SHEEHY

"Extraordinarily good reading . . . 115 case histories . . . Intimate, always intelligent."

—Publishers Weekly

PASSAGES

#1
Bestseller

"A stunning accomplishment . . . The hope, wit and demythification of adulthood that permeates Sheehy's book makes *Passages* a work of revelation."

—Front page, *Washington Post Book World*

"*Passages* is an antidote to future shock—and few adults will read it without glimpsing themselves in its pages."

—*Glamour*

"If you read *Passages* you will be in less danger of living the unexamined life that Socrates decried."

—*The New York Times*

"Even the periods of painful crises are viewed as merely the opportunity for creative change . . . Every seven years or so, I intend to read this book. So should you."

—*Newsday*

PASSAGES

Predictable Crises
of Adult Life

GAIL SHEEHY

ISBN 0-553-20138-7

Published simultaneously in the United States and Canada.

Bantam Books are published by Bantam Books, Inc. Its trademark, consisting of the words "Bantam Books" and the portrayal of a bantam, is Registered in U.S. Patent and Trademark Office and in other countries. Marca Registrada. Bantam Books, Inc., 666 Fifth Avenue, New York, New York 10103.

PRINTED IN THE UNITED STATES OF AMERICA

PASSAGES: PREDICTABLE CRISES OF ADULT LIFE

*A Bantam Book | published by arrangement with
E. P. Dutton & Company, Inc.*

PRINTING HISTORY

*E. P. Dutton edition published May 1976
15 printings through March 1977*

*A selection of the Literary Guild, May 1976; Macmillan Book
Club, September 1976; and Psychology Today Book Club,
September 1976*

Portions of this book previously appeared in:
BRIDES' MAGAZINE, SKY MAGAZINE, FAMILY CIRCLE, THE
WHARTON MAGAZINE, BOOK DIGEST, GLAMOUR MAGAZINE,
MCCALL'S MAGAZINE, NEW YORK MAGAZINE, *The Miami
Herald and Field Newspaper Service.*

*Bantam edition | June 1977
25 printings through April 1981*

Grateful acknowledgment is made to the following for permission to reprint published materials: "The Kid," copyright ©
1953, 1970 by Conrad Aiken from the book Collected Poems
by Conrad Aiken, reprinted by permission of Oxford University Press. In Praise of Darkness by Jorge Luis Borges, translated by Norman Thomas di Giovanni, copyright © 1969, 1970,
1971, 1972, 1973, 1974 by Emece Editores S.A. and Norman
Thomas di Giovanni. Published in the United States by E. P.
Dutton & Co., Inc. "Once More, the Round," copyright © 1962
by Beatrice Roethke, administratrix of the estate of Theodore
Roethke, from the book, The Collected Poems of Theodore
Roethke, reprinted by permission of Doubleday & Company,
Inc. "Only You (And You Alone)." Words & Music by Buck
Ram and Ande Rand, TRO—copyright © 1955 by Hollis Music,
Inc., New York, N.Y. Used by permission. Cartoon, copyright
© 1974 by Jules Feiffer, distributed by Field Newspaper Syndicate. Portions of this book previously appeared in NEW YORK
magazine.

PRINTED IN THE UNITED STATES OF AMERICA

34 33 32 31 30 29 28 27 26

To my mother and my father

CONTENTS

CONTENTS

CONTENTS

AUTHOR'S ACKNOWLEDGMENTS

The seed of this book was planted by the late Hal Scharlatt, a fine editor and superb human being who encouraged me to explore the adult condition without haste. Upon his untimely death, Jack Macrae stepped forward. Beyond hundreds of hours of his wise editorial counsel, he brought to the personality of the book his special qualities of even temperament and taste.

Flesh was given the book by all those who took the time and courage to contribute their life stories. They cannot be acknowledged by name. I can only hope that I have done them justice.

Those who helped to educate the book were many. I owe a primary professional debt to Daniel J. Levinson, Margaret Mead, and Roger Gould. Special thanks are due Bernice Neugarten, George Vaillant, Margaret Hennig, James M. Donovan, Marylou Lionells, and Carola Mann for the kind offers of their expert knowledge.

I am deeply grateful to Carol Rinzler, Deborah Maine, and Byron Dobell for reading the book in one draft or another and helping me to refine it. Comments were also graciously offered by Jerzy Kosinski, Patricia Henion, and Chota Chudasama.

Many long nights and early mornings found Virginia Dajani typing, Lee Powell transcribing, and Ella Council running off copies of what seemed at times a ramshackle effort that would never take shape. My thanks to them for never saying so, and for their indefatigable good spirits.

Financial assistance was offered by the Alicia Patterson Foundation in the form of a fellowship, when the book was only a cloudy gleam in my eye. The Foundation gave moral support as well, and to its director, Richard H. Nolte, I am more than professionally grateful.

I do not really know how to thank Maura Sheehy and Clay Felker for their endurance. But having cheerfully sacrificed my attention at home and on holidays while I wrote, anguished, rewrote, dreamt, and lived this book, they are truly its godparents.

New York, N.Y.   —GAIL SHEEHY
February 1976

Part One

MYSTERIES OF THE LIFE CYCLE

**What web is this
Of will be, is, and was?**
—JORGE LUIS BORGES

1
MADNESS AND METHOD

Without warning, in the middle of my thirties, I had a breakdown of nerve. It never occurred to me that while winging along in my happiest and most productive stage, all of a sudden simply staying afloat would require a massive exertion of will. Or of some power greater than will.

I was talking to a young boy in Northern Ireland where I was on assignment for a magazine when a bullet blew his face off. That was how fast it all changed. We were standing side by side in the sun, relaxed and triumphant after a civil rights march by the Catholics of Derry. We had been met by soldiers at the barricade; we had vomited tear gas and dragged those dented by rubber bullets back to safety. Now we were surveying the crowd from a balcony.

"How do the paratroopers fire those gas canisters so far?" I asked.

"See them jammin' their rifle butts against the ground?" the boy was saying when the steel slug tore into his mouth and ripped up the bridge of his nose and left of his face nothing but ground bone meal.

"My God," I said dumbly, "they're real bullets." I tried to think how to put his face back together again.

2

Up to that moment in my life I thought everything could be mended.

Below the balcony, British armoured cars began to plow into the crowd. Paratroopers jackknifed out of them with high-velocity rifles. They sprayed us with steel.

The boy without a face fell on top of me. An older man, walloped on the back of the neck with a rifle butt, stumbled up the stairs and collapsed upon us. More dazed bodies pressed in until we were like a human caterpillar, inching on our bellies up the steps of the exposed outdoor staircase.

"Can't we get into somebody's house!" I shouted. We crawled up eight floors but all the doors to the flats were bolted. Someone would have to crawl out on the balcony in open fire to bang on the nearest door. Another boy howled from below: "Jesus, I'm hit!" His voice propelled me across the balcony, trembling but still insulated by some soft-walled childhood sac that I thought provided for my own indestructibility. A moment later, a bullet passed a few feet in front of my nose. I hurled myself against the nearest door and we were all taken in.

The closets of the flat were already filled with mothers and their clinging children. For nearly an hour the bullets kept coming. From the window I saw three boys rise from behind a barricade to make a run for it. They were cut down like dummies in a shooting gallery. So was the priest who followed them, waving a white handkerchief, and the old man who bent to say a prayer over them. A wounded man we had dragged upstairs asked if anyone had seen his younger brother. "Shot dead," was the report.

Something like this had happened to my own brother in Vietnam. But the funeral took place in the bland Connecticut countryside, and I was a few years younger. So neatly had the honor guard tricornered the victim's flag, it looked like a souvenir sofa pillow. People had patted my hands and said, "We know how you must feel." It made me think of the strangers who were always confiding in me that they were scheduled for surgery or "taking it easy" after a heart attack. All I had for their pain were the same words: "I know how you must feel." I had known nothing of the sort.

After the surprise massacre, I was one among trapped thousands cringing in the paper-walled bungalows of the Catholic ghetto. All exits from the city were sealed. Waiting was the only occupation. Waiting for the British army to perform a house-to-house search.

"What will you do if the soldiers come in here firing?" I asked the old woman who was harboring me.

"Lie on me stomach!" she said.

Another woman was using the telephone to confirm the names of the dead. Once upon a time I was a Protestant of strong faith; I tried to pray. But that silly game of childhood kept running through my mind . . . *if you had one wish in the whole world* . . . I decided to call my love. He would say the magic words to make the danger go away.

"Hi! How are you?" His voice was absurdly breezy; he was in bed in New York.

"I'm alive."

"Good, how's the story coming?"

"I almost wasn't alive. Thirteen people were murdered here today."

"Hold on. CBS News is talking about Londonderry right now—"

"It's called Bloody Sunday."

"Can you speak up?"

"It's not over. A mother of fourteen children was just run down by an armoured car."

"Now look, you don't have to get in the front lines. You're doing a story on Irish women, remember that. Just stick with the women and stay out of trouble. Okay, honey?"

From the moment I hung up on that nonconversation, my head went numb. My scalp shrank. Some dark switch was thrown, and a series of weights began to roll across my brain like steel balls. I had squandered my one wish to be saved. The world was negligent. Thirteen could perish, or thirteen thousand, I could perish, and tomorrow it would all be beside the point.

As I joined the people lying on their stomachs, a powerful idea took hold: *No one is with me. No one can keep me safe. There is no one who won't ever leave me alone.*

I had a headache for a year.

When I flew home from Ireland, I couldn't write the story, could not confront the fact of my own mortality. In the end, I dragged out some words and made the deadline but at an ugly price. My short temper lengthened into diatribes against the people closest to me, driving away the only sources of support who might have helped me fight my demons. I broke off with the man who had been sharing my life for four years, fired my secretary, lost my housekeeper, and found myself alone with my daughter Maura, marking time.

As spring came, I hardly knew myself. The root-lessness that had been such a joy in my early thirties, allowing me to burst the ropes of old roles, to be reckless and selfish and focused on stretching my newfound dream, to roam the world on assignments and then to stay up all night typing on caffeine and nicotine—all at once that didn't work anymore.

Some intruder shook me by the psyche and shouted: *Take stock! Half your life has been spent. What about the part of you that wants a home and talks about a second child?* Before I could answer, the intruder pointed to something else I had postponed: *What about the side of you that wants to contribute to the world? Words, books, demonstrations, donations —is this enough? You have been a performer, not a full participant. And now you are 35.*

To be confronted for the first time with the arithmetic of life was, quite simply, terrifying.

It is unusual to find yourself in the middle of a

shooting war, but many of life's accidents can have a similar effect. You play tennis twice a week with a dynamic 38-year-old businessman. In the locker room a silent clot throttles an artery and before he can call for help, a large part of his heart muscle has been strangled. His attack touches his wife, his business associates, and all his friends of a similar age, including you.

Or a distant phone call notifies you that your father or mother has been hospitalized. You carry with you to the bedside a picture of the dynamo you last saw, clearing land or dashing off to the League of Women Voters. In the hospital you see that this dynamo has passed, all at once and incontrovertibly, into the twilight of ill health and helplessness.

As we reach midlife in the middle thirties or early forties, we become susceptible to the idea of our own perishability. If an accident that interrupts our life occurs at this time, our fears of mortality are heightened. We are not prepared for the idea that time can run out on us, or for the startling truth that if we don't hurry to pursue our own definition of a meaningful existence, life can become a repetition of trivial maintenance duties. Nor are we anticipating a major upheaval of the roles and rules that may have comfortably defined us in the first half of life, but that must be reordered around a core of strongly felt personal values in the second.

In normal circumstances, without the blow of a life accident, these issues affiliated with midlife are revealed over a period of years. We have time to adjust. But when they are thrust on us all at once, we cannot immediately accept them. The downside of life comes too hard and fast to incorporate.

In my case, the unanticipated brush with death in Ireland brought the underlying issues of midlife forward in full force.

If I tell you about the week, six months later, if I

report the observable facts—while dashing out the door to catch a plane to Florida to cover the Democratic National Convention, a healthy, divorced career mother finds one of her pet lovebirds dead and bursts into uncontrollable tears—you might say, "This woman was cracking up." Which is precisely what I began to think.

I took the aisle seat in the tail of the plane so that when we crashed, I would be the last one to see the ground.

Flying had always been a joy to me. Plucky one that I was at 30, I had taken to parachuting out of bush planes for sport. It was different now. Whenever I went near a plane I saw a balcony in Northern Ireland. In six months the fear of airplanes had blossomed into a phobia. Every news photo of a crash drew my attention. I would study the pictures in morbid detail. The planes seemed to split at the front; I made it a rule to sit in the tail. From the safety of the entrance canopy I would call in to the pilot, "Have you had experience with instrument landings?" By now I had no shame.

I did have one comfort. The upsets of the first half of my 35th year were vaguely classifiable. I could attach the anxiety to real events. My flight phobia fell under the convenient umbrella of conversion reactions (the process by which a repressed psychic event is converted into another symptom). The sense of uprootedness could be explained by the fact that I'd had four different addresses in the previous two years. All my life-support systems were in flux.

By that July, however, I had put on the brakes. Things appeared to have quieted down. On the contrary, very little was going on near the surface, but no less than everything was shifting below it.

An outburst of weeping over a dead lovebird was the signal. What was wrong with me that I couldn't even keep a lovebird alive? Somehow, I connected this loss to the unexpected departure of my housekeeper.

7

Could I ever replace her? If I couldn't, my own work would have to cease. How would my daughter and I survive?

For the moment Maura was safely installed with her father. Despite our divorce, or perhaps as a result of it, we had the kind of long-running love that transcends pettiness because it is built on a shared conviction. Even in the raggedness of pulling apart, we had agreed that we would know each other forever as the mother and father of a child. Together we had made this contract; it was unalterable; it superseded all others. And so we had come to enjoy the special qualities of respect and friendship that grow out of putting another's well-being first. There was nothing out of the ordinary in Maura's spending a week with her father, but I missed her severely. The power to discriminate between a temporary separation and an absolute ending had abruptly left me. A dark thought took its place: Whatever it was that had ruptured inside me had released a sinister force that threatened to destroy my whole jerry-built world.

On the flight to Miami, no sooner had I single-mindedly willed the 727 to clear Flushing Bay than the intruder was back, rummaging around in my psyche and sniffing at the value of my resources: *You've done some good work, but what does it really add up to?*

Too nervous to eat, what I didn't know was that a combat between two opposing medications had begun in my abdominal zone. One had been prescribed for a lingering intestinal flu; the other, by a different doctor, after the Ireland trauma. Onto the angrily separating oils and waters of that digestive system, I threw cognac and champagne.

Once inside the hotel room, to be mindlessly mechanical seemed the best idea. Fill the closets. Clear a work space. Set up, as they say, a new "home base." Open the suitcase. But right there, opening my suitcase: paralysis. I had thrown in on top of a white skirt a new pair of red leather sandals. They had bled

8

into the skirt with a blazing stain. I shrieked. Suddenly I couldn't coerce myself into making schedules, taking phone messages, meeting deadlines. Which story was I writing for whom anyway? Unknown to me, the clash of medications had begun to register. The dizziness, the gouging stomach cramps. My heart lurched into manic rhythms and began leaping around inside my chest like a frog in a jar.

The room was on the twenty-first floor. Walls of glass opened onto a balcony. The balcony hung recklessly over Biscayne Bay. Beneath it was water, nothing but liquid. There was an eclipse that night.

I was drawn out onto the balcony. With morbid fascination I monitored the eclipse. Even the planet was suspended in an unstable condition between intervening forces of the universe. I watched the heat lightning spark off the towers of Miami Beach. The impulse was to let go, float with it. Parts of myself buried alive with an unreconciled parent, severed husband, misplaced friends and loves, even my unexplored ancestors, broke the surface and heaped on me in a mass of fractured visions, all mixed up with the bloody head of the boy in Ireland. I sat through the night on that balcony in Miami, trying to get a fix on the moon.

The next morning I called both doctors who had given me pills. I wanted a nice, neat medical explanation that would make sense of this free-floating fear. Once I had the diagnosis, I could lie down and make it all go away. They confirmed that the two drugs (one a barbiturate and the other a mood elevator) were colliding in a violent chemical reaction. I should stay in bed for a day. Keep stimulation to a minimum. Rest. Yes. But the medical diagnosis did not make it go away because "it" was much bigger than a day's illness.

Then I tried an old technique. I would write the demon out of me. Writing had always served as a way of understanding what I was living. For what seemed like no appropriate reason, I had brought along notes for a short story. In fact, I felt almost compelled to write this particular story while I was in Miami. It was taken from an incident described to me by an intern ten years before. These were the notes:

An exceptionally alert and active woman of 60 had lived a long and comfortable married existence in the Fifth Avenue Hotel. Her husband died. She found herself, overnight, without the funds to carry on. She had no choice but to leave her home and all her friends of forty years. The only relative who could take her in was a disagreeable sister-in-law down South. Despite this abrupt and total dislocation, the widow went gracefully about closing up her New York life. At dinner the night before she was to leave, her minister and friends praised her remarkable strength of character. The next morning they came by to drive the widow to the airport; no one answered the door. They broke in and found her sprawled on the bathroom floor in her underclothes. No bump, no bruise explained it as a slip. She was simply unconscious.

Baffled, her friends drove the widow to a hospital. The intern found nothing on preliminary examination. The widow, by now conscious, had to be set to one side of the busy emergency room. Her freshly coiffed hair became disheveled. Her eyes grew vacant. She let the johnny coat fall open. Her friends sat patiently, waiting for those with knife wounds to be cauterized; but confronted with life in the raw they were wholly out of place. They were nice silk-print-dress people, as was the widow—before this. Now she began to alter even beyond the recognition of her friends. She fumbled over simple questions, confused names and dates, and eventually lost her orientation altogether. Her minister and friends retreated in polite horror. Within a matter of hours she had disintegrated into a babbling old woman.

I couldn't write a word of the story.

Watching television was about all I could do. At midnight I snapped off the TV. For what happened next there is a simple mechanical explanation, but at the time, the steadying handle of cause and effect was beyond my reach.

I passed in front of the TV and bent over to pick up a metal belt. A hissing sound escaped from the set. With head over toes I looked back, and saw an apparition. A jellyfish of fiendish hues was spreading across the screen, eely blues and poisonous greens, stinging hairs of sulphuric yellow—*stop!* I bolted upright, reeling, and felt an explosion go off inside my head.

"That's it," I said aloud, "I've come unstuck."

The phone was in the other bedroom, beyond the window wall with its balcony hung over the water. The sliding doors were open. Wind sucked at the curtains, teasing them out over the bay. Suddenly, I was terrified to walk past that window wall. If I so much as went near that balcony, I would lose my balance, go over the edge. I crouched down. Crablike, clutching at the feet of furniture for handgrips, I edged across that gaping room. I tried to tell myself this was ridiculous. But when I stood, the simple fact was that my limbs collapsed. The thought persisted: *If only I can reach the right person, this nightmare will go away.* I was hanging on to shreds and I knew it.

Ireland could be explained simply: Real bullets had threatened my life from the outside. It was an observable event. My fears were appropriate. Now the destructive force was inside me. I was my own event. I could not escape it. Something alien, horrible, unspeakable but undeniable, had begun to inhabit me. My own death.

Each of us stumbles upon the major issue of midlife somewhere in the decade between 35 and 45. Though this can also be an ordinary passage with no outer event to mark it, eventually we all confront the reality of our own death. And somehow, we must learn to live with it. The first time that message comes through is probably the worst.

We try to flee the task of incorporating our own shortcomings and destructiveness, as well as the world's destructive side. Rather than accept the unacceptable spooks, we try to drive them away by resorting to the coping techniques that have worked before.

The first is: turn on the lights. It always made the spooks go away in childhood. As adults we translate that technique into acquiring the correct knowledge. I looked first for a clear and simple medical explanation. Only part of my symptoms were ascribable to a chemical reaction to pills; I wanted that part to be the whole explanation. It wasn't, and turning on the lights did not take the fear away.

A second technique is to call for help. When the child is afraid he calls a Strong One to interrupt the fear and make it vanish. Then he learns the technique for himself and is able to dismantle most irrational fears. Now what happens when we come to a fear that we cannot make vanish? No one has any magic against mortality. Everyone to whom we assign that task disappoints us. My call from Ireland, of course, failed.

A third method is to ignore it by keeping busy, pretending to carry on as if nothing has changed. But the same sensations are likely to persist. I couldn't shake the questions about where I had been and where I was going, the overall feeling of losing balance. Balance is, speaking symbolically, standing on one's own two feet. It is the status we first achieved as children breaking in our first hard soles. Even then, by virtue of learning how to take over some of the responsibility for ourselves, we felt both winners of grand new powers and losers of our protective supports. The major task of midlife is to give up all our imagined safety providers and stand naked in the world, as the rehearsal for assuming *full* authority over ourselves.

The fear is: *What if I can't stand on my own two feet?*

The thought of death is too terrifying to confront head on, and so it keeps coming back in disguise: as pitching airplanes, swaying floors, precarious balconies, lovers' quarrels, mysterious backfires in our physical equipment. We elude it by pretending to function as before. Some people press down harder on the career accelerator. Others play more tennis, run more laps, give bigger parties, find younger flesh to take to bed. I flew on to a political convention. But sooner or later a rockslide of thoughts, distorted and sharp-edged visions of aging, aloneness and death, can gather enough force to temporarily crush our most basic assumption: *My system is in fine working order and I can stand up whenever I wish.* What happens when we cannot rely even on that? The struggle begins in earnest between a front-door mind that tries to brush them away and the piercing questions of the second half of life that keep tumbling down the backside of the mind, saying: *You can't forget about us!*

Work is another way of keeping busy. In my case, fear made work impossible. The story that I was trying to write in Miami concerned a woman coming to the end of her rope. One who is left alone, falls unconscious, loses her faculties, and is transformed with a Dorian Gray stroke into an old lady.

The story was the inner psychic drama that I was living. My structure, too, was disintegrating all at once. I was leaving that whole world of the girl I wanted to think I was—the loving, generous, fearless, ambitious "good" girl who lived in a silk-print, sensible, humane world—and now I was seeing the dark side. The unfathomable fears were: *I'll lose my stable pattern and all the skills that work for me . . . I'll wake up in some alien place . . . I will lose all my friends and connections . . . Suddenly, I won't be me anymore . . . I'll be transformed into some other, execrable form . . . old woman.*

Well, I wasn't. I survived. I grew up a little, and all that seems a hundred years ago. An awesome life accident had coincided with a critical turning point in my own life cycle. It was this experience that made me eager to find out everything I could about this thing called *midlife crisis*.

But no sooner did I begin seeking out the people who are the case histories in this book than I found myself drawn into a subject infinitely more complicated. There were crises all along, or rather, points of turning. The more I interviewed, the more I noticed similarities in the turning points people described. Not only were there other critical points than at midlife, but they came up with a relentless regularity at the same ages.

People were baffled by these periods of disruption. They tried to connect them to outer events of their lives, but there was no consistency to the events they blamed, whereas there was a striking consistency to the inner turmoil they described. At specific points along the life cycle they would feel stirrings, sometimes momentous changes of perspective, often mysterious dissatisfactions with the course they had been pursuing with enthusiasm only a few years before.

I began to wonder if there were, in fact, turning points in the lives of adults that were *predictable?*

Is There Life after Youth?

It occurred to me that what Gesell and Spock did for children hadn't been done for us adults.

Studies of child development have plotted every nuance of growth and given us comforting labels such as the Terrible Twos and the Noisy Nines. Adolescence has been so carefully deciphered, most of the fun of being impossible has been taken out of it. But after meticulously documenting our periods of personality development up to the age of 18 or 20—nothing. Beyond the age of 21, apart from medical people who are interested only in our gradual physical decay, we are left to fend for ourselves on the way downstream to senescence, at which point we are picked up again by gerontologists.

14

It's far easier to study adolescents and aging people. Both groups are in institutions (schools or rest homes) where they make captive subjects. The rest of us are out there in the mainstream of a spinning and distracted society, trying to make some sense of our one and only voyage through its ambiguities.

Where were the guidelines on how to get through the Trying Twenties, the Forlorn Forties? Could folklore be trusted, for instance, when it tells us that every seven years we grown-ups get an itch?

We have been taught that children develop by ages and stages, that the steps are pretty much the same for everybody, and that to grow out of the limited behavior of childhood we must climb them all. Children alternate between stages of equilibrium and disequilibrium. As parents, we are educated not to blame these extremes of behavior on a teacher, the other parent, or the children themselves, but to accept them as essential steps to growth.

Yet having applied this understanding of personality growth chapter and verse to guide our offspring from crib to college, we leave them at the door to adulthood like windup dolls: technologically proficient, geared for problem solving, trained to maneuver around obstacles. But equipped with any real understanding of the *inner* works, of the notion that even as grown-ups we may alternate between being in step and being off balance both with ourselves and the forces in our world—no, that's not part of the cultural programming.

The years between 18 and 50 are the center of life, the unfolding of maximum opportunity and capacity. But without any guide to the inner changes on the way to full adulthood, we are swimming blind. When we don't "fit in," we are likely to think of our behavior as evidence of our inadequacies, rather than as a valid stage unfolding in a sequence of growth, something we all accept when applied to childhood. It is even easier to blame our periods of disequilibrium on the closest person or institution, our mother, our marriage, our work, the nuclear family, the system. We seize on the cop-out.

Until recently, whenever psychiatrists and social scientists did address themselves to adult life, it was only in terms of its problems, rarely from the perspective of *continuing* and *predictable* changes. The concepts handed down by Freud were based on the assumption that the personality is more or less determined by the time a child reaches the age of five.

What do these concepts have to offer the 40-year-old man who has reached his professional goal but feels depressed and unappreciated? He blames his job or his wife or his physical surroundings for imprisoning him in this rut. Fantasies of breaking out begin to dominate his thoughts. An interesting woman he has met, another field of work, an Elysian part of the country—any or all of these become magnets for his wishes of deliverance. But once these objects of desire become accessible, the picture often begins to reverse itself. The new situation appears to be the dangerous trap from which he longs to take flight by returning to his old home base and the wife and children whose loss suddenly makes them dear.

No wonder many wives stand aghast, spectators at this game of chance, able only to label it "my husband's craziness." No one ever told them that a sense of stagnation, disequilibrium, and depression is predictable as we enter the passage to midlife.

And what do traditional Freudian concepts have to say to the 35-year-old mother who, having tried to provide the ideal Petri dish for the growth of her children's egos, suddenly feels her own to be about as solid as a boiled turnip? No matter what your age, you might identify with the apocryphal experience of a 35-year-old woman named Doris.

For the fifteen years of her marriage, Doris's husband had never pressed her to entertain or to go with him to business affairs. One night he came home with the news that he was being considered by his firm's major competitor for its top spot.

"And listen to this," he said. "The retiring president has invited both of us to a dinner party next week. This will clinch it."

"Omigod," Doris said. "I haven't had dinner with anybody above waist height for years. What'll I talk about?"

"C'mon, honey," her husband said, "all you have to do is glance through last week's newspapers."

Dutifully, Doris read four weeks' back issues of the news of *The Week in Review*, and every night before she went to sleep, she memorized the name of another Arab leader.

The party was studded with the worldly and the wise. Her dinner partner was the company head. "Oh no," she thought, but valiantly she plunged in and began expounding on the problem of air rights when cities start using solar energy. The man's mouth was full, so she went on to explain Hubert Humphrey's philosophy of democracy for the Third World. Taking a breath, she noticed to her delight that she had the full and transfixed attention of all the dinner guests at her end of the table. Encouraged, she ad libbed for five more minutes. The president was obviously impressed. In fact, he couldn't take his eyes off her.

She looked down modestly. And discovered that all the while, out of habit, she had been cutting up the man's steak.

The pith of this story, and the man's predicament before it, concerns something we might have sensed but were never told to expect: that life after adolescence is *not* one long plateau. Changes are not only possible and predictable, but to deny them is to be an accomplice to one's own unnecessary vegetation.

A new concept of adulthood, one that embraces the total life cycle, is questioning the old assumptions. If one sees the personality not as an apparatus that is essentially constructed by the time childhood is over, but as always in its essence developing, then life at 25 or 30 or at the gateway to middle age will stimulate its own intrigue, surprise, and exhilaration of discovery.[1]

The mystics and the poets always get there first. Shakespeare tried to tell us that man lives through seven stages in the "All the world's a stage" speech in *As You Like It*. And many centuries before Shakespeare, the Hindu scriptures of India described four distinct life stages, each calling for its own fresh response: student; householder; retirement, when the individual was encouraged to become a pilgrim and begin his true education as an adult; and the final state of *sannyasin*, defined as "one who neither hates nor loves anything."[2]

The first psychologist to view the life cycle by stages was Else Frenkel-Brunswik. Drawing on the intellectual opulence that was Vienna in the 1930s, she later brought her insights to theorists at the University of California at Berkeley. Hers was a pioneering effort in the linking of psychology with sociology. Working from the biographies of 400 persons—a dazzling cast that included Queen Victoria, John D. Rockefeller, Casanova, Jenny Lind, Tolstoy, Goethe, and Goethe's mother—she examined their histories in terms of external events as well as subjective experiences. Frenkel-Brunswik's conclusion was that every person passes through five sharply demarcated phases.[3] The phases she described foreshadowed the eight stages (three of them for adults) in the life cycle later outlined by Erik Erikson.[4]

It was Erikson who began to make the life cycle a clear and popular concept with the publication of his first book, *Childhood and Society*, in 1950. We know only obliquely of Erikson's own suffering in the lifelong effort to build a personal identity. The son of a Jewish mother and a father who abandoned the family before his birth, he repudiated the name of his German

18

Jewish stepfather. He created his own name—Erik, son of Erik—thereby casting himself as his own father. After leaving Europe in 1939, a victim of Nazism, he became an American citizen in California and at Berkeley began to concern himself with the universal crises of development.[5]

Erikson constructed a chart showing life unfolding in observable sequence. Each stage was marked by a crisis. "Crisis" connoted not a catastrophe, but a turning point, a crucial period of increased vulnerability and heightened potential. He was careful to point out that he did not consider all development a series of crises. He claimed rather that psychosocial development proceeds by critical steps—"critical" being a characteristic of moments of decision between progress and regression. At such points either achievements are won or failures occur, leaving the future to some degree better or worse but in any case, restructured.

In describing the three stages of adulthood, Erikson used only a few paragraphs. He set out the central developmental issue of each period, the ground that the personality could gain or lose. In the first adult stage the key issue is *intimacy,* and the alternative isolation. His next criterion for continued growth is *generativity,* the process by which the individual becomes paternal and creative in a new sense, feeling a voluntary commitment to guide new generations and younger associates. The final stage presents the opportunity for *integrity* and might be said to represent the point at which the midlife crisis has been successfully resolved.

I was encouraged to discover that Erikson had called upon others to flesh out his seminal theories. I felt a natural affinity for the works of Frenkel-Brunswik, Erikson, and others they had inspired. My own mentor was Margaret Mead. I realized that something very important had been missing in the way I was accustomed to writing about people; I had been dealing in fragments, a chapter from each life. What would have explained a great deal more was the perspective of people *moving across time*.

Plodding through the maze of print on marriage, divorce, the family, death of the family, and so on, I was brought up short one day by a flatfooted statistic from a Bureau of the Census abstract:

> "The median duration of marriage before divorce has been about seven years for the last half century."[6]

The computer had caught up at last with folklore. How many other breakthroughs, studies, statistics, and raw, unrecorded adult histories were out there begging to be brought together? That settled it. I leaped at the opportunity to accept a fellowship from the Alicia Patterson Foundation and turn to full-time study of adult development.

One evening in the spring of 1973 I attended a symposium called "Normal Crises of the Middle Years." The Hunter College auditorium was packed with vague but hoping faces—an assortment, one imagined, of seekers, blamers, self-doubters, deserters, second and third marital offenders, abandoned middle-aged women, and fidgeting "menopausal" males. All were anxious to hear what was normal about a crisis they had thought afflicted themselves alone.

A shy, attractively graying professor of social psychology from Yale, Daniel Levinson, began to describe what life is about for men from the ages of 18 to 47. He and his team had been studying forty men in different occupations for several years. Just as there are basic principles governing development in childhood and adolescence, Levinson asserted, so do adults develop by periods, each period engaging them in specific tasks. Many changes can take place *within* each period. But a person moves from one to the next only when he starts working at new developmental tasks and builds a new structure for his life.[7]

And no structure, according to Levinson's calculations, can last longer than seven or eight years. Once more, science had ratified folklore.

I was excited by Levinson's work, although it raised a riot of questions in my mind. It turned out that Else Frenkel-Brunswik had been his mentor. When I approached him for guidance on how to work with the biographical method, he was generous with his time, and he read some of the first biographies I collected. "They're excellent interviews with lots of good quotes," he said, "which means you're getting the person in his fullness or emptiness." That made me happy. "But don't introduce abstract concepts. When they want to talk about something important, let them go on." That made me wonder if I'd be a geriatric case before I got all the tapes transcribed.

Although the subject of adult development was only in the germination stage, spurts of theory were welling up at Harvard, at Berkeley, Chicago, UCLA. As I visited those academic centers, I was surprised to find out how little cross-pollination had taken place. The phenomenon of simultaneity was clearly at work.

But most of the research was being done by men who were studying other men.

Men and women may be isolated for the purpose of a scholar's study, but that is hardly how we live. We live together. How can we possibly expect to understand the development of men until we hear also from the people who bring them into the world, from the women they love and hate and fear and perform for, depend on and are depended on by, destroy and are destroyed by?

At UCLA I discovered an exception in psychiatrist Roger Gould, who had done a preliminary study of white, middle-class people from 16 to 60 that included women. Because no depth interviews had been done, the results were intriguing but sketchy. Gould later agreed it was vital to interview both men and women. He asked to read some of the histories I was collecting and offered his detailed interpretations.[8]

I settled on three major objectives for the book. The first was to locate the individual's *inner* changes in a world in which most of us are preoccupied with externals—to rediscover the obvious and somehow put words to it. Was there some way to demystify professional jargon? To make a lively and healing art of self-examination available to people who, like me, were finding themselves caught in the snarls of growing up adult but, having no guide, were holding themselves or their partners to blame?

The second aim was to compare the developmental rhythms of men and women. It soon became glaringly obvious that the tempo of development is not synchronized in the two sexes. The fundamental steps of expansion that will open a person, over time, to the full flowering of his or her individuality are the same for both genders. But men and women are rarely in the same place struggling with the same questions at the same age.

It was a natural progression to the third objective: to examine the predictable crises for couples. Especially if Dick and Jane are the same age, they are much of the time out of sync. During the twenties, when a man gains confidence by leaps and bounds, a married woman is usually losing the superior assurance she once had as an adolescent. When a man passes 30 and wants to settle down, a woman is often becoming restless. And just at the point around 40, when a man feels himself to be standing on a precipice, his strength, power, dreams, and illusions slipping away beneath him, his wife is likely to be brimming with ambition to climb her own mountain.

Because this asynchronous pattern is so often the case, and because the book follows the life cycle chronologically, it may appear to the reader during the first half of the book that I am more sympathetic to women. That is because I observed more outer restrictions and inner contradictions for women during the first half of life. Quite the reverse is often true in the second half of life; hence, the second half of the book may seem more consoling to men.

• Use of the word *crisis* to describe the strategic interplay of stable periods and critical turning points has caused some confusion. "What about me? I didn't *have* a crisis," people will often say rather defensively. Our culture's interpretation of the Greek word *krisis* is pejorative, implying personal failure, weakness, an inability to bear up against stressful *outside* events. I've replaced that confusing label with a less loaded word for the critical transitions between stages, and called them *passages*.

My own work progressed in stages. It began with an innocent's excitement. Then I published an article titled "Catch-30" in *New York* magazine, outlining the subject I was studying. The responses and hundreds of letters from people of all ages who said, "You're writing about *me*," gave me a touch of messianic fever. Which was quickly followed by panic. Suppose ten people took what I said seriously? Most of us don't influence ten strangers in our lives. The responsibility was awesome. I became a grind: reading psychiatry, psychology, biographies, novels, longitudinal studies, and bloody dull statistical printouts. I was a million laughs at dinner parties, so I stopped going, or shut up and passed the pistachio nuts.

Gradually, I weaned myself away from dependence on the authorities. I came to rely on the richness of the life stories I had collected to test and inform the theory and to add original insights. I began to feel comfortable with my own authority.

In all I collected 115 life stories. Many of the couples I saw together, after first reconstructing their biographies separately. Those sessions supplied a fascinating complexity and threw a good deal of light onto individual psychology.

The people I chose to study belong to America's "pacesetter group"—healthy, motivated people who either began in or have entered the middle class, though some began in poverty, even ghettos. I chose this group for several reasons.

First, I had to make a choice of one stratum of American society in order to be able to trace consistencies by exploring laterally within it.

Second, the people in this group become the carriers of our social values. They are also the major exporters to other classes of new life patterns and attitudes. Roughly five years after ideas emerge in the middle class, as a Daniel Yankelovich study shows, working-class young people inherit these new opinions on sex and family, work and life-style expectations.[9]

Finally, I chose this group because the educated middle class has the greatest number of options and the least number of obstacles to choosing their lives. They are not hemmed in by traditions, as are those born rich and socially powerful, nor do they enjoy the same stability. And they are not deprived of education or economic advantages, as are the near-poor working class, nor do they hold the prerogative of some members of that class who have kith and kin to call upon when they are in trouble.

If any group has options to change and improve its life, it is the American middle class. And yet with freedom comes turmoil. Hence in the stresses, victories, and defeats of people in the middle—people with the luxury of choice—we would be likely to see most clearly the way they move from one stage to another as variations on the theme of adult development, rather than as reactions to outer obstacles or the regimentation of class behavior.

The people in this book range in age from 18 to 55. The men include lawyers, doctors, chief executives and middle managers, ministers, professors, politicians, and students, as well as men in the arts, the media, the sciences, and those who run their own small businesses. I sought out top-achieving women as well and also followed the steps of many traditional nurturing women.

Almost all of the people I interviewed asked to

remain anonymous. In an effort to avoid any possibility that a reader might recognize them, I tried at first to alter their professions as well or to change the geographical location. But the occupations that people choose and the places they live are too intimately linked with the personality that explains them and the fabric that shapes them. There is no such thing as a precise equivalent. And so only their names have been changed, and all the quotations come straight off the tape recorder.

Although many of my respondents were raised in small towns, the urban centers to which they have gravitated include New York, Los Angeles, Washington, San Francisco, Chicago, Detroit, Boston, New Haven, and Dayton, Ohio, the city considered by pollsters the home of the average American couple. Some have moved to the suburbs, and a few others to the woods, the Rockies, the beaches of California. Over half have been divorced. Some have no children, and a number of the women head their own households. It is difficult to pinpoint the religious distribution because so many people have left the faith of their childhood or changed it or are seeking new forms of spirituality. Roughly a third came from Protestant backgrounds, and another third each from Catholic or Jewish homes.

Some of my subjects were flamboyant; some of a paler feather. Complexity can be found in the most plainly clothed life, just as there is a thread of commonality in the most bizarre. And from out of the most crushing setbacks, people often gather a dignity of intention.

I fully expect a vocal group of dissenters. Loudest among them will probably be those who argue: "You are trying to systematize something so variable that it's all baloney." There is no factual rebuttal to that statement. People who explore the human personality are dealing not with science but with art, observation, hunch, insight. When there have been many studies of adult development and a framework has been set out by enough explorers in this field, we will have something worth arguing about. It will be a long time before universal dimensions emerge.

There is also something in this book to offend everyone. Even some of the people whom a description fits precisely won't like it, won't accept it, won't welcome receiving an underlined copy in the mail from an ex-mate. But that's all to the good. If you read all the way through and still feel complacent, the book will be a failure. The stuff of our everyday lives is a volatile subject, and it's natural that our reactions to such material are subjective. I must admit, however, that I was puzzled when the first few comments on the same biographies, given to me by friends and colleagues, were so blatantly inconsistent: "Loved him, hated her," and "I just can't connect with the guy who was a failure in business," and "your men are all childish," and—this from an ambitious single woman writer of 30—"your women lack initiative."

Then I spoke to a friend who writes books about explosive contemporary subjects, using case histories from his psychiatric practice. When he sent around his first manuscript to some of his colleagues, they all came back with disparate responses. Each one found fault with a different case history and warmed to another. By the time he'd written a second book and received the same mixed, inconsistent responses to the case studies, the reason became obvious. These were not comments on the validity of the material, but Rorschach tests of the people reading it.

Furthermore, it is sometimes difficult to sympathize with people who enjoy enviable positions in the most luxurious nation on the planet. Most of the people who gave their stories to this book have the opportunity at some point in life to use their judgment and creativity. Their minds are trained; their bodies, relatively sound; in their work is little of the torpor and dehumanization that afflict the mill worker, the factory worker, the line lady in an assembly plant. And yet—they bellyache. Why?

Well, for one thing, when guaranteed anonymity, the people I interviewed welcomed the chance to go right to the core of their doubts, hopes, conflicts, emotional disabilities. They didn't dress themselves up in public personae. Some of the people I talked with said, "You will know more about me when we're through than I've ever revealed to anyone."

The last interview I did serves as a good example. I was looking for an educated woman who had chosen to be a wife and mother and remained happy with that choice straight through to midlife. I found her; she had written the following biographical sketch for an alumnae newspaper: "Four children. I'm an English teacher. In my spare time (ha ha) I practice the piano, play tennis, do needlework. I just gave up smoking. My college years were wonderful. I'd like to go back and do it all over again! Right now!"

When we sat down and talked for eight hours, what came out was: Her husband had left her the year before. He said that he had grown and she hadn't. She feared that with her husband gone, she would simply wither away as a person. She was terrified about breaking into the business world at 40. One night her daughter tried to persuade the electrician to spend the night because "Mommy has a big bed and she's very lonely." The cheery biographical sketch for her alumnae newsletter had been written (ha ha) at the lowest point of her life.

Everyone has difficulty with the steps of inner growth, even when the outer obstacles appear easily surmountable. What's more, the prizes of our society are reserved for outer, not inner, achievements. Scant are the trophies given for reconciling all the forces that compete to direct our development, although working toward such a reconciliation hour by demanding hour, day by triumphant day, year by exacting year is what underlies all growth of the personality. I count my own fortune now in the treasury of lives opened to me in trust. They live in me, resonate in me, teach me every day that no age or event can of itself prevent the human spirit from outstretching its former boundaries.

We all have an aversion to generalities, thinking that they violate what is unique about ourselves. Yet the older we grow, the more we become aware of the commonality of our lives, as well as our essential aloneness as navigators through the human journey. Gradually, the fragments of lives of people I had previously written about and those I was busy interviewing began to come together as parts of a coherent composition. Generalization scared me less and less. I reread an observation by Willa Cather with a mixture of amusement and startled recognition:

"There are only two or three human stories, and they go on repeating themselves as fiercely as if they had never happened before."

2

PREDICTABLE CRISES OF ADULTHOOD

We are not unlike a particularly hardy crustacean. The lobster grows by developing and shedding a series of hard, protective shells. Each time it expands from within, the confining shell must be sloughed off. It is left exposed and vulnerable until, in time, a new covering grows to replace the old.

With each passage from one stage of human growth to the next we, too, must shed a protective structure. We are left exposed and vulnerable—but also yeasty and embryonic again, capable of stretching in ways we hadn't known before. These sheddings may take several years or more. Coming out of each passage, though, we enter a longer and more stable period in which we can expect relative tranquillity and a sense of equilibrium regained.

Everything that happens to us—graduations, marriage, childbirth, divorce, getting or losing a job—affects us. These *marker events* are the concrete happenings of our lives. A developmental stage, however, is not defined in terms of marker events; it is defined by changes that begin within. *The underlying impulse toward change will be there regardless* of whether or not it is manifested in or accentuated by a marker event.[1]

A person's life at any given time incorporates both

external and internal aspects. The external system is composed of our memberships in the culture: our job, social class, family and social roles, how we present ourselves to and participate in the world. The interior realm concerns the meanings this participation has for each of us. In what ways are our values, goals, and aspirations being invigorated or violated by our present life system? How many parts of our personality can we live out, and what parts are we suppressing? How do we *feel* about our way of living in the world at any given time?

The inner realm is where the crucial shifts in bedrock begin to throw a person off balance, signaling the necessity to change and move on to a new footing in the next stage of development. These crucial shifts occur throughout life, yet people consistently refuse to recognize that they possess an internal life system. Ask anyone who seems down, "Why are you feeling low?" Most will displace the inner message onto a marker event: "I've been down since we moved, since I changed jobs, since my wife went back to graduate school and turned into a damn social worker in sackcloth," and so on. Probably less than ten percent would say: "There is some unknown disturbance within me, and even though it's painful, I feel I have to stay with it and ride it out." Even fewer people would be able to explain that the turbulence they feel may have no external cause. And yet it may not resolve itself for *several years*.

During each of these passages, how we feel about our way of living will undergo subtle changes in four areas of perception. One is the interior sense of self in relation to others. A second is the proportion of safeness to danger we feel in our lives. A third is our perception of time—do we have plenty of it, or are we beginning to feel that time is running out? Last, there will be some shift at the gut level in our sense of aliveness or stagnation. These are the hazy sensations that compose the background tone of living and shape the decisions on which we take action.

The work of adult life is not easy. As in childhood, each step presents not only new tasks of development but requires a letting go of the techniques that worked before. With each passage some magic must be given up, some cherished illusion of safety and comfortably familiar sense of self must be cast off, to allow for the greater expansion of our own distinctiveness.

What I'm saying is, we must be willing to change chairs if we want to grow. There is no permanent compatibility between a chair and a person. And there is no one right chair. What is right at one stage may be restricting at another or too soft. During the passage from one stage to another, we will be between two chairs. Wobbling no doubt, but developing. If I've been convinced by one idea in the course of collecting all the life stories that inform the book, it is this: Times of crisis, of disruption or constructive change, are not only predictable but desirable. They mean growth.

This is not the only alternative, of course. If the work of adult life seems too hard, one can always settle back in a "permanent home," arrange one's whole life system around it, the job, schools for the children, social activities, and all the rest of it. Then, when the rumblings of a new stage of development begin within, one can point to the impossibility of change.

When financial reverses prompt a young person to quit school and go to work, when marriage does not happen at the hoped-for time, when a child is born unusually early or late, when people simply can't seem to find themselves and their occupational achievement is delayed—these are what we might call *untimely events*. They upset the sequence and rhythm of the expected life cycle. People whose lives have been oddly shaped by such untimely events grope for some handle to explain what they did not anticipate.

"I'm a late bloomer," we often hear. "She peaked early," or "he's a burnt-out case," or "she's a cradle snatcher." Even when the outcome is favorable—the gnome of Wall Street blossoms late as a sculptor, or the seasoned bride and her young prince are transported to delight—there is a nagging sense of something being out of whack. For one thing, people who zigzag off the familiar course of development are offered little support by society. Gossip sets them apart as strange because they challenge conventional wisdom and threaten the rest of the flock. Moreover, as social psychologist Bernice L. Neugarten observes, we talk a great deal about sex-role identity but rarely mention the mighty influence of "age-role identity."[2]

What of the driven individual whose extreme path is an applauded one: Can he too be tripped up? The wunderkind hell-bent on reaching his goal, having spent little time on building emotional attachments, may ignore through his rocketing years the hollow feeling inside the nose cone of his success. Society goads him on. Or her—think of Dorothy Parker, Marilyn Monroe, most movie queens for that matter. Having spent their energies on speeding along one narrow trajectory, the superachievers may be shocked at the passage to midlife to find they are really behind. On the other hand, people who commit deeply to a goal and play it out to their satisfaction sometimes flourish in midlife when their neglected emotions are released. It can give them a second lease on life.[3]

There are other events that the individual is powerless to prevent: a war, a Depression, the death of a parent or child, husband or wife, or a real threat to one's own life as I experienced in Ireland. I call this a *life accident*.

Because the blow of a life accident hits harder if it coincides with a critical passage in the life cycle, it may force us to resolve the issues of that passage more effectively.[4] However, some of the men who were only half way out of the parental family and groping for a jobhold when the Depression of the 1930s blasted the bedrock out from under them, found themselves permanently afflicted with the jitters over job security.

Two Couples, Two Generations

Besides age, stage, and gender, our personality development is influenced by generation and social change. Usually, we rely on the simple and obvious method of placing people by their generation: "He's an old '30s radical," or "she's a child of the '60s." My emphasis is on the more subtle inner changes that are common to our chronological development. They deserve attention, not because they are necessarily the weightier influence on our development as adults, but because we usually ignore them.

In my research I found a traditional family, dreamers of the American dream with no manifest crises on their record, and studied each member. I shall call them the Babcocks. Everything but their names remains unchanged. It was useful to compare two photos from the Babcock family album. One was taken in 1947, the bride and bridegroom Ken and Margaret. The other, taken in 1974, is of their son Donald and his fiancée Bonnie. Between these two couples stretch twenty-five years of history and changing value systems. What are the differences in their dreams? What visions of marriage, what goals for the future, what overall view of themselves single out each couple as it sets sail into the adult world?

Some would say that the two generations could be easily recognized. Here are their own words:

Couple A

Of himself at 22, the man says: A lot of things rubbed off from my father. He heavily encouraged my participation in athletics and competition. He had been on the swimming team at Yale. He wanted me to do the same thing. Even though I was doing really well in science, he prodded me to take extra help sessions. "Develop a long suit" was the advice he gave to all his children—an ace in the hole for financial security.

What made me decide to get married? Well, it was meeting her and falling in love. Knowing that this was what we ought to do, spend the rest of our lives together. And I wanted a tighter family. I mean, the bonds of my family weren't as strong as in hers, and I was attracted by that.

For my own future it was all a question of goal attainment. I wanted to see some of my own ideas carried out; it was a matter of working hard and following through. I was very excited in college about doing my own research. But when my friends approached me with the idea of going into business, I was already coming to realize that just doing research was not enough.

She puts in a comment: What research lacked was financial reward.

He: I looked at business as a vehicle more than anything else. You could call it a shot at the big time. I really don't like to have to worry about money. And I like to keep her happy.

Her view of his dream: All right, I knew he really loved his research. But after six months of his working on starting his new corporation, he said to me, "I'm doing this because I want to be able to give you everything you want"—meaning material things. I said, "But do you really *want* to do it? I know you love your research." Then I realized that the business venture was really a big challenge for him. He had developed a love for business machines.

He inserts a correction: Well, an interest.

She: A very big interest.

He: I saw it as a tool.

She: That's one thing we used to argue about. I told him he was getting carried away. It was stifling.

On her own goals and ambitions: There were a number of fields that really interested me. Especially psychology. But I just couldn't plan that much in the future. I pretty much followed him. That's why I transferred colleges three times. Because his career came first. I really love to work with disturbed children, any children actually. My idea was to work until 30, and then I would be with children into my forties—a real mother and typical housewife.

Couple B

Of his dream at 21: I was taught as a small boy to strive for financial success. To be a good provider for my family. Stand on your own two feet and make good. This was drummed into me at an early age, and this was the goal I had in mind—to have children, support my wife, have a nice house, send my kids to Yale like my father did, and be a success in business.

What made me want to get married? When we met, we were both very young and immature. My father thought she was the greatest ever. My family was of more modest means.

Her point of view: I was very lonely growing up. One of the reasons I wanted to marry him was to have a big family. I was very attracted to the closeness I saw between his parents and the four children in his family.

On how she saw his dream: I had great hopes for him. I believed he would rise to the top of any business he was in. He was so dynamic. He came across with the idea that he could do anything.

He protests: Well, I can.

She corrects herself: Yes, I do think he can do a tremendous amount. But you never know where it's going to lead.

Her aspirations: I had a year of college, majored in television and radio. Then I gave up all ideas of a job to do with that field. I went to work just to make some money. Nothing jobs. I really wasn't dedicated to what I was doing. I wanted to get married and have a big family.

Couple A is the son, Donald, and his fiancée, now 22 and 20. Couple B is the mother, Margaret, now 46, and the father, Ken, 48. If you had any trouble sorting out the dreams and values of the two generational pairs, it is a confusion that troubles the Babcocks themselves.

As the father points out with pride, his son is following precisely in his own footsteps. "I graduated from Yale one week, married the next. Donald's in the exact same position I was."

While each of us is continually growing up or growing old, the interior life system has its own stubborn idiosyncratic clock. At one time or another probably all of us feel like the inner man who howls, unheard, in a Jules Feiffer cartoon (*see page 38*).[5]

Yet events that demand a leap of action before we're ready often have the happy effect of boosting us on to the next stage of development in spite of ourselves.

As we shall see, each person engages the steps of development in his or her own characteristic *stepstyle*.[6] Some people never complete the whole sequence. And none of us "solves" with one step—by jumping out of the parental home into a job or marriage, for example—the problems in separating from the caregivers of childhood. Nor do we "achieve" autonomy once and for all by converting our dreams into concrete goals, even when we attain those goals.[7] The central issues or tasks of one period are never fully completed, tied up, and cast aside. But when they lose their primacy and the current life structure has served its purpose, we are ready to move on to the next period.

Can one catch up? What might look to others like listlessness, contrariness, a maddening refusal to face up to an obvious task may be a person's own unique detour that will bring him out later on the other side. Developmental gains won can later be lost—and rewon. It's plausible, though it can't be proven, that the mastery of one set of tasks fortifies us for the next period and the next set of challenges. But it's important not to think too mechanistically. Machines work by units. The bureaucracy (supposedly) works step by step. Human beings, thank God, have an individual inner dynamic that can never be precisely coded.

Although I have indicated the ages when Americans are likely to go through each stage, and the differences between men and women where they are striking, do not take the ages too seriously. The stages are the thing, and most particularly the sequence.

Here is the briefest outline of the developmental ladder.

PULLING UP ROOTS

Before 18, the motto is loud and clear: "I have to get away from my parents." But the words are seldom connected to action. Generally still safely part of our families, even if away at school, we feel our autonomy to be subject to erosion from moment to moment.

After 18, we begin Pulling Up Roots in earnest. College, military service, and short-term travels are all customary vehicles our society provides for the first round trips between family and a base of one's own. In the attempt to separate our view of the world from our family's view, despite vigorous protestations to the contrary—"I know exactly what I want!"—we cast about for any beliefs we can call our own. And in the process of testing those beliefs we are often drawn to fads, preferably those most mysterious and inaccessible to our parents.

Whatever tentative memberships we try out in the world, the fear haunts us that we are really kids who cannot take care of ourselves. We cover that fear with acts of defiance and mimicked confidence. For allies to replace our parents, we turn to our contemporaries. They become conspirators. So long as their perspective meshes with our own, they are able to substitute for the sanctuary of the family. But that doesn't last very long. And the instant they diverge from the shaky ideals of "our group," they are seen as betrayers. Rebounds to the family are common between the ages of 18 and 22.

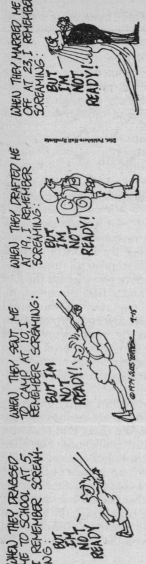

38

The tasks of this passage are to locate ourselves in a peer group role, a sex role, an anticipated occupation, an ideology or world view. As a result, we gather the impetus to leave home physically and the identity to *begin* leaving home emotionally.

Even as one part of us seeks to be an individual, another part longs to restore the safety and comfort of merging with another. Thus one of the most popular myths of this passage is: We can piggyback our development by attaching to a Stronger One. But people who marry during this time often prolong financial and emotional ties to the family and relatives that impede them from becoming self-sufficient.

A stormy passage through the Pulling Up Roots years will probably facilitate the normal progression of the adult life cycle. If one doesn't have an identity crisis at this point, it will erupt during a later transition, when the penalties may be harder to bear.

THE TRYING TWENTIES

The Trying Twenties confront us with the question of how to take hold in the adult world. Our focus shifts from the interior turmoils of late adolescence— "Who am I?" "What is truth?"—and we become almost totally preoccupied with working out the externals. "How do I put my aspirations into effect?" "What is the best way to start?" "Where do I go?" "Who can help me?" "How did *you* do it?"

In this period, which is longer and more stable compared with the passage that leads to it, the tasks are as enormous as they are exhilarating: To shape a Dream, that vision of ourselves which will generate energy, aliveness, and hope. To prepare for a lifework. To find a mentor if possible. And to form the capacity for intimacy, without losing in the process whatever consistency of self we have thus far mustered. The first test structure must be erected around the life we choose to try.

Doing what we "should" is the most pervasive theme of the twenties. The "shoulds" are largely defined by family models, the press of the culture, or the prejudices of our peers. If the prevailing cultural instructions are that one should get married and settle down behind one's own door, a nuclear family is born. If instead the peers insist that one should do one's own thing, the 25-year-old is likely to harness himself onto a Harley-Davidson and burn up Route 66 in the commitment to have no commitments.

One of the terrifying aspects of the twenties is the inner conviction that the choices we make are irrevocable. It is largely a false fear. Change is quite possible, and some alteration of our original choices is probably inevitable.

Two impulses, as always, are at work. One is to build a firm, safe structure for the future by making strong commitments, to "be set." Yet people who slip into a ready-made form without much self-examination are likely to find themselves *locked in.*

The other urge is to explore and experiment, keeping any structure tentative and therefore easily reversible. Taken to the extreme, these are people who skip from one trial job and one limited personal encounter to another, spending their twenties in the *transient* state.

Although the choices of our twenties are not irrevocable, they do set in motion a Life Pattern. Some of us follow the locked-in pattern, others the transient pattern, the wunderkind pattern, the caregiver pattern, and there are a number of others. Such patterns strongly influence the particular questions raised for each person during each passage, and so the most common patterns will also be traced throughout the book.

Buoyed by powerful illusions and belief in the power of the will, we commonly insist in our twenties that what we have chosen to do is the one true course in life. Our backs go up at the merest hint that we are like our parents, that two decades of parental training might be reflected in our current actions and attitudes.

"Not me," is the motto, "I'm different."

CATCH-30

Impatient with devoting ourselves to the "shoulds," a new vitality springs from within as we approach 30. Men and women alike speak of feeling too narrow and restricted. They blame all sorts of things, but what the restrictions boil down to are the outgrowth of career and personal choices of the twenties. They may have been choices perfectly suited to that stage. But now the fit feels different. Some inner aspect that was left out is striving to be taken into account. Important new choices must be made, and commitments altered or deepened. The work involves great change, turmoil, and often crisis—a simultaneous feeling of rock bottom and the urge to bust out.

One common response is the tearing up of the life we spent most of our twenties putting together. It may mean striking out on a secondary road toward a new vision or converting a dream of "running for president" into a more realistic goal. The single person feels a push to find a partner. The woman who was previously content at home with children chafes to venture into the world. The childless couple reconsiders children. And almost everyone who is married, especially those married for seven years, feels a discontent.

If the discontent doesn't lead to a divorce, it will, or should, call for a serious review of the marriage and of each partner's aspirations in their Catch-30 condition. The gist of that condition was expressed by a 29-year-old associate with a Wall Street law firm:

"I'm considering leaving the firm. I've been there four years now; I'm getting good feedback, but I have no clients of my own. I feel weak. If I wait much

41

longer, it will be too late, too close to that fateful time of decision on whether or not to become a partner. I'm success-oriented. But the concept of being 55 years old and stuck in a monotonous job drives me wild. It drives me crazy now, just a little bit. I'd say that 85 percent of the time I thoroughly enjoy my work. But when I get a screwball case, I come away from court saying, 'What am I doing here?' It's a *visceral* reaction that I'm wasting my time. I'm trying to find some way to make a social contribution or a slot in city government. I keep saying, 'There's something more.'"

Besides the push to broaden himself professionally, there is a wish to expand his personal life. He wants two or three more children. "The concept of a home has become very meaningful to me, a place to get away from troubles and relax. I love my son in a way I could not have anticipated. I never could live alone."

Consumed with the work of making his own critical life-steering decisions, he demonstrates the essential shift at this age: an absolute requirement to be more self-concerned. The self has new value now that his competency has been proved.

His wife is struggling with her own age-30 priorities. She wants to go to law school, but he wants more children. If she is going to stay home, she wants him to make more time for the family instead of taking on even wider professional commitments. His view of the bind, of what he would most like from his wife, is this: "I'd like not to be bothered. It sounds cruel, but I'd like not to have to worry about what she's going to do next week. Which is why I've told her several times that I think she should do something. Go back to school and get a degree in social work or geography or whatever. Hopefully that would fulfill her, and then I wouldn't have to worry about her line of problems. I want her to be decisive about herself."

The trouble with his advice to his wife is that it comes out of concern with *his* convenience, rather than with *her* development. She quickly picks up on this lack of goodwill: He is trying to dispose of her. At the same time, he refuses her the same latitude to be "selfish" in making an independent decision to broaden her own horizons. Both perceive a lack of mutuality. And that is what Catch-30 is all about for the couple.

ROOTING AND EXTENDING

Life becomes less provisional, more rational and orderly in the early thirties. We begin to settle down in the full sense. Most of us begin putting down roots and sending out new shoots. People buy houses and become very earnest about climbing career ladders. Men in particular concern themselves with "making it." Satisfaction with marriage generally goes downhill in the thirties (for those who have remained together) compared with the highly valued, vision-supporting marriage of the twenties. This coincides with the couple's reduced social life outside the family and the in-turned focus on raising their children.

THE DEADLINE DECADE

In the middle of the thirties we come upon a crossroads. We have reached the halfway mark. Yet even as we are reaching our prime, we begin to see there is a place where it finishes. Time starts to squeeze.

The loss of youth, the faltering of physical powers we have always taken for granted, the fading purpose of stereotyped roles by which we have thus far identified ourselves, the spiritual dilemma of having no absolute answers—any or all of these shocks can give this passage the character of crisis. Such thoughts usher in a decade between 35 and 45 that can be called the Deadline Decade. It is a time of both danger and opportunity. All of us have the chance to rework the narrow identity by which we defined ourselves in the first half of life. And those of us who make the most of the opportunity will have a full-out authenticity crisis.

To come through this authenticity crisis, we must reexamine our purposes and reevaluate how to spend our resources from now on. "Why am I doing all this? What do I really believe in?" No matter what we have been doing, there will be parts of ourselves that have been suppressed and now need to find expression. "Bad" feelings will demand acknowledgment along with the good.

It is frightening to step off onto the treacherous footbridge leading to the second half of life. We can't take everything with us on this journey through uncertainty. Along the way, we discover that we are alone. We no longer have to ask permission because we are the providers of our own safety. We must learn to give ourselves permission. We stumble upon feminine or masculine aspects of our natures that up to this time have usually been masked. There is grieving to be done because an old self is dying. By taking in our suppressed and even our unwanted parts, we prepare at the gut level for the reintegration of an identity that is ours and ours alone—not some artificial form put together to please the culture or our mates. It is a dark passage at the beginning. But by disassembling ourselves, we can glimpse the light and gather our parts into a renewal.

Women sense this inner crossroads earlier than men do. The time pinch often prompts a woman to stop and take an all-points survey at age 35. Whatever options she has already played out, she feels a "my last chance" urgency to review those options she has set aside and those that aging and biology will close off in the *now foreseeable* future. For all her qualms and confusion about where to start looking for a new future, she usually enjoys an exhilaration of release. Assertiveness begins rising. There are so many firsts ahead.

Men, too, feel the time push in the mid-thirties. Most men respond by pressing down harder on the career accelerator. It's "my last chance" to pull away from the pack. It is no longer enough to be the loyal junior executive, the promising young novelist, the lawyer who does a little *pro bono* work on the side. He wants now to become part of top management, to be recognized as an established writer, or an active politician with his own legislative program. With some chagrin, he discovers that he has been too anxious to please and too vulnerable to criticism. He wants to put together his own ship.

During this period of intense concentration on external advancement, it is common for men to be unaware of the more difficult, gut issues that are propelling them forward. The survey that was neglected at 35 becomes a crucible at 40. Whatever rung of achievement he has reached, the man of 40 usually feels stale, restless, burdened, and unappreciated. He worries about his health. He wonders, "Is this all there is?" He may make a series of departures from well-established lifelong base lines, including marriage. More and more men are seeking second careers in midlife. Some become self-destructive. And many men in their forties experience a major shift of emphasis away from pouring all their energies into their own advancement. A more tender, feeling side comes into play. They become interested in developing an ethical self.

RENEWAL OR RESIGNATION

Somewhere in the mid-forties, equilibrium is regained. A new stability is achieved, which may be more or less satisfying.

If one has refused to budge through the midlife transition, the sense of staleness will calcify into resignation. One by one, the safety and supports will be withdrawn from the person who is standing still. Parents will become children; children will become strangers; a mate will grow away or go away; the career will become just a job—and each of these events will be felt as an abandonment. The crisis will probably emerge again around 50. And although its wallop will be greater, the jolt may be just what is needed to prod the resigned middle-ager toward seeking revitalization.

On the other hand ...

If we have confronted ourselves in the middle passage and found a renewal of purpose around which we are eager to build a more authentic life structure, these may well be the best years. Personal happiness takes a sharp turn upward for partners who can now accept the fact: "I cannot expect *anyone* to fully understand me." Parents can be forgiven for the burdens of our childhood. Children can be let go without leaving us in collapsed silence. At 50, there is a new warmth and mellowing. Friends become more important than ever, but so does privacy. Since it is so often proclaimed by people past midlife, the motto of this stage might be "No more bullshit."

Part Two

PULLING UP ROOTS

What matters it that all
  around
Danger and grief and
  darkness lie,
If but within our bosom's
  bound
We hold a bright unsullied
  sky. . . .

—EMILY BRONTË

3

BREAST
TO
BREAKAWAY

Drinking, sex playing, competitive sports, hot rodding, street-ganging, joining the army, joining the Peace Corps, joining sororities and fraternities, smoking dope, popping pills, backpacking through Rajasthan, religious quests, rioting, streaking, seeking bliss consciousness—each of these experiments satisfied something of young people's need to test their capacities and seek their own truth. The context offered by history varies when each of us is ready to take the step away from home, but the inner shift demanded by this passage remains the same.

In gradually detaching ourselves from the family, we initiate the search for a personal identity. This is usually thought of as a crisis of adolescence. Yet the full achievement of identity is not merely a matter of deciding who we are and what we are going to do in the world; those decisions are subject to change over the course of a lifetime. There is a more highly refined dimension of growth that is only possible and appropriate after we have had time to profit by years of life experience. It is called by Jung *individuation*,[1] by Maslow *self-actualization*, by others *integration* or *autonomy*. I speak of it in this book as *gaining our authenticity*. By that I mean the arrival at that felicitous state of inner expansion in which we know of all our potentialities and possess the ego strength to direct their full reach.

From the broad perspective of the life cycle, how long does this take?

We are children until we reach puberty. We are adolescents until we reach that point in our twenties when we take hold of a provisional identity. And somewhere between the late thirties and early forties when we enter midlife, we also have the opportunity for true adulthood, whereupon we proceed either to wither inside our husks or to regather and re-pot ourselves for the flowering into our full authenticity.

If you have already left home, you will probably be muttering to yourself, "What is this nonsense? I *am* an adult!" "Don't I earn a paycheck?" "Aren't I taking care of a child of my own?" "Don't I live my life as I please, no matter what my parents think?" These and other external demonstrations of becoming an adult are easy to point out. The complicated steps of internal growth are another matter.

Each child arrives in the world an outlaw. He strives to center the universe about himself and to make it what he wants it to be: his own inner circle. For the first few months of life, this is easy. The infant *is* the world, and there is no awareness of "self" as distinct from "other."

Gradually, though dimly, this first circle comes to include primitive images of the caregiver—the first other—usually the mother. The baby cries out to its caregiver, who responds by feeding, soothing, and removing discomforts. Naturally, the need and response will not always dovetail. This allows the child to make his first rough reckoning of the balance he must expect in life between satisfaction and discontent. With the discovery that most of his needs will in time be met, the child gains the fundamental resource from which his development will proceed: a sense of basic trust.[2]

This trust becomes the cushion enabling a new kind of exchange, in which both the self and the other are acknowledged; psychologists call it *mutuality*. An early example of mutuality can be seen when a baby smiles. The mother returns the smile, whereupon the child rewards her with an even more enthusiastic response. The essence of mutuality is that each needs the recognition of the other to complete the transaction. The child has now written the first page in a long story of intimate exchanges.

Our Merger and Seeker Selves

With the debut of the first separate sense of self about the age of two, we are endowed with an extraordinary gift: the makings of our own individuality. The price of cultivating this seed is separation, the gradual and painstaking process of separating the inner reality of *me* from the glorified images of *them*. Therein lies the rub. Glorification of our parents is encouraged by the very fact of our dependence on them, and our consequent need to cast them as the omnipotent Strong Ones.

Something in us yearns to remain an infant fused with mother, yearns to drive off anything strange and indulge only our own cravings for pleasure or power. The urge is so strong that now and then the young child is willing to forego his own inner imperatives and dissolve his budding distinctiveness. Why not? So long as we bathe in our own egocentric circle, we know nothing of problems. We can only know problems when forces in our inner life come into opposition. And that happens when the self begins to divide.[3]

It helps to think of these forces as under the management of two different sides of the self, as different as two floor managers on opposing sides of a bill in Congress. The impulse on one side of us is to merge. Its manager might be called our *Merger Self*. The opposing impulse is to seek our individuality; that side is our *Seeker Self*. These impulses are driven by contradictory wishes that set up the push-pull underlying all steps of development.

One is the universal wish to be attached to an-

stance, how to get across the street without being hit by a car. The process goes something like this:

"Stop! Don't run into the street!" shouts the mother the first time the curious child runs ahead of her toward the traffic at the end of the block. Startled by her tone of alarm, the child stops short. After one or more excursions to the same corner, the child halts before the curb and parrots exactly the mother's words: "Me 'top, wait for Mommy." The child does not cross the street. But now, instead of the control coming from outside, there is a controlling presence inside: a phantom parent. The command of the other has been partially incorporated into the self.

By taking in the "Don't cross the street" prohibition and thousands of other forms of behavior through identification, we all end up with a constant companion we might call our *inner custodian*. It curtails our freedom and in that respect is a dictator. But in exchange, it can foretell the future ("You'll be hit by a car if you cross on the red") and so also protects us from danger; therefore, it is a guardian as well.

The inner custodian has other powers beyond the familiar cautionary ones. Our parents also tell us throughout childhood: "Watch me; be like me," or in some cases, "Don't be like me." Directly or indirectly, a father may communicate the message: "If you don't go to medical school and become a doctor, you won't be respected." By the same token, a mother whose lot is to be a domestic may drum into her child the directive: "Study your English, Maria. Read. Learn. Do you want to grow up and be a maid like me?"

From then on throughout much of life, even when things are running smoothly outside, our internal world may be in a state of agitation over the competing urges of the Seeker and Merger Selves, as well as the face-off with the inner custodian.*

---

* In psychoanalytic terms, we are talking now about the concepts of self and object that originated with Freud. On first exposure, such concepts are infuriatingly abstract. Beyond the abstract words, though, their pro-

Eventually, of course, we all violate the "Don't cross the street" taboo. Violating it is the only way to end up with a judgment based on our own experience. Dangerous or not, we must find out if it's possible both to cross the street *and* to avoid being hit by cars.

The first time we make it safely to the other side of the street on our own, the authority on that particular subject begins to shift from the inner custodian to the self. Imagine our self compartment overtaking an inch or so from the compartment controlled by our phantom parent. By experimenting, we find out how to watch for speeding cars and what to do if we get caught in the middle when the light changes. Now we are on the way to trusting our own dictates and relying on our own guardianship, so that eventually we can play in the big traffic of the world. We no longer hear Mother's voice telling us to stop. It is what psychiatrists call an *integrated identification*. Each time we confront that archaic directive with the truth of our own experience, we become freer to enjoy riding a bike, taking the bus to school alone, and some of us eventually to attempt skiing, skin diving, or piloting a plane.

Learning to cross the street is comparatively easy. Coming to trust our own judgment in volatile matters such as sex, intimacy, competition, the choice of friends, loves, career, ideology, and the right values to pursue is a much longer and more demanding process.

Breaking Away from the Inner Custodian

By the time we are ready to leave home, we have learned to administer the protections of the inner custodian and to choose directives for ourselves—or so we

---

fundity eventually makes it possible to stretch a person's biography over a theoretical framework and to see the underdesign of a person's development along with some of the original sources of snags and knots. I have tried to put the theory in less abstract terms, substituting "inner custodian" for "object," and to apply it to the stages of adult life to add a deeper dimension to the tasks we face in each passage.

think. It is this internalized protection that gives us a sense of insulation from being burned by life, from being bullied by others (and even into midlife, from coming face to face with our own absolute separateness). The illusion can serve us well while we are young, but it is also very tricky.

This inner custodian is a two-faced image. Like the self, it has two sides. The benevolent side of our internalized parent is felt to be the *guardian* of our safety. The *dictator* side of our internalized parent has the menacing face of an administrator of shoulds and should-nots. Its influence is prohibitive.

Think of Janus, the ancient god of entrances and exits. His two bearded profiles, back to back and looking in opposite directions, represent two sides of the same gate. But is inside the gate safety or entrapment? Is outside the gate freedom or danger? This is a riddle with which we struggle throughout life, for the answer is yes, no, both, and not entirely either.

Particularly in the Pulling Up Roots passage, in which we are shedding an old familiar life system for the first time and feeling exposed and uncertain, we are tempted to take on the form of our phantom parent along with all its weaknesses. We fool ourselves by insisting that it is our choice alone or that we are really quite different. This can be a step backward on the way to a progressive solution, as we shall see. However, many who allow themselves to lapse into this form and accept passively the identity preferred (directly or indirectly) by the family, wind up locked in.

None of us wants to go too far, too fast beyond the value system of our inner custodian, to become too much an individual. Because then we cannot crawl back into the sanctuary when the growing gets rough. This is the conundrum of Pulling Up Roots, indeed, of all the decades well into the middle of the fifth.

The passage in which we are earnestly in transit between the intimate circle of family and the adult world extends roughly from the ages of 18 to 22. The tasks during this time are to locate ourselves in a peer group role, a sex role, an anticipated occupation, an ideology or world view. We generally begin at this stage by claiming control over at least one aspect of our lives that our parents can't touch. Parents can offer lessons and clubs and family trips to Yosemite or the Caribbean, but in the giving somewhat contaminate almost anything they give because it is an extension of their rules and values.

Each time we master an undertaking that replaces the parental view of the world with our own evolving perspective, we overtake another inch or so from our inner custodian. But it is not so simple as a one-to-one transfer. Underlying each of these tasks, there is also the fundamental conflict *within us:* while our Seeker Self urges us to confront the unknown and take chances—pushing the young person to all manner of extremes—our Merger Self beckons us back toward the comforts of safety and the known—and the possibility of locking in prematurely.[6]

A First Solo Flight

On the brink of the Pulling Up Roots passage, the familiar universe seems stale. The conviction is that *real* life is somewhere out there, away from family and school, "waiting to happen to me." Young people who can't wait to put a continent between themselves and their parents and childhood friends are impelled by the desire to defeat the power the family still has to reclaim them. In extreme cases, they choose authoritarian spiritual groups that demand total allegiance and a complete break with past associations. The attractions are the promise of absolute truth, repudiation of parents, and a substitute for the safety of home.

Donald Babcock, the young man we met in Chapter Two who was about to repeat his father's pattern, provides an example of how the Merger Self

56

can overwhelm before the Seeker Self has a chance to kick up its heels.

Donald was graduated from the Hotchkiss prep school and then entered Yale because that was the *family destiny*. If the father is Joseph P. Kennedy, the family destiny is that the eldest son become president. If the mother is Judy Garland, that the daughter be a star. In many instances, the family destiny will define, not a particular occupation, but rather a certain value to strive for: intellectual achievement, creative independence, contribution to one's race, or sheer self-reliance. At the gateway to the twenties, the young person will have to figure out some way to incorporate this parental mandate with his own inner imperatives (or reject it for the time being) if he is to cultivate his own budding distinctiveness.

After finishing his first year at Yale, Donald's motto was loud and clear: "I have to get away from my parents." The getaway vehicle was his parents' car. He wasn't looking for an authoritarian family or for spiritual levitation; he was simply seeking the *real* experience of driving across the country to take a summer job in California. Like most Americans of an age to leave home, Donald set out swaddled in the magical protection we all carry along from childhood. Most of us at that age believe we should have all the powers we presume our parents to possess. We, too, should be able to forecast the future and know where absolute safety lies.

"Be sure to rotate drivers," were his father's final instructions. "That way, nobody will fall asleep at the wheel."

They were going ninety when they left the road. They had just rotated drivers: *I don't know what happened I was asleep at the time I woke up hanging from a seat belt staring at my friend's bloody face I tried to move but nothing would, not my back, my neck, my wrist, oh Jesus, we just laid out there in the desert for two hours*. He could hear others crying from somewhere else in the metal squash. He didn't know it then, but his neck was broken. And also his back.

With all the illusory protection the 19-year-old carries on his first solo excursion, not even this temporary paralysis can be believed. After all, the hero always walks out of the debris, blood-crusted but grinning, and oh what a story to tell some beautiful girl.

"The accident was a setback for me in a lot of ways. I couldn't take the job I had waiting in California. In fact, I couldn't do much of anything. That accident ended my athletic career. I lost fifty pounds. And I was back in a dependent state, living at home again, needing a lot of care. My father would come back after he checked into the office and shave me. My mother would come home during the day from her job; my grandmother was always looking in. It was kinda nice, it brought the whole family closer together. But after a few weeks, it began to drag on. I was immobilized in traction."

Donald's assumption that he could stand on his own two feet had been knocked out from beneath him, although as he saw it from this stage, it was only temporary. It meant that he would have to be propped up a little bit longer by his parents. When fall semester began, he wasn't strong enough to go back to school.

"My father came through with a job for me as a security guard on a museum estate. As a Republican committeeman, he has a lot of jobs to give out. I was against the idea, but here I was in a back brace. My job was to keep people out. Nobody ever came in except horseback riders. Looking back at it, it's weird, but the accident was probably a good thing. In that I got a chance to meet Bonnie."

Bonnie loves to tell the tale of their meeting in an enchanted forest.

"My place to ride on the estate was the Wonderland. I called it that because all the shrubs were shaped like animals. I would get off my horse and let her graze while I wandered under the giant pine trees and around the perfect little pond. It was a place for fantasies. For me, it was love at first sight. I saw somebody there, a boy, sitting against a tree and playing his harmonica. He looked so *passive*. When I rode away, I just couldn't forget his face. I had to go back every day."

What better fairy tale than to bring life to a slightly wasted swain?

For Donald, banished to seclusion in a forest inhabited only by scuttling creatures and small, nervous birds, Bonnie's appearance was a vision of strength. She was the certainty of youth that he had misplaced. How recklessly she galloped toward him bareback; yet dismounting from her horse, she was so ineffably feminine, blonde, soothing as butter on burned fingers.

"She was beautiful. We met in the woods every day for three weeks. Then I had an operation. I was trying to take care of myself. I knew I had to wear a back brace for two more months. I was still literally a cripple. I felt—powerless."

Bonnie didn't know about the back brace until their first public date. She led him to an amusement park. "He was trying so hard to impress me by going on all these crazy rides that I love. Suddenly I realized that this man was in agony. I knew he didn't want mothering . . . but even now I tell him that he shouldn't be sleeping on a waterbed."

How strange it all was for Donald. What a startling contradiction to the syllogism he had worked out for his life before the accident. About not getting married for seven years after graduation, he had been absolutely definite. He was a modern man. But then, abruptly, he had again become a boy, one who needed taking care of. His own parents would not do. To allow such a lapse would be to risk falling back into the old childhood dependency. By transferring the need to a girl his age, Donald could replace the soothing functions of his family. We are all particularly susceptible to "take care of me" contracts at such times. Donald, being now the very picture of 22, settles for a far simpler explanation: "Love is a strange thing."

It seems that his need to recover a sense of safety led Donald to give up his own vision of how to make his way in the world. Almost to the wire before graduation from Yale, he was engrossed in oceanographic research and determined to make an original contribution to the energy problem. But instead of carrying out his plan to go to graduate school, he decided to marry Bonnie a week after finishing college and go into business—just like his father. Although his father welcomed this repetition of the family pattern, Donald's mother was disturbed by it. She tried to search her son's mind for the kind of marriage he envisioned.

Donald told her, "This may surprise you, but I really would like a marriage pretty much like yours."

"That's flattering to hear," his mother admits, "but Donald hasn't a clue about what a marriage like ours is. He's seen what he wanted to see. How can my son know what it's like to live with a lack of communication?" Although Donald tells her he hasn't altogether abandoned the idea of graduate work but wants first to "take a shot at the big time" and build financial security, his mother foresees for him a duplication of the narrow, risk-fearing path taken by the man she married.

Ken Babcock didn't dare wrestle with identity questions when he was a young man either. Today, his is the slugged face of a man who has led with his chin for a quarter century in the big ring of American business. Always a contender but never quite champion, never imagining what it would be like to say what he really felt. It is only in middle age that Ken Babcock has broken out of the I-must-become-president mold mandated by *his* father. Only at 48, for the first time, is he beginning to feel comfortable living within his own contours while asking, uncertainly, for confirmation that what he has become is enough.

And so while his son Donald has also avoided any

early turbulence by passively accepting the family destiny *in toto*, it is but a temporary comfort. Heading off an identity crisis at this passage only inhibits one's development. Other young people who can accept the experience of a crisis at this turning point generally emerge stronger and more in control of their destinies.

4

PLAYING IT
TO
THE BUST

I know another Hotchkiss graduate. As far back as hē can remember his father always called him a no-good black pup. The old man pumped a broom for eighty-four dollars a week, that was at his peak; and all the boy knew of his father was that he looked like something dug out of a mine collapse. Whatever basic values the boy had to work with came from a figure of blunt impact, 240 pounds of it, forever shouldering the children toward some vague goal of social upgrading with the subtlety of a pro linebacker. No one, *no one*, tangled with Mrs. Watlington; she was the terror of the neighborhood. And that was what the boy first wanted to copy about his mother: her physical strength.

The world was four blocks of clean, new housing projects in East Harlem. People there did their dancing and cursing and drinking and kissing and killing in public. The boy grew up messing around with seven or eight dudes just like himself, thinking life was not-now-but-going-to-be something beautiful. But how? He studied the television screen for clues. "Leave It to Beaver" and the other programs in which parents automatically turned on warm water taps of understanding were some kind of TV-man lie; they didn't apply.

It never occurred to the young Watlington boy that they were poor. He had no idea in his tight little world where everyone had the same apartment and the same street furniture—the playgrounds, the gossip benches, the body-to-body swimming pool, the garbage cans overflowing with pinto beans, navy beans, food stamp beans, and the whiff of meat eaten only on Sundays—no more idea of his social pocket than a boy coddled behind the artificially lit frangipani of Beverly Hills can conceive of a family without a therapist.

Rich was not what he dreamed of being, cool was. Loose and cool like the boys who sat around getting high with his older brother. "Those dudes would just sit there nodding and scratching and acting stud to all the girls—playing it to the bust. I couldn't wait to be like them."

Mrs. Watlington had different ideas. She expressed those ideas by "whoppin' ass" with an ironing cord. She whopped until the boy's hide became too hard, "until you got too old and your parents couldn't do nothing more with you," as he says, "and then you went on to be whatever you were going to be. And that was their influence in its entirety."

In most households, this rupture between parents and child would come in the mid-teens. Mrs. Watlington's son was 11. All he thought was, "We're unlucky. One of these days we're all going to pull out—like any success story. But as the years go on, you realize that your eight friends aren't going anywhere except on welfare or into jail or the ground."

The name is Dennis,* the spirit inextinguishable. In 22 years, his collected identities have ranged from showpiece of the neighborhood youth center, to smack peddler, to football star, to being the "black experiment" at a fancy prep school. Back to bum. Then a messenger boy. From there to war councillor for a coalition of street gangs, he built right on up to di-

---

* Dennis Watlington permitted the use of his real name.

rector of the youth center that spawned him. Not long ago, his father shook his hand for the first time.

I offer the story of Dennis to sharpen the focus on denominators common to all classes and colors in the Pulling Up Roots passage. He was not from a benign middle-class background with caring parents and wide opportunities for pursuing whatever course inspired him. He was a boy with one big outer obstacle course before him. Nevertheless, presented with all the tasks of development outlined in the previous chapter, he comes through. The question is why? The answer lies in the way he engages the steps of *inner* growth.*

The voice buried deepest in Dennis's memory of childhood is the one that constantly described the incontestable purpose of all good acts as—"goin' roun' white folks." Mrs. Watlington tied it to every admonishment. She and her janitor-husband were unschooled and locked in early. Consequently, the family destiny she hammered into Dennis was a directive for getting out. School was the vehicle for being like white folks, synonymous in her view with being clean, smart, safe, and not powerless. The message was: *Don't be like us; be like them.*

Parents in economically comfortable families invite identification with themselves. Ken Babcock, for instance, was only too pleased to have his son Donald follow his path—by going to Yale, making the swimming team, marrying young, and forfeiting graduate school to go into business where he could "earn some money, and learn to put bread on the table." If such

---

* A further reason for choosing Dennis as an illustration is the unusually close access I had to the state of his feelings throughout this passage, from the time he was 17 until he turned 22. Intending at first to write an article about him, the research grew into friendship, and the friendship took us over years when it wasn't at all clear how things would turn out for Dennis. I drove him back and forth to prep school dozens of times. When I wasn't around to talk to, he sent his feelings on tape. There were times when I could be helpful to him and other times when he put the finger on certain of my preposterous attempts to duck contradictions in my life. There was also a time to pull away. I was, after all, another one of "them," an adult.

a complete identification "takes," it assures the father that his own status will be perpetuated by his son and serves as an endorsement of his own life.

Things are quite different in families handicapped by class or color or both. Where the burning aim is to boost their offspring up the class ladder, the parents may discourage or even prohibit identification with themselves.[1] They point instead to models of higher privilege.

When Mrs. Watlington could no longer control Dennis with the ironing cord, her recourse was to throw him out of the house. He slept on the stairs, in the park, or in a church. The streets became his substitute for the circle of family, until a black man from the neighborhood, combining the full weight of his mother and father, picked him up by the collar, dragged him off, and gave him a bed. Chuck Griffin was brand new in the youth center business. His idea was to dig out the biggest troublemakers before they hit 12, harness their crazy energies in football pads, and teach them how to beat every honky school on the northeastern seaboard. His initiation method was to beat the living daylights out of each boy and then give him love. An oilcloth sign stretched across the center, spelling out how the coach wanted his boys to see themselves: Home of the Chargers—Number One on the Planet Earth.

In Dennis's estimation, Chuck was the supreme intellect and singular moral power of his universe. Chuck was also, no secret about it, the complete substitute father. His plans for the destiny of his boys keyed in with Mrs. Watlington's idea. He, however, knew how to accomplish it, how to badger the boys into hitting the books so they could play in the games so he could parade their athletic skills up and down New England and ingratiate them into white prep schools on scholarships. This was a reinforced variation of the message: Conduct yourself, not as *we* do, but as *they* do.

Before Dennis and his generation, about the only

boys who escaped East Harlem were those who went into the army or those who took a trip into their own veins and, more often than not, found it a dead end. Of course, that was not how the young Dennis saw drugs. The dealer (along with the pimp and the numbers runner) was king of the ghetto. And that was where Chuck ran into competition.

"The average ghetto kid sees the hustler on the corner with the tailor-made suit and his El Dorado double-parked, and that's money," Dennis explains. "He can *see* it. Suddenly, going to school seems like a drag. I hustled dope for a while before I started using it, and I thought I was on top of the world. I was making more money than my *father*. Two, three hundred dollars a week."

He was 14.

Dennis was always big for his age, one of the biggest and darkest sticks of dynamite in the project. He looked much older. This commanded spontaneous respect from both friends and enemies. There were other innate qualities. He was homely as a boy, a liability he worked hard to overcome by developing his flair for the dramatic. He was intelligent, seething with vitality, quick with wit. Dennis could charm a cop into calling him "Mister" and he built on it.

That is to say, he built a style that attracted other people to him. But where was he going to lead a bunch of boys as energetic and unfocused as himself? The question was, as it is for everyone at this age, which of all the competing identifications would Dennis select for his own behavior? How does anyone sort out the conflicting cues and make sense of what he or she is supposed to be?

Dennis needed to affirm his worth and his strength by becoming a leader. One way of leading would be as a drug hustler. Another way, Chuck's way, would be to break out of the ghetto, absorb all the education possible, and return home to act as a catalyst for other boys just like himself. Copying either hero required a big step. That is why models have such importance.

We are pulled into an identification when we are ready to be triggered; something about the model's behavior helps to channel our capacities and coincide with the impetus to take the next developmental step.

Before Dennis could make such a selection, he reached out, as is usual, for the support of his friends. Among the boys he ran with the strongest was Noel Velasquez. Noel was short but put together like a hydrant. He was a brooding, emotional Puerto Rican boy, passionate as Zapata. That was the nickname Dennis gave him. He pulled his weight on the street by fighting with everything that moved while waiting for an equal opportunity in the narcotics trade. This was the only place where Noel could scratch together some kind of identity. As he confided, "To whitey, I'm a spic. To the brothers, I'm a hick. So where have you got to go? I got it together through dope. In the drug world, there's no color."

Noel became another of Chuck's reclamation projects. Pouring his energy and anger into football, he began to enjoy acceptance at the center for excelling in an approved form of combat. Still, there was a dangerous residue of fury. Noel's father had been brutalizing the boy, by fist and by ridicule, since infancy. His mother whimpered but dared not interfere. The boy had never learned to trust.

Chuck was an insider. Tough as a thug himself, fierce as any sting artist, he also had a good product. He was selling pride. And he wouldn't give up. Night after night he thumped through the projects, bellowing into doorways wherever he caught the scent of a reefer or sensed a needle or spotted one of his boys knocking out elevator lights. "I don't want to see a boy on the streets after eight-thirty, d'ya hear? Anybody wants to smoke, that's five paddles. Drinking is ten. Tomorrow we play Choate. Just remember, you're all part of something."

It was a cliff-hanger. But at that time American society supported Chuck's view. It was 1969, and in the pitching seas of the civil rights movement, sentiment was rolling still toward integration of black youth into the world of white education.

Dennis was on the last curl of the wave.

Eight weeks after Chuck pulled Dennis and Noel off heroin, he was shooing them into the hallowed dorms of Hotchkiss. They were the very first, to use the term then newly popular, "Afro-Americans" to be admitted from the ghetto. Social conscience had come to the school of the Fords and the DuPonts.

By an accident of cultural history, then, the first round trip out of the family universe took Dennis Watlington to the same school Donald Babcock attended. But for Dennis, the pitch between family and the social order was considerably steeper. The angle of ascent was from the pulsing streets of the projects to the remote hills of rural Connecticut, where the windows went dark at ten and all the preppies went to bed with a dependable destiny beneath their Huey Newton posters. The view was beautiful. But in such a rarefied atmosphere, a ghetto boy can get dizzy, if not lose his breath altogether.

The little white boys panted at Dennis's heels like pups. He was streetwise. This, coupled with his repertoire as a gifted role player, made a tremendous impact.

"A lot of people up there are scared of me and let me get my way because half of them have never seen anyone like me," Dennis recounted on his first holiday weekend back home. "They think—Harlem—dives and dope, machine guns and tanks. Pleasing them is very easy. I'm just an act. If some big shot comes to the school, they put me right up top on the reception line. I start smiling, and they say, 'He's happy, see?'"

Very quickly he was caught in some empty social corridor, between two peer groups as different as black and white, between two competing value systems and views of the world that didn't remotely touch. Dennis Watlington yearned to merge somewhere but didn't fit quite anywhere. The day the

Chargers bused up to play Hotchkiss, the sudden collision of forces nearly left his spirit lame.

He was the junior varsity quarterback. Noel had made running back, but Dennis was the star. The Hotchkiss boys had first seen him in action the year before, back when they thought they had the weaknesses of the unknown Harlem team doped out. Coming from *down there*, these exotics would have no discipline and no skills, just brute strength. The preppies were not prepared for the opposite. The bodies of the Chargers were punctured, winded, in terrible shape. But the will and teamwork dinned into them by Chuck's incessant skull sessions were dazzling. The Chargers had won.

This year it was a different ball game altogether. Project boys pitted against their own ex-stars, their great black hopes gone north, arrived half-wishing to find their heroes had sprouted the wings of Vulcan and Mercury. Dennis and Noel had the impossible task of upholding this idealization while simultaneously proving they could not, would not ever (please, Lord!) become that most despised variant of their race— Oreos.

To top it off, Dennis's girl came haughty and sniffing. A gifted singer who intended to marry well and make the best of the world's goods hers, she wanted Dennis to know that Hotchkiss wasn't all that red hot in her book. It wasn't as "fly" as Choate, for instance.

It was after Hotchkiss won the game and the day lapsed into dusk, when Chuck and his Chargers had piled back into their bus and Dennis was left with Noel outside—truly outside, extraneous, suspect as a counterfeit—that the ache of isolation went to spasm in all the boy's fibers. Dennis stood shaking on the school lawn, his face contorted into a smile. Lumping up around the back window of the bus, his old friends waved and watched the face grow small, smaller, disappear into the blot of trees. Gone. Dennis belonged to something else now, something he wanted to hate and hated to want.

"Say I do become successful," he argued it out aloud. "I'll have a whole lot of money, a beautiful house, I'll probably have a lot of broads, but it won't mean a thing. Because I won't be accomplishing anything for my people. Where would I live? White folks aren't going to accept me. And if I go back to Harlem with big bucks, they aren't going to accept me either. So the more money I make, the more I isolate myself."

Struggling to make sense of all the conflicting expectations, he fastened on Chuck as his cue. "I'll make money, but I'm not going to change. You won't see me in silk suits and a Cadillac. I'll have a simple car and a simple life, and I'll go back down to Harlem and work with simple people like myself—the way Chuck worked with me."

Loneliness is the most common companion during one's first year as a tenant in society's circle. Most of us spend that year in college, a job or the army. Dennis had also been placed in a class two years behind his age group, a fact made painfully evident by the contrast between his size and experience and the chickadees in his dorm. Their maximum reach outward had yet to go beyond a beer bust. "Nifty," they called his antics. His loneliness was intensified by the terrible space between the "I can do anything" covering act and his real inner feelings. He could so easily fail.

And did fail—the biology exam, right before Christmas recess. The rest of the students were stampeding for the airport or waiting beside bulging laundry bags for cars to pick them up. Dennis locked himself in his room with Beatles records and wept. He began in a drone to tape a Christmas message for me.

"This is a depressing-assed place. The worst thing about failing up here is you're doing it all for other people. Back home, people will fill you up with 'I'm sorry' and 'Bad break' and 'What happened?' You don't want to face them. All I can do is, I can work harder or leave. I'm sitting here making the decision.

I think I can be just as useful when I grow up without getting all the reputations from the good schools. Money doesn't mean that much to me. All it takes for me to live is a place to eat, somewhere to sleep, and a pack of cigarettes. What I want to do I can't put my finger on . . . but I know I don't want to do this. I'm pretty fucking shattered."

A few days later, Dennis was staring at his reflection in the jukebox at Juicy Lucy's Roadside Rest. "Does it look better?" he asked me. He had spent the morning with a push comb, raking his Afro into a fierce nimbus in preparation for the trip home to New York. But reentry to that familiar circle was like nothing he expected.

All over wasted East Harlem, his friends were dying. It is hard to find someone there who dies a natural death. Six of his buddies had OD-ed, leaving only himself and Noel from the old gang. All of a sudden, they were standing on the rim of hell, looking in.

This bombardment of world views served to innoculate the two boys against slipping back into the drug life, but it also deprived them of their old sanctuary. Between the old spontaneous slap of palms, a beat was missing. The boys at the center either resented them or idolized them. In either case, they fit scarcely better here than at Hotchkiss. They had to continue seeking because there was no place to merge. Back again at school, the two boys became inseparable. In Dennis's words, "We lived for each other."

After that first close year, everything went awry between the two survivors. The easy flip of a peer from conspirator to betrayer, a normal experience at this age and stage, was in their case particularly painful.

The administration cast Dennis, he being the crowd pleaser, as the model the wayward Noel should copy. Dennis bathed shamelessly in this shower of new-found esteem. He couldn't stop himself. The better he performed, the gaudier grew the praise. The more he permitted comparisons at the expense of his soul brother, the wider grew a fatal gap between the two boys.

Noel withdrew. Numbed into a powerlessness of which he was made every waking moment aware, sick with apathy for the school and all it stood for, his devotion to Dennis curdled into revenge. The day he ran away from Hotchkiss, Noel vowed to become king of the streets.

Partly to close the gap before he became too different too quickly, and partly as an act of contrition, Dennis dropped out of school in Noel's footsteps. He found himself in an eerie limbo, back in New York City. "For so long I'd gotten by on being charming and witty and an athlete. But without school to take care of me, I discovered I didn't know how to work or fend for myself. I was a bum. Just another bum without a job."

About here, Dennis began the serious search for that often described but hard to locate sense of identity. He would have to sort out the contradictory identifications with his parents and his substitute father (incorporated as the inner custodian), with Noel and the boys of Hotchkiss and Harlem (who alternated between being buddies and betrayers) as well as the expectations of both black and white worlds.

After some months as a bum, he swallowed a lump of humiliation and sent a distress signal to me. I found him a job as a messenger for the summer at a magazine. On the magazine's baseball team, he gained attention as the heavy hitter. He hardly saw his old friends uptown and began dating white girls. "I was with the type of people I had met at Hotchkiss, around white folks. And they really souped my stuff up. I thought now I knew the game thoroughly, but it was just a new, highly modern form of 'dance, nigger, dance.'"

We all play to the role expectations of the group. Here was Dennis, once more adhering to his mother's dictates by goin' roun' white folks and playing up to their stereotyped expectations. Knowing the act that brought him applause was just that, an act, not an authentic way of being, he nevertheless felt limited to the kind of behavior for which the group would give him recognition. He was the entertainer.

Until Dennis could gather the wanted fragments from his varied and competing identifications, he could not compose his own identity—a *consistent* way of behaving and feeling that would make sense both to himself and to others who meant the most to him. In the meantime, he would pitch and toss from one extreme to another. Most people in the Pulling Up Roots passage do.

The recognition given to Dennis at the magazine was not as a messenger, but as a prep school star destined for loftier position. Buoyed by this playback, Dennis returned, undefended by his conspirator Noel, to complete his last year at Hotchkiss. He was leaving himself wide open to new influences.

Fortuitously, a teacher took him in hand. He had the name of a Viking prince. "A jive-assed Viking, Leif Thorn-Thompson—now how's a street dude going to get tight with any cat wearing a hyphenated name?"

But this TT was a rugged individualist, young, a woodsman, himself something of a thorn in the school's side. He had been officially named Dennis's school advisor. TT persuaded the authorities to allow Dennis to be a day student and take a room off campus with the advisor's family in what was lovingly referred to as "the ranch." Together they hacked down trees and rode bikes hard; TT had been a professional racer. At night, they studied and drank tequila and rapped about life.

"TT became my tutor, my best friend; he's a brilliant man. And that's when the real change began. TT was the person who introduced me to the idea of breaking it down myself, finding out what you are in the things you do."

Dennis came to love the mud on his shoes and the ice-throttled hush of winter woods, a peace broken only by philosophical combat, man to man, in an atmosphere of pure trust. It was, for once, a safe, tight fit. Not that he became a monk. There were still a few run-ins with the state police: mischief, no criminal intent. But after this bucolic interval, upon graduation, Dennis had to come back down to the cement of the projects—and he had forgotten his street smarts.

"Here's the amazing part. The moment I stepped out of the cab from Hotchkiss in front of the center, Noel dragged me into the basement. He said, 'There's a whole lotta rough shit goin' down here. We got this gang called the Slumlords . . .' "

A runner called Cheko comes running in with the message "There's a rumble on 120th and Second—" and Noel heaves a heavy lead chain at the uprooted country boy. Dennis has seen nothing like this since he was 14. The gladiators are all wrapping their chains around their wrists in cold, slow ritual while he watches, having no idea of what is going on. He can't ask. There is no time for a gradual reentry. All at once they are on the street, stalking the Prison Brothers of West Harlem, eyeballed by a phalanx of edgy police. Dennis tries to stuff the chain up under his shirt—what the—the damn thing keeps jumping out like a trick snake.

"Not a half-hour after hitting the city, I was in there swinging that chain. I was just following."

Noel appointed him that day war councillor for the Third World. The Slumlords were no less than the parent body for thirty gangs and chartered to do the negotiating for 7,000 boys. Noel was president. Dennis was to make the decisions on when and where the gang wars would happen. They were the brass.

Dennis was plain naked scared. Scared that first day, scared every day for most of the year that followed. And for good reason. It began immediately to reveal itself: the integration swindle. All those folks who had put money on black boy futures, who had

told Dennis he was chosen to go forth and get the
superior education and come back and save, had sold
short. They were into black power now. His stock had
dropped to zero; in fact, it was a liability.

What's more, Noel had an old score to settle with
the black preppie. Dennis had been the star in an
arena where Noel had failed. Now the playing field
had moved to the cement pen, and here Noel, true to
his vow, had become king. Here, one moment's hesitation between blow and counterblow to think things
through could be fatal. That was Dennis's penalty for
the Hotchkiss years. They both knew that Noel could
destroy him with it.

"I felt like a fool—I couldn't get started," Dennis
confessed. "What was scaring me outa my ass was re-
membering what I had just recently come from, which
was so different and so much safer. I never had to
worry about even a fistfight. Now here I was down
with dudes who were dying to shoot off their rifles,
real rifles, and shotguns and monogrammed derringers.
It got that deep, man. I got to the point of being so
scared, I had to revert to blind ghetto. Now I realize
that I just wanted to belong to them again. I'd been
gone so long that I wasn't special anymore. I was 19
and nothing."

Nineteen and nothing—that was his sense of self
in its entirety. The dictate of his inner custodian (com-
prised of Mrs. Watlington and Chuck) to educate
himself like white folks now stood to lose him the belongingness to his peer group, unless he eschewed
college and embraced the doctrine of black power
gangs. This boomerang of expectations stopped Dennis
in his tracks. He remained stalled there for a year.

"I remember trying to find somebody to take a
picture of me in a big pile of trash. I related there
because I really felt like that."

Every impulse generated its own countermand. He
was at once in search of and in flight from closeness
with others. He hungered for commitment, yet could

not commit himself. He needed a deferment to assemble the many fragments of his makeup before he could take hold. And fortunately, he took it.

Though the Pulling Up Roots experiences of Dennis Watlington were offbeat, his *reactions* are typical. In our confusion over how to answer the "Who am I?" questions of this passage, we are likely to grow excessively dependent on a friend or a group of contemporaries ("Noel and I lived for each other," as Dennis admitted; and on returning to his street companions, "I just wanted to belong to them again"). We may run away (as Dennis did from prep school). We may defer commitments rather than accept stereotyped roles (both the "dance, nigger, dance" role and "blind ghetto" gang leadership were repugnant to Dennis). And many of us experiment with borderline delinquency.[2]

A surprise in one study of highly successful men was that most of them went through a delinquent period as boys.[3]

"Stop the world, I want to get on!" is what we would often like to shout at this point. Our instincts are good. Stopping is probably the best thing to do.

When Dennis at 19 felt himself to be nothing—a bum in a big pile of trash—he was actually involved in a constructive process. Taking time out to sort through the many and contradictory influences of his childhood and early adolescence, he remained for a year in the developmental position psychologists call *moratorium*. It is a delay of commitments. A stop-out. But for Dennis it was also dangerous.

The Slumlords' claim to fame was having five convicted graffiti artists in their junior gang. Their work was recognized, their identity named; they had been convicted and therefore titled as artists. When they weren't emblazoning their *noms-de-rue* the length of five subway cars, they were painting the freedom jackets of their fellow gang members. Each party had its own emblem, a name stenciled in livid hues and embellished with iridescent bijouterie. They traveled like birds of a species held together by the special color of their wings. "Flying our colors" was the term.

As they moved into deep ganging, Noel seized every chance to color Dennis glaring white. To mark him in front of the group as contaminated by the enemy in the way he talked, walked, thought. "Where Dennis comes from, they don't even fight, much less war."

When plots being hatched had to be bilingual to include the Spanish-speaking members, Noel would mark Dennis with his up-classed culturing. "Don't forget French. That school Dennis went to, they say *s'il vous plaît* before they fart."

And there were other giveaways that Dennis could not unlearn, did not want to in fact. How to finesse the gatelatch on a tennis court, for instance. Or how to carry a briefcase into the city bureaucracy as a youth "liaison," which he did, coming back with a few thousand dollars in funding to keep the center open as an alternative to gang terror. He couldn't see the sense of playing with chains and guns and he said so.

Like Jerzy Kosinski's "painted bird," Dennis became one of the innocent victims loosed each day only to be attacked by their own kind because their coloring differs.[4] He was captive to Noel who sought to cast him out, wings smeared with these alien markings, into the suspicious ghetto flock which would no longer recognize him as one of their kin. Which sooner or later, it seemed likely, would tear him apart.

How he hated their ignorance.

Dennis hid his suffering. Chuck, his substitute father and former epicenter of his universe, now had to be compared with TT, the advisor from Hotchkiss.

"What happened was I began to outgrow Chuck. But I couldn't say that to him, not even then. You idealize someone, totally idealize him, and then other people take your thinking higher. It's like losing an illusion forever. I'll never be as close to anyone, and that disillusionment set me back."

This is one of the painful but liberating tasks of

this period: to de-idealize the parent (or parent substitute) so that one can learn to have confidence in one's own judgment.

"I had looked up to Chuck as the supreme moral power. Now he and his wife were splitting up and he was prowling around like a teenager. He began to share talk with me about things grown men usually keep from boys." In Dennis's reaction, we hear the sudden puritanical intolerance that comes over the young when Mom and Dad expose themselves as human. To complicate matters, Mom and Dad's midlife crisis usually coincides with at least one child's adolescence.

An interlude now. So much of Dennis's passage had been consumed with seeking, his Merger Self was more than ready to take over for a while. An older woman offered Dennis her love and comfort. A professional in the city agency where he acted as a neighborhood liaison, she fluffed pillows in his most squalid corners and let him lie back for a cherished spate of passivity. "It was like being supported," Dennis says, "I could take the feminine role." Such transitional figures often help us through a difficult passage.

Dennis resisted the trap so beguiling to many of his contemporaries who are unable to wait out a moratorium. He ran with the gang, but the gang never ran him. By never losing contact with what was inside, Dennis was able to hold on to his free will and to the thread that would lead to his own personal definition. Once his fragments coalesced, he could attach his leadership ability to a commitment that felt right.

Not so Noel. He allowed the group to define him too early. Playing with identity is also playing with fire. Not infrequently, this fire play is for keeps.

The day Noel died, a portent hung over the projects like a darkening of sky just before it rains, but it never rains, it only remains dark. The imbroglio was strictly personal. A paltry blowup, apparently over a girl; it was really a contest between two gang leaders defending their reputations. Noel thought that the bigness of his name, plus showing a small derringer, would put enough of a scare into his rival to cool things. The rival had friends waiting. They blew out Noel's right lung with a shotgun.

"Noel's death was the end of an era in our lives," Dennis says. "I became very straight, hardworking, loyal to my woman, a good provider, got my own place, fixed it up, the whole trip. Damn, I did a lot of growing up in that time."

The age now is 22, the occupation director of a youth center and part-time student at an Afro-American acting school. You can see the pieces coming together. The ironies of his journey through the first passage do not escape Dennis, and he speaks of them with nostalgia.

"When I was 19, I thought I knew everything. And you see, I didn't know *nothing*. Noel would have come to that realization, too. But he got cut off. It begins to frighten me because life goes on. Things seem so set, pat, safe, definite today, but it doesn't stay that way. I'm not the same person I was then, and I thought then was forever."

5

"IF I'M LATE, START THE CRISIS WITHOUT ME"

The crisis model of young people caught in a turbulent passage between their late teens and early twenties has come to be equated with the normal process of growing up. We all recognize hallmarks of this sensitive condition: kids who are at once rebellious, listless, and jumpy. Kids who are seized by sudden and riotous swings of mood. When cramped by anxiety, they cannot sleep or work. They may suffer from mysterious maladies and hold to inflexibly high ideals. Often they seem to be gripped by a negative view of themselves and by hostility to the family. They are likely to drop out of school, the job, the romance, or to stay in and be actively resentful.

In short, it's like having flu of the personality. And since we all think of flu as something to be inoculated against, obvious questions are raised.

Is all this psychic havoc typical of development during the Pulling Up Roots period? No.

In that case, is tumult essential at some later time if one is to achieve identity? Probably yes.

Can't a person get through life without suffering one of these mental blitzes? Yes, if you are willing to let others define you and take care of you—and provided there is always someone whose interest lies in doing so.

Let me explain my answers. First, because the behavior of those late adolescents who are in turmoil is so upsetting to them and alarming to their parents, it can't help but draw the greatest share of our attention. Yet among the general population in this age group, the classic crisis of identity is rather rare. That was the conclusion of a survey of recent studies of adolescent development made by a Harvard research director, Stanley H. King. In his own study of Harvard students, King found the most common pattern to be a gradual and progressive identity formation.[1]

The typical student was a young man who, when faced with present problems, coped in ways he had found to be successful in past experiences. He made friends easily and was able to share his feelings with them, which helped him to work out gradually the kinks in his relationship to the family. Mood swings he would have, but he was not at their mercy. By throwing himself into sports, theater, writing, fun, or enjoying a good laugh at himself, he worked off his depressed feelings. Nearing college graduation, many of his previous self-doubts, as well as the inflexible armor that may have covered them, had begun to fall away.

He knew by now that he could have an effect on people and events and therefore felt a surge of confidence, competence, and personal power. His interests had deepened, interests that did not violate his values. From taking the old, arrogant "I'm absolutely positive" stands, he had relaxed enough to be able to enjoy the prospect of personal freedom to change his moral decisions.

But let us not forget that King was looking only at young men, and at some of the most highly privileged young men in the nation. When these Harvard seniors come to *know* they can have an effect on people and events and thereby feel an increase in self-esteem and a sense of power, they are absolutely correct in their assumption. For most college students outside the privileged corridors of Ivy League schools, and certainly for young women, there is no such guarantee of graduating into the "old boy" network that to a large degree runs the country. And for those who don't have a college diploma, a good deal of scrambling is required simply to get a toehold in the system, never mind assembling an identity.

If a full-blown identity crisis is uncommon during this passage, and evidence of a gradual, progressive identity formation comes only from Harvard men, then where do most of us stand? J. E. Marcia, associate professor of psychology at the University of British Columbia, made an important addition to Erikson's work by distinguishing four "normal" positions in which people are likely to find themselves during the identity formation process.[2]

Some will be in the *moratorium* group. They have not yet made commitments or invested much of themselves in other people, and about their own values they are still vague. But even while delaying their commitments, they are actively struggling toward finding the right ones. They are in a crisis that has yet to be resolved and are taking a stop-out, as Dennis did.

The *identity-foreclosed* group appear very sure of what they want to be, as Donald Babcock was (and probably a good many of the Harvard seniors in the King study). They have made commitments without a crisis, but not as a result of a strenuous search. They have passively accepted the identity their parents cut out for them. The son of a Republican investment banker, for example, becomes a runner on Wall Street and joins the young Republicans. Or the daughter of a suburban California housewife and a landscape architect marries a young man in the local nursery business. Predictably, people with foreclosed identities are more authoritarian than any other group. I call these people *locked in*. Until recently in our culture, this was the slot into which most young women were trundled early.

82

The *identity-diffused* group have shrunk from the task of defining what they want or how they feel. Parents, teachers, or friends expect from them something other than what they can give or want to be. They are not able to rebel against their parents (or other authority figures) or to struggle with them toward resolving the conflict. They perform well enough in school and social roles. But they always feel like misfits. Often, in the early attempt to define themselves, they become immobilized by feelings of inferiority or alienation. But unlike those in moratorium, they do not seem driven to do much about it and are not in a state of crisis. Young women with the opportunity to attend college are frequently, by graduation, in a state of identity diffusion.[3]

The *identity-achieved* group has been in crisis and come through it. They have developed a sustained personal stance with regard to their sense of purpose and view of the world. They are also likely to be a good deal older.[4]

As young people try to fit themselves into, or prove themselves outside of, such categories, they usually pipe up with at least two more questions.

Suppose I do have all the Sturm und Drang *up front. Will it unhinge my later development?* On the contrary. It will probably facilitate it. Students who come down with a classic personality upheaval at this age generally recover quickly, before the senior year of college is out. And they are likely to become well-integrated adults.[5] Harvard psychiatrist George Vaillant, who has been deciphering the results of a fascinating study of 268 men across the span of thirty-five years, finds that a stormy adolescence, per se, was no problem to the normal progression of the adult life cycle. In fact, it often boded well.[6]

If I don't have the crisis at identity-crisis time, must it erupt during a later passage? If you're lucky. A crisis appears to be necessary before identity can be fully achieved.

Seeking an Idea to Believe In

For as long as there has been adolescence, we belonging to its self-conscious legions have had the problem of hiding our gruesome little secret (inadequacy) while trying to appear as the attractive, confident, convivial persons we all want to be all the time. How do we humor ourselves through this contradiction between the ages of 18 and 22? We seek an idea to believe in, heroes and heroines to copy, and we begin to rule out what we don't want to do with our lives.

Most young people search avidly for a cause greater than themselves, in the service of which it will make sense to be an adult. Movements claiming to predict the future of the universe are the most beguiling, for once that monumental matter is settled, the halfway person can throw his energies into managing the messy details of growing up.

Through the 1950s in America, family and society had a fairly integrated impact on the young person. Both reinforced the ideal of building upon the family destiny and of gaining credentials from the proper institutions to be admitted to the adult world. The Silent Generation dedicated themselves to the ideas of *qualifying* for the real world while seeking *togetherness* at home. Drinking and hot rodding, as the chosen experiments, were obvious rehearsals for inheriting the privileges of their parents. The young were doing what their parents did, only somewhat more recklessly. If they were rebels, it was generally without a cause.

In 1960, the traditional pressure to follow in the parents' footsteps was counteracted by a sparkling president with a dedication to offer the young. Kennedy said, in effect, "Follow me in a cause greater than yourself." That cause became egalitarianism in both its meanings: equanimity and equality. Or peace and freedom.

Supporting the egalitarian idea was a go-go affluence that made possible a heightened idealism and raised the expectations of every social class, race, and gender within one young generation to a degree seldom before paralleled in the world. The educated young expected work to be meaningful, institutions to be changeable, liberation for all to be achievable, and life to afford a series of peak experiences.

But the hated war in Vietnam dragged on. And then the money dried up. The causes dissipated. The leaders were dead or deceiving. When the war ended, relief mingled with exhaustion. With the 1970s, the young were washed back in the apathetic aftermath. No more utopias. Some observers say that as a result of their reduced hopes, college students today have a revived sense of optimism.[7] It remains to be seen what and whom they will invent to put their faith in.

The current ideology seems a mix of personal survivalism, revivalism, and cynicism. Uppermost, once again, is the pragmatic—gaining skills as the means to a paying job.

Dennis, in riding the last curl of the egalitarian wave, was carried along by the early interpretation of that idea in the black community, the belief that the best way to make up for ghetto disadvantage was to get an excellent white education. Although that idea has been abandoned in favor of strengthening a separate black identity, it did provide Dennis with a vehicle to make an illuminating round trip between family and society.

His triumph was in refusing to succumb to an absolute definition by any group or its ideology. Instead, he let go to the inner process by which his selffragments could begin coming together. It need hardly be stressed that the temptation to be defined by our peers is hard to resist.

When does a peer group become a deviant peer group? The prevailing sociological theory is that individuals learn to commit crime when the people whose good opinion they most value and the groups to which they belong (peer, family, or neighborhood) believe that criminal behavior is desirable.[8] The premise neatly fits our conception of ghetto kids, but haven't we seen the same principle operating among the most privileged of our middle- and upper-class young? Or among the felons of the White House "family" in the Watergate era?

When revolutionary fever caught the imagination of a generation of American college students, it quickly became contagious. The adult society was seen not only as alien but also as fatally corrupted. By 1968, the group that classified its members as revolutionaries or radicals included almost one-eighth of all college students and about one-tenth of the noncollege youth.[9]

The affinity groups that formed on campuses to carry out trashings and bombings and the Weathermen and the Black Panthers were all deviant peer groups held together, like the street gang, by the common belief that unlawful behavior was desirable. The purpose may differ, demonstrating machismo in a gang versus making a political impact by destructive means, but the necessity of the group as a buffer remains constant.

Erikson strongly favors a moratorium period and even describes the positive effects of delinquency.

Each society and each culture institutionalizes a certain moratorium for the majority of its young people. . . . The moratorium may be a time for horse stealing and vision-quests, a time for *Wanderschaft* or work "out West" or "down under," a time for "lost youth" or academic life, a time for self-sacrifice or pranks—and today, often a time for patienthood [psychiatric treatment] or delinquency. For much of juvenile delinquency, especially in its organized form, must be considered to be an attempt at the creation of a psychosocial moratorium.[10]

Yet Erikson's statement assumes that society in its beneficence grants license for hell-raising to both sexes. Girls stealing? Girls expected to be delinquent? Not in most families. Traditionally the prodigal is the son.

Consider the girl from a conventional background who wants to involve herself totally in a cause. Suppose that she, like Patty Hearst, is exposed to the prolonged, intensive proselytizing of a revolutionary group, people her parents would consider wholly disreputable. Imagine the group's leader to be a wounded Robin Hood. One who would name her, costume her, and teach her resistance. One ruthless enough to defy her parents *for* her. To that delicate footbridge leading back to the sweet suffocation of her family he would take the ax. Would not she, suspended in the breach, leap with a cry of joy to a negative identity?

If the persona held to be fitting by her parents and community was truly distasteful, possibly yes. Unless there are also strong positive feelings about one's parents and one's self, along with the doubts, the young woman or man may rebel by becoming the very opposite of what they are supposed to be. As Robert W. White puts it so succinctly in *The Enterprise of Living:* "When one cannot bear to be a white sheep, it is preferable to be a black sheep than to be no sheep at all."[11]

All too often, a young woman feels unable to polarize herself sufficiently to make the separateness from her family circle stick unless buttressed by a Stronger One, be he guerrilla chief, addict-boyfriend, pimp, or simply the man idealized as superior. She glorifies him as the rival of her parents and empowers him to speak for the "bad" self that she cannot risk expressing. In this way, she evades her own painful developmental task. Consequently, no shift of authority takes place internally from other to self. It is merely an external transfer of control from other (parents) to other. It may look like rebellion, but it's really a forfeit of the self in the vain hope that someone else will direct her to *real* life and absolute truth.

About the outcome of a delinquent period, Erikson is quite sanguine: ". . . the young individual may feel deeply committed and may learn only later that what he took so seriously was only a period of transition; many 'recovered' delinquents probably feel quite estranged about the 'foolishness' that has passed."[12]

I am skeptical about the ease of recovery from being part of a delinquent group. If the young rebel is deft enough to stay out of jail or has well-connected parents who can smooth things over, he or she may pass through this transition unscathed. But when one is prematurely marked by busy authorities as a member of a deviant group ("promiscuous," "junkie," "disturbed"), the amazing tensile strength of the group identification is reinforced. Even the best efforts by agencies to rehabilitate young lawbreakers, to snap the chain of attitudes linked by friendship or neighborhood, have generally met with failure. One explanation for this resistance is offered by James Q. Wilson, professor of government at Harvard: "A deviant peer group—one that encourages crime or hell-raising— would regard any effort by society to 'reform' it as confirmation of the hostile intent of society and of the importance of the group."[13]

Which Model, Hero, or Heroine to Copy?

As the need to de-glorify the parents becomes pressing, an impetus builds to replace them with heroes and heroines. In Dennis's eyes, his school advisor became a "brilliant man," eclipsing his substitute father, Chuck. Though the transfer of idealization from parent to model can be painful, it is an important part of the process by which a foreclosed identity can be avoided. Models close at hand and commonly chosen are an encouraging teacher or charismatic coach, a libertarian aunt or eccentric uncle (the kind who is never shocked).

But the more extreme the new models, the more exotic the guru or ruthless the revolutionary, the easier they are to identify with. For one thing, their exaggerated style is simple to mimic. More important, they beckon the young seeker over a moat, in the imagination at least, where the bridges leading back to the sanctuary of family would be burned. And so the young may be as easily beguiled by the conspicuous glamour of sports and movie stars, artists, and tycoons, as by the scruffiness or sexual flagrancy of young entertainers; by the money and daring of gangsters and prostitutes; by the seething hatred of contemporary Robin Hoods. They are also vulnerable to the charisma of a politician who offers a crusade or to an infantile charlatan who offers them eternal childhood.

It is so much easier to identify with a person rather than with an idea. Given the raw clay of adolescent sensibility, minds as yet undeveloped, moist and yearning for the imprint of an ideal, it is easy for charlatans with commercial interests to exploit the young simply by promising them a bogus new destiny, or a way to "happen" overnight.

The effects of such mind manipulation can waylay youthful development well past the exploratory stage. Many of the "acid heads" who followed the piper of dropping out were well through their wasted twenties before Timothy Leary was exposed.

The spell of idols is binding not only on the seekers of exotic rebellions. "What are all those nice, clean-cut kids doing passing out leaflets on the street corners?" people wanted to know when the Reverend Sun Myung Moon came to New York.

"I come to America by the will of God. I receive a revelation to bolt America. I do my mission unto my death."[14] Thus began the Reverend Moon's message, delivered unto 20,000 youths stacked up to the roof of Madison Square Garden in September of 1974. After an hour of revelation, the Reverend began to lose his congregation. But not his converts. Although limited in number, theirs were the faces that chilled. Deathly solemn, expressionless except for flinches of contempt and a lip-set of distrust, they scoured the crowd with Secret Service eyes from the aisle seat of each row.

These too were American kids, between the ages of 16 and 22 one guessed, but somehow they all resembled young brown-shirts.

Once they might have joined the Peace Corps or been bused to GOP convention galleries to chant "four more years." They have fled the current thickets of bi-, homo-, and even heterosexuality to live in sexually segregated quarters, protected by a pledge of celibacy (until forty days after marriage) from the terrifying freedom to explore the flesh. Their sex roles, occupation, and ideology are utterly defined by the self-proclaimed redeemer.

All have become members of the Reverend Moon's "family." They have given up their own families, and in many cases their savings, to venture without risk. Traveling the world in tightly structured "teams," the converts are trained to spread the gospel by rote public relations. There is room, too, for circumscribed aggression. The boys act as security guards at the revival rallies, where any dissenter is labeled by reflex as a "Communist devil" and summarily silenced.

The acolytes of Moon have found in their other, that authority they cannot as yet grant to themselves.

"What Am I Going to Do with My Life?"

Most of us during this period of exploration are vague, if not void of ideas about what we want to do. We generally begin by defining what we *don't* want to do.

"You won't see me in silk suits and Cadillacs," Dennis was certain at 18.

Other people will say they knew they didn't want to be "a digit in a big corporation" or "a dental hygienist like my older sister" or didn't want to "spend the rest of my days in Dyess, Arkansas."

For sons and daughters of people who are well known, the process of elimination usually begins with a statement like one from the heir of a family of Southern politicians: "All I knew was that I did *not* want to stay in the South and be John Dey Manning's son and Jay Manning's grandson and so-and-so's great-grandson. It was time to go someplace else and see if I could make a name on my own."

Most of these responses fall into one of two slots: the "all I knew is I wanted to get out" vow or the "all I knew is I didn't want to be like" oath. Another basic desire is to prolong a while longer the delicious irresponsibility of youth.

We hear the haunting presentiment of a dutiful middle age in the current reluctance of young people to select any option except the one they feel will impinge upon them the least. In the words of a Columbia University student slouching toward graduate school: "I live from day to day. I don't have a panorama of the future ahead of me, and I don't want it!"

6

THE URGE
TO
MERGE

Until recently, seeking has been done primarily by boys and merging by girls. Girls could seek scholarship so long as it didn't interfere with popularity. It was fine to take a summer job, but not to embark on a serious career. They could train their talents in dance lessons, drama clubs, piano recitals, church choirs, any of which would suit them well for a lifetime of pleasing. Unless—and this apprehension lurked always in the back of the mind—they turned out to be gifted. For then they would be forced to make a painful choice: either marriage or mastery of their art. Most of them gave up the lessons.

Boys learn basic skills of teamwork and competition on the sports field, skills that later serve them well in business and political organizations. They are also introduced to buddyism in the locker room. In activities approved for girls, there has been little practice with competing and even less opportunity for comradeship. Girls rarely found themselves in situations comparable to a football game or military service, in which the adventure involved great-enough risk to demand interdependency. Sharing an apartment with a roommate was mild by comparison and usually perpetuated the competition for boyfriends.

All You Need Is Love

The mass cult of songs, soaps, poems, pulp, flicks, scents, ads, art, and miscellaneous hype extols LOVE as all a girl needs. This has a far broader impact than the most exquisite thinking of any social scientist, for instance Abraham Maslow.[1]

In his "hierarchy of needs" theory, love and belongingness follow right after food and shelter and safety. Yet there are two more rungs beyond love on the ladder of human needs. One is *esteem,* the desire for achievement, mastery, competence, and confidence, as well as for the respect and recognition of others. Beyond that is the need for eventual *self-actualization.*

Most theorists agree that more than anything else, it is successful work experience that helps a young person resolve the conflicts of dependency and establish an independent identity.[2] But while young men have been encouraged to make the search for a lifework their first priority, young women have been expected to be content with, and adjust to, a sense of identity bootlegged from their sex role. The message has been: You are who you marry and who you mother.

True, alternate models for girls now enliven children's books, magazines, the TV screen, even congressional hearings. But in the excitement over new heroines, it is easy to overlook one fact, as simple as its power is stunning: The very first image every girl identifies with, her model at the earliest and most penetrating stage of development, is mother—a woman who unmistakably had a child.

How does a young woman pull loose from her phantom parent and establish her own identity if the only occupation fully endorsed for her is to become her mother in her own married household? The answer is, of course, that most women up to recent times did not pull loose.

It was barely conceivable, before the 1960s, that

a girl child could embark on Being Somebody before her father had escorted her to the altar under a fingertip illusion veil. The door to adulthood would be magically unlocked by wedlock, a piece of doublethink endlessly celebrated. This form still persists as the most favored route to female identity: the *"complete me" marriage*.

But if only mothers and fathers and society push young women into wedlock, how do we explain all the daughters of today's wiser parents who warn them to wait, but to no avail? An even subtler coercion works on young women: their own inner timidity.* They *want* to believe that a man will complete them and keep them safe. Marriage is a half step, a way to leave home without losing home. Somehow a substitute world is going to materialize spontaneously out there, a playhouse, important friends, excitement. What such a marriage brings instead is a foreclosure of identity. The commitment to being a wife is made before the individual is allowed, or allows herself, to struggle with and select from the possible life choices. The pull is back toward safety and sameness, a highly seductive pull in the late teens and early twenties.

The problem has been that most young women wouldn't dare or weren't allowed to have an identity crisis. And so they never quite grew up.

The Piggyback Principle

Throughout the film *American Graffiti*, the high school hero wavers about pulling away from his steady girl and the whole comfortable universe as he knows it to depart for college 2,000 miles away. The drag and thrust is punishing. The boy hesitates, falls back into the arms of his sweetheart; they cling. Throbbing

---

* A distinction is intended between fear—of real and observable dangers (i.e., the streets are icy; is it safe to drive the car?)—and inner timidity, which I have used to mean the inner picture one has of a situation and the meaning one assigns to it.

through the soundtrack is a wishful theme song that
repeats the romantic logic:

> "Only you make this change in me,
> For it's true, you are my *destinee*." ©

The longing to merge with a lover is perfectly
natural at this stage (as is the impetus, previously
described, to seek a cause greater than oneself and
people and ideas to put one's faith in). But particularly
for young women, that natural impulse has grown into
a full-blown assumption.

The assumption is: we can piggyback our development by attaching ourselves to a Stronger One.

Serena was a small-town girl who went away to
college in Champaign, Illinois. She wanted to believe
in the piggyback principle, too. How she craved in the
formlessness of freshman year to have her hometown
Jim beside her. Spinning through the library carrels,
through the sex maze and value systems of people from
practically everywhere, Serena was no longer the big-
fish high school leader. She was one of 36,000 minnows
swept along in the tides of a Big Ten university. "I
desperately wanted somebody there to understand
what I was going through."

Jim, apparently the strong, detached one, wrote
back from his own distant university, "You can't keep
hanging on to me."

Serena had a strong advantage over girls who are
encouraged to lean. She was the eldest daughter, and
firstborn daughters are often brought up with privileges and expectations no different from a son's. Their
fathers are likely to emphasize abilities rather than
sex role, to teach them sports, and to encourage them
to seek excellence. They are given chores and often
expected to earn their own way, as Serena was. Frequently, fathers seem to be seeking in a firstborn
daughter the comradeship they can't have with their
wives because their wives are always starting dinner.
A phenomenon observed in some of the biographies I

collected was also noted in a University of Michigan study of successful men. While their wives were definitely expected to be noncompetitive and non-achieving, the men took pride in a competitively successful daughter. She was often the favorite because she, unlike a son, could reflect well on her father without becoming a rival.[3]

The outstanding event of Serena's freshman year was this: all turned out in businesslike brown, even to the matched stockings and executive-height heels, Serena marched into the school newspaper to impress the editor. He, in his Bolshevik jeans, laughed but gave her the job. She was good at it, very good. The longing for Jim subsided (but not much). She wrote him fourteen-foot-long letters on the wire service rolls.

Love at 18 is largely an attempt to find out who we are by listening to our own echo in the words of another. To hear how special and wonderful we are is endlessly enthralling. That's why young lovers can talk the night away or write fourteen-foot letters yet never seem to come to the end of a sentence.

Then the snapback. Home from the first year's stretching at college to the old ties of high school: the Indian summer of childhood.

"When Jim and I got back together that summer, we were suddenly bumping into each other, not fitting in." They slept together for the first time, but sex would not cement the gap between them. Serena and Jim spared themselves falling victims to the Piggyback Principle. The chafe of their uneven growth was too evident.

At a new coffeehouse in town, for instance: "Why can't you wear lower heels?" Jim was shorter than Serena, a discrepancy he had never mentioned before. Now he seemed determined to cut her down to size.

"I'm already in flats."

Like all the rest of their friends, Jim hadn't the first inkling of what he wanted to do. Serena was the exception; she knew. When she bounded across the coffeehouse to interview the manager, Jim blew up.

"Why do you have to look for a story on a date with me?"

"But I'm"—hateful words, envied identity—"a newspaper reporter."

Jim began taking an interest in another girl. He clearly resented the conversion of Serena from hanger-on to entity, and one who dared to match him intellectually.

"It was suddenly a snapping period," she says. "The puzzle pieces had all reshaped themselves, and we didn't fit together anymore. I decided that we both needed a lot more room."

And with more room, both of them flourished. From the vantage point of her mid-twenties, Serena can say, "Jim was probably the first person who helped me to grow up." She also acknowledges that every young girl she knows tries to smother her first love in possessiveness. Oh, what tears and rejection await the girl who imbues her first delicate match with fantasies of permanence, expecting that he at this gelatinous stage will fit with her in a finished puzzle for all the days. Serena was fortunate.

Jailbreak Marriage

Although the most commonplace reason women marry young is to "complete" themselves, a good many spirited young women gave another reason: "I did it to get away from my parents." Particularly for girls whose educations and privileges are limited, a *jailbreak marriage* is the usual thing. What might appear to be an act of rebellion usually turns out to be a transfer of dependence.

A lifer: that is how it felt to be Simone at 17, how it often feels for girls in authoritarian homes. The last of six children, she was caught in the nest vacated by the others and expected to "keep the family together." Simone was the last domain where her mother could play out the maternal role and where her father could exercise full control. That meant good-bye to the university scholarship.

Although the family was not altogether poor, Simone had tried to make a point of her independence by earning her own money since the age of 14. Now she thrust out her bankbook. Would two thousand dollars in savings buy her freedom?

"We want you home until you're 21."

Work, her father insisted. But the job she got was another closed gate. It was in the knitting machine firm where her father worked, an extension of his control. Simone knuckled under for a year until she met Franz. A zero. An egocentric Hungarian of pointless aristocracy, a man for whom she had total disregard. Except for one attraction. He asked her to marry him. Franz would be the getaway vehicle in her jailbreak marriage scheme: "I decided the best way to get out was to get married and divorce him a year later. That was my whole program."

Anatomy, uncontrolled, sabotaged her program. Nine months after the honeymoon, Simone was a mother. Resigning herself, she was pregnant with her second child at 20.

One day, her husband called with the news, the marker event to blast her out of the drift. His firm had offered him a job in New York City.

"Then and there, I decided that before the month was out I would have the baby, find a lawyer, and start divorce proceedings." The next five years were like twenty. It took every particle of her will and patience to defeat Franz, who wouldn't hear of a separation, and to ignore the ostracism of her family.

At the age of 25, on the seventh anniversary of her jailbreak marriage (revealed too late as just another form of entrapment), Simone finally escaped her parents. Describing the day of her decree, the divorcée sounds like so many women whose identity was foreclosed by marriage: "It was like having ten tons of chains removed from my mind, my body—the most exhilarating day of my life."

Openings

Springing up from the multiple attitude revolutions in the last decade, a lively tolerance for diversity now supports more openings: pilgrimages and communes as a temporary way of life, living together, staying single, becoming a bachelor mother or remaining a childless couple, experimenting with bisexuality or homosexuality. People who can prolong their schooling or who qualify for tempting career apprenticeships are marrying later, having children later, having fewer children, or planning none at all.

Barbara, now 31 and still single, is of the first generation of women to be more relaxed about making such departures from the old mold. She also had five willful aunts and a family history that supported the idea of eccentricity. Although her mother wanted Barbara to be "gorgeous" and marry rich, her father took pleasure in explaining complicated information to the precocious little girl. "I think he wanted me to be a kid, and stay that way as long as possible and never ask him for money."

Very early on, Barbara had an important presentiment: "The great thing about being a kid is that you have a long apprenticeship—if you'll take the trouble to put yourself through it." She began at 18 teaching herself to write fiction. Her stories were terrible, naturally, but that bothered her not in the least. Craft is everything, she had been told by an older friend who was a writer, and once she got craft down, everything else would follow.

Her ideas about what she didn't want to be could not have been stronger. "I wasn't going to end up like the kids I knew in the suburbs, who were spoiled and dumb and whose parents' values were idiotic. I had no interest in being a normal, average kid." But she was typically foggy on how to go about getting what she wanted, "which was, I suppose, an apartment and a job."

And so she made the break with her family, at 19,

by dropping out of college and running off with an older man. "I didn't want to live with him particularly, although I tried to talk myself into it, but I knew I didn't have any choice. I had no money, no job, no skills, nothing. To get those things through the normal channels, you go to college for four years. I just didn't see that for me." Of course, she did have a choice. What she saw was an older man who would be the vehicle to transport her into the adult world; once there, she broke off with this transitional figure and before the year was out, found her first official apartment, roommate, and job. "I got off pretty clean, though to this day I don't feel terribly honorable about it."

By the time Barbara was 25, she knew her craft and knew what was publishable. She had returned to school and was just now finishing up. She took a summer job as an office temporary and wrote up a storm. That fall, her first story was purchased by *The New Yorker*. Deliriously happy, she ran off with another man, thinking "this was a blazing love," and hit ground rather hard. At 29, she began to bring to her love life some of the discipline that had always characterized her writing life. She had met a wonderful man. "I was very glad I took a year to get to know him, a year in which my first book appeared and I fell in love." At present, Barbara and her beau are about to throw their possessions together. What she is feeling is terror—"I don't know if I'm fit to live with; who knows?"—but for the first time, she feels her emotional life is grounded.

For all her initiative and stick-to-itiveness, Barbara was not without ambivalence in her merging instincts. All along she wondered, "Why couldn't I have been the sort of person who just settles down and doesn't give anyone a moment's trouble, meaning, have a baby and the whole thing. I didn't want it. But I felt that I should have. In my happiest moments, I wouldn't have traded my life for anybody's.

In my most unhappy moments, I would say, 'Well, it's clear that you're just nuts and no one will ever have you.' But I was always very smart, cold, clear, and uncomplicated about my own work. I love to write. I want to have everything. And I don't see why I can't."

Considerable support among young people of Barbara's generation has shifted away from being locked in and toward the pattern she chose. A person may keep his or her options open and move from one tentative commitment to another, actively seeking people, ideas, and some endeavor to believe in but maintaining a transient status.

Yet even today, sociologists report that many women between the ages of 18 and 24 live as if suspended. They can't bring themselves to make career commitments, or any extended plan for that matter, until they know whom they are going to marry.[4] And although today there are many trial marriages, as Gary Wills says, there is no such thing as a trial child.

The Complete-Me Child

When it becomes imperative in the late teens to prove that one can *do* something, make something work on one's own, the easiest place for a young woman to turn is to her uterus. The occupation of baby maker is always available. It gives her a clear identity. Motherhood may be a very satisfying occupation, but it is also one behind which all those fears about not measuring up in the outside world can be hidden.

Contemporary theories advanced to explain the desire of women to use their anatomy range from Erikson's controversial concept of a woman's "inner space" (a perpetual vacuum asserting her emptiness until it be filled) to a more varied list of reasons proposed by Edward H. Pohlman in *Psychology of Birth Planning.* A woman may wish through having a baby to prove her competency, to assert her gender, to compete with her mother, to ensnare a husband, to gain attention, to fill up her time, to punish herself or others, to become immortal.[5] Striking by its absence from this list is the universal wish to attach to another.

Great leaps of the last fifteen years in technology and ideology have given us the brand new "contracepted woman" and a profound feminism, followed by antimotherhood books and even antifertility rites. The revolt against automatic motherhood has spread to all classes. In a 1973 survey by Daniel Yankelovich, only 35 percent of college women and an astoundingly low 50 percent of noncollege women agreed to the proposition that "having children is a very important value." How much of this is their heads talking? Career counselors say that young women students today may *know* that motherhood is no longer a lifetime career, but they still cannot feel that way about it.

The thrall of motherhood has subsided very little among girls from 15 to 19. The birthrate plummeted by one-third in the 1960s for girls between 20 and 24. Yet married teen-age girls continued to turn out babies at an amazing and almost consistent rate over the same period. And nearly half the brides in this age group are rushed to the altar by shotgun.[6]

Girls from poor families aren't the only ones preoccupied with their reproductive powers, although for them the compulsion is all the more poignant for the literal lack of anything else to do with themselves. Once they leave high school, there is no job, no further schooling, no higher goal even suggested within their milieu than to carry a nice boy's child, preferably their husband's.

But things are definitely changing. After tonsillectomy, abortion is now the second most frequently performed operation in this country.

Compulsory Graffiti

What now is the story for Ms. Average American Girl? She is likely to be graduated from high school but not from college. She will find a tentative job, become a wife at the age of 21, and exit from the work world shortly thereafter to start a family. She will remain in this domestic setting until her mid-thirties. What girls aren't told is the plot of the second half of their lives.

The average American woman is likely to return to work at 35 when her last child enters school. She can then look forward to a career, or more probably clerk-work, for the next *quarter of a century*.[7] This paragraph should be written on the walls of the girls' washrooms in every high school in America.

Boys have the urge to merge, too. For almost every female identity foreclosed by early marriage and maternity, there is likely to be a young man tied into an occupational slot before he has had time to experiment with his latent talents. A study of 5,000 high school graduates found that those who went right to work or into full-time homemaking were more constricted, had less intellectual curiosity, and less interest in new experiences.[8]

At least temporarily, such young people surrender the battle to invent themselves and take on instead the form proffered by father, mother, teacher, religious leader, or the group. They find themselves in the position I describe as locked in. (This correlates with the "identity-foreclosed" status defined by Marcia). Understandably, one of the most popular routes out of the locked-in position is divorce. Teen-age marriages are nearly twice as likely to end in dissolution as contracts made at later ages.[9]

The College Woman

Although it appeared the best chance to seek was to be had by those with advanced educations, that liberalized notion backfired on many college women. What a shock it was when the early instructions to be as bright and industrious as boys were reversed, at least implicitly, to read: Be pleasing, not competitive; be loved, not ambitious; find a man, not an occupation (unless it was teaching, because, it was said, one could always combine teaching with raising a family).

Is it any wonder that most women came out of college with their identities diffused? Discouraged by the external world and debilitated by their inner fears, they gave up searching for their own form and commitments. They could not, therefore, have the crisis and growth that search provokes. Upon graduation, most college women were searching for a man and, if anything, had a "Why aren't I married?" crisis. Once that was resolved, their identities were usually foreclosed, at least for the time being.

In 1969, a study comparing male with female personality development in college finally broke the grantsmanship barrier. (Funding had been withdrawn from a previous such study because the foundation thought the results disturbing.) Anne Constantinople took a cross-sectional look at 952 undergraduates at the University of Rochester, using Erikson's measure of personality development to score each student. These were her findings:

Although the women seemed more mature when they entered college, only the men moved consistently over the four years toward a resolution of their identities. The academic environment supported and coaxed the male student toward making career choices and gaining assurance. The same pressures and opportunities led many female students to a prolonged sense of identity diffusion. (The identity-diffused, as described by Marcia, are unable to rebel against their parents, teachers or friends, who expect from them something other than what they want or how they feel; hence they perform well enough but always feel like misfits.) Many of the young women felt they had to choose between a career and being a parent, a choice no young man is asked to make. So long as the women students could not make this decision or put it off, they were unable to resolve their identities.[10]

Finding My "True Self"

Why can't we hurry up and find absolute truth at 21?

The notion of a true self embodying all real goodness is a romantic fiction. The best of all parents have not shielded us from wrestling with the problems of security, acceptance, control, jealousy, rivalry. The strategies for living that we develop, some causing us to be tender and loving and others egging us on to be competitive and cruel, form parts integral to our distinctive character by the end of childhood.

To "know thyself" in the full sense, one must eventually allow acquaintance with all these parts. This is the opportunity presented to us as we move through a series of critical passages. But although a writer finds it convenient to assemble a great variety of studies and biographies into a concept such as passages, the person moving through the steps one at a time is absorbed by the developmental tasks of whatever period he or she is in. And even as one part of us seeks the freedom to be an individual, another part is always searching for someone or something to surrender our freedom to.

7

BEGINNINGS
OF THE
COUPLE PUZZLE

The near-perfect face of a young woman turns fitfully in the California morning, the lids over her glassbright eyes shoot back. The world, glaring, ultraviolet, is open to her. But something intrudes. Her pledge. She had vowed to awaken on this birthday with the direction of her life settled. Instead, she lies still (this thistle of a girl who has rarely topped 100 pounds), feeling fat and stymied. Outside her bungalow, the physical culture fanatics are already dancing their way to the sand and there is nowhere to hide from the relentless optimism of this southern California sun. Only a few years ago it matched her outlook exactly.

Adventure and thrills and strength and romance and intelligence—those were the words Nita had used to describe her dream. They might be said to epitomize the dream of the twenties. But although Nita is now 25, developmentally she is still in the Pulling Up Roots passage and not yet able to tackle the work of the Trying Twenties. This is not unusual. Although rough age norms have been given for each period, individuals may vary considerably. Again, the sequence is the thing.

Ian awakens, is up and immediately in action. She watches her husband's back. How precisely he goes about his morning routine, uniforming himself in his stiff white intern's lab coat, rolling the EKGs into his briefcase. For his disciplined side she envies him. It is his reckless side, though, that deeply excites her.

It was Ian who introduced her to risk, through the kayak, the surfboard, rock-climbing, backpacking, skiing like the wind. It was amazing to watch what her body could do. With Ian in the lead, she found herself shooting rapids, dangling from a rope while whacking pitons into inhospitable granite. The effervescence of being equal to it all!

In his aura she can feel always the surge of energy. How strange this exchange of electricity; it is almost as if she absorbs his juice. The optimism begins rising again.

Ian always has to get to the top of the mountain or round the final bend of the river; this is his thrust in all things. Having no such finite goals of her own, she has coupled herself to his.

"It was a substitute way of feeling good about myself. He was so proud of me. And I felt we had reached a very mature relationship because he wasn't anything like my father. My father's pursuits were, how would you say it, more civilized. Ian demands of me in a lot of adult ways."

But he will not tell her how to do her life.

To understand why Nita, earnest as she is, feels so blocked and tormented, one must measure the gap between her family's instructions and the tall image she has set for herself. For the first 18 years, the dimensions of Nita's universe were exceedingly small. The family was solidly Catholic, the California town tiny and provincial, the parochial girls' school sheltered. No one knew why out of the blue she chose the most radical of exits. She might have begun pulling up roots less brutally, gone away to a religious college or to a more traditional campus. Berkeley was as far away in spirit as she could get.

One major break was not enough; she rushed on to another. Thrown together with a sexually sophisticated roommate, Nita was determined to amputate her own moral code. She promptly coerced her high school steady into sleeping with her. Months into her new realm, Nita was reeling. Shocked at herself. Deprived of the easy confessional, having eschewed all that, she had to reach even farther back. "I wanted my mother to say it was okay."

She pressed on, presenting a brave front through the People's Park sleep-ins, facing the police lines and the rest of the commonplace violence. Yet beneath Nita's ritual sponsorship of the "fuck the system" banner compulsory to that time and place, there was a little and good girl scared to death she'd be found out.

Although it was the last thing she could have admitted then, "Berkeley absolutely took the wind out of my sails." Her leap had been too grand. She needed a retreat, quiet, a period of hibernation to catch up with herself. She quit her summer job in San Francisco and gladly went back home. "What I wanted to do was hide."

As a hedge against the future, she applied to Stanford, convinced she would not be accepted. This would give her an easy out to sidestroke for a while, she thought, maybe travel a bit. Clearly, Nita was trying to create a moratorium. Stanford did not cooperate. It accepted her.

Here was an environment so benign—good God, the girls wore nylons to class! and talked about fixing her up with a "hunk"—that Nita was by their definition a patented hippie, without even trying. She decided to play the role. Hooking up with another apparently advanced young woman, the sophisticated Jessica from New York, she would announce to her marveling dormmates, "We're splitting for the night to break windows." And in fact they did turn up at all the trouble spots, as dutifully as if they were pouring for sorority teas. They didn't trash, curse, never broke a thing. Nor did they get arrested, for that would have cut off the support from their parents.

In the summer of her junior year, Nita agreed to

make another jump, this time across country with Jessie to start a drama workshop for children. At the last moment she backed out of her seven-league boots. It wasn't until late August, yearning to mend the tear in their bond, that Nita crossed the continent to visit her friend in Boston. Jessica ignored her.

With some amazement, Nita confessed in her senior year, "I still don't feel independent."

Each one of us has our own *step-style*, the characteristic manner in which we attack the tasks of development and react to the efforts we make.[1]

Some of us take a series of cautious steps forward, then one or two back, then a long skip up to a higher level. There are those of us who thrive on setting up sink-or-swim situations: "I can't do it without a deadline," or "When my back's against the wall, I always manage to come through." Others, when face to face with each task, sidestep it for a time in a flurry of extraneous activity.

Nita's step-style is to take a giant leap and then retreat. No sooner does she begin to recover, forgetting her trepidations, than she requires of herself another overextension. And is miserable if she cannot execute it. We have seen her repeat the design. (She throws herself at Berkeley and at her high school boyfriend, then runs for cover at home and accepts refuge at Stanford. She commits herself to Jessica's far-off scheme, then withdraws, and later tries to make amends.) She keeps fooling you because it looks as if she is taking steps. On second look, one wonders if she is an escape artist.

By her senior year Nita had made a good deal of progress in testing out her own sexual code. Giving shape to her aspirations was far more intimidating. Zoology was her major. As a secure career prospect it left something to be desired. Enter here an influential figure (almost an archetype), an English professor. Having spied an exceptional term paper of hers, he sought her out to join his special class.

"He took me under his wing. He thought I was a good writer. That was very appealing."

Although the ability was there, Nita was certain that each time she wrote something good it was a fluke.

"I never really knew it was a good paper until someone put an A on it. I was grasping. I didn't believe in my talent, and I didn't know what to do with it. My indecision seemed to make the professor uncomfortable." And then comes Nita's refrain: "He couldn't tell me what to do with my life."

"You could publish," her teacher urged at last.

Freeze.

From that moment until the end of the term, this young woman who would feel adequate only if she became all at once a Lessing or a Vonnegut could not write another line for his class. "I was afraid he'd find out I didn't really have what he thought I had."

With all the proclamations of feminism as her shield, in this area she is still up against the terrifying opposition of both phantom parents. Nita wants to express her ambitions, to have a career and win her own way in the world. But aggressiveness of this sort, for a female, has no antecedent in Nita's life. She has an authoritarian father who believes that nice girls don't have careers, and a traditional mother whose programming never varies from telling Nita she should want to be a good wife.

What if she blatantly violated their instructions on what it means to be "nice" and "good"? Suppose she were to succeed in becoming altogether different from her mother? An oddball poet of acknowledged passion, let's say, who lived in a pea green houseboat on bean sprouts and a small sinecure from the local arts college. Would anyone want a creature so possessed, a woman who was so blatantly, all by herself . . . adequate? Certainly not a man, as Nita says, with the qualities "to replace" her father.

On the other hand, if she were to throw all her chips blindly into the gamble on her talent, believing that on the strength of success she could later claim her reward in love (as men do), what if, within inches of mastering the discipline, she turned out to be a second-rate player? What becomes of aspiring women who fall short? To be consigned to a limbo between dependent wife and independent achiever, unvalued in either realm, no children for an excuse, no man to take care of her, the charms of her twenties spent—this is a fate too punishing even to contemplate.

A great deal of effort on the part of many college women goes into avoiding either one of these fantasied fates. The simplest and what appears to be the safest option, though it is not safe at all, is the one to which Nita was drawn. Rather than risk failing big, she retreated from the attempt and failed small.

At the end of her senior year, Nita felt "the whole world was open to me. And then I started getting scared. I never did spring out into the world. I had a great many ideas about what I could do," she says, "but I didn't have the determination, the guts, the emotional energy to put them into effect."

Who would tell her how?

She met Ian in Palo Alto shortly after graduation. Not on impulse alone was she attracted to him; she knew of him by his legend. He was the Lochinvar of her home town, older by five years and superlative by reputation. Not that Nita was seeking a man to live for. Clearly, to do so in the 1970s would have been heresy. By that time, Nita was a thoroughgoing feminist. Ian was the first man she had ever met who sensed what he had to gain from a liberated female.

"I wanted to be my own person. But I also wanted to go with him. I thought he would *force* me to be independent."

Beyond this dubious piece of reasoning, there was a further contradiction in Nita's thinking. Adventure and thrills and strength and romance and intelligence —the words she had used to describe her dream— were exactly the qualities she saw in Ian, *already plugged in.* He was one live wire, this young man; that very week he was flying off to a medical internship. Nita felt as though he turned some switch in her works that animated her down to the last skittish neuron. What's more, she was sure she would lose him if she didn't follow.

She followed Ian. Her mother approved. In fact, their first date had been arranged by her mother and his. With this sanction in mind, Nita gathered the grit to live with but not marry this near stranger. Soon after began the parental campaign.

"They played to my lowest instincts. Intellectually, I didn't buy all that nonsense about how he'd marry me if he truly loved me and that would prove I was a nice girl. But emotionally their argument got to me. I wanted it and didn't want it at the same time, so I married with tremendous reservations."

Ian wasn't looking for a contract either, but since her parents insisted—and a man could hardly find a more infectiously eager companion. Ian believed Nita would do whatever she set out to do.

In that sweet, soft hammock of their first summer together, she luxuriated in timelessness. Guilt began to intrude only when the rhythm of the school year resumed. Should she get a job, or remain flexible and available to Ian? She decided to remain available and sign up for a few classes. The very idea of bounding out into the workaday world for fifty weeks a year frightened her. Furthermore, it seemed a trap. Going back to school was the thing.

"I know I want to get a Ph.D.," she would rake it over and over on her Sundays with Ian. "The question is, in what?"

"It's your decision, honey."

"I like marine biology, and I like English"—nudging always toward his authority. "What do you think would be best?"

In weak moments, he might say, "Well, if you like to write, why don't you write?"

"I'd flop. I'm too normal."

112

She could be, no *should* be, an ichthyologist, a playwright, a brain surgeon, a concert timpanist. Another brand new "should" that Nita has adopted from her generation is one concerning children.

"I can't imagine having a child until I could support it on my own. No one should have to stay married because of children. If I had a career, a way of being responsible, I think I would probably like being a mother."

Instead of trying to compose the divisions between her self and her inner custodian, Nita would simply turn back to her husband to extricate her from the dilemma.

"I.can't tell you what to do with your life," was the way he usually answered.

And she knew he was right, but damn his neutrality!

A year passed. Eventually, she let the decision be made for her by a school advisor. Nita went into Early Childhood Education. And hated it.

"Once I got in as a Ph.D. candidate, I felt safe." But a year later, "I was feeling incompetent, one minute inferior and the next minute superior. It wasn't rational." All that summer, her mind was in tangles trying to extract the one perfect career that would meet all specifications. It had to harmonize with Ian's schedule, gain his respect, excuse her from housework —Eureka! Driving down Santa Monica Boulevard one day, she was seized with a burning idea.

"What I really want to be is a doctor!"

In her own inimitable step-style: "I wanted to plow full speed ahead and take every premed course immediately." Three weeks after leaping into the new program, Nita felt shaken and sure she would fail.

Her mother reinforced her guilt and fearfulness. "Instead of wanting to be a gourmet cook and having the best garden in the neighborhood, you're going to medical school. It doesn't sound right for you at all." Her mother's words, Nita says, struck her deeply.

"You won't stick to it," Ian said. "You're not compulsive enough." He thought it was just as well, after all, when she quit trying.

"It made me feel bad when Ian said that, but I was in no position to deny it." Numbly, she went back to education.

So long as she kept her complaints theoretical and focused on her betrayal by family and society, her husband was sympathetic. "Parents groom daughters for servitude so they can get you off their backs financially," she would rail. "Being supported makes it so easy to get into a dependent role. You become chattel, with no skills or motivation. It makes me furious, and who understands it?"

Ian said he understood.

As polemics wore thin, Nita began to blame Ian for being the one who got her into this fix.

"I'm jealous. You got to go to medical school with everyone's support. I want somebody to tell you what my mother tells me: 'Oh, he works so hard, he deserves to have a clean house and a wife who cooks dinner for him.'" Then she would turn angrily to her husband: "I want the same respectable sanctions you have. Why can't you help me more?"

This, Ian didn't understand at all. "What right have you to make things more difficult for us? I'm working as hard as I can. Why can't you make things easier?"

He's right, Nita has begun to think. Disgusted at her own vacillation, confused about why it should be so, she is growing desperate. "I'm behaving in a way I don't like and nobody else could like. It's going to destroy all my relationships. I have to get up really fast or I'll sink."

She would also love to be the vibrant hostess who doesn't find out an hour before the party that the candles are stubs and ice cubes are what she forgot to make while rushing to finish a paper on Piaget. Sometimes she sees her married and happily jobless friends as the incipient frumps she will never be. At other times she is not at all convinced their values are fraudulent. In fact, "It kills me not to be able to give nice dinner parties."

Nita allows no room for semi-failure or less than signal success. Like so many young women, she feels that in order to justify being different and having ambition she must be able to do all things brilliantly. It's all or nothing. Intimidated into inaction by the voices of her inner custodian, she sees escape only in magical terms: Somehow, she must be transformed into a person of such accomplishment and assurance that the inner custodian would be silenced once and for all.

She might have said, "Okay, one step at a time. I'll get my credentials as an early childhood educator and let myself feel safe in graduate school, while I'm learning to guide small children like my mother did. But I'll also make it my business to write adventure stories about what I know, the outdoor life, and try submitting them to magazines and newspapers. If and when I feel confident about my talent, I might leave the security of teaching and be a writer."

But what she is saying to her inner custodian, instead, is this: *I will be emancipated, liberated, sexually free, career-directed, and not have children—I will be the opposite of you.* Her custodian answers by withholding the inner permission: *Try to be that different and you'll pay for it, fail, be left stranded and alone.*

A favorite way of twisting an intimate relationship out of shape is to invite our partner to replace our phantom parent and tell us what to do. Or what not to do, especially when it's something that we're looking for an excuse to avoid anyway. Men as well as women slip into this common knot.

No matter what answer the partner gives, it can be used against him or her. "It's your fault that I failed; you should have known I wasn't ready." Or, "Why didn't you let me, when I had the opportunity?" A mate is not the one to let. The way to grow is to let ourselves.

It is fortunate to have a mate who resists being cast in the role of the authority (as Ian does). Many

115

mates are more easily manipulated. The well-meaning partner can be jockeyed into playing the heavy. And the bossy wife or authoritarian husband can be goaded into becoming a monster.

"It didn't start looking as if I would fail, that I lack goals and direction, until now," Nita says. Even upon Ian she now looks with resentment. Always she is watching his back. He is ahead, sure, strong, agile, slicing parabolas in the snow, teasing a roll of the surf with a perfect glissando, the pure athletic tension of his shoulders upping toward the summit; and yes, even his distracted good-byes at the hospital—"Loved seeing you, kiddo, but I've got a spinal tap to do before grand rounds"—and then his back again, disappearing down the corridor.

The perversity of it all does not escape her.

Having promised herself she would settle on a direction and be forging ahead by her 25th birthday, Nita is moving backward instead. She has stopped doing her work for graduate school. She has even stopped jogging.

On the surface, Nita would appear to be a young woman struggling between a career and marriage. But she could quite easily have both; the division is deeper. Unlike Dennis Watlington from Harlem, Nita has everything going for her in the outside world. She becomes angry at her husband but can elicit no solution from him. She implores him to give her permission for independence, but he is not the one withholding it. Frustrated in her halfhearted attempts to make Ian the problem, she grasps for some other outer switch that will illuminate her one true path.

"This is Ian's main argument: I'm always looking for one gimmick that is going to turn the lock. If I find the right major, or the right psychiatrist, or the right anything, the whole world is suddenly going to click."

It is idiosyncratic of Americans to think that every problem has a solution if one can only push the right button. Feeling unfulfilled? Change majors, change jobs, change love mates, switch sexual habits, move out of the filthy city to the safe suburbs, move back from the boring suburbs to the vibrant city. Yet we so often find ourselves slipping back into the old problem once the push-button effect has worn off.

The origin of Nita's deadlock is not the wrong major or the wrong mate, and deep down she knows it. When all the false others have been exhausted as scapegoats, she begins to creep up on the real villain.

"I divide against myself."

Stalled though she is at the moment, Nita may well come out ahead later on. At least she hasn't resigned herself to a foreclosed identity; she is still determined to find her own form. But she might also tire of the effort and let her escapist side prevail. In that event, we would probably find a frustrated woman five years up the road, intent on making others pay for her own default. We would all like to know the end of her story, but there isn't any end. This is where she is, almost at the very start.

Part Three

THE TRYING TWENTIES

What can be known? The
  Unknown.
My true self runs toward
  a hill
More! O more! visible.
—THEODORE ROETHKE

8

GETTING OFF
TO A
RUNNING START

The Trying Twenties confronts us with the question of how to take hold in the adult world. Incandescent with our molten energies, having outgrown the family and the formlessness of our transiting years, we are impatient to pour ourselves into the exactly right form—our own way of living in the world. Or while looking for it, we want to try out some provisional form. For now we are not only trying to prove ourselves competent in the larger society but intensely aware of being on trial.

No matter how different the forms we choose, our concentration during the Trying Twenties is on mastering what we feel we are *supposed* to do. The distinction is between the previous transition, the Pulling Up Roots years, when we knew what we *didn't want* to do, and the next transition, into the thirties, which will prod us toward doing what we *want* to do.

Graduate student is a safe and familiar form for those who can afford it. Working toward a degree is something young people already know how to do. It postpones having to prove oneself in the bigger, bullying arena. Very few Americans had such a privilege before World War II; they reached the jumping-off point by the tender age of 16 or 18 or 20 and had to make their move ready or not. But today, a quarter of a century is often spent before an individual is expected or expects himself to fix his life's course.[1] Or more. Given the permissiveness to experiment, the prolonged schooling available, and the moratoria allowed, it is not unusual for an adventurer to be nearly 30 before firmly setting a course.

Today, the seven-year spread of this stage seems commonly to be from the ages of 22 to 28.[2]

The tasks of this period are as enormous as they are exhilarating: To shape a dream, that vision of one's own possibilities in the world that will generate energy, aliveness, and hope. To prepare for a lifework. To find a mentor if possible. And to form the capacity for intimacy without losing in the process whatever constancy of self we have thus far assembled. The first test structure must be erected around the life we choose to try.

One young man with vague aspirations of having his own creative enterprise, for instance, wasn't sure if his forte would be photography or cabinetmaking or architecture. There was no sponsor in sight; his parents worked for the telephone company. So he took a job with Ma Bell. He married and together with his wife decided to postpone children indefinitely. Once the structure was set, he could throw all his free-time energies into experimenting within it. Every weekend would find him behind a camera or building bookcases for friends, vigorously testing the various creative streaks that might lead him to a satisfying lifework.

Singlehood can be a life structure of the twenties, too. The daughter of an ego-boosting father, taught to try anything she wished so long as she didn't bail out before reaching the top, decided to become a traveling publicist. That meant being free to move from city to city as better jobs opened up. The structure that best served her purpose was to remain unattached. She shared apartments and lived in women's hotels, having a wonderful time, until at 27 she landed the executive job of her dreams.

121

"I had no feeling of rootlessness because each time I moved, the next job offered a higher status or salary. And in every city I traveled, I would look up old friends from college and meet them for dinner. That gave me a stabilizing influence."

At 30—*Shazaam!* The same woman was suddenly married and pregnant with twins. Surrounded by a totally new and unforeseen life structure, she was pleasantly baffled to find herself content. "I guess I was ready for a family without knowing it."

The Trying Twenties is one of the longer and more stable periods, stable, that is, in comparison with the rockier passages that lead to and exit from it. Although each nail driven into our first external life structure is tentative, a tryout, once we have made our commitments we are convinced they are the right ones. The momentum of exploring within the structure generally carries us through the twenties without a major disruption of it.

I Should Be . . .

I should get my experience in a big corporation first.

I should work to change the system.

I should be married by now.

I should wait to get married until I've accomplished something.

I should help my people.

I should be running for president; that's what Harvard prepared me for.

Now is the time I should be free and try everything.

The shoulds are defined by the family destiny, the press of the culture, and/or the prejudices of our peers. Of course, cultural instructions change. When the revolution of attitudes reached its peak in the last decade, many young people of both sexes exchanged shoulds. For a time, young American men were fugitives from their society's every ideal and institution. The enemy was known: It was big business, big horsepower, the big lie in Vietnam. While young men of the counterculture were learning to reject the Lieutenant Calley machismo and dropping out to resist the old American success model, however, many of their female contemporaries were flooding into the marketplace to scoop up the vacant positions. The opportunity was there; the feeling was they should take advantage of it. In the current social climate, young women seem to feel they should run for Congress, whereas many young men are looking for "meaningful relationships." And the contracepted, consciousness-raised couple believes that people should live together first, not marry, not have children.

One of the terrifying aspects of the twenties is the conviction that the choices we make are irrevocable. If we choose a graduate school or join a firm, get married or don't marry, move to the suburbs or forego travel abroad, decide against children or against a career, we fear in our marrow that we might have to live with that choice forever. It is largely a false fear. Change is not only possible; some alteration of our original choices is probably inevitable. But since in our twenties we're new at making major life choices, we cannot imagine that possibilities for a better integration will occur to us later on, when some inner growth has taken place.

Two impulses, as always, are at work during this period.

One is to build a firm, safe structure for the future by making strong commitments, to be set. This is the way to keep faith with our cautious Merger Self. Yet people who slip into a ready-made form without much self-examination are likely to find themselves following a locked-in pattern.

The other urge is to explore and experiment, keeping any structure tentative and therefore easily reversible. In this way we satisfy the cravings of our

Seeker Self. Taken to the extreme by people who skip through their twenties from one trial job and one limited personal encounter to another, this becomes the transient pattern.

The balance struck between these two impulses makes for differences in the way people pass through this period of provisional adulthood and largely determines the way we feel about ourselves at the end of it.

The Power of Illusions

However galvanizing our vision in the early twenties, it is far from being complete. Even while we are delighted to display our shiny new capacities, secret fears persist that we are not going to get away with it. Somebody is going to discover the imposter.

To have seen the vivacious, 24-year-old junior executive at her work in a crack San Francisco public relations firm, one would probably not have guessed the trepidations underneath: "I realized that I had not grown up. I was amazed at how well I functioned at work. When clients would deal with me as an equal, I'd think, 'I got away with it,' but the feeling wasn't one of joy. It was terror that eventually they would find out I was just a child. Simply not equipped. The other half of the time, I would have tremendous confidence and arrogance about who I was—a hotshot out there accomplishing all sorts of things and everybody thinking I was so terrific. I was like two people."

Many of us are not consciously aware of such fears. With enough surface bravado to fool the people we meet, we fool ourselves as well. But the memory of formlessness is never far beneath. So we hasten to try on life's uniforms and possible partners, in search of the perfect fit.

"Perfect" is that person we imbue with the capacity to enliven and support our vision or the person we believe in and want to help. Two centuries ago, a fictional young poet in Germany, torn by his hopeless passion for the "perfect" woman, drank a glass of wine, raised a pistol, and put a bullet through his head. It was a shot heard round the world. The lovelorn dropout who fired it was the hero of Goethe's novel *The Sorrows of Young Werther*, which contributed to the romantic movement that colors our expectations of love to this day. Goethe himself was a poet of 25 when he wrote the story. And like the fictional Werther, he suffered from an infatuation with a married woman, an unreachable woman, whose very mystery invited his fantasies of perfection. Goethe's hero struck such a chord in young people throughout Europe that a wave of suicides followed the book's publication.

Today, as then, it's enlightening to speculate on the degree to which a young man invents his romanticized version of the loved woman. She may be seen as the magical chameleon who will be a mother when he needs it and in the next instant the child requiring his protection, as well as the seductress who proves his potency, the soother of anxieties (who shall have none of her own), the guarantor of his immortality through the conversion of his seed. And to what degree does the young woman invent the man she marries? She often sees in him possibilities that no one else recognizes and pictures herself within his dream as the one person who truly understands. Such illusions are the stuff of which the twenties are made.[3]

"Illusion" is usually thought of as a pejorative, something we should get rid of if we suspect we have it. The illusions of the twenties, however, may be essential to infuse our first commitments with excitement and intensity, and to sustain us in those commitments long enough to gain us some experience in living.

The tasks before us are exciting, conflicting, and sometimes overwhelming, but of one thing most of us are certain in our twenties.

Will power will overcome all.

Money may be scarce. The loans and laundry endless. The evil bait of selling out may tempt the would-be doctor, writer, social worker. But clearly, or so it seems, we have only to apply our strong minds and sturdy wills to the wheel of life, and sooner or later our destiny will bend under our control.

A self-deception? Yes, in large part. But also a most useful *modus operandi* at this stage. For if we didn't believe in the omnipotent force of our intelligence, if we were not convinced that we could will ourselves into being whatever kind of persons we wish to be, it wouldn't make much sense to try. Doubts immobilize. Believing that we are independent and competent enough to master the external tasks constantly fortifies us in our attempts to become so.

It is only later we discover that logic cannot penetrate the loneliness of the human soul.

One True Course in Life

If and when we feel we have made a friend of the real world and are about to fix our course, a tone of optimism and vitality propels us forward in giant steps. We are most brimming with aliveness when we are just about to gain a solid form.[4] This applies throughout life and to the different forms we may take. But upon discovering our very first independent form, we may assume it is the forever one and cling to it obstinately.

That is why people in their twenties commonly insist what they are doing is the one true course in life.[5] Any suggestion that we are like our parents raises our hackles. Introspection is a dangerous thing. It doesn't disappear, of course, but it is not a signal characteristic of this period. Too much introspection would interfere with action. What if we were to find out the truth? That the parental figures, unknowingly internalized as our guardians, provide the very feelings of safety that allow us to dare all these great firsts of the twenties. They are also the inner dictators that hold us back.

To tell such a thing to most 25-year-olds will call

forth howls of denial. This is precisely the interior reality from which each of us at this stage is trying to make a break. We are utterly convinced that all our notions spring full blown, as if by magic, from our own unique selves.

At all costs, any parts of our personality that might interfere with our chosen "one true course in life" must for the time being be buried. We cannot, will not, dare not know how strongly we are influenced by the deep tugs of the past: by identifications with our parents and the defense mechanisms we learned in childhood. Indeed, if there is a blemish on our behavior or something annoying about the one we love, this is the age when we are certain all that's needed is to have it pointed out.

"If there's something about me you don't like, just tell me," says the newlywed anxious to please. "I'll change it." If he or she is not forthcoming with such an offer, the other one is determined to change it for the partner. "He may drink a little too much now," the bride confides to her friend, "but I'll reform him."

Examination of the internal forces acting upon us will resume in the thirties, when we are more stabilized externally. Well into our forties, we will still be dredging up exactly those suppressed parts we are now making every effort to ignore.

9

THE ONE TRUE COUPLE

These are the seesaw years for the couple. The ups are breathtaking, rapturous, triumphant breakthroughs of "We can!" The downs are surprise thuds. We try to deny and dismiss them because the last thing we want to accept at the summit of our illusions is that there are some things we can't. Optimism rides as high now as expectations. This *will* be a happy time. We never know until we leave the twenties whether or not it was.

Ignorant of our own and our mate's inner life, we are ruled largely by external forces at this stage. And because the adult world is not in the mental health business, it rarely presents the young couple with opportunities that serve equally each one's readiness to individuate and need to feel secure. Occasionally there will be the perfect compromise. Much more often, the growth spurts will be uneven. When he is moving up, she is likely to feel herself slipping; and just when she feels ready to soar, he may descend into the sloughs of despond. Trying to stabilize—that is what the twenties are all about.

The parallel-development view of love is quite the opposite, presenting, as the model, partners who grow together. It is this idealization with which we have been afflicted, a view abidingly popular with marriage counselors, sociologists, women's magazines, and many psychology courses.

Growing in tandem is virtually impossible in a patriarchal society, as ours has been. Only one-half of the couple has the use of that remarkable support system known as a wife. Added to this basic determinant of tempo is the rate of social change. Even in a relatively stagnant society, the odds are minimal that any couple can enjoy matched development. Subscribing to that view in his book *Future Shock*, Alvin Toffler goes on to point out that the odds take a nose dive when the rate of social change greatly accelerates, as is happening in America: "In a fast-moving society, in which many things change, not once, but repeatedly, in which the husband moves up and down a variety of economic and social scales, in which the family is again and again torn loose from home and community, in which individuals move further from the religion of origin, and further from traditional values, it is almost miraculous if two people develop at anything like comparable rates."[1]

The crucial factor in our gathering dismay over uneven growth, viewed developmentally, is this notion that we should not have any inner turmoil. And when we do, it must be evidence of our own badness or, a far more appealing assumption, the fault of our mate.

The first year of marriage generally finds happiness at its peak. Somewhere in the second year, satisfaction ordinarily begins drifting downward in a U-shaped curve that reaches its lowest point in the late thirties. If the couple divorces before then, the split is most likely to occur seven years after their union, during the Catch-30 passage.

Such probabilities, based on a summary of studies and statistics, do not jibe with the state of continuing bliss most of us anticipate when we are 22.[2]

What we may learn, if we stay at it long enough, is some facility for that most delicate and enigmatic balancing act of all: the art of giving to another while still maintaining a lively sense of self. Or, to put it another way, the capacity for intimacy.

Before one can give and accept real intimacy, one must have secured a reasonable sense of personal identity. Early marriage often short-circuits young people's work on themselves as they slip under a grid of obligations to act as spouses and parents.* It was 1950 when Erikson proposed that developing the capacity for intimacy was the central task linked to the twenties and thirties. But at that time, the value system underlying psychoanalysis vaguely described "genuine intimacy" as a selfless devotion to the other. The self was a blurred concept. Now that the focus has shifted to autonomy, contemporary couples in their twenties must figure out how to balance the seesaw by themselves. A feat they are quite certain, being of the age of certainty, that they are uniquely qualified to perform.

Serena Carter (the young woman whom we met in Chapter Six) assured me that she and her husband were just about crisis-proof. Her letter came in objection to an article in which I had described common snags faced by the couple at 30. Serena neither sympathized nor identified:

> Your men are childish, unrealistic, insecure people who blame everything bad that happens to them on their wives, and everything good that happens on their own superior judgment. . . . I can't imagine my husband sidling up to me when I turn 30, with a college degree, and no children, nudging me in the ribs and saying, "Hey, honey, get cultured."

---

* The average age at which women marry has recently risen to 21; for men, it is 23. But apart from this broad national average, there is evidence that more of our well-educated young people are waiting a few years longer to complete their schooling or to start career apprenticeships before pledging their troth.3

Her letter had the unmistakable ring of a person in the twenties, certain that her current life course is the correct one and that rational efforts will accomplish all.

"My hunch is that you and your husband would be the ideal representatives of the twenties point of view," I wrote back. "Can I persuade you both to be part of the book?"

They consented with enthusiasm. They were both 24 and curious, recently transplanted from the singularism of the Protestant Midwest to the boiling, multitongued street life of Manhattan's Upper West Side. Serena came to her door poised and erect. Her shy blond husband, Jeb, was refinishing a rocking chair. Each assured me in the same words that there was no problem for which they couldn't find the "happy medium, mutually beneficial" solution. Yet at the end of our first session, Serena fixed me with a puzzled frown and uttered what might be a motto for this stage:

"Why does it come out sounding as if I'm constantly in doubt, when I'm really very sure of myself?"

Underneath the armor of optimism, that is the way most people feel in their twenties. The truth is, neither Serena nor Jeb Carter has been a stranger to the predictable crises of growing up. The good news is they were able to help each other through the last passage without knowing it. And by alternating between independence and dependence, each is helping the other right now to stabilize around a new balance.

You couldn't have told Jeb Carter at the depth of his funk that it was a gift to have his crisis neat and clean and all up front at 21. Until that time, intimacy was an extravagance the boy could not afford. Not after catching his old man with the floozie on Illinois Highway 17 like that. And watching the sight suck the color out of his mother as if the garage door had banged shut on a twenty-five-year-old marriage and asphyxiated her. But the boy was already on his own, as he says, meaning he was in college; he would survive.

Driving back home from a Big Ten campus upstate, the universe of his boyhood had startled him with its smallness. The population was still 750. The one and only highway coming into town still deadended in the Mississippi; nothing had changed. Yet to his mind's eye, tantalized by glimpses of other ways of life, the place looked suddenly like a toy sailboat squeezed into a glass bottle. Part of him longed to crawl back inside. Another part feared he too would shrink and cease to breathe here. Beyond downing a few at the bar of the River Vu restaurant, there was nothing to do in this town but work on the lock and dams or keep walking until you drowned. The civic event of greatest commemorative significance had been the opening of a laundromat in 1965.

How much all this humdrumery had to do with his father's drinking problem the boy couldn't say. There was a fierce pride in the man that he did not enjoy exposing to the corrosions of reality. He did his shedding and bleeding silently. The boy had never known him any way but bald, never heard him express, even once, a personal thought.

His father worked for the Army Corps of Engineers, flushing boats through the lock. He worked the night shift mostly and seldom stopped home even to change out of his twills before hitting the taverns for thirty miles around. For companions, he had the big, blunt men he worked with and a mistress called Pabst's beer. Though a series of minor car accidents gave his wife a case of nerves whenever he stayed out all night, she had never gone after him. It came out of the blue, then, when Jeb was home for vacation, that she insisted on finding the old man.

Jeb waited in the car while his mother went inside the gin mill and saw the evidence of her latest competitor, this time a woman. Back home his father assumed the posture of the wounded innocent. His parents fought. But everyone fights. It would pass, Jeb prayed.

In the morning, from his bed, he heard his father express himself for the first time. "I'd like a divorce," he said. "That's the way I want it."

Shock. A fulcrum of anger against his father, followed by numbness; the rest fades out until Jeb's next visit to his mother. Having obtained a transfer in her job with a feed company, she was moving the family trailer to another town.

"Now Jeb Carter," she said to her son, "don't you go crying on my account. I'm just fine."

Jeb's sympathies, as always, rested with his mother. He was the last of four boys and the small one; four foot ten and head to head with his mother until he finished high school. Around her he was an easy cryer. She didn't laugh. Around everyone else he held back.

The one thing he was afraid of was that they would find out a little dink like him had big-as-you-please "I could be president" dreams. And so except for the times when he could empty out his feelings around his mother, he adopted the carapace of the old man.

"I never displayed much of my inner self to people. That way, if they laughed, I knew it wasn't really me they were laughing at."

The mask was effective until Jeb Carter turned the corner of his senior year of college and began to think he was going off the deep end. For reasons he couldn't fathom, Jeb had taken a mixed discipline in engineering and law. When the guidance counselor had warned, "Engineering is a mistake, your Kuder tests show that you like people, and engineers like things," Jeb had said, "Thanks a lot," and then proceeded as though deaf through four years of training for his father's profession. ("You keep thinking it will all work itself out in the end.")

One dutiful summer after another, he had made

reports at the John Deere plant in Moline on why the holes didn't come out an inch apart on the paint cans the way the engineers' drawings showed. By the summer after his senior year, he didn't give a damn. "The operator had a hangover," he would write on his reports, enjoying for the first time the destructive potential of his independence. The trouble was, once Jeb scrapped engineering as a goal, he had no tenable dream to replace it. "No interest in getting ahead, working up to management, feathering the nest in the suburbs, nothing."

He was estranged from his father. The mother whose smile was his only source of reassurance had all she could do to put her own pieces together in a small hot trailer. Jeb moved in with his brother, who had just divorced a perfectly nice Missouri girl and could talk only of how he suddenly felt nothing for his own three kids. That made it one silent, drowning summer. The deep end.

Much as he might have believed the identification with his father had been killed off, there was still a powerful draw toward that old familiar sanctuary. A friend offered to get Jeb a job with the Army Corps of Engineers. He was tempted, began slipping back.

He had taken the law boards only because it was expected of him. You could have knocked him over with a pencil point when he came out with the highest score in his class. The dean couldn't wait to write him a recommendation.

"But it's not me," he told the dean. "Law school and that slick Wall Street image is just heading too far away from everything I've been raised for." An accurate assessment of what he was up against, which was a classic identity crisis.

For Jeb, the push-pull of seek and merge forces left him with several options. He could turn back down Illinois Highway 17 clear to the Mississippi and become a government engineer just like his father. Or he could break dramatically with that familiar form and, ready or not, drag himself off to an elite law school on one exotic coast or the other. He could also stay right where he was until he caught up with himself. Left to its own youthful resourcefulness, Jeb's psyche invented a tailor-made therapy to pull him out of his crisis:

"For some reason, I had an urge to work at a gas station."

This was muscle work, outdoor work. The ice cooler in back was always stocked with beer and he drank with the guys, light but steady, all day. "I like to drink," he discovered, and without permitting himself to see the obvious connections, began living as a facsimile of his father.

It was just about now that Jeb's first intimacy began to develop.

"She was the first female I felt safe about opening myself up to. She never laughed." It is Jeb's considered opinion that Serena is what changed him.

Funny, but Serena is dead certain that she had nothing to do with it. When the question comes up even today of who was the Strong One, the answer is clearly all in the eyes of the beholder.

"When I first met Jeb," Serena will explain, "I had just finished a disastrous romance. I started going from bed to bed and going on crying jags in between. It was bad because I had always felt fairly stable." She was 20. "There were two people who pulled me out. My roommate—she was a substitute mother. I would sit there bawling 'I'm going crazy,' and she'd say, 'You're out of your mind; you're just the same as you were yesterday.' The other one was Jeb. I cried on his shoulder."

Jeb's initial reaction was, "I liked Serena, but I don't enjoy that role, the strong figure."

To which Serena replies, "Jeb is still the only man I've ever met who gives me the option of disagreeing and is not insulted or threatened. I'm forceful and I need somebody who can reason with force."

With an astonished blink, Jeb says, "I don't consider myself a strong person."

"I think you're much stronger than other men," his wife persists.

"Even today Serena has no concept of the fog I was in when we met."

"He straightened himself around; I just happened to be there."

"If Serena hadn't been there, I would have thrown in the towel."

And so on. The beauty of it is, they are both right. What really happened with Serena and Jeb is that each was able to be strong in an area in which the other needed support.

In career directedness Serena was head and shoulders above all her friends at college. She was already working press, not just a gossip picker for the school paper but meeting deadlines for a city editor downtown. In Champaign, Illinois, she was a big fish. All that stood between her and the dream of jumping into the whirlpool of world events as a journalist was, she thought, one year more of school. In the romantic area, however, the same natural ebullience had left Serena rather badly maimed.

She had a habit of falling for young men who professed to want a free-minded woman and then turned out to have sniveling fiancées back home with the silver pattern all picked out. The last such swain had left her wondering if she were pregnant, fortunately a false alarm. When she told him later about her lonely vigil, he berated her for dispensing her favors too liberally. Upon meeting Jeb she was feeling lower than a whore. More than anything she needed a period of revirgination. Jeb was an innocent.

What did he know about sex, coming from a Methodist pinpoint on the Midwest prairie where the raciest thing they taught in the schools was Shakespeare? "I wouldn't say it was easy for me, but with Serena I felt safe. She was a little hesitant at first . . ."

That first spring they were only buddies. "I didn't want him to be the rebound who would take care of me," Serena decided and therefore cut it off. Come

June they went separate ways, Jeb into his deep-end summer, Serena back home to pursue her revirgination by playing the chaste belle to a retrograde Southerner.

It all clicked into place one night the following fall. Serena roared into the gas station shorn of ambiguities, full of zest, and threw her arms around the short, shy boy in the Standard Oil uniform. Shortly thereafter Jeb moved into her apartment. He feasted like a refugee on the sense of oneness regained with another. Soon enough he found himself proposing.

Now why, one might ask from the "realistic" perspective, would an ambitious journalist and a floundering gas station attendant see fit to marry?

"I'd found a person I felt free to open up to," Jeb says, "and I didn't want to lose her. I think that's love."

For Serena's part: "I was so tired of putting my all into relationships that didn't go anywhere. I decided I'd do almost anything to make this work. There was enough there for me to say, 'Let's do something with it, not just live together, get married.'"

To which Jeb adds, with the lapse in introspection so characteristic of the twenties: "It was the thing to do. Whether or not I wanted to marry Serena was quite independent of where I went and what I chose to do with my life."

Almost as an afterthought, the couple recalls that before they exchanged vows, Jeb did apply to law school and was rejected. It turned out that the dean of the engineering school had given him a poor recommendation. For both of them, it was the ideal setback.

"This way Serena could finish school where she was and keep her newspaper job," Jeb explains. "And it was fun for me working at the gas station for a year."

He liked his companions, especially the big-liquor-gut boss who could drink him under the table at will. Jeb switched to the night shift, and he liked that too. He didn't stop home even to change out of his monkey suit before hitting the local sawdust bar to drink until closing. He was always joined by Serena, his wife, who enjoyed that year too.

When any one of us is shedding an old familiar life structure and sense of self, feeling exposed and fearful, we are tempted to take on the form of our phantom parent along with all its weaknesses. Exactly what Jeb did. But by slipping back temporarily into his father's form, working with his hands and drinking hard just as the old man had done, he was able to live out the "bad" parts of his parental identification and retain the "good" ones. He learned that he could drink without becoming an alcoholic, enjoy physical work without wanting to become an engineer, express his feelings without being cruel to his wife. He, Jeb, had his own validity.

This personal moratorium was what enabled Jeb to take a progressive step the next year. Having gathered the courage of his own instincts, he was ready to risk becoming something altogether different from what he had been raised for. A trial lawyer, the big dream. And if anyone laughed, so what? He had Serena to believe in him now.

"Before the year was out I knew where I was going. I was going to get into a prestige law school. And I did—this time I was accepted at Columbia. New York. I began to be excited about the country boy going to the big city."

The perfect stop-out for Jeb had synchronized brilliantly with Serena's needs. She had needed a man who would value her friendship before he insisted on being a lover. She was also able to complete her schooling in a place where she felt important.

The only mistake the One True Couple might make now is expecting that this lucky synchrony will continue.

Going Through Changes with the One True Couple

No two people can possibly coordinate all their developmental crises. The timing of outside opportunities will almost never be the same. But more importantly, each one has an inner life structure with its own idiosyncrasies. Depending on what has gone before, each one will alternate differently between times of feeling full of certainty, hope, and heightened potential and times of feeling vulnerable, unfocused, and scared.

This is the Carters' current dilemma. For the first time, two people who believed they were crisis-proof as a couple find themselves in a situation that just may *not* respond to the perfect "happy medium, mutually beneficial" compromise. And hating to admit it.

"Serena was afraid of the move to New York," Jeb begins guiltily, "afraid it would change us."

Which it fortunately has.

"I had always felt more than ready up to that point to take a chance," Serena says defensively, "ready to go away to the academy, to high school, to college. But I wasn't ready to come to New York. I guess I was afraid. I felt totally like a fish out of water. I thought I was going to die. And here was Jeb depending on me."

Well, Serena didn't die. And Jeb has since been learning to depend on himself. The balance in their intimacy is changing before this couple's very eyes. When they were 21 and ensconced in a familiar college town, Serena made it possible for Jeb to be dependent while he got his bearings. At the moment, Jeb's end of the seesaw is up. His sense of self has grown more consistent in law school. Now he is not only clear about his occupational form but is seeking the most prestigious fit within it. With mounting confidence, Jeb is tempted to stay in the Big Apple and shoot for a job in the U.S. attorney's office.

Now Serena is the uncertain one. Although she appears a most resolute young professional, as we have viewed her up to now through her husband's eyes, Serena's actual step-style is something else. She is fearless, competent, and competitive—until she reaches the top of the ski jump, symbolically speaking.

Then she invents an impossible comparison with the most glorified model (I'm not Jean-Claude Killy, so I can't be good enough) and steps back from the edge.

"When I was 12, I was offered a scholarship to art school. At that point I had to ask myself how talented I was."

And again at age 14: "My dancing teacher wanted me to join a performing company. My mother's effect was her lack of effect. So I had to decide. Both times I decided I probably wasn't good enough. I'd never be Margot Fonteyn."

Yet the achievement drive remained strong, as it commonly does with the eldest daughter in a family of girls. Serena's father had treated her no differently from a boy. She was expected to fix the motorboat, clean up the yard, cement walls, and distinguish herself in field hockey and basketball. Before finishing high school, she had fixed on journalism as her dream.

Despite her surefooted progress in moving from the college paper to a city beat, and what with all her determination that no man should make her a sacrificial lamb, Serena turned out to be the one who promoted marriage. Emotionally she was raw. Sexually she was disillusioned, unfairly labeled as promiscuous. And then, even her covering act as the polished professional was questioned.

"That's the first sign of a bad reporter," her editor had carped when she found herself too involved in a racial story to write it. The criticism might have stimulated an "I'll show him" reaction in some apprentices. Given Serena's step-style, the words cut easily through her bluster of confidence and let out all the air.

"That's the first time I realized, I'm not great. Before I could make up my mind about marriage, I had to decide again, how good was I? As a reporter. Good in the sense that Mozart was good, or Tallchief or Fonteyn or Nureyev."

Again, the impossible comparison as a way out. If she married this young man for whom she also felt love, she wouldn't have to. Wouldn't have to attempt being great, risk emerging as mediocre, chance disappointing her father or scaring off men with her competitiveness. For the time being she could avoid both failure and success. Serena found an easy rationalization for deferring her own dream: "To be really good at something, you can't be married. I believe that, along with Katharine Hepburn. But I felt this relationship would be more important to me than all the prizes."

Four years later Serena Carter is stuck in a little job in a big city and trying furiously to convince herself that once more, together with Jeb, they will work out the perfect compromise. The question is: Will they move to a smaller city where Serena can break into newspapering? Or will they stay in New York so that Jeb can try for his dream spot in the U.S. attorney's office?

Most days Serena is sanguine about their discussions. "We can always talk in 'if' terms. If such an offer comes to Jeb, we'll consider it very carefully and do what is mutually best."

On nights when she comes home cranky from her job in "communications" (which in the corporate world means that every time somebody sneezes, it must be Xeroxed), Serena has to stamp out little brush fires of discontent.

"I did anticipate that when we came to New York I would lose my identity, but then I tried to deceive myself that I wouldn't. I felt the opportunity for Jeb outweighed any temporary disadvantage for me." The word *temporary* catches in her throat. "People are always talking about things being temporary that turn out to be permanent." Serena has been in this job for two years. "I'd like to get back into reporting. But I've told myself to sit back and observe rather than fight it."

Only when pressed on the issue does Serena dare a glimpse beneath the perfectly ordered structure of her life with Jeb. There is something underneath all this talk, something amorphous, that Serena cannot yank out with the pliers of her will power and that may therefore be disruptive.

"I can't foresee anything getting in our way—unless, I just suddenly have to pursue my career much hotter. Which is a possibility. I might have to go after it and sacrifice everything else."

The demons vanish when Jeb walks in the door, tossing his hang-down hair out of his eyes, sweet and pale in his corduroy pants with the orange patches.

Jeb aspires to the pattern of an integrator. He is trying to balance his commitments to the woman he loves and the achievement he desires. Like all integrators, he does not want to become possessed by his work and endanger the closeness with his mate; on the other hand, he does not want to be judged incompetent and left behind on the pyramid.

We shall meet integrators both male and female at other critical points along the life cycle, but their view from the twenties is generally as Jeb sees it: "At one level, I'd like to be the next Edward Bennett Williams. But at another level, I don't have the need to achieve to the extent that I'd overwork myself to get there. More than anything I'm worried about my relationship with Serena, maintaining that at a full level. At the same time I certainly don't want to be an incompetent lawyer."

Up to the very recent past, integrators had children, too, which made balancing personal and professional development an even greater acrobatic feat. The Carters are terrified by the idea of children. Given Jeb's dream of opening his own law practice by the time he is 30 and Serena's determination that by that time she will be a reporter for the *New York Post*, they have simply shut the door on this tempest of a subject as if to pretend it isn't there.

"I see no children," Serena says.

"I don't either," Jeb says.

"At all. Ever."

"I've told her I'm liberated to the extent that I'm willing to help with all the chores. But if it comes to children, I'm not willing to split that time."

"I feel fortunate at least that Jeb will not make the demand on me to have children if I don't want them."

Upon actually passing 30, she very likely will want children. Then their negotiations will have to be far more existential because the demand will be coming, not from the other, but from that mysterious, unpredictable, previously hidden inner self.

On the question of who will get favored position on the seesaw of career opportunity, Jeb is beginning to hang on less tightly to their joint illusion.

"That's one problem we haven't solved yet," he admits once out of his wife's earshot. "Quite frankly, we haven't reached a happy medium."

The Carters are a prime example of the seesaw at work. It smoothed out very nicely for them in the previous passage. It can balance out for them in the future—if they come to recognize that each of them will have periods of inner turmoil and that it is not evidence of one partner's badness nor the fault of the other.

Serena, who up to the time of their move was the more directed one, is now floundering professionally. But she is also stabilizing emotionally, and that stability was probably necessary before she can take the next outer step.

Resolving the issues of one passage does not insulate us forever. There will be other tricky channels ahead, and we learn by moving through them. If we pretend the crises of development don't exist, not only will they rise up later and hit with a greater wallop but in the meantime we don't grow. We're captives. If the growth work *has* been done on the developmental tasks of one passage, it bodes well for meeting the challenges of the next one.

Not until the passage to the thirties will the

Carters sense that there are other forces in life, phantom forces, inexplicable passions and fears that will have their way. For Jeb to acknowledge now even this much—that everything is not going to work itself out in perfectly matched development—is probably the best chance they have of remaining the One True Couple.

10

WHY
DO MEN
MARRY?

Ever since romanticism replaced the arranged marriage, the assumption has been that people marry for love. This is largely a myth.

Any marriage can evolve into the mutual love of watching each other live. But first marriages are often a matter of conforming to the shoulds of the twenties. Until recently, few people felt free *not* to marry at this age. My conclusions are based on a synthesis of the 115 interviews. When I asked "Why did you marry?" the answers given by men who married in their twenties were quite consistent. (Their present ages range from 30 to 55.)

"I made a head decision," explained a writer. "This was the time. I didn't really have any deep desire to get married, but I thought I should. Doris expected it." He is now middle-aged and divorced.

A lawyer admitting to the same automatic response was uncomfortable about parting with his romantic illusions; he is only 30. "Within six months before or after our graduation from law school, all but one of my friends got married. I don't think it could be that everybody met the right girl by coincidence. There must have been an element of its being the right time. Not to take away from Jeanie. . . ."

Each man thought that the shoulds were particular to his religion, region, or class background.

"Being married was just the way you lived as an upper-middle-class WASP in Cooperstown."

"If you grew up in the East and had a good Catholic school education and you came from the professional middle class, it was expected that you would marry and have children."

"Getting married was the natural thing you did when you were from Philadelphia, middle class, and Jewish."

The other real forces urging young people into marriages generally sift down to one of the following: the need for safety, the need to fill some vacancy in themselves, the need to get away from home, the need for prestige or practicality.

Safety

Again and again, from men as often as from women, one refrain is heard: "I wanted someone to take care of me." The collection of wishes carried by the phrase "take care of me" obviously comes straight out of childhood. Those of us raised in the child-centered middle-class American home have an appetite for attention so devouring, we scarcely hear what we are saying. Anything that intensifies the loneliness and the sense of lost security that accompany leaving the family (finishing school, entering the service, falling ill, finding ourselves in a strange place, seeing our parents' marriage come apart) increases the urge to recover the absolute safety of home.

But our dependency problems are bigger than this. With the affluence of the last twenty-five years, dependency became a systemic disease in America. The notion has flourished in all classes that one has the right to be taken care of throughout life. Beginning with the GI Bill or scholarship that would buy the education and the FHA loan that would buy the mortgage on a house, one would then be taken care of by the union, the corporation, the bureaucracy (as part of the vast army of government employees) or welfare until the time came to draw social security benefits and cash in on one's pension.

Falling into marriage as a safety net is by no means exclusive to women. So attached is Jeb to his Serena, so totally has he imbued her by now with the magical properties that can no longer reliably be ascribed to his parents, he cannot imagine a single misfortune they couldn't overcome so long as she is by his side. But remove Serena—

"Do you feel you could pretty well meet any road-block that presents itself from here on in?" I asked him at the end of all our interviews.

"I think so," he said. As we talked, Serena quietly fixed dinner.

"Suppose you suddenly failed in law school?"

"I'd wring the professor's neck." He laughed easily.

"Suppose you were robbed or Serena were mugged?"

"If I were burglarized, I'd use my insurance and not worry. When an emergency comes up and we don't have the money, we just say, 'It'll work out.' Now as far as Serena being mugged—" He tugged on his moccasin. "I would guess I'd be better equipped emotionally to deal with it if it happened to me."

"And if your father died?"

"I'd just go on," Jeb replied implacably. But the question had triggered a truly dangerous invasion of his safety base. "If it were Serena who died"—he sat awhile with that bayonet of a thought stuck in his mind. His optimism was suddenly penetrated. "That's the one thing I'm not prepared to do, go on without her."

Eventually, if Jeb is to end up with the safety inside himself, he will have to acknowledge the original source of his imagined protection: his mother. But he is not ready to challenge his inner custodian on the safety issue. Few of us are, in our twenties. He finds it easier to believe that all those protective powers are carried by his mate. So long as Serena is healthy and able to maintain a strong sense of *her* self, she can uphold the illusion.

If the magic mantle of the Strong One is passed back and forth between the couple, as we saw happening with Jeb and Serena, there will be progress both in sharing and in independence. The combination is what allows genuine intimacy to flourish. But people who enter into "take care of me" contracts may not get that far. The dynamic can also work this way: Panic. Marriage for safety. Backfire.

Here is a man of 23. The graduate of a mediocre college, Al was ill-prepared for his vague dream of being a college professor. "I was afraid I was going to fall through. It was terrifying to face having to be something. So I got married to a big, bright, ambitious girl because she was pragmatic. She knew how to deal with life. Together I knew we could survive. On my own I knew I couldn't. A year later she had a nervous breakdown. I'd married mother and ended up with baby."

Fortunately, it doesn't often happen that the backfire is so brutal. But then again, when we are young, most of us would dismiss the notion that it could happen at all. We are cheered on by testimonials such as this one, given by Bernard Berkowitz and Mildred Newman, authors of the best seller *How to Be Your Own Best Friend:*

BERNIE: Would you mind if we told everyone that simple but wonderful resolution we made when we married? We decided that we would *take care* [author's italics] of each other. I can't think of a better basis for a marriage.

MILDRED: There's a great deal that goes into taking care of each other. We each need some babying sometimes.[1]

And so we do. But there are many pitfalls to swallowing this conventional wisdom whole. It encourages our inclination in the twenties to value a spouse according to how well he or she takes the place of a parent. This can be disappointing and ultimately dangerous. It coaxes us to remain children who look for permission and excuses ("He won't let me" or "If it weren't for her") and who expect our protection to come from another, rather than from the development of ourselves.

Expecting a mate to replace our parents does nothing to break the power of the inner custodian. It merely fills us with demons, which is how Roger Gould depicts that whole set of unintegrated identifications locked away in the compartment owned by the other. Demons related to sex, intimacy, competition, the right values to pursue, and all the other volatile matters on which we have not yet established our own authority. And demons they will remain so long as we adhere to the warning of the inner tyrant (as Gould phrases it): *"If you don't break my taboos and stay where you are and don't intrude into this territory that I own as the object* [other], *you will be safe and taken care of and believe in illusions and everything will be all right."*[2]

And it may well be, so long as we have a mate onto whom we can project those demons. And so long as there is no disturbance in his or her life that prevents this mate from taking care of us.

The desire to have a spouse perform the soothing functions once ministered by one's parents does not disappear with the passage into the thirties. Indeed, it is one of the things people are most angry and anxious about as they enter into their forties. Each partner resents being depended upon as a substitute parent by the other and, in the same breath, fears the gathering evidence that he or she is in fact all alone.

Let's jump ahead and listen to the poignant confession of a 43-year-old artist. Being in command of his own firm, even being an early student of the human potential movement has not cloistered him from this common couple knot. Yet it is only in the chaos of his midlife passage that he can see the knot and know it for the first time.

"Michele has always counted on my parental qualities, my support, my strength, the sense that I knew what I was doing and where I was going. Any manifestation of weakness on my part was very destructive in our relationship. If I was insecure or weak or fearful, then Michele's fear of being depended on by *me* would make her more panicky. That would mean, of course, my anxiety increased. This kind of knotting has been very dangerous for us. Weakness on my part would reinforce danger on Michele's part. It's a system that tends to destroy."

It comes as a rude shock in midlife when the father-husband no longer wants to play the role of omnipotent protector or when the child-wife grows up and talks back. Or the reverse: when suddenly he doesn't want to be mothered anymore or she doesn't want to be Mommy. Any one of these may be a fine, healthy step toward full adult development, but the partner who is still dependent on the old contract feels betrayed.

Then the unspoken response may be *take care of me or else:* "I'll deny you in bed"; "I'll cut off your allowance"; "I'll slowly mutilate you with razor-sharp remarks in public that leave no trace of blood."

The irrationality inherent in our romanticized "take care of me" contracts leads social theorist Philip Slater to a devastating prediction of the outcome:

In relation to women, men have taken the stance assumed by the warrior-aristocrat toward the peasant: "If you feed me, I will protect you." Before long, of course, every protection contract becomes a protection racket: "Give me what I want and I will protect you against me."[3]

To Fill Some Vacancy In Themselves

The assumption behind this reason for marriage is that personal qualities are transferable. Marry her mercifulness, and you shall be spared anxiety. (But who is to allay her anxieties?)

"I called her a year-round fireplace," the former husband recalls wistfully, "the original Gray Lady who was always ministering to others' dreams and needs and hurts."

Fifteen years later he was ready to take a daring jump and try starting his own business. His wife balked. Having for so long been contained in the Gray Lady role, which made it possible for her husband's personality to stretch, she was by then a mass of insecurities. The marriage came to an end.

Marry her vitality, goes another assumption, and the batteries will be yours:

"I had reached an age [25], a certain readiness to change the terms and conditions of my life," explained a frustrated artist who eventually established his own small business. "It was her vibrancy, it was like warming your hands over a flame. I'm a little phlegmatic." The placidity of married life in the suburbs soon reduced his wife's vibrancy to a gentle simmer. "Something happens with women who are at home," he found. "You come in from the office and you feel like she's plugging in to *you* like a storage battery."

But his wife became again so animated in their middle years that it literally gave him a new lease on life. She plunged into a new career after twenty years at home. With her encouragement, the thwarted artist sold his business and sat down to let his inward eye take him where it would. "If I flop, okay, but I don't have to feel that I'd be punishing her. She's self-reliant now."

To Get Away from Home

Although jailbreak marriages are most commonly made by young women, the escape motive was also noticed among the men.

"Why did I get married? To get away from home! I was an insecure, shy kid. And here's a popular girl that liked me. I really stumbled into it."

This man happened to be, by his own admission, a prisoner of his Jewish mother. But the answer would often come out the same way from sons of "Mrs. Forsyth" or "Mrs. O'Leary."

Prestige or Practicality

The mate will confer a higher status, or help in a concrete way to foster his or her ambitions. A good bet.

"I was trying to prove to myself that I could become president of the company," explains a man who hadn't gone to college and was painfully aware of the handicap. "A friend introduced me to a very attractive and rich girl. I've spent thousands of hours [since their divorce] trying to decide how much I was influenced by the fact that she stood to inherit a great deal of money."

"Well, marriage," says the doctor who needed a helpmate through medical school, "it was a practicality. People always seem to come back to it as the final answer, just like democracy."

"When two people are under the influence of the most violent, most insane, most delusive, and most transient of passions," wrote Shaw, "they are required to swear that they will remain in that excited, abnormal, and exhausting condition continuously until death do them part."

No man I interviewed who was over 30 mentioned that he was in love with his wife when he married her. Nor did anyone suggest that sex had been an inducement. The amnesia factor in recalling past emotions is part of the explanation, but the profound changes that occur in interior perceptions as people move on to more intricate stages are also reflected.

Except for the absence of sex as a remembered motivation, my sampling supported the conclusions drawn by psychiatrist Don D. Jackson and writer William J. Lederer in their outstanding work using the systems concept with hundreds of married couples. They write in *The Mirages of Marriage* that people "like to think of themselves as being in love; but by and large the emotion they interpret as love is in reality some other emotion—often a strong sex drive, fear, or a hunger for approval."[4]

That is not to say love doesn't develop. Many of my respondents talk about loving their partners now, ten or twenty or thirty years further along in their own personal evolution. Once the myth of the all-purpose marriage bursts of its own burden of dependencies, it becomes possible for people to enjoy each other simply as being. Or a second match is made with less concern for conventionalities and with a lot more privacy. One of the conventions that often goes out the window is marriage itself. Many people find it easier to live together when that commitment is voluntarily renewed.

The caring of experienced partners goes less into roles and more into enhancing the special qualities and endearing idiosyncrasies that brought them together in the first place. It is not a federal case if he refuses to see her loathsome relatives, has interesting women friends, skis badly, likes spending Saturday in the garage assembling something he calls sculpture, makes love passionately some mornings and some nights falls asleep. Nor does the roof fall in if she gets a promotion, takes a ski trip alone, goes seriously back to art school, sits reading the newspaper while he clears the table, or spends Saturday night playing the oboe in a room of her own.

But that's not how we see things in the twenties. Young people are constantly talking about their lives as puzzles. Remember the young woman a few chapters back who described the breakup with her home-town boyfriend after she had taken a job with her college newspaper? "We were suddenly bumping into each other, not fitting in. The puzzle pieces had all reshaped themselves, and we didn't fit together any-more."

The comforting thing about assembling the pieces of a jigsaw puzzle is the inexorable logic of it. There is only one choice—the right one. With enough patience, the puzzle can be solved once and for all.

In life, however, the pieces are constantly chang-ing shape or slipping out of our hands. No sooner do we think we have assembled a comfortable life than we find a piece of ourselves that has no place to fit in. Or the supporting structure tilts, we slip away from our mate, our children expand and want more room, our parents begin to shrivel and remind us they will leave a terrible empty space. Sometimes we have to start all over again.

The unsparing rule is that we must be willing to outgrow what no longer fits and to let others do the same. This stretching is rewarded in time. Men and women who do continue to grow eventually pick up the personality parts that were earlier suppressed.

Some of those suppressed parts are linked to sex roles. The shoulds are very different for men and women in the Trying Twenties, which has a great deal to do with where they come out in their forties. In an effort to make these critical distinctions clear, Chapters Eleven and Twelve will take a broader view of the life cycle.

11

WHY CAN'T A WOMAN BE MORE LIKE A MAN AND A MAN LESS LIKE A RACEHORSE?

Men must. Women don't have to.

A man in his twenties must funnel his energies into making an independent way in the world or else be ridiculed. He must continue this expansion at the expense of one illusion after another. Every guidepost tells him that the twenties and thirties are the years granted him to seek mastery, the time to earn the credentials that will win him approval from others and rewards from society. If he burns with the desire to gain recognition as well, a man must be faithful and endlessly attentive to his real loved one: the career. All our traditions and institutions help to pave the way by recommending, applauding, and giving full permission to men who pursue such a course.

A woman doesn't have to find an independent form in her twenties. There is always a back door out. She can attach to a Stronger One. She can become the maker of babies and baker of brownies, the carrier of her husband's dream. If she resists this pattern, she runs into the contradiction between permissions for development given to men and women. The achieving woman has always been exposed to intimidation by the same threat that hangs over the underachieving young man: *No one will want to marry you. You will end up 60 years old and all alone.*[1]

How do any of us gain the confidence necessary to tackle the many tasks of the Trying Twenties?

Confidence is gradually built throughout this period on successes in proving competence. Men, and a smaller number of women, who are determined to gain a niche in the outer adult world, stick tightly to their chosen work structure—proceeding from law school to clerk to junior partner, for instance, or from typist to researcher to junior copywriter—and the tightness of this early structure makes it easier to stabilize.

The imprint of people and experience on those in their twenties who are out in the world, working at their expansion, is vastly different from the limited and repetitive imprint left on people who stay at home or remain in school. Eager beavers in business, quick to offer fresh ideas, are at first crushed when they are told, in effect, "Go away, kid, you bother me." The expectation that ability will be justly recognized bursts. A graduate student in a school of photography, worshipful of the professor who is committed to art and above the seductions of crass commercialism, is conditioned to look upon editors and agency heads as the enemy. After some years of actual working contact with such people, the young photographer may look back on that same vaunted professor as a man who has never been outside the womb of self-perpetuating academia ("He's never covered a war or even worked!") and part with the illusion of the former hero.

By the time a man (or an achieving woman) reaches 28 or 29, a series of such jolts has weaned him away from many of the illusions he once needed. In working at his dream, he becomes less of a dreamer. Soon he will be ready for the momentous step of converting the dream into concrete goals, or redefining it.

As Levinson pointed out when I interviewed him, a career timetable in itself delineates a series of stages and indicates the appropriate time one should spend in moving from one stage to the next. It gives a source of order and shape to the individual life course.

The woman who marries early in her twenties with an undivided commitment to being a wife and mother is in a more nebulous position. She must improvise a timetable around the needs of others. If she is a married woman with a small child and is also trying to balance an outside commitment, she can seldom be faithful to a career in the way a man can. She is not yet practiced or confident enough in any area to integrate all her competing priorities. The career that provides her husband stability may throw her into pandemonium.

When Levinson introduced the "Dream" as a crucial element in the development of young adults, he also spoke of two key relationships for a man in his twenties: the mentor and the loved woman. "The loved woman may serve developmental functions similar to those of the mentor. She may help to define and carry the Dream, to create a life within which the Dream can have a place." He added a passing acknowledgment: "Of course, the relationship will be durable and further his development only if it also furthers hers."[2]

Surely that is one of the biggest "of courses" in the evolution of mankind. If women had wives to keep house for them, to stay home with vomiting children, get the car fixed, fight with the painters, run to the supermarket, reconcile the bank statements, listen to everyone's problems, cater the dinner parties, and nourish the spirit each night, just imagine the possibilities for expansion—the number of books that would be written, companies started, professorships filled, political offices that would be held, by women. Indeed, most women of high achievement have expensive housekeepers who perform many of these wifely services.

In recent years young people have been trying out important variations on the old sex roles. There are women who stay single until their careers are established, and husbands who do a fair share of the diapering and vegetable dicing. There is even out-and-out role reversal: the artist-husband who stays home and works in between putting the children down for naps and whose wife calls from her office to say she's bringing someone home for dinner.

The instructions one culture gives to any one generation have a good deal to say about which parts of the personality, in particular, a person suspends in the early years. Too often such personality traits are associated with biases about the differences between masculinity and femininity.[3] Even the terms active and passive seem sociologically loaded.

A more precise distinction is between behavior that is *initiating*—in which one seizes the initiative, opens the transaction, seeks to implement one's wishes —and behavior that is *responsive* to other people's needs and wishes. Neither characteristic is exclusive to one sex. That the two continue to operate, at variance, within each individual, simply demonstrates the ongoing tension between the seeker and merger selves. But it is certainly true that our culture emphasizes initiating behavior at the expense of responsiveness in young men, while the reverse is approved for young women.

Let us focus for the moment on women and men who made the decisions of their twenties before the sexual revolution. In particular, people who were somewhere between eighth grade and voting age at the beginning of World War II, and who are today's middle-aged.

The Bad Old Days

Young men bluffed their way into the adult work world. Only then began the long process of matching their skills and adjusting their expectations against actual experience. Gradually, as they gained and exhibited competence, they were given validation from many sources: from the older men who promoted them, from the contemporaries who competed with them, and from the wives who depended upon them. By the time they reached 30, most educated men were generally confident that they were on their way in the world of accomplishment.

Most women went a different route. After a couple of working years to pay for her placemats and flatware, or attending college if she were so unusual,* a woman married and retreated from the outer adult world to nurture one man and 2.9 children. She too was busy proving her competence: learning how to still the howls and train the bowels of a helpless infant, how to perform the organizational feat of turning out her own first Thanksgiving dinner, how to live on the household allowance, and hundreds of other firsts that were novel and scary. For a time, it was satisfaction enough simply to master each skill of the caregiver. But the young married woman was isolated and dependent on very few sources for recognition and self-esteem; whereas her husband was proving himself in a sphere so large and remote that eventually he couldn't even explain it to her.

The evidence of how such disparate experiences of passing through the twenties shaped the personality development of men and women was revealed in a major longitudinal study conducted by the Institute of Human Development of the University of California at Berkeley. It focused on a random selection of 171 men and women who grew up in the San Francisco Bay area and who were, it turned out, more than usually upwardly mobile for their historical time in America. Their lives were followed from birth over a period of thirty to forty years.[4]

The trends that occurred for men only were these: Across the years from junior high school into their thirties, their personal confidence steadily increased.

* Ninety per cent of women who were between the ages of 30 and 44 in 1972 did not have a college degree. (U. S. Dept. of Commerce, 1973)

They made strides toward greater social control and certainty. They became (in the words of the study) more dependable, productive, and assertive, increasingly valuing their independence and finding themselves capable of giving advice to their colleagues. By their thirties, the men were aware of their own social and sexual powers and quite satisfied with themselves. At the same time, their control was achieved with the loss of some tenderness and self-expressiveness.

In contrast, the women in their thirties were *less* sure of themselves than they had been as young adolescents, when they were far ahead of the boys. They had become "submissive, fearful, guilty, over-controlled, and hostile." Their only developmental gains were those associated with being a wife and mother: They were more protective, introspective, and sympathetic. But even those gains were accompanied by reciprocal losses. Their sexual enjoyment had declined. They had lost their youthful assurance that they were exciting and attractive as women and by now felt secure in only one role: They were mothers.

The Brave New Days

But isn't this the unisex generation? Don't boys find it much easier to be tender and self-expressive? And how often people say, "It must be so much easier to be a young woman today."

It is certainly different. But easier? It all depends on whether one is looking at the external obstacles, many of which are in the process of being removed, or at the battle to be done between a young person and his or her inner custodian, which can be truly fierce.

Beneath the contemporary young woman's most adamant rhetorical goals, there is still the quicksand of the old "you don't have to" message. Even when she is aware that the back door out (leading away from the dangers of individuation) may be a trapdoor, there is usually little in her childhood training that encourages her to resist the temptation.

One could go all the way back to the earliest Oedipal period to trace the origins of this developmental conflict. But to be brief about it, let us pick up from the point at which a pilot light in the loins ignites in us the awareness of ourselves as sexual beings.

It is commonly accepted by behavioral theorists that both boys and girls have their primary attachment to mother. Both sexes have masculine and feminine attitudes as well as masculine and feminine Oedipus complexes. And both wish to restore the original attachment to mother. In puberty, when this primitive desire takes on an actively sexual cast, boys no less than girls are prevented from carrying out their wishes, but there is a vast difference in the reasons they can't and in the compensations offered.

For a boy it is a cultural taboo that says incest is not allowable for very good reasons that have nothing to do with his adequacy. He could, but he may not. When his father and rival intervenes, there is an implicit compensation to soften the blow. The boy will have to wait until he takes his own wife, whom he can then possess in the way he now wishes to possess his mother. Long before that he may unconsciously substitute for her by sexual initiation in the arms of an older woman. Or if not actually cradled in the flesh by a prostitute or Mrs. Robinson (of the movie *The Graduate*), he can fantasize about it in the manner of Turgenev's love-struck boy in *First Love*. Thus encouraged, when the boy eventually does abandon the sexual love for his mother, his Oedipus complex is shattered. He identifies with his father and goes on to inherit the prerogatives of a man in a man's world. The sequence is a progressive one: mother to father to manhood.

For a girl the Oedipal story has a loop. If she is to end up identifying with her own sex, as healthy psychological development would have it, she must jump from mother to father and back to mother. And that raises the controversial issue of penis envy, controversial mainly because Freud's term makes it sound as though all the fuss is over an appendage rather than a set of privileges.

The subject of penises came up once at bath time with my ten-year-old daughter.

"Have you ever wished you had one?" I asked, straining to pick up from this reliable source any evidence of the mutilation fantasies they write about in textbooks.

"No," she said blithely. Then considered a moment. "But there are certain advantages. You can pee outdoors in the summer without it running down your leg."

A perfectly rational assessment, although she has not yet made the connection to the different powers and privileges accorded to men and women. A young girl is disappointed to learn that she cannot implement the love for her mother, for a reason that is not at all clear when puberty brings on a rush of clitoral sensation. She may try, giving her mother passionate movie-clinch kisses, but mother is not moved, except perhaps to put her off in embarrassment. Psychoanalyst Juliet Mitchell has extended this interpretation in a thought-provoking essay on Freud's theory of the distinction between the sexes:

> No prohibition shatters her love for her mother, but she learns that she possesses nothing with which to implement it. A sense of her inferiority . . . sets her on the path towards femininity. The girl's positive Oedipus complex (love of the father) is entered into only by default; it is not as strong as the boy's Oedipus complex nor is there any reason fully to give it up—on the contrary . . . [she] finds her cultural place in a patriarchal society when she finally manages to achieve her Oedipal love for her father.[5]

Fathers are not unwilling to collaborate in keeping this fictional romance alive—fair to say that the devotion of an innocent young girl is irresistible.

Perhaps the filial fighting, so common between

mother and daughter during a girl's adolescence, erupts not only because she learns to be jealous of mother as her rival, but also because she is rather dismayed at where this leaves her. Because the handicaps she has in initiating her wishes are the same as her mother's, somehow mother is implicitly to blame for them. Nor can the mother fully compensate her daughter—there will be no wife for her later on.

Somewhere in this Oedipal loop, any girl can become confused about the transfer of affections. There is no good reason to give up the love for her father except that it tends to keep her a little girl for life. If the culture is in an antipatriarchal mood, going back to the traditional mother as a model isn't attractive either. People have already warned her that's a dead end. The process of jumping from mother to father and back to mother may immobilize her with doubts.

Who on earth shall she be like?

The mother who has developed a strong grasp on her sense of self can offer the young girl a vigorous and provocative model. And there are more and more mothers like this all the time. Bleaker prospects are in store for daughters of those resigned mothers who have little identity of their own. The young woman who wants fervently to reject her mother's form must make haste before that comforting inner voice lures her back into the old familiar sanctuary. The quickest way out of this danger zone is to jump into someone else's form. And where is the closest ready-made mold? He's across the living room reading his newspaper.

Eureka! I'll be like him. *He* has it all together. If I become his replica, so will I. I'll be inside him and charged by all his juice. Then I will be confident and respected.

Just listen for those women who exclaim they have suddenly found the way to complete themselves. You will often hear lawyers' wives consumed with the necessity to enter law school. Not necessarily to practice law, just to finish—both law school and themselves. You will hear academics' wives yearning for their own advanced degrees, businessmen's wives talking about running their own boutiques or real estate agencies. And often doctors' wives (like Nita, in Chapter Seven) want that medical degree, too. Even when it fits over their own talents no more closely than a cloak.

Like many young women in their twenties today, Nita compares herself with her mate and says, If he can, why can't I just as easily? The fact overlooked is that her husband is a man doing what men *should* by everyone's measurement. His father, his mother, his friends, teachers, and society are all allies supporting him in taking that direction. Reality is a prop to him. But the very realities that today give a girl like Nita the permission to have a career—the professor and the husband who say it is okay—demand that she break her ties with mother and give up the little-girl love for her father. Reality is in many ways her enemy at just the time when it is imperative to make reality a friend.

Fear of Success

The fear of success in women was first demonstrated by Matina Horner in 1968. As a doctoral student at the University of Michigan, she showed that the motive to achieve in women college students was complicated by ambivalence. To be tops in academic performance, particularly under competitive conditions, and most especially when the competition was with men, might result in a loss of love and popularity. The more competent the woman, the greater her conflict about achieving.[6]

But there is more to it than the worry that no one will marry a woman if she's too successful and independent. We must remember that Horner's subjects were college freshmen. The evidence in the biographies collected here is that the combined fear of success and of failure can carry over even after a woman finds an encouraging mate (as Nita did) and often continues to inhibit women who have been married, either happily or miserably, for a decade or two.

The deeper psychological dilemma has to do with defying the inner custodian. A woman who was taught by her parents that her proper role is to please a man runs a great risk if she becomes too independent. Just as she is about to seize control of her own destiny, that inner custodian, thwarted by her disobedience, might run amuck. It might show its nasty tyrant side and make a fool of her. Or punish by causing her to fail: *I told you so.* In her darkest fantasies, she would be left stranded, lost, alone.

Fear of Softness

Boys too are invited to suppress certain aspects of their personalities, in particular, anything that might interfere with action and complicate the display of virility. Added to the demand that a boy renounce the primary attachment to mother, he learns that to please the traditional father and/or to gain approval in the world, he must cauterize many of his emotions. Men are to be strong, not soft.

One of the most useful defenses of the self is denial. When boys feel weak or fearful or about to cry, they are taught to deny the emotion, project it onto an outer obstacle, externalize it.[7] When boys first scrimmage on the football field, they are not encouraged to admit any doubts about injury they might do to themselves or to empathize with the opposing players they leave in a heap of pain. And surely, no one in command of B-52 pilots in Vietnam encouraged those young men to think about the unseeable devastation they were leaving below. The B-52 may be the maximum technological expression to date of the militaristic man's continuing refusal to be human.

Although denial and externalization are immature defense mechanisms, they serve the young person's need to wall off inner doubts while the first major outer risks are run. Action is more easily possible when one is unencumbered by much introspection or empathy, even though this means that fluency with one's emotions is forfeited, at least in youth.

Looking Past Our Noses

If our personalities and life courses were fixed for good by the end of our twenties, it would be a pretty drear existence for us all. Bright young men might spend the rest of their days victimized by their own outer success, still racing like horses around a track with no finish line and possessing approximately the same capacity for emotional depth. Women who married young and had children, if they remained stuck in the coop, quite likely would become convinced of their inadequacies and grow fat on self-loathing. This happens. But it only happens to people who will not risk further growth, which in any case is difficult to avoid if only to survive life's accidents.

Let's jump ahead.

For most of those in the twenties, a fantastic mystery story waits to be written over the next two decades. It races with excitement and jeopardy, fools us with false villains, diverts us from the real villains that are the divisions within ourselves, mugs us with surprise changes in our perspective, and leads us down secret passageways in search of our missing personality parts. Even at the end, we are never quite sure whatdunit.

Somehow, the source of our identity moves from outside to inside, and it is this psychological movement in sense of self that is the key to the mystery. It causes many men and women to switch from the opposite poles of their twenties to a different set of opposites by their forties.

This switch is strikingly revealed by the way in which men and women tell their life stories. The differences were particularly distinct in the way all of them spilled out the histories of the first half of their

lives. The men talked about the actions they had initiated. The women talked about the people they had
responded to.

That is, the men reconstructed their tracks according to the career line they had followed. They
measured themselves at each step against the timetable
approved for their particular occupational dream.
Love partners were filled in as adjuncts to their real
love affair: courting the dream of success and seeking
their identity through their work. The men talked
about their wives and children largely in terms of how
they helped or hindered the dream, but they rarely
spoke, without prompting, about the needs or nourish-
ing of the human beings closest to them. These human
connections seldom converged with what a man saw as
his main track of development until he had reached
his forties.

Women, by contrast, spun out their stories around
their attachments to, and detachments from, others:
parents, lovers, husbands, children. The central thread
running through their young lives was the state of
these human connections. The pursuit of an individual
dream was most often a stitch that was picked up,
dropped, perhaps picked up again. It was what they
did before they married, between babies, or after the
divorce. Women whose lives incorporated a vital
career line generally described that line as the either/
or choice they had to make, the profession they
doggedly pursued instead of marrying Peter or the
exit route they took from Paul or the detour they
made from family commitments and for which at some
point they feared they would be charged a toll. Loaned
time. It was rare to find a woman under 35, even a
talented and successful one, who felt complete without
a man.

Until very recently in our culture, most men and
women spent a good part of their twenties and thirties
living one of two illusions: that career success would
make them immortal, or that a mate would complete
them. (Even now, those illusions die very hard.)

Men and women were on separate tracks. The career as an all-encompassing end to life turned out to be a flawed vision, an emotional cul-de-sac. But did attaching oneself to a man and children prove to be any less incomplete as life's ultimate fulfillment?

Each sex seemed to have half the loaf and was uncomfortable about the half they were missing. Did the missing halves even belong to the same loaf? Men had the credentials with which to barter for external advancement. Women had the perceptiveness to say: "What good is becoming president if you lose touch with your family and your feelings?"

The woman was jealous of the man's credentials. The man was disturbed by the woman's truth.

As men and women enter midlife, the tables begin to turn. Many men I interviewed found themselves wanting to learn how to be responsive. And a surge of initiating behavior showed up in most women. What happens?

Here is a sneak preview.

12

SNEAK PREVIEW: MEN AND WOMEN GROWING UP

Inside the educated 35-year-old married woman is a young girl who remembers what it was like to win at word games or get the highest mark in the class, to control a spirited horse, or to do twenty piqué turns around the stage with her blisters raw and pounding into the bluntness of her toe shoes but it didn't matter because everyone applauded. A girl who used to have confidence and dreams and write in her diary, "I'm going to be Sonja Henie when I grow up" (or Esther Williams or Lois Lane or Elizabeth Taylor), and who probably became the mother of someone who now says, "I'm going to be Billie Jean King."

How is it this woman is now in her mid-thirties and still has to ask a man for her allowance? What does he do with those rosebuds in his office all day that makes him come home saying, "I'm too tired tonight, honey"? Doesn't he know that under the stretch marks her sexual engines are racing as never before? Why must she murder the dullness of her days? Killing time is a suicidal act. The time she is killing is all she has left to live.

Demanding to be admitted in this conventional midlife woman are her so-called bad parts ("I don't know what I believe in anymore" or "I'm not even sure I like my children") and her assertive side—the initiating kind of behavior that will allow her to direct more of her own life (and require that she take more responsibility for it). The words change from woman to woman, but stripped down, there is a great deal of similarity to the longings underneath. "Let me into the world! I want to be smart and important and have value placed on my time and talents, too. Is it possible to pick up where I stopped learning? Do men still find me appealing? I wish someone would take me seriously. I wish someone would help me to stop being afraid."

Inside the tough-talking, hard-jogging man of 40 who is identified largely by his work, there is a boy trying not to cry, "Time's running out!" A boy who often wants to say, "Hey, I'm sorry about some of the things I have to do, like kowtowing to the brass and backstabbing the young talent, like pushing memos around my desk and superfluous products into the world when I'd rather be somebody's best friend (my kids', for instance) or add just one iota of real value to the world. But time's running out. If I don't hurry up and become the manager, or write that best seller, I'll be a failure. A loser waiting to be junked. I'm not so proud either of leching after every firm bottom that steps on the elevator when my own wife at home would give anything for just a touch. But I only know how to perform, be on top, and, Jesus, I can't even count on the old screwing machinery anymore. It's apt to go soft on me just when I need it."

The voices demanding to be admitted, acknowledged, absorbed somehow by this midlife man are those he could not allow himself before. His responsiveness and vulnerability and also his dark side. "I wish somebody would let me be what I am, tender sometimes, and dependent, too, but also vain and greedy and jealous and competitive. I wish somebody would accept that I'm not always the stronger one. I wish someone would take this panic away."

The only one who can do this, for both men and

women in midlife, is one's self. Letting go of the fantasy projections onto others is not easy earlier in the life cycle, when essential elements of our sense of self are tied up with parents, peers, mates, children, or mentors. By the time we set off on the second half of our journey, we will have sustained repeated separations and losses in our attachments to these others. Attachments we once thought were vital to maintaining our being are not, we discover, and with that discovery it becomes not only possible but compelling to seek an honest unity within our selves.

Carl Jung was the first major analytic thinker to view middle life as the time of maximum potential for personality growth. We yearn at that time for the undividedness of self that has always been lacking. As the hope of finding security in another vanishes, the conflict is brought to a head. Consequently, many of our archetypal images of "feminine" and of "masculine," images we unconsciously project upon a mate, can be withdrawn. Jung talks about the necessity to "confront our own contrasexual aspect" and to integrate it, which makes possible an extraordinary enrichment of all experience.[1]

At the very least, it is an unsettling process. "It is not hard to imagine what will happen when the husband discovers his tender feelings and the wife her sharpness of mind," writes Jung. He goes on to warn that when middle-aged men become effeminate and women belligerent, it is an indication that these persons have failed to accord their inner life due recognition.[2] Levinson also cites the acceptance of the feminine in himself as one of the major tasks for a man in midlife transition.[3]

Many men find formerly suffocated feelings pushing up through their narrow public personae once they pass midpoint. The forties is a time for discovering the emotive parts of themselves that didn't fit with the posture of the strong, dynamic, rational young men they were supposed to be at 25. Many of those parts they temporarily displaced onto the women in their lives, whom they could then love, fear, or hate for having these qualities.

Federico Fellini was able to articulate this process most sensitively after he had reached his own middle age, when he made the nostalgic film *Amarcord* about his boyhood, a film that has been hailed as his most complete.

"Man has always been accustomed to look at woman as a mystery onto which he projects his fantasies," Fellini says. "She is mother, wife or whore, or Dante's Beatrice or the muse. Man through the ages has continued to cover woman's face with masks that to his subconscious probably represented the unknown part of himself."[4]

It is a critical step, then, for the man in midlife to be able to look behind the masks and recognize the unknown parts he sees. That in itself shows some strength. One afternoon I met a man at exactly that point in his life.

The Responsive Man

Millions of Americans hear him every evening give an account of the world. He is a star, a television newscaster, a face better known than most of the President's cabinet members. He can afford to tan it in the Caribbean on an income nearly ten times the peak of his father's earnings (his father rarely had the wherewithal to get beyond his front stoop). He can tint out the gray in his hair, tone up the doughy muscles of middlescence on the most exquisitely devised exercise tables in Manhattan, take the woman of his choice out to dinner at "21," and take back any traces of psychic discomfort to a Park Avenue psychiatrist. The day our paths crossed, he had been asked to sit for a portrait. It will hang with the likenesses of two dozen other men and women in an exhibition of prominent members of his profession. The portrait is just another testimony by which the world is telling him, at the age of 46, that he has placed near the top of the heap.

It is not enough.

"I'm near the top of the mountain that I saw as a young man, and it's not snow. It's mostly salt," he blurted out.

"Most guys I talk with who are successful—whatever the hell successful is—left their personal lives way behind them. They stopped growing at age 12 or 14, when they were overcome with the crying ambition to do something. Professionally, they're terrific, but their personal lives are in a *mess*. There should have been concomitant growth, and there wasn't. The idea now is to bring both parts of their lives together. *That* is the struggle.

"You see, now I'm getting ready for the day when I get kicked off that salt-capped mountain. My whole life was predicated on *getting there*. Now I want to have a goal and somebody to share it with who will bolster me on the way down," he said, forcing a mock-Bogart laugh, "because I'm going to need a little help."

This man was wrestling with questions one hears over and over again from men his age. To the newscaster, the meaning of his membership in the success club changed completely over the midlife passage. His marriage of twenty-one years, a marriage he had hoped would last for fifty, came apart. He realized that he had never put enough of himself into it.

"I married her when I was in college. She was a good girl, but it's just that I was dumb and she was too. My syndrome was, I always had to establish distance. I'd come close a little bit and then withdraw. When she got mad because I'd pushed her back too far, I'd break the wall down and come after her, right? It made me feel like a good boy again. Then I would get frightened and shove her off. It was like a yo-yo. You can't do that to a human being."

I told him the yo-yo syndrome was more prevalent than he thought.

"Why in hell do we have so much trouble with

173

the opposite sex?" he exploded. "The most important
thing to a man next to his job, and even higher than
his job if he really will admit it"—the newscaster
paused, being of an age when he finally could admit
it—"is the personal relationship with his woman. Why
is that the area he's dying in?"

"Men are not given awards and promotions for
bravery in intimacy," I commented.

"And I'm angry about it." He jumped to his feet,
forgetting the portrait, forgetting everything but the
urgency to express a neglected side of himself. "We get
accused of being untender and ungentle, and we're
not all those things," he insisted. "The other side never
got a chance to grow. All we heard about was drive,
success, work." By the illustration he then gave, it was
clear that he was trying, at 46, to be comfortable in
letting out these new feelings.

"I can go out on a city street and yell at the top
of my lungs, 'I hate you, you s.o.b.!,' and nobody will
turn around, right? But get out there and start yelling,
'I love you!,' and fifteen people will stop in their tracks
as if I just held up a bank." He smacked a fist against
his palm. "That's not right!"

It is important to note that the issue of how to
express love and tenderness is one that grips women's
attention in their twenties. Here are the opposites
mentioned before.

This man's sense of himself at 40 was shaken on
all sides at once. He was plunged into that de-
illusionment chamber from which only the rare man
can escape without facing up to the gap between the
vision of himself in his twenties and the actuality of
himself at 40. Even when a man has not *objectively*
fallen short of his goal, he must wrestle with inco-
herent feelings of futility. Witness this man, whose
mountain peak had been reached when he won a
television news slot.

"You're discontent, and you don't even know what
you're discontent about," is how the newscaster recalls

the first signals. "It's the gnawing sense that you're not getting all out of life that you should be."

Is there nothing more? he asks, fearing that whatever the answer, it is too late to change. It is *not* too late, but some of the changes could have been allowed earlier. In the newsman's life, it was too late at 40 to correct for the compulsive philandering that had driven his wife to despair in her solitary cell in suburbia. The whole structure crumbled. He unloaded a misunderstood wife and took on an understanding analyst.

He is now living with a successful career woman his own age who makes him proud but doesn't crowd him. They have been together for three years, exactly since he turned 43 and pulled out of the panic of midlife transition. She knows his destructive habits. At the first hint of withdrawal in his voice, she simply smiles and says, "Are you funny today?"

"And the biggest help"—the newscaster withdraws for an instant from revealing any more—"this is very intimate, but why not? You're making love, and all of a sudden you're tired, you lose interest, you say, 'Why don't we just go to sleep?' Without having to feel you've just committed a terrible crime!"

The artist and I applauded.

"But if the people out on the street who watch knew all that, what would they think?"

"They're not watching," I reminded him. "Intimacy is not a TV performance."

It was refreshing to see a man so excited about discovering access to his barricaded feelings. With a newly stabilized life structure and a knowing woman who has a good sense of humor, he seems to be broadening his capacity for feeling.

The mess he left behind was not so hopeful. Shortly after I published a brief account of the newscaster's dilemma, I received a call from his wife. She wanted to see me and give her side of the story.

"That was one of my little revenges when he left

175

me," she began as she removed her coat. "I had my mink remodeled." She has the face of a Big Ten cheerleader, slightly corrugated now and cosmetically florid. Her body is generously curved; she is a pretty woman. But she speaks as if anesthetized except when describing one of her huband's more flamboyant transgressions. Then her eyes fly open and floodlights come on. She is humorous and animated, but only when speaking of the past.

I asked about her present situation. She ignored the four years since her husband left and started in describing their last bloody year together. Time stopped there. She stopped there, and is still placing blocks in her path to individuation. Many of the blocks are real: four children and a dormant woman left in the wake of a man's midlife crisis. But she stacks them in a way that prevents one turn from leading to another and to the eventual escape from her "prison," which is how she has come to think of the suburban gadget dream after having twenty years of it. "Our whole marriage was one hour a week of conversation about the lawn or the next move."

That was not how it was supposed to be, back in their dull industrial town, when she had a job with the telephone company and a crush on a "tall, strong, beautiful" firebrand who was going to college. "I'd do anything to make him notice me. I did have my own dream of moving to New York and being a career woman. It was impossible. My father was a factory worker, we were poor." She finally met him at a bus stop in her 18th year. When they set off into the twenties, it was all wrapped up in the standard illusions and tied with the ribbons of stereotype: He was the go-getter and she the caregiver, piggybacking her dream.

"He struck me as being a man of ambition who would accomplish something, and I could be a help. I had been an editor of the high school paper, and journalism was very much a favorite pursuit of mine. It seemed to be a good fit. His grammar was atrocious.

I was very patient about correcting him. His dream was to emulate Edward R. Murrow and also to be a millionaire by 40. He was very romantic with me until the moment of marriage. Once I became the woman in his house, I became mother, in his head. And his mother represented the person who always said no."

She was dead right about this. I had already heard it from the mouth of the newscaster, who had only recently been able to see the real lock himself.

"The terror starts with mothers," he said. "For me, it's the fear of being suffocated. Mothers love you, but they smother you. They don't let you fall down and get hurt. I see women in terms of mothers, as someone who is always going to ask where you were, who you were with, why you were doing that. It's the fear of being made to feel like a bad boy. You're afraid your woman is going to make you feel the same way, like you've failed at making her totally happy, constantly."

By moving his wife into the position of mother, he created a convenient scapegoat on whom he could blame his own fears and limitations. The "she wouldn't let me" excuse, once affixed to his mother to explain why he couldn't be a professional ballplayer, was in time transferred to his wife. She wouldn't let him be a movie star. She never took an interest in his activities. When his wife made a point of trying to slip this lock, he would yo-yo.

"Where are you going?" he would say, finding her in the car.

"I thought I'd come along today and watch you play ball."

"None of the other wives come."

"I'd really like to."

"Do you want to sit in my lap for every broadcast, too?"

Like most of us, the newscaster became a master at handling the tools necessary to maintain his lock. Taking the part of delinquent boy and telling his wife every time he had been "bad" made it easy to keep her at a motherly distance.

177

"I was feeling up this girl in front of the library—" he would begin.

"What are you talking about!"

"Oh, you know, all the guys do it; it's just bullshit."

"If it's bull, then why do you spend so much time at it?" Her anger, diluted by weakness and dependence, was easily mollified. And his confession would enable him to feel like a good boy again.

But he couldn't touch his own wife. Not with tenderness and affection. "I didn't realize I was ducking and weaving," he had told me. "Deep down I thrive on loving and touching in a tender way, but guys are frightened to death that if they give this to their wives, they'll be smothered." The risk is easily enough avoided by performing one's intimacies outside the immediate circle, with a dim face in a hotel room or other men's wives, safe women.

His wife recalls: "It was almost as if he was saying, 'Here's my conscience; it's up to you to take care of it while I go play hooky.'"

A whole string of such secret delegations build up between any husband and wife: "My wife is the gregarious one. I let her take care of our social calendar." Or "I'm a creative person; thank God I'm married to an organizer!" In most instances one assigns to the other what he or she doesn't want to be bothered with, which may be fine. The process becomes destructive when one partner delegates a *necessary* ego function to the other. If the newscaster had taken the responsibility for his own conscience, he would have had to give up the philandering by which he created distance from intimacy. By delegating to his wife the responsibility for stopping him, he could continue to be the indulged, delinquent little boy. No sooner had he confessed than he would be off on another rampage of assignations, repetitious as a chain letter and just as casually broken.

For maintaining distance with his mistresses he had another mechanism. He would nitpick. "At one point I was going with a lovely Australian girl, a fine human being," he had explained. "Her calves were just a little bit heavy. For a year it didn't bother me, and then the destruct cycle took over. Those legs got bigger and bigger, so big I finally couldn't see anything but her calves. With another woman it might be her hair or her way of dressing. For six months or a year I'd be the most giving bastard in the world, until my nitpicking gave me a reason to say, 'This is not for me.' I would start getting wooden, distant, cold. Subconsciously I would have invested the woman with qualities that my mother or sister had, and that would drive me away. Not her. It wouldn't be anything she did. It would be me looking for a reason to get out."

At home, of course, his wife was always pitching soft ones across the plate. Whether flaw or endowment, he could always knock it out of the park. Her skirts were too short; her breasts, too large. She was not seductive enough at home, or she was coming on too strong, which reduced him to impotence. He refused to allow contraceptives to interfere with her "spontaneity," then threatened to leave if she didn't have the results taken care of. So went the yo-yo until she had a second abortion at 32.

"I think I knew then the whole thing was falling apart," his wife says today. But she stayed put through the Age 30 passage, believing her husband to be her safety. Her attempts at broadening were limited to learning to drive and taking a job in a bank. A trickle of confidence did begin to accumulate as she discovered she learned rapidly and made friends easily. And then they moved again.

"I was planning all along that when I felt comfortable, I'd explore my own fulfillment," she says. The statement might more accurately read: *I was postponing all along exploring my own fulfillment because of my own internal timidity*.

In the settling-down years of her thirties, she coaxed him into buying the standard developer's colonial in the suburbs that would anchor her security.

"As his work took him more and more away from

home, we didn't have to confront each other. Things were peaceful. And having grown up poor, I could now see financial rewards on the doorstep. I could play indoor tennis and go to lunch with my friends. I settled for it. The distance just got worse as he approached the forties. It came to a crisis for me after two years of dreadful neglect. He wouldn't even hold my hand. I'd say, 'My God, our young lives are going by. Can't we talk, can't we touch? What is it, did you kill somebody?' "

He confessed, at 43, that it was another affair. This time his wife howled and cursed and clawed at the suburban night. The next day he left. The four children grouped around his wife like a color guard. He shouted from the back door, "I can't stand you, the kids, this dump of a house. I've got to get out!"

There are other ways of breaking a couple lock, but because much of our training in adult relationships is taken from movies and TV, one method that naturally suggests itself is to go through the door like Charles Bronson. Episodes following such a dramatic exit are not often shown, for in real life they concern the body's reaction to anxiety and the human capacity for degradation.

Every day he phoned asking to come back. "I'm sick. I can't get through meetings. I have this terrible diarrhea."

She made his return conditional on his visiting a psychiatrist at least once, and then she waited in the family room, expecting this moment to be the climax of her life. He would apologize, praise, give testimony at last to the significance of her existence.

"Where's the mail?" was his reentry line. "What have you got to eat?"

It was as if he had never left and the crisis had never occurred. More than that, in her two weeks alone she had made a startling discovery. Her husband was not her safety. Nothing changed with the removal of his corpus; it merely formalized the emotional absence that had always been.

"He still had his life; I still had the suburb and the children. Nothing had changed, and that was shocking. Oh, I cried. But the upset was realizing the kind of life we had been living. Now I'd really have to face it."

He left five times that year.

Her comfort came, not from making the most of her freedom to expand (she took a real estate course and then did nothing with it), but from institutionalizing her martyrdom. "Each time he left I would pretty up my prison."

They went together to a marriage counselor, but what he really had in mind was a counselor for the defense, an authority who would pronounce him the victim and her the villain. "Why didn't you let me—" is how he began most of their sessions, pointing at his wife. Nonetheless, because he had suggested an interaction that goes by the name of "therapy," his wife clung to it as a sign of hope.

The therapist said, "It never ceases to amaze me how long some women will wait."

When the last piece of furniture was in place and the shutters on her prison repainted, she decided to give a party—her first. It had been his custom to seek entertainment and contacts only in his public life. He never wanted the kind of friends one would invite home—too close. This burst of defiance on his wife's part augured well for her growth: "I was beginning to get stronger and stop being the passive pushover I'd been all those years. He didn't know how to deal with me." To hell with his permission. She invited fifty guests and a caterer and threw herself a wingding of a 41st birthday celebration. He attended, subdued. But it was too much strain on the yo-yo. He never did bounce back.

"When my husband deserted—" The repetition of this phrase seems to be one of her prime sources of pleasure. "When my husband deserted, I didn't know it, but he was already living with that other woman." There follows a recitation of woes ranging over money, one daughter's car crash, another daughter's abortion, all of which are directly attributed to the man who has by now been absent for four years. "The telephone company calls periodically to turn off our phone; my attorney calls his attorney, who calls his accountant. That's been my life since."

What is the point, one wonders, in wasting more years listlessly tossing bombs in a war that is over? Why can't she just get on with her own expansion? The same reason comes up so often. If she loses him as the enemy on whom she can blame all her troubles, then she must realize that the enemy is *inside*. So long as this possibility remains unacceptable, she will continue to battle with a phantom villain.

The woman I have just described is a caregiver. This is the pattern chosen by women who have no intention of pursuing a dream of their own. They elect to be auxiliaries to a husband's career and growers of children, in exchange for financial support. There are many women who choose the caregiver's pattern and later find it possible to stretch toward a broader definition without a marriage breakup. There is also the caregiver who manages to get past the midlife passage without having any authenticity crisis at all. She doesn't control her own identity, and she doesn't want to. It is always possible to go on letting others define one and take care of one, so long as there is always someone whose interest lies in doing so.

When suddenly there is not, the sound you are likely to hear in the midlife years is the plaint of a caregiver such as the newscaster's wife: "I loved being a mother and I loved being a housewife. I just needed to be cherished. I never felt cherished."

The Initiating Woman

But that is only half the story. What of the women over 35 who do take the risks of admitting their assertive side? Those I talked to had found all sorts of capacities and extensions beyond their attachments to men and children. Some had struck out into painting, writing, photography, creative pursuits of all kinds. Some had gone back to school or to teaching with a new vigor of commitment. Others had put their family-management skills to broader use in public agencies or started their own businesses, or they were selling real estate or running for office. Against the fading orchids of ladies who had "married well" but remained dormant inside their hothouses, these hardy and second-blooming begonias were more beautiful, more mysterious, more exciting than they had ever felt themselves to be in the bloom of youth.

Mia is such a woman. The next to last time I saw Mia, she had stopped believing in her own worthlessness. I knew it the moment I saw her across the room. We were at a party called to plan an event for the international women's art festival. Many of the others there were rich wives who would take what importance they could from being sponsors. Mia was different, an artist in her own right.

"What's happened?" I asked.

"Everything! All at once. This week a book of my pictures goes to press. The publisher came to me! I'm doing a one-woman show next month, and *Camera 35* is devoting half an issue to my work. It's like a dream."

She rushed on, the heat of her exuberance so direct that I had to remind myself of the journey that brought her to such a place. This was a woman who for thirty-five years had performed one escape attempt after the other in the effort to avoid claiming her own authority. At the midpoint, she had risked the disintegration of everything she had been taught to believe guaranteed her safety and enrichment. She left her husband, a man idolized by others, and endured years of estrangement from her children. Recently, she told me, she had even pulled free of the mentor who first put a camera in her hands. Upon discovering her talent to be superior to his, he had become abusive.

"I have a lover who lives on the other side of the country," she was saying now. "We met at a creative workshop. He's one of the venerated professors in the field, and he respects my work. I don't have to pretend anymore that I'm less than the best I can possibly be. He doesn't distract me; I don't crowd him. And when we do get together, it's—*whoosh*—like swimming nude for the first time. My children like me again, and I don't even care that my breasts sag. I'm 41 and I'm flying. I catch myself laughing on the street!"

The urge to soar had been there at 30, but so was the safety net of her own making. In its snarls, like so many women, Mia was caught up and stalled. She could not break through and develop in a progressive way because so many of the preliminary steps still had to be taken. And so what she had was a standing-up nervous breakdown.

There was no point to her being in Puerto Rico that summer. Not with three babies at the lifting and diapering stage in a two-room apartment off the beach where the sewers emptied out in San Juan. Not when her husband was quartered hours away at a camp in the rain forest. But it was like him to volunteer to be where he could best help humanity in the aggregate; he was an activist minister. Once a week the Reverend would fly down to visit his family. Mia saw him only for dinner. The rest of the time he would be at the beach, in the water, perfecting his "Peace Corps float."

The August heat pressed down. The cockroaches multiplied into a squirming carpet, and her back went bad. All week she screamed at the children. When the Reverend came on Sundays she would throw blunt objects at the mirror. He stopped spending the night. One visiting day she blew sky high.

"If I have to bend one more time to pick up the baby, I'll break in two," she howled. "Or pitch him over the roof." No response. "You won't talk to me. Please! I'm getting scared. I'm ready to crack."

Her warnings failed to bestir the Reverend. This much she knew about him by now: He was one of those people who could exercise compassion only from a safe distance. To the multitude of college students who sat beyond his lectern, plucking at each silvery philosophical fruit as it ripened in his fertile mind, he was the man with all the answers. He could comfort the parents of suicidal freshmen, inspire the young to global causes, soothe the dying. But for pain or need in his immediate circle, the Reverend had no tolerance whatsoever. He couldn't see. He didn't hear. Around his personal emotions there was a fender of steel.

Such people often go into the ministry, politics, psychiatry, or other forms of counseling, professions that allow them to help others from a detached, guru position but protect them from the dangers of one-to-one intimacy.

Had Mia attended to her first instincts on this score, she would never have married the Reverend. But openness and intimacy were not what she craved most at 22; authority was. A voice of authority to do what she could not, which was stand up to her father. Mia's father was a renowned musician who toured the capitals of the world and effortlessly dominated all those around him. His ego was devouring. It was easy to please him; all she had to do was say yes.

Yes, she wanted to be on the stage. Upon uttering those words at the age of five she was sent off to study dance, and from the age of 11, she was trained even to the exclusion of school. What did they talk about in school? she longed to know. She was parched with loneliness. Having gone through the contortions of puberty alone, Mia was a long time in catching up with her peer group. Many years later she would still be dipping back into the candy bin of adolescence to fill up on the fun she resented having lost.

Physiology spared Mia the ballerina's life her father had in mind. Mounds rose on her chest. Her hips swelled like donuts, and pads of flesh parted her thighs. She came out of puberty beautifully shaped for a lover's embrace but of a shape that was not going to approximate Markova no matter what. The family destiny was adjusted. She would be an actress.

"I also wanted to please my mother," she can say

at 41, "but that's taken me until *now* to recognize. She was the one who said, 'Stop biting your nails; no one will marry you. Stop reading books; no one will marry you.'"

At 22, Mia was living out her official dream as a member of a Broadway cast and colossally bored. That was the point at which the Reverend came into her life, with his articulate professor friends, his Proust and Dostoevsky, his riveting tales of the torments of war and poverty in a world that was totally foreign to her. But it was something else about the Reverend that captivated her.

One day she heard the young man talk back to her father. Instead of oozing in deference, as did all the other sycophants, he stated his opinions flawlessly and without fear. Mia felt like Rapunzel.

"This would save my life! He was a respectable, acceptable, solid, officially recognizable *counter*authority. He would make me safe. He would do all my saying no to my father for me. My instincts told me at the last minute there was something unreal about our getting married. I didn't want it, but I thought I should. He had the same reservations, as it turns out. He didn't tell me about them for twenty years."

Mia spent her twenties trying to substitute for her self, that once-upon-a-time dream who existed only in her father's mind and had been extinguished by marriage. She manipulated her husband into making her pregnant. "I was desperate to have something to reassure me I was real." She had one child, then two more in rapid succession. Frightened then by the helplessness of such a brood, she threw herself into running a soup kitchen and filled the house with her husband's students. It was amusing; it kept the place alive. What scared her was that everyone went home.

"There's something we have to talk about," she would begin gently.

A flicker of panic in his eyes. Then, as though her words were an injection of morphine, he would fall into a wooden sleep.

"Can't we have a normal fight about it?" she would sometimes plead.

"You're as big as what makes you mad," was his answer. Racism could make him mad, Vietnam, famine in Pakistan, but the slow starvation of one woman whose flesh twitched at night immediately next to his—no, to permit her a world of private chaos might have forced open his own inner chambers.

"After seven years I found myself being drawn to other people," Mia remembers. "I had just emptied out. I couldn't give him anything. I'd supported all fifteen of his causes, but to me they were fifteen mistresses. They took up all his time, his energy, passion, guts. There was nothing left."

If one cannot dare the broadening that is a universal urge in the passage to the thirties, the inner demand must be diverted in compulsive activity or secondary escapes found or a soothing regressive trip taken back to an earlier stage. In any one of these ways, the confrontation with the inner custodian can be postponed. Mia tried them all.

Before the seams could crack in Puerto Rico, Mia packed abruptly and returned home, masking the rupture by making recordings for the blind and speeches for the Peace Corps and hovering oppressively over her children. "Keeping busy was the most important thing. I thought, When he comes back in November, he'll see that I made a great effort to un–crack up, and we'll start over."

The notion that our personalities can be changed on command belongs to the twenties. Mia was getting too old for such illusions. On New Year's Eve she slipped into a brief, listless nonaffair with one of her husband's associates. His status was similar to hers. They loved the same man and resentfully picked up the pieces of his personal life while the Reverend collected all the professional acclaim. They met secretly in cars pretending their conspiratorial crush was romance. The plain fact was, Mia had no sex in her life whatsoever. For all the joy her ripe flesh afforded, she thought, she might better have been a miserable flat-chested dancer.

The day before Easter, with the penitential Lenten season coming to an end, Mia sensed a funny silence in the house. The Reverend called her upstairs to the bedroom. It was the first time he had addressed her in such an intimate way.

"I've figured out that the only way life is bearable for you is because you're seeing _____," he said. "I know about it, but I don't want you to feel guilty. I had an affair in Puerto Rico."

His confession summoned no absolution from his wife, nor did it assuage her guilt since she felt none.

"I couldn't leave because of the children," she explains. "They were too young. At some level, I might have known it was a matter of time."

For the duration of this passage, Mia's behavior slipped from regression into self-degradation. She shopped. Every day a full-hipped woman without expression could be seen wandering about downtown staring at window displays like a teen-ager with nothing more important to do than pick out the right shoes. Her car was routinely towed away. Her children waited at school, forgotten. At night, with enough liquor sopping her brain to take up all powers of discrimination, she would make herself available to the faculty. Every encounter was the same: quick, dry, anonymous. The only way she would know the name of the last man who bedded her was to look it up in the faculty directory—if she cared.

"I was dying on all levels. And then, one day when I was 31 years old, I fell in love. Utterly, completely, never-again love. And I realized what I'd been missing. It was an impossible situation. He was a 19-year-old student. But he understood me the way nobody ever has, including my mother. He saw my weaknesses; he knew how to deal with my guilt. While my husband was upstairs writing his sermon, we'd drink tea and talk for seven hours in the kitchen. Suddenly I was able to see things and say things about myself. My relationship with the children improved because I was getting fuel from someone. For three years I lived a double life."

It was a toboggan slide back to adolescent love, which is mostly conversation. In this exploratory, narcissistic, one-to-one alliance, which she had missed as a young girl, uncomplicated by the demands of marriage, she could begin to define herself through the feedback from another.

Thirty-five was the watershed year. The guilt of living off the fuel of a young man had caught up with her, and into her life was introduced an entirely new kind of vehicle for self-expression. An artistic vehicle. An independent way to seek achievement, mastery, confidence, and the recognition of others. Being thoroughly accustomed to seeking for such expansion through men and children, she describes this new object of love in the same words one would use for a lover:

"I was seduced by photography."

There was good reason for the confused association. It was a man who put the camera in her hands and showed her how to use it, a mentor who also became her lover.

All the studies agree that the presence or absence of such a figure has enormous impact on development. For a man in his twenties, the mentor, a guide who regards him as a younger adult but not as a boy or son, supports the young man's dreams and helps him put it into effect in the world. He is a nonparental career-role model. He also offers a critical leg up in helping a young man overcome the father-son polarity. The lack of mentors, Levinson has concluded, is a great developmental handicap. There is a further developmental handicap that men are spared, however. For them, the mentor and the loved one (the other key figure) are generally two different people.

Fewer mentors are available for women. Indeed, when I brought up the question of mentors with women, most of them didn't know what I was talking about. Female mentors have been particularly scarce. And when a man becomes interested in guiding and advising a younger woman, there is usually an erotic interest that goes along with it. What follows from that are many combinations we can easily recognize: producer and star, professor and graduate student, doctor and nurse, director and actress, and so on. The kicker is that the relationship of guide and seeker gets all mixed up with a confusing sexual contract.

What happens if she becomes confident enough to do without me? the mentor often fears. He can keep a finger on the control valve by criticizing her performance or by cutting back on his emotional support. The woman may have a difficult time finding her own equilibrium because her professional, emotional, and sexual nourishment are all piped in from the same person. And eventually that person is too much like a father for her own developmental good.

On the other hand, career women who haven't had a mentor relationship miss it, even if they don't know what to call it. Roughly 80 percent of the judgment jobs are hidden in the unpublished job market and reached only through the grapevine or the mentor system.[5] Almost without exception, the women I studied who did gain recognition in their careers were at some point nurtured by a mentor.

The same finding was made by Margaret Hennig in her Harvard doctoral study (1970) of twenty-five high-level women executives.[6] *All* had attached very strongly in their early careers to a single male boss. And once in the protective custody of this mentor, they subordinated all other relationships to it. The mentor helped these women to believe in their abilities and also acted as a buffer against clients and other company members who felt threatened by able women.

Mia's intertwined romance with a mentor and a camera initiated a crisis of growth, stretching and testing her for the next five years in all the ways that the midlife passage can. It began with a joyful ventilation, as described in a letter from her mentor:

I showed you the simple alchemy of light, silver, and certain chemicals. But you had to find your own way with photography. I wanted it to give you what it had given me. I wanted you, in the middle of the intense and exhausting busy-ness of going nowhere, to be able to hold something finished in your hand, something you had seen and fixed. . . . All this time, and for years before, something had been growing in you. It was the kind of pressure that can lead to things like alcoholism or suicide or, occasionally, art. Happily, it began to find its way out through your photography.

For Mia, taking pictures began as something she could do that pleased her lover. Within a year it became her own sustenance. She realized it was all that stood between her and complete emotional collapse; for by now, in every other area of her life, she was barely functional. She agonized over what to do about the children. There are other women who could leave sterile marriages and find the energy to manage a household of children while training themselves in a new profession, she told herself, but in a much later breath admitted, "I'm not one of them." Given her present condition, she knew she could only be destructive to the children. To work her way out of this dilemma, she made a decision that most of us would find unthinkable. She left the children in the care of her husband.

She tried to explain to them: "You know how much Daddy and I fight. It's wrong to scream at you when we're really angry at each other." The littlest boy, who was nine, began asking to dress like his older sister. She was the favorite; if he duplicated her, it might persuade his mother to stay.

They all stood waving outside the faculty house the day she left. Her eyes burned and her blood raced and she drove directly into the sun. She was a hobo. In a sterile white high rise in Manhattan she found one room and put away her books and cameras. She set up a darkroom. Except for classes or to shoot pictures, she saw no one and went nowhere.

"I had to collect a portfolio, and if that's what I was going to do, I had damn well better do it. I was exhilarated but I felt scared too."

Do you hear the sound of opposites again? This might be the voice of the 25-year-old man, seeking his niche in the adult world by sticking tightly to a narrow career goal and subordinating everything else.

But for Mia there were also the rocky days when her children came to town to visit "kooky Mommy." She wondered if they would ever forgive her for leaving them. Her mentor didn't turn up again until she was all settled. "We were in that strange freaky state," she recalls, "where you wonder why things are not what they are said to be."

Her pictures were becoming good, and her love life went bad because of it. Her eyes, when she was working, were the sulfurous blue of a struck match. She was her own discovery. But to her mentor those same working eyes represented a betrayal. The originality of their vision had surpassed his influence. He was good, but Mia was gifted.

"How do you do it?" he later wrote. "I've asked you that often, knowing while I asked that it's a damned silly question to begin with. Simply, you seem to tune with what is around you. . . . It's like trying to analyze a haiku—one can't."

They couldn't go on a picnic because she would find the remarkable in trees that seemed to him commonplace. At parties she was terrified lest someone praise her work within his earshot. When they returned home he would rage, drunk, and strike at those eyes that saw what he could not. The point came where they couldn't walk down the street together.

Sooner or later every apprentice must refute the absolute power of the mentor if he (or she) is to emerge as owner of his own authority. Levinson says a man cannot have a mentor after 40. Women in business who outgrow their guides are more likely to reach top management. Those who remain reliant cannot advance to the top position and are likely to become a lodestone to their mentors, who usually in the end discard them.[7]

Maintaining the pretense that she was not superior to her teacher was a torture for Mia, but the lingering dependence on him was part of a much larger issue she had to resolve in midlife. She could not make the break with her mentor until she dared to defy her inner dictator.

It took her forty years of living on the same earth to say no to her father. She brought her fist down on the dining room table and shouted one night, "Who do you think you are, God?"

"Yes," her celebrated father replied.

"Well, you're not," she said, and the great man's magical powers over her were broken.

Today, Mia is admired by other women for what she has dared to be, for her passion and intensity and pride of self, for her strong-mindedness and truth. But it would be remiss of me to leave you believing that Mia has found everlasting harmony between love and work.

Her authenticity, attained only at the price of torment, throws a scare into men. Even men like the professor. When they met at the creative workshop, it seemed that here at last was a man who would be secure enough to rejoice freely in Mia's talent. It was her spirit that attracted him in the first place. But what attracted soon began to frighten, even repel. In fits of something like revenge he tries now to cut away at the painstakingly rigged confidence Mia has built around her work. He turns for reassurance back to his stupid gentle girl students. "They swoon the minute he walks into the room."

Recently Mia and I met for lunch. She looked tired but resolute in her working jeans, boots, untinted glasses. Out of her portfolio came the lustrous monograph, just published, a public recognition of her vision as art. It is a time of sweet triumph. She talked about being wildly busy hanging her first one-woman show, but there was a cloud over her effervescence. The professor was in town. Deliberately ignoring these great events in Mia's life, he expected her to be ready on a phone call's notice to join his itinerary. She was angry, wary. Why should he behave this way?

"He drinks too much, smokes too much. He drives his car all over the freeways of Los Angeles with a death wish in his eyes." Mia went on reciting the danger signals of a man at the self-destructive peak of his own midlife crisis, as if forcing herself to heed them. "I'm seeing him now through his work. He's an artist, and his work is a perfect reflection of the way he treats life. The figures are plastered on top of one another, disintegrating. They're cruel, obscene. I scare him because I don't like his work. It's dehumanized. And once in a while when I tell him, he panics."

The famous professor, like the celebrity Reverend before him, like Mia's father, sounded to me like an infant god. I had come across several such men whose tremendous public success had partitioned them off from a sense of their humanity. His subordinates continually tell this man in so many words that he is a god. They do not make demands on him that he be emotionally in touch or touchable. They do not bring him pain or domestic confusion. Eventually, everyone he surrounds himself with is a subordinate. As soon as a germ of depression or anxiety threatens to invade his sterile field, he goes back to work, where people reassure him that he is a corporate "giant," a movie "mogul," a creative "genius." The depression goes away. Little by little he regresses into believing that he *is* an infant god who can have anything he wants. And less and less does he want to go home to his wife, because she will demand that he be human.

The professor is married. He is 43. At a period in life when everyone has fearsome questions to face, he would naturally be looking for reassurance. But given the particularly precarious status of an infant god, it is probably all the more upsetting for him to acknowledge Mia's independence. He calls at five in the morning as if to teach her her place as a subordinate.

"It's me."

"I know who it is. So what?"

An alarm goes off in her head. Instinct tells her that beyond the professor's obvious attraction as an artistic and sexual companion are perils which appeal to her weakness.

"For me, being around him is like standing on the edge of a cliff and *wanting* to jump, knowing it could destroy me. But I'm not going to let that happen."

How easy it would have been in the past for Mia to go on laughing like a little girl, lured to the cliff's edge by a man so dominating and egocentric that eventually he would overpower her, sweep her off her feet. With a child's cry of joy, she would submit, leap, begin falling, fall into emptiness, and with a howl of recognition for her folly realize too late that he would not be there to catch her. And worse—that she might never, no not ever, stand on her own two feet again.

Although Mia has not yet found the ideal partner (life, after all, does not pass out partners equitably so that we all end up in matched developmental sets), she has found her self. She trusts now in her instincts for preserving that self.

"It took me too long, too much psychic sweat to get where I am now emotionally and professionally. I'm not about to let someone erode that. Life's too short. So I'll be alone for a while. There are worse things than being alone."

Which is an altogether new perspective on life and time and self-awareness, an unimaginable perspective to the 25-year-old who believes that life will go on forever and that not to be loved is the worst thing in the world. It is a view that can be glimpsed only while peering into the abyss from the edge of that precarious passage to the middle years.

Life does end. Time is short. Each of us travels alone. No one else can always keep us safe. And there are some parts of our personalities that we cannot change or ignore, even when the price is separation and loss, if eventually we are to find unity within ourselves.

Part Four

PASSAGE TO THE THIRTIES

He plunged to the center,
and found it vast.

—CONRAD AIKEN

13

CATCH-30

"What do I *want* out of this life, now that I'm doing what I ought to do?"

A restless vitality wells up as we approach 30. Almost everyone wants to make some alteration. If he has been dutifully performing in his corporate slot, he may suddenly feel too narrowed and restricted. If he has been in a long period of training, such as medicine, he may wonder at this point if life is all work and no play. If she has been at home with children, she itches to expand her horizons. If she has been out pursuing a career, she feels a longing for emotional attachments. The impulse to broaden often leads us to action even before we know what we are missing.

The restrictions we feel on nearing 30 are the outgrowth of the choices of the twenties, choices that may have been perfectly appropriate to that stage. Now the fit feels different. We become aware of some inner aspect that has been left out. It may make itself felt suddenly, emphatically. More often it begins as a slow drum roll, a vague but persistent sense of *wanting to be something more.*

Both the vagueness and the persistence, the unmistakable sound of a man in the Age 30 passage, pervade George Blecher's short story, "The Death of the Russian Novel":[1]

> Sometimes I sit down with myself and say, "Look, you're thirty now. At best, you've got fifty years more. But what are you doing with it? You drag yourself

from day to day, you spend most of your time wanting, wanting, but what you have is never any good and what you don't have is marvelous. Why don't you eat your cutlet, man? Eat it with pleasure and joy. Love your wife. Make your babies. Love your friends and have the courage to tell those who seek to diminish you that they are the devil and you want no part of them. Courage, man, courage and appetite!"

During this passage, which commonly spans the years between 28 and 32, important new choices must be made and commitments altered or deepened. The work involves great change, turmoil, and commonly, crisis—a simultaneous feeling of rock bottom and the urge to break out. The transition initiates the more stable and settled period of Rooting and Extending.

One common reaction to the transition into the thirties is tearing up the life one spent most of the twenties putting together. It may mean striking out on a secondary road toward a new vision. It often means divorce or at least a serious review of the marriage. People who have espoused the joys of singlehood or childlessness are often startled to find themselves wanting an old-fashioned marriage, or eager to stay home with a child.

Years later we wonder why so much confusion and doubt surrounded making changes that, in retrospect, seem obvious. That is because there is much more to this transition than changing the external circumstances. The voices from within become more insistent now. And in the thirties we begin to let down our guard. The iron gate we tried to shut against the Janus faces of the inner custodian when we were hell-bent on proving our identity to be wholly our own inspiration can now be opened a crack. On our side, we are a little more certain of ourselves. The other side, in turn, is beginning to lose some of its menace as a dictator and some of its seductiveness as a guardian. We can begin to see and hear its influence, little by little, to recognize it.

And so begins a courageous, though often clumsy, struggle with the gifts and burdens of our own inheritance. The challenge is to sort out the qualities we want to retain from our childhood models, to blend them with the qualities and capacities that distinguish us as individuals, and to fit all this back together in some broader form. The widening and opening up of our inner boundaries makes it possible to begin integrating aspects of ourselves that were previously hidden.

The combined evidence of many interviews, studies, and statistics suggests that the opening-up process starts in the late twenties and culminates in a restabilization and closing-off process that begins in the early forties. When Else Frenkel-Brunswik first delineated this border phase, she characterized it as the most fruitful time in professional and creative work. A great deal happens at the beginning of it (nearing 30), so that its entrance is clearly defined, usually, by the final and definite choice of vocation. Although many personal relations are acquired before this time, she observed that they are usually only temporary. It is in the transition to the thirties that most people choose a definite personal tie and go on to establish a home.[2]

But not before they reappraise.

Almost everyone who is married will question that commitment. In some instances the real question is whether or not one wants to stay in any marriage. At the very least, the contract needs revising to allow for new things we know about ourselves. Or don't want to know, for our illusions die hard.

Nonetheless, the passage to the thirties stimulates a subtle psychological shift on all fronts. "Me" is just starting to take on as much value as "others." The urge to widen is beginning to overtake the need for safety. An aliveness is rising from within. And what about the change in sense of time?

Blecher speaking again: "The fear of death rivets

me to the sidewalk. . . . Yet it doesn't make me live better."[3]

That is because death at this stage is still an abstract fear. There is still time to do it all. New continents of experience await discovery. We are impatient, yes, but not yet urgent.

Another surprise awaits all of us as the Trying Twenties draw to a close. Will power and intellect cannot overcome all obstacles, as we thought. As Bertrand Russell must have thought at the age of 27. By then he was well along in the analytical breakthroughs that eventually produced his *Principles of Mathematics*. He and his wife were living with Alfred North Whitehead. "Every day was warm and sunny," as Russell described it in his autobiography, and his nightly discussions with an older and wiser man were intoxicating. The autumn of his 27th year he felt to be "intellectually the highest point of my life." One day that winter everything changed, and a mysterious new dimension broke through the control of his mental powers. He returned home to find Mrs. Whitehead in agony from a recurring heart ailment. For five minutes, shaken to the core, he felt the impenetrable loneliness of the human soul.[4]

> At the end of those five minutes, I had become a different person. . . . Having for years cared for exactness and analysis, I found myself filled with semi-mystical feelings about beauty, with an intense interest in children, and with a desire almost as profound as that of the Buddha to find some philosophy which should make human life endurable.

The words of a fine writer put flesh on the sterile study. Frenkel-Brunswik found the passage into the thirties to be "the culmination period for subjective experiences," and Gould concluded from his study that a "marked subjective experience" reveals to people that life is much more difficult and painful than it was thought to be in the twenties.[5]

Life does indeed become more complicated, but it is in this complexity that we find possible a new richness. Russell was invigorated rather than depressed by his new awareness.

> A strange excitement possessed me, containing intense pain but also some element of triumph through the fact that I could dominate pain, and make it, as I thought, a gateway to wisdom. The mystic insight which I then imagined myself to possess has largely faded, and the habit of analysis has reasserted itself. But something of what I thought I saw in that moment has remained always with me.[6]

CATCH-30 AND THE COUPLE

If individuals sound baffled at this turning point, the confusion only increases when it comes to the couple. It makes itself loudly heard in the shattering of marriages. For the past fifty years, Americans have been most likely to break out of wedlock when the man is about 30 and the woman 28.[7]

What is this thing, this whirlpool of inconsistencies, that seems to catch so many? Catch-30, as I came to think of it.

The men and women we hear from in this chapter married in their early twenties. It was understood that she would stay out of anything but peripheral participation in the adult world and reproduce a family world for him. Roughly seven years later he is feeling competent as a man, an acknowledged, if still junior, adult. The press of the outside world has taught him how to maneuver around his professional illusions. He knows now, for instance, that vivid displays of intelligence are not as well rewarded as loyalty because many older men are afraid of younger men. But in his earlier twenties, when he wasn't sure about those professional illusions, he didn't dare tell his wife. To do so would have jeopardized the safety that both of them needed to believe he could provide.

Now, invigorated by his newfound confidence, no longer in constant need of having his loneliness taken care of, and becoming bored with a substitute mother, he changes the instructions to his wife: Now you must be something more, too. Be a companion instead of a child and mother. Be capable of excellence, like me.

"Why don't you take some courses?" is the way it usually comes out, because he still doesn't want her to stray too far from the caretaking of him (and children if they have or plan them). But what *he* sees as encouraging her, *she* perceives as threatening her, getting rid of her, freeing himself from her.

She is at war with her own Age 30 inner demons, feeling narrowed and impatient, although probably ill-equipped to be something more. As part of their original contract, she was told she didn't *have* to get out into the world in any full sense. So long as she does not make any strenuous efforts to individuate, she can partake of all those illusions that she brought along from her mother that make her feel safe. Anyone who pushes the other way is goading her toward danger. Therefore *he*, the husband who has suddenly changed the instructions to "You have to," must be the villain.

Now her experience is betrayal. She is being kicked out of her own house. She is 18 again, filled with all the anxieties that the 18-year-old has in leaving home. Little lessons in the culinary and creative arts lead nowhere except to the end of the course and back to the house. This is not being something more. It is being diverted into something else. She still has no impact on people and events in the larger realm, no access to the hierarchies of accomplishment, no *focus*. Her confidence has deteriorated. What does she have to offer the world? And even if there is a chance the world would take her seriously, is it worth leaving the security of home?

This is an important point: The willingness to risk is based on a history of accomplishment.

Her attention span shortens as the inner agitation builds. Women friends may be a consolation (so long as they're not achieving much of anything outside the home either). Maybe a lover is the cure for what ails her (and would serve to punish her husband at the same time). Business entertaining only rubs salt in the wounds. When the men talk in their knowing way of how to run things better—the country, the company, the union, the university—she feels she has nothing informed to add from her own experience. The easiest available diversion from her real problem is to pump all her hostile vitality into running a tight ship at home, because she is too fearful to attempt running things anywhere else.

Deep down her husband knows he could not tolerate her nonproductive life style. "I was concerned that Didi, who had an excellent mind and worked at the Guggenheim Museum when I married her, was not *doing* anything," one man recalled. Another businessman, whose wife had welcomed marriage as an excuse to stop answering casting calls, remembered a change in his attitude six or seven years later. "In that period I wanted from my wife a sense of her own independent contribution to the union." But he usually wants the contribution at no cost. It is hard for the man of 30 to imagine making enough room to allow for the serious training of his wife as a lawyer, designer, professor, actress, corporate hotshot. Even more forbidding, suppose she were to become just as preoccupied by and competent in her work as he?

The contradiction between what he wants and what he fears makes him feel guilty. Spinning into the whirlpool now is her envy, oppressive enough so that almost all men married to caregivers mentioned it. "I began at 30 to see a future for myself in the academic world, in a responsible position," is the way a burgeoning administrator described it. "I think there might have been some envy on my wife's part that I had a vision of myself. She stopped being supportive. Well, she still participated, but without showing much enthusiasm for the responsibilities of being my wife, such as entertaining. She still had nothing of her own. She was feeling frenzied."

He wants the problem to go away. It distracts him from his own Age 30 dilemmas. Having done all his shoulds as the apprentice, he is impatient to broaden his realm of responsibility.

First, he must begin honing his dream into definite goals, or discard the old dream for a new one, or broaden it or diversify it. Whatever the direction, it calls for major decisions. And it often calls for a move. There simply isn't enough time to play social worker to his left-behind wife. Or rather, he hasn't enough interest to make the time. He takes the necessity plea: "I'm too busy trying to build a future to solve your problems, too."

Later on (usually after the divorce) husbands will insist, "I *did* encourage her." And complain that she never followed through.

"Thirty was the time when I was on the make," recounts a man who made the vice-presidency of a major American corporation by the tender age of 35. "As long as the kids were taken care of I was happy; I wanted them out of my way. Suddenly you win an award, and you get this nice feeling—Jesus, people know my name.

"I thought my wife ought to do something. Be more structured. My wife had gone to art school, but she was turning out to be just a dull housewife. A bright girl who never does anything to capacity; whereas I was always pushing beyond capacity. She's a great weaver, great drawer, great cook—and never finishes anything! She'd start a project, drop it for six months, start something else. 'Let's make bread now.' So we'd have all kinds of great bread for a few months, and then we're through the bread kick. Drives me crazy! We discussed her getting a job, briefly, or going to school. I think she interpreted that as my wanting her to go out and earn money. My point was to make herself more interesting, more productive.

"On the other hand, I must have been one of the worst fathers around. Even when I was home, I was always working ahead. I remember once describing my life as a comic strip. 'I have this comic strip going, and I've got to keep ahead of publication. When I am home, I'm in my room, which is set up as a studio, and I'm working on what the hell am I going to do next week? next month? to keep the comic strip going.'

"My wife and kids just weren't that interesting. I told her my work was the most important thing to me. She took it okay. She's a nice, placid lady, and she was never on my back to earn more money.

"A dream of her own? If she has one, I'm not aware of it. I suspect that her dream was: Wouldn't it be nice to have a terrific husband?"

The same blind exasperations were expressed by a man called in the marketing world "a golden boy." Born poor, he married a Powers model and placed her in a suburban stage set. By the age of 30 he had become president of a major food-processing company.

"Oh, hell, the woods are full of courses my wife started. And the hospital groups, church groups, they all wash out—and how, I suggested them! Sure I criticized her. 'Don't start something you don't follow out on,' I told her. 'But more important, the reason you should do it is to broaden your interests. You're wasting your bloody life!' "

When the same man, several presidencies and twenty years later, looks back on what he really wanted from his wife at 30, the motives are clearer. And far less altruistic. "I guess I told her to take courses to buy peace. It's easy to say what I would have liked."

Would he have liked his wife to develop as a true peer back then, to have found a purpose in the world quite independent of her commitment to him?

"I'd like to say yes to that question. But I honestly don't think I could have handled it then."

Did he actually want a woman who was totally

supportive without getting in the way or growing dull?

"Yes, exactly."

If the woman does not act on her own impulse to broaden during this passage, the bind doubles. Sensing that to give vent to any solid ambition—to devote the time, love, and discipline necessary to make it work—will invite a jealous backlash from her husband, she retreats instead to the safety of her un-grown-up stage. And tries to reel him back in with her: "Why don't you stay home more?" He senses that as a trap. What he formerly saw as safety, he now resents as danger. Now her whole effort is to hang on to the arrangement and hate him.

Who is right? They both are. The classic Catch-30.

The Testimonial Woman

Enter a third figure, who can offer the man a convenient lift out of his knot: the Testimonial Woman. Because the transition from the twenties to the thirties is often characterized by first infidelities, she is not hard to find. She is behind the secretary's desk, in the junior copywriter pool, in the casting call lineup, in the next lab coat. The root of the word *testimonial* is *testis* (plural *testes*). I read somewhere that when one aboriginal man bumped into another, he cupped the sexual parts of his tribesman in greeting. It was a "testimonial to manhood" and the original basis for the handshake. Whether or not it's true, the Testimonial Woman offers the same service: She fortifies his masculinity.

The wife bears witness to the embryo who was. Even if she doesn't confront him, he looks into those memory-bank eyes and recalls his faults, failures, fears. The new woman offers a testimonial to what he has become. She sees him as having always *been* this person. She is generally younger, subordinate but promising. He may be able to take the part of teacher.

Then she can become more and more like him, further affirming him as admirable and worth emulating.

The traditional wife, at home with children and dependent on her husband, literally cannot afford to know what she half knows. It has the makings of a very angry situation.

A classic description of the Testimonial Woman spilled out of a 36-year-old advertising executive: "The big change in my life at the age of 29 was, I was no longer faithful to my wife. Everything started happening at once. I found out I could write copy, damn good copy. My salary climbed in one year from $10,000 to $24,000. Power comes with ability, and the more power you get, the more attractive you become to women. I began to screw around indiscriminately. It was terrific. Here I had a wife at home who was concerned only with the kids. Then a really significant thing happened. I met a girl who made me realize I would not stay married, although she ended our affair brutally. Two years later the lady came along. I hired her as my secretary. Used all the tricks there are to use with power. 'Go cash my paycheck.' I taught her how to write. I started her.

"What was tearing me apart was seeing what I was doing to my wife's life. Making it miserable without explaining it to her at all. Laying blame on her for not having made something of her life. You know, 'How many times have I asked you to go to school?'"

What did his wife say to his exhortations?

"She said, 'My life is devoted to the children.'"

If his wife suddenly *had* changed her whole mode of life, I asked him, would he have been able to take it?

"I can't answer that," he said gravely. "Because of things I now know about myself. And because, since we've divorced, she *has* changed."

After hearing that comment over and over again from men, I began to wonder if divorce is a *rite de passage*. Is this ritual necessary before anyone, above all herself, will take a woman's need for expansion seriously? The Changed Woman after divorce was a familiar figure to come out of the biographies, a dynamic figure, and one who usually held considerable allure for her startled former husband.

What's this? *She's lost weight, cut her hair, opened a shop, and from what I hear, seems to be playing around with all kinds of men. It kills me if I let it. She's not even trying to get married again! She says she doesn't want to be tied down.*

He would have you believe, as it is popularly assumed, that he outgrew his wife and that they had to divorce because she was a clinging, uninteresting person. Yet the Changed Woman is anything but dull. She has mystery. In fact he is amazed to see, several years out of their marriage, how much dimension she has gained. The superficial reason for their split seldom holds up once he has learned more about himself. It has very little to do with his wife, whoever she was.

With the advertising executive, it is a clear-cut battle with the powerful mother on whom he allowed himself to remain financially dependent until he was 27. It should be no surprise that the adman is having similar problems with the woman for whom he left his wife. After living with his Testimonial Woman for four years, he says, "I can't promise her I'll be faithful, either." His dream now, as he works feverishly to establish his own agency, is to have a million dollars by the time he's 45. It is significant that he projects 45 as the end of the dream period. Perhaps he won't be capable of any deep mutuality with a woman until that time. Very likely it will take him until then to work out his own autonomy. But not for the reason he anticipates, that by the mid-forties he will be so rich he can't possibly be dependent on his mother. It will be because, if and when he faces that emotional dependence, he will begin to understand himself.

When people become aware of their own complexities, they can see a mate as more than their personal object of gratification. Only then can they begin to understand that any mate is also a separate and complicated person who comes with a history, who has a cycle of life to play out.

Divorce, however, is not a cure-all for the predictable disequilibrium of this passage, as we shall see in the biographies.

Wives' Work

When the Age 30 passage stirs in a married woman the push from within to expand, a struggle of massive proportions begins. Many counterforces oppose her expansion. The real needs and unrestrained possessiveness of small children, for one. The thinly disguised jealousy of other women who are too dependent to dare rocking the boat, for another. Often one's own mother offers the cruelest disapproval. "My mother is practically ashamed of me," laughed a 30-year-old who felt ready to put her training into action. "She thinks I'm an inferior mother because I want to practice medicine and have a housekeeper to help with the children."

And then there is the whole trick bag, part real and part imagined or projected, of a husband's opposition. Some of the double messages he is likely to send out are not unlike the contradictory wishes parents communicate to their adolescent children: *Take responsibility for yourself—but—don't let that something take you away from me*. Husbands, like parents, enjoy an irreplaceable ego boost from being idealized by their dependents. If a woman begins to say to a man, in effect, "I'm no longer going to look to you as the one who has the right answer all the time; I'm going to test my own capacities and challenge you on issues," she is taking away a man's free ride to feeling big.

But that is exactly where most women have to begin. When the husband has been made heir to the parental sovereignty, the wife, like the adolescent wrestling for a sense of self, is going to have to place her world view, her friends, her idea of a meaningful course to pursue in competition with the presumptions of the person she has empowered as the Strong One. It is a necessary precursor to her independence. And it must be seen as necessary. Many women, by denying the necessity of this developmental step, eventually blight the very marriages they are trying so hard to preserve.

And if she does act on her inner stirrings? If she declares her need for an individual destiny and strikes out to find it? She may be astonished to discover that her mate feels relieved. A man often finds himself delighted not to have a wife waiting at home for him to bring her a world of accessible joys and money. But during the transition he may perceive malice where none is intended. In her first clumsy attempts to sort out and declare her individuality loudly enough so that she herself will believe it, he may hear himself being depreciated. Most men operate on the fantasy or at least the wish that their wives want what they want: *She should want to take care of me and the children because that's what I want from her.*

There is only one way to find out how much of the impediment is actually her husband and how much is her own mistrust of what lies on the other side of the status quo. And that is to take the risk. To do some serious thinking about how to increase herself, not just how to lose weight or jolly up her days with a lover. As psychoanalyst Allen Wheelis says, there is no question that the world will bend to a committed psyche. But the commitment must have the ring of reality.

If a woman in truth doesn't want to expand, that's another thing. Her out is easy. She can retreat at the first grunt of displeasure roused in her husband, or at the first setback in her efforts to finish a poem or complete her degree or carry off a boycott. She can take the cloak of victim. A mountain of current books, films, and magazine articles will back her up. And so long as she can convincingly blame the tedium of her life on men, she doesn't have to change.

Closed-Dyad Disease

Other problems beset the couple that has wallowed into the valley of the closed dyad: the in-turned husband-wife, mommy-daddy pair of the idealized American family. The closed couple is fine for rapid success and social climbing, but it tends to work against the building of community. What these pairs get in return for their upward mobility is a loss of lateral supports (real friends, neighbors, extended family). And without the support of the remainder of the community, the closed pair can become a *folie à deux*.

Anthropologist Ray L. Birdwhistell, a pioneer in the study of nonverbal communication between men and women, has spent tens of thousands of hours scrutinizing behavior within the closed dyad. He believes that the closed aspect is what makes this a diseased social form. The intensity that characterizes the early period of a relationship, the very thing that closes the dyad, is naturally reduced when two people face openness. But closed pairs regard it as illegitimate to have strong emotional feelings for *anyone* outside the family.[8] Haven't we heard it said a hundred ways?

HE: "You're always on the phone with your girl friends."

SHE: "Another business trip? You never spend any time with your family."

HE: "I can't bear another Thanksgiving with your mother."

SHE: "Why do you have to go out to dinner with people you see all day at the office?"

The individuals are only reaching out for lateral supports in friendship and vertical supports with kin. But if all such supports are considered flimsy or disloyal, the pair has nothing but each other and "associates" or "contacts," which means nothing but sanitized relationships. A deadly but familiar fix.

The usual defense is to justify all outside supports

in terms of what they will do for the family. They must bring in money or prestige or possible opportunities for advancement.

HUSBAND: "I need the contacts I make on the golf course. You don't appreciate it, but I'm working my tail off out there!"

WIFE: "I'm only going back to work so we can send Jennifer to private school. I'm sure I'll be a better mother for it."

So often a woman gives up her friends when she starts a family. Although the sisterhood cultivated by the women's movement has made friendships among women not only possible but precious, the old convention was to view women friends as fill-ins when there wasn't a man in her life. It is still common to let lapse the warm, nonsexual, buddy closeness she once had with a man friend because, well, her husband wouldn't understand.

Denials, justifications—the sad truth is, people are afraid to admit the satisfaction they derive from such outside relations.

ROOTING AND EXTENDING

Only in the early thirties do we begin to settle down in the full sense. Life becomes less provisional, more rational and orderly. Accomplishments are expected of us by now. As an actress put it, "After 30, there are no more advantages to be gained from simply being younger than other people."

And so most of us begin putting down roots and sending out new shoots. People make major investments in a home, both financial and emotional, and become very earnest about climbing career ladders. A major part of the settling process involves converting the dream into concrete goals. That is, assuming one has been lucky and the trials of the twenties have added greater substance to the dream.

An artisan who had spent six years "really scuffling" to get his own business off the ground described "how that began to change about the time I was into my early thirties. By then the business was a fairly substantial one, not making a lot of money but a decent income, with good acceptance. My wife and I found the apartment we've been in for fifteen years. In that period everything seemed very cohesive and rational. The pieces all seemed to make some kind of sense. Friends were good. We went to a lot of parties, and we had a feeling of community. There was a lot of aspiring, too, but with goals in sight. That period was probably as close to the dream of my life as I've ever had."

The artisan was fortunate in being able to deepen his commitments in the passage to the thirties. He was his own boss; his business had not failed; nor was he dissatisfied with the direction he had taken in his twenties. He had waited until 29 to choose a wife. During the Rooting and Extending period marriage was a new extension for him, and friends took the place of the children this couple did not want to have.

For many men, the early thirties is the blue-suit period. They set a timetable for fulfilling their goals. It is of consuming importance to become acknowledged as a junior member of their occupational tribe. Men who continue to focus narrowly on their external goals can be, more than at any other time in their lives, shallow and boring.

Americans in corporate life run into a particularly mean conflict during the Rooting and Extending period. Settling down runs directly counter to the uprooting that is required of corporate gypsies. The man logs so many hours on airplanes, he can barely remember how to eat without pulling down a tray. He doesn't make friends; he makes contacts. The corporate wife, doing time on the "GE circuit" or with "I've Been Moved" (wives' vernacular for IBM), doesn't have an office to go to where she might find new acquaintances through her work. The neighbors she resolutely tries to cultivate vanish into the transfer pipeline. And before she has a chance to hang curtains in the new house, it's off to another town, another set of schools for the children, another Newcomers' Club. The only place in the world her name consistently appears is on property transfer lists.

Yet people will find ways to root that are instinctive. It is healthy to root. Those who felt the need to tear up the structure of their twenties are particularly keen to build a solid base. Says a divorcée of 34 who is redecorating her apartment, "I want to feel I'm a very stable citizen."

Another woman who divorced during the Age 30 passage and was just beginning to enjoy settling into her first decent apartment, with a room for her child that didn't look out onto a tenement wall, found out just how deep runs the need to root during this period. She was 32, but the man in her life had just passed 40. "Please, you've got to move in with me," he insisted all of a sudden. "There's plenty of time for that," she said in the calm of her stabilized period. "But we might all be dead tomorrow!" said he in the panic of his midlife crisis. Sensing his terrible urgency, but with vague misgivings, she did move in with him. A week later she felt like a letter that had been slipped under his door with no return address.

It is also unwise to ignore the Age 30 passage and attempt to move directly from the Trying Twenties into Rooting and Extending. Those who do so, often locked into their "secure" marriages, too fearful or self-indulgent to widen, may feel a lack of heroism in their daily lives and complain there are no more surprises. But rather than engage the inner impulse to broaden themselves, they bury the message in exterior changes: It's time to rearrange the furniture in their lives. And so they move from garden apartments to the suburbs or build houses or renovate brownstones, believing this in itself will give them a clear purpose in life. While the husbands concentrate on "making it," the wives are induced into what John Kenneth Galbraith calls "a competitive display of managerial excellence."[9]

Just as people find many routes into the turmoil of Catch-30, there are various ways to pull out: a few noisy but successful ways that address the problem directly, and the more common cooling techniques that keep the lid on while the fermentation continues.

14

THE COUPLE KNOT, THE SINGLE SPOT, THE REBOUND

The Couple Knot

And now they were 30. He, an upstanding Wall Street lawyer chafing to work for the public good. She, a diverted case, a lover of politics and veteran of campaigns, but a mother, a clipper of part-time want ads. They had married at 25. And for several years they seemed to be typically eager people enjoying the new experiences of a typical marriage within the professional class.* I knew them as friends, but nothing about the quality of threads that bound them as a couple. Except to sense that by now they had their tangles like the rest of us.

There were brief moments to go by, nothing consistent. Rick seated at a luncheon in his parents' summer home, dutifully quiet while the well-known father expounded on how to win a class action suit. Occasionally his father would say, "Rick dug up that

---

* Striving for symmetry in the outer life structure of subjects who illustrate the couple situation, I chose, from all the biographies, three couples involved in the same professional "family." By keeping the profession constant, we can see the inner line of development more clearly. The men are all lawyers: an aspiring student (Jeb) in the Trying Twenties; a junior partner in the passage to the thirties; and a man who leaves his own practice to run for public office in the passage to midlife.

citation for me." The rest of the time Rick would press creases in his napkin. Ginny's place would be at that end of the table where the heads barely clear plate height, the children's end, the conversational junkyard. At moments she looked like a little old woman.

But later they would be a young couple frolicking on the beach, different people. Ginny with her pixie hair scrambled and her slender legs cutting up the sand like scissors, playing Frisbee, playing out her girlhood. Rick would hoist their small son to his shoulders and beam with the contentment of carrying the world on his head.

From time to time a comment would suggest the vast inner space of their marriage, the disconnect points in their dream, the shadows of separate demons.

"The concept of being 55 years old and stuck in a monotonous job drives me wild," Rick would say, "not so much the money, but the *claustrophobia*." Or another man's wife would express the wish to go to law school. "Great idea, those were the best years of my life," Rick would say, rushing into the young woman's wish and invigorating it with advice, contacts, the full weight of his approval.

"Everybody else's wife can go to law school, but not your own." In dropping the remark, Ginny would take apparent pleasure in exposing a contradiction.

Trapped, Rick would make a weak joke. "Ginny's way of expressing herself is to get into a fight."

I talked with Rick Brainard first. The idea of being an attorney was one he'd had since he turned 13. His parents gave him one share of stock in a major league baseball team, and upon receiving his first proxy form, he went to the ball park and told the coach how to run his team. Newspapers ran interviews with this little free-lance reformer. Rick was tickled at stealing for a day the kind of publicity usually focused on his father, a lawyer who had never succumbed to the temptation to run for public office and

therefore held his status as a leading independent reformer in their city. As the only son with several
sisters, Rick had a powerful model with whom to
compete.

Graduating from college with mediocre grades
and a political science major he considered useless,
Rick took off for some wandering abroad, which he
found a strong learning experience. Even before entering law school, though, his direction was further
shaped by a professor who didn't flinch from taking
unpopular positions but who demanded excellence of
written expression. The professor was a master at em-
ploying language creatively to support his argument.
Rick added this to his aspirations.

"I've always had three goals. I like power. I'd like
to have money. I don't think either of these excludes a
third, which is, I want to be in a position to work for
the public good."

I asked if he consciously thought of himself as
"running for president."

"I used to think I wanted to run for government.
But it was never a goal; it was a dream I've given up
on. My present goal is to get to a position where I can
call up the mayor and say, 'Look, I recommend this.'
I have a mentor in the law firm who operates this way,
and he bedazzles me."

Apart from his professional goals, there are rumblings in Rick's life system at 30 that he couldn't have
predicted. For one thing, he is eager to increase his
family. "The concept of a home is very meaningful to
me. I love my son in a way I couldn't have anticipated.
And I want more children. I could never live alone."

Another change is the tension building between
him and his wife. "I don't think Ginny anticipated the
concern she has about her role. Or the degree of time
I put into my work. I've told her that I'd like to be
more taken care of. She feels, and intellectually I
agree with her, that I should help more with my son.
But emotionally, I'd like everything to go away."

Most upsetting to Rick is the change from feeling that there is plenty of time to do it all to the sense of time pressure. Just to be able to try a case and to be thought competent was enough in his twenties. Now he's impatient to branch out.

"I'd say that 85 percent of the time I thoroughly enjoy my work. But when I get a screwball case, I come away from court saying, 'What am I doing here?' It's a *visceral* reaction that I'm wasting my time. I keep saying there's something more. And I'm afraid I might not get the opportunity to find out what, unless I make it."

He is considering leaving the law firm. If he waits much longer, it will be too close to the time of reckoning on whether or not he becomes a partner. "And that's like getting married to the firm."

Had he talked to Ginny about these visceral changes? I asked. "I haven't talked to her about the internal workings of my mind in this because she's not going through it, and she can't go through it. The input will have to come first from other people."

What would he most like from his wife at this point? "I'd like not to be bothered. It sounds cruel, but I'd like not to have to worry about what she's going to do next week. Which is why I've told her several times that I think she ought to go back to school and get a degree in social work or geography or whatever. Hopefully that would fulfill her, and then I wouldn't have to worry about her line of problems. I want her to be decisive about herself."

Ginny's girlhood was far less complacent. For the first eleven years she was an only child, and then her parents began building a second family.

"The first time I saw my mother drunk was right after she bore the first of four more children. It just got worse with each child. It became more obvious and difficult—Mother always going out on some pretense of grocery shopping; Dad literally dragging her out of bars. Whenever I was home I had to work, diapering, vacuuming, cooking, being a second mother to my brothers and sisters. I got into a terrible competition with my mother because I was more patient and clever at managing the little ones. She would yell and scream." Ginny felt smug but always guilty; she had replaced her mother in a role on which the mother had defaulted. Nonetheless, she did take over in a difficult situation and seemed to be on her way to becoming a strong individual.

The bright spot was that she had a lively mind and an excellent academic record, which her father avidly fostered. He stayed up late with Ginny after the housework was done and prepared her for tests. She was especially good in math, and he was an engineer. They became intellectual mates. But he was never satisfied if she brought home less than 100 percent on a math test. At 17, Ginny yearned to break free of her tedious family responsibilities, but she was allowed to stray only as far as her own backyard. Her father insisted that she go to the hometown university where he was an employee.

"I was very scared of being a math major. Math was for boys. All the girls in my social group were history majors. But I did so well in my first math course, I began tutoring two boys. Then, I don't know what happened. I flunked the final exam." The teacher insinuated she had cheated to do well in the first course. He said he would give her a C if she promised not to continue in math the next year.

"It was a shock to fail the math exam because I'd always done so well. I decided I wasn't as smart as I thought I was. I'd switch to history and get decent marks and not rock the boat. My father didn't care anymore. I had failed him badly. It was an end to something."

One night when she was combing her hair before a date, her father said he guessed that she was just going to college to have a good time and find a husband. She wailed at him, "How can you say that?" But there was no changing his mind. What registered with Ginny was, "I guess I'm not as smart as he thought I was." And when it came time to deliberate about how to get a scholarship to a graduate school, her father's testy recommendation was: "Be a stewardess."

With little choice of occupation and no further financial support, her only vision was: "No matter what happened, I was going to New York." Making the rounds of employment agencies there, she was told over and over, "You're overeducated, and you can't type." She fell into a master of arts in teaching program and eked out her degree on a stipend. But this led her into a job she found absorbing. She teamed up with a black teacher in a Harlem school, and together they became a model team, committed to making a social contribution through early childhood education.

A year later she met Rick. "To me, it was a choice of Rick or the job. And I wanted to be with Rick." Having left her teaching post guiltily, she grew restless after the first exciting year of married life. She decided to apply to law schools. Rick said, "Well, try it, if you get through the first year, maybe you can find a way to take it part time."

"His one condition—I don't know if I agree with it or not—was that I could only apply to Columbia, Fordham, and NYU. He said, 'If you can't get into one of those three, then you're probably not meant to be a lawyer.' I thought there were others in the acceptable range, but couldn't apply. The fact that I wanted to become a lawyer was minimally important to what he was doing, in terms of impact on his life and his success. He was concerned about the time I'd have left for him.

"I studied vigorously. Everything was coming together for the first time, my continued interest in politics, my analytical mind, my social service bent, and law school became so appropriate. I felt I had a direction, a goal."

The next episode in her life Ginny recalls vividly, even to the dialogue. A month before the results of her boards came back, she visited the doctor with mysterious symptoms. She phoned Rick at his firm.

"I'm pregnant."

"Gin, that's thrilling!"

"But it may not be very convenient. I think we should discuss it."

His voice thinned. "Discuss—what?"

He came home that night well prepared for the defense.

"You're going to make a superb mother, Gin. Don't panic. Your qualms are just based on feelings of inadequacy. Believe me, I have absolutely no doubt—"

She flew at him, crying, raging, "I'm not ready to have a baby! You did this. You're forcing me to choose."

"What are you saying?"

"You made me pregnant to eliminate any possibility of my going to law school."

"That's unfair." He argued the case with that legalistic sleight of hand which assures that nothing is lost sight of except the point. "Isn't it true that you haven't been accepted yet? It's not as though I found out that Columbia accepted you and did something to prevent it. These occurrences that you're anxious about haven't come together yet."

"We could have an abortion," she said.

His face lost all expression. With an almost clinical detachment, his eyes fixed on his wife, carrier of his seed, hysterical vessel.

"We could try again later," she added.

He led her to the living room sofa, his voice firm. "This is a very bad idea. Right now you're a little upset and afraid."

She sobbed on his shoulder, knowing that his refusal to fight would be her defeat. She did not go to law school.

After reconstructing their histories separately, we agreed it would be illuminating to sit down together and talk about the central points of conflict in their marriage.* There were several issues on which each had offered me a dramatically different interpretation: children, work, time.

Who really wants children in this family? How badly? And what are you willing to give up?

RICK: I want at least three, if not four. Very badly. Not just for personal satisfaction, but because of how I grew up. Being the only male Brainard of my generation, I do feel pressure. I'd like to have two sons and one or two daughters as well. I don't know what I'm willing to give up. When I was a boy I didn't see much of my father. Once I figured it up and had a confrontation with him. I said I only got to see him seventy-two hours a year. He began taking me away for one weekend every year, just the two of us. I envision something like that for my sons. And daughters. But I'm not willing to give up the kind of commitment I have for my own profession. Obviously, something has to give at some point.

GINNY: I have a much more reserved commitment to having children. I'm being honest with myself and Rick when I say that I want to see how I react to the birth of each child before I have another one. If everything goes fine, then I'm willing to have four. But I have a stronger respect for how family life can deteriorate if you have more children than you can successfully handle.

RICK: Right now we've worked out a satisfactory arrangement around our son's nap schedule. I try to see him for half an hour in the morning and half an hour at night.

---

* One thing that is especially revealing of how we jockey ourselves into developmental knots and then work at maintaining them is the dialogue between couples. For that reason I have reproduced at some length the dialogue between Rick and Ginny (fictitious names). Like most people, they remember selectively and hear what they want to hear.

GINNY: I find it totally unacceptable that your relationship with your father, or your son, is based on fixed periods. It's saying: "Here's your chance, and if you don't take it now, that's tough cookies." I think parents have to be there when they're needed.

Who first brought up the subject of children?

GINNY: You did, right?

RICK: The only thing I remember was Ginny and her roommate in college talking about having eleven children each, opposing football teams.

GINNY: It was more than a joke. I imagine it had a lot to do with bragging about our ability to produce. But Rick tells me now that he assumed I was going to maintain this pact, that I've reneged.

Who wanted Ginny to give up the job she had before she married?

RICK: I think Virginia's job took more out of her than practicing law does for me. She had a total commitment. And I felt to some extent that's inconsistent with marriage and raising children.

Were you attracted by the kind of work she did, because it was with children?

RICK: No, what attracted me was that independent woman who had a commitment. I'm in favor of that.

GINNY: Rick still doesn't see the contradiction.

RICK: Well, my understanding was that Ginny quit because there were lots of premarital details to work out. It was also the first time she had any degree of financial ease; she might have enjoyed that.

GINNY: I enjoyed being with you as much as possible. So the choice became either cut back on seeing you or give up teaching. You had also let me

know that you didn't think it was possible for me
to balance the two commitments.

RICK: I honestly don't recall. It wouldn't surprise me.

*How did you feel, Ginny, about being free for
once to have fun?*

GINNY: I liked that. Very much.

*Deep down, did any part of you welcome the
chance to pull loose from the responsibilities of
being a mother to the schoolchildren, as you had
been at home for your brothers and sisters?*

GINNY: That's possible. But intellectually, I had enormous disrespect for a woman who did nothing.
Rick and I both agreed after the honeymoon that
there was nothing admirable about a woman
vegetating. He anticipated having an interesting
wife who was involved with volunteer activities or
some sort of part-time thing. One of the main conflicts is that Rick doesn't see why I have to be
paid. I don't get much satisfaction out of volunteer work.

*How did each of you see Rick's future when you
married? What part would each of you play in it?*

RICK: I know I told Ginny I envisioned working long
hours and becoming, hopefully, well known. And
doing things to make New York better—not necessarily as a politician, but on the periphery of
politics.

GINNY: Not on the periphery! When we got married
our social life revolved around election parties.
People were always talking to me about your
future in politics. And you discussed with me
yourself whether you might go to the Justice Department. This was the kind of life that being
with you represented.

RICK: As I hear it, most of what Ginny focused on was attending parties and being involved in political discussions. I don't think my projection was that I would be the next Senator Kennedy.

GINNY: You were accustomed to having people look to you as someone who would grow up and have an impact, which fascinated me.

RICK: It's true that some of my parents' friends had transferred their desire to get my father to run for public office to encouraging me.

GINNY: Yes, and they started including me in whatever they were projecting for you. All of a sudden it became, What's yours and Rick's future in politics? My vision of myself was being part of campaigning, decision making, issue resolving. I would have something to say on the topic and be listened to.

RICK: That startles me! I can't see how Ginny got that input. I saw a very different kind of participation on her part. More of the hostess role. My goal was similar to what I'm doing now—except that there's not as much time to make a social contribution as I'd like.

Here is a strong example of the disparity in the way two people see what appears to be the same dream. Ginny saw herself as being a politician through her husband. Rather than strike out or stay out on her own, marriage seemed a more comfortable form for working out her wish to be a social activist who would be listened to in the world. And so she selected from the conversation that surrounded Rick the vision of her husband-as-candidate. Rick, on the other hand, was attracted to a woman who showed independence and who was making the kind of solid commitment to good works that he wanted to see himself make. But what he really wanted at the time, it would seem, was a wife who would be content to perpetuate his family dynasty and provide the support system so that he could become successful, recognized, and rich. And so he chose out of Ginny's conversation the one joke that intimated she wouldn't mind having eleven kids.

Why doesn't Ginny go to law school? Who "won't let" her? Or what is she afraid of?

RICK: I gather I was alleged to have told Virginia to apply only to three top law schools?

GINNY: You don't remember giving the impression that going to a lesser school would have been demeaning?

RICK: I don't deny it. I just don't remember.

Suppose that Ginny were to talk about going to law school now?

RICK: I'd love it. But I'd be frank to say I don't think she'd make a good lawyer. I do recall telling her that. I would not sponsor her as a member of the bar.

What do you think she would be really good at? As opposed to what it would be convenient to have her do?

RICK: Two things I've found she does very well: She interrelates with children, young children, and I'm sure she's a fine teacher; she also seems to have a facility for administration, organization. The reason she wouldn't do well as a lawyer is that she's not skilled at writing.

You talked, Rick, about the professor you patterned yourself after. He instilled the idea that excellence in law went hand in hand with excellence in written expression. Aren't there other useful kinds of lawyers?

RICK: The best lawyers in my firm can turn a paragraph from a hammer into a sledgehammer.

Was it threatening to you to have Ginny want to become what you are?

RICK: I can't say there wasn't a subconscious threat there. She seems to think there was.

GINNY: He all but said at one point that failing might devastate me, so that I should not attempt it at all. He also told me that three years of concentrated effort would not be compatible with being a wife.

RICK: Let me cut into that. I'm sure I did tell her that my experience in law school was of fully devoting oneself. It was like teaching had been for her.

GINNY: At this point our positions are almost institutionalized. I'm the wife and mother now, so it's my expectation to defend my home. To defend the amount of time Rick gives to our son and to me. So I have a right to be his conscience in this area. Oh yes, and to defend his health.

RICK: That's not how I view our differences of opinion. My attitude is colored by the fact that I want to be successful, both financially and in terms of my own self-image. I see nothing wrong with my hours. They're high, but within the norm of our office.

GINNY: I'm not going to let you get away with that. The second year you lawyered, you had by far, by *far* the largest number of billed hours. So much so that a partner had to tell you to take it easy. You should never have told me that because then I could say Aha! See? Your hours are not normal. You can be successful and still not kill yourself.

Meaning, you can be successful without running away from me?

GINNY: Yes.

RICK: Ginny and I don't have as much time together as if I were a teacher, but there are trade-offs. We can travel; Ginny can have someone come in to clean. Our son will be able to go to a good school. Plus the personal satisfaction of knowing that I'm handling more interesting cases. My attitude is, you've got to put in long hours so you get the best work.

Maybe what Ginny is hearing is the last part. That the major reason you work longer is, not to provide her with luxuries, but to elevate yourself to the position where you can handle the more interesting cases.

RICK: You're absolutely right about that connection. Unless I handle difficult cases now, chances are I'll be stuck when I'm older without the expertise or the opportunity.

GINNY: To me, that can also be interpreted as, "I enjoy work more than I enjoy home."

Do you think this matter of whether or not Ginny goes to law school or broadens herself in some way is central to the ongoing conflict about how much time she expects you to spend at home?

RICK: No. I just don't think Ginny would make a good lawyer.

Suppose she were a second-rate lawyer, or a store-front lawyer, or a paraprofessional, but enjoyed it?

RICK: I'm not going to help her out the door without protest. But I'm not going to stand in her way. I don't think our conceiving the baby was my way of stopping her from going to law school.

GINNY: Well, I specifically remember how the baby was conceived. Do you?

RICK: You refused to make love to me earlier in the evening.

GINNY: Right. And the way it finally happened added to my feeling that this was a coercion. Rick had a subconscious interest in creating the situation. But Rick doesn't believe in psychological motivation.

RICK: The motivation there was very simple. I was—

GINNY: Interested in making love at the time! Not for the entire month, but at that particular time of the month. We didn't stop so I could put in the diaphragm, which was rare. And I got pregnant. One shot.

RICK: Very true.

GINNY: Very potent. Right? Do you remember the discussion after we got pregnant? I all but accused you of doing it so we wouldn't have to face my going to law school.

RICK: Wouldn't surprise me.

GINNY: You don't remember sitting on the couch? You had me in your arms, and I was crying.

RICK: Vaguely. All I really remember is going out for dinner afterward to celebrate.

GINNY: Unbelievable! I don't remember the celebration dinner at all.

(An uncomfortable silence)

How much of what you feel, Ginny, is envy that Rick has in his work something very involving and exciting to do?

GINNY: A great deal is envy. Especially if he comes home really proud of a case he's won. As a mother I can be proud of my son, but then I'm accused of being vicarious. Why am I taking credit for another human being's development? And yet Rick is always advising *other* wives to become attorneys.

RICK: I don't do it to everybody. I wouldn't encourage somebody who I didn't think should go.

GINNY: Are you implying then that they're smarter than I am?

RICK: You're the one who attaches the words "smart" and "admirable" to being a lawyer. In my concept a lawyer, teacher, housewife—they're all equally good.

The obvious echo Ginny hears in Rick's words is the judgment of her father: "not that smart." She tries to resolve the questions left hanging with her father by reenacting the argument with her husband: Why did she default on her father's belief in her intellectual quality? Was it the fault of her nasty male teacher? Did she want to fail in order not to be a social outcast? Or was she really "not that smart"? If it were only an external problem, she could easily resolve it. She doesn't have to be the kind of lawyer her husband is, the polished writer of briefs. She could work in community law or start a citizens' action group tomorrow. Rick is correct when he says that lawyer isn't the only thing synonymous with being smart and admirable. That is *his* form, which she idealizes. She is also ambivalent about the motherhood role, for obvious reasons. Now that her son is here, she loves him, but she is panicky about being expected to produce a dynasty for Rick. Given the model of her mother, that way lies possible destruction.

Rick is overloaded with steering decisions of his own. And as he admits, he would like all the problems with his wife and son to go away. He uses various devices to create this disappearing act. He neutralizes Ginny's arguments with legalistic maneuvering and refuses to be goaded into a confrontation. He reinforces her apprehensions that she is only good enough to produce children. And he plays on her fear of failing (again, as she failed her father). But he also indicates from time to time that he is not as inflexible as Ginny makes him out to be.

By continually inviting her husband to be the authority, Ginny conspires with him in disempowering her. Toward the end of the long evening, they acknowledged as much.

GINNY: You could interpret this argument between us as: Without Rick's sanction it would be impossible for me to go out and have a career, therefore, he has co-opted the authority to make that decision.

RICK: You cooperated. You decided you wanted to have the baby.

Do you put it together, Rick, that what you're doing is engrossing, gives you solid goals and a sense of mastery, and that makes Ginny jealous, because she can't find anything like it in part-time or volunteer work to give her self-esteem? And so long as she has to stay back, she will do everything in her power to take back your time and attention?

RICK: I don't think in those terms. Whatever the motivation, the effect is the same. Do you want to know what my perception is? Ginny is defensive of those roles—wife and mother and protector of the family life—because they're *desirable* roles. I don't resent her doing it. There is tension. But there has to be.

GINNY: I've come to look at it as an established tension too. I'll try to get as much as I can of him, and he'll try to evaluate the legitimacy of my complaints.

If Ginny has to be like her mother and have more children than she can handle and have contempt for herself because she's "doing nothing" in the world, then she feels she has the right to complain, just as her mother did. Rick seems to concur that this price is worth being free to do exactly what he wants to do. It's the making of a shrew.

Where do you see yourselves at 35?

GINNY: I see no job for me in the immediate future. Kind of resigning myself to a given, and not starting over again. I don't feel I have the opportunity to change. Rick, on the other hand, is broadening his goals.

RICK: The odds are good I'll end up as a partner of the law firm. And not doing as much public service work as I'd like.

You both see yourselves in five years, then, trying to resolve the same conflicts you're working on now?

RICK: I don't think I'll ever fully solve them.
GINNY: I think mine are more potentially solvable—once the children start growing up.

That is one response to Catch-30 for the couple: to stay in the marriage, to resist change, to take inelastic positions that eventually will tighten into a knot until, as Rick prophecies, "obviously, something has to give at some point."

The Single Spot

But what of the person who stayed single through the twenties? The next biography is of a 35-year-old woman I shall call Blair.

"I was going to be on the cover of *Time*, but I was also going to have four children."

Blair is now aware that this is called a conflicted vision. She is older. No such awareness penetrated during the early years when she was racing to the top. In 1954 she was 16 years old and fresh out of high school. She fell in love, not with a man, with the notion of becoming a success fast.

"I had a dream of myself as someone singular."

At 16, she had no time for college, nor did her parents encourage it. She started work as assistant to an auto dealer. A few years later Blair was ready to take on all of General Motors. She opened her own auto business with another woman. Immediately she drew the responses she wanted, which were more of the same she had enjoyed at home from her father. She idolized him as an intellectual, a political radical, and most of all, a success. His ethos was to run on one's wits and to get there first. He was particularly charmed when Blair skipped two grades at school. That put her way ahead; she had started out as the firstborn of the family.

After a few years in the gamey auto business, she decided to scale one of Chicago's glossier pyramids. She chose a middle-sized advertising agency. Was she "running for president"? I asked.

"I would never have said president. When my boss took me to a birthday lunch, he asked me, 'What do you want to be when you're 25?' I told him, 'Vice-president of this ad agency.' That was the biggest thing I could think of."

Her boss became the central figure of her twenties. He gave his blessing to her highest aims. She gave him back adoration. He breathed in, she breathed out.

"I had an enormous attachment to that man. He made reading lists for me, and I just soaked it up. We traveled together. He would even stay over at my apartment. But no sex. He had an iron-clad rule that one doesn't dip the pen into office ink."

The poet was the one who hurt. He went on about the toils of the soul as leader of her Great Books group, but when it was discovered that he had made her pregnant, he went away.

It was a dichotomy that continually plagued her. "Men were attracted and then they would say, 'You're too much for me.' Whereas in business I could never do too much. People loved me for my ideas and gave me prizes. In one world I was revered; in the other I was a freak."

Bear in mind this was the 1950s. The suffragette movement was dead, and the feminist movement hadn't been born. Blair was daring to make a bold assertion of ambition while the bulk of women were engaged in one of the greatest back-to-the-kitchen slides of American history.

Her father ran off with a Mexican dancer. She

took it as a personal rejection. She also began to suspect that he wasn't the intellectual or the political radical she had thought. But even as Blair feared she might turn out just like her father, all flash and no sustaining personal investments, he was the parent with whom she most consciously identified.

If guardedness had been her hallmark where men were concerned, she became now as impersonal as a Holiday Inn. "Drop by anytime you're in town," she would say, "come for dinner, spend the weekend, whatever," creating the impression she was fine whether a man was there or not. Any man should feel free to leave. When he did, she bled inside and was baffled.

The costs in shallow love affairs and two shabby abortions were high. Yet in this fledgling period, when proving herself a competent executive absorbed all her resources, it was less painful to suffer the costs of leaving her sexuality unexamined. What could she do with it? Make a marriage and join the handicapped? Watch her boss look her in the eye, as at one whose affliction was always suspected, and say, "No sense training you; you'll just leave to have a baby." The dictates of her unconscious were to leave all those emotions in some distant reservoir. To let them erupt might have sunk her into a wash of unresolvable contradictions.

Blair compensated for her childlessness by lavishing attention on her nieces and nephews. She concentrated on the satisfaction of being bolder and more professionally accomplished than any other woman she knew. One day the powers that be would deliver to her door a fantastic gift box. The card would read: "To someone truly singular."

The time came, when she was 26, to overcome the dependence on her mentor. Or to go backward. He had been raided for a better position with another firm. But the offer, he said, did not include bringing along a woman whose status and salary might foment a revolt in the typing pool.

"Years later he admitted that in the beginning he'd had no idea I would advance enough to be a challenge. And there I was, vice-president. He was afraid if he took me along I'd outstrip him."

She moved out, and up, to the vice-presidency of a more prestigious agency, where she supervised national accounts. Quite by surprise, when the door opened on her 27th year, she found herself one floor above her dream. Directions please!

No new plan suggested itself. "It wasn't that the right man came along. I had gone beyond my imaginings in business, and everyone else was married. I had to live out all my fantasies of what a wife was."

A wife, so often, is her mother. Blair's mother and younger sister had both married the promise of model homes, higher status, and permanent security. "Just the worst! I was never going to have a marriage like that. But I ended up doing the *same thing.*" Her choice was a hard-driving businessman with political ambitions.

Blair gave up her job shortly after the wedding. She filled the wifely role to malicious perfection.

"You don't seem very enthusiastic about giving all these business parties," her husband would say.

"I'm doing exactly what you wanted!" she would shout back. "I'm being the fashionable wife; I'm in the newspaper. It was *you* who wanted someone who didn't work."

All of which baffled her husband. He had enough to contend with in swerving toward the age of 40.

"Why don't we go away then and live a quiet life?" he would suggest when the din of her socializing had abated with the day and they were in bed. "I'm fed up myself with performing for clients."

Blair would curl up like a conch and pretend sleep.

"You don't love me," he would say, waiting for a refutation that was not forthcoming.

The convoluted truth she could not explain was that Blair was busy living out her mother's life and hating it. Once she had gained recognition as an executive whiz, she felt something else missing. Instead of sifting out the parts of her own femaleness that she might have enjoyed, and trying to integrate them with her professional activities, she threw herself into the "bad mother" role. She had to become a parody of that inner custodian in order to end up being more the woman she wanted to be.

This is not at all unusual. People in the passage to the thirties may convert suddenly into living out a mother's or father's life without recognizing the origin. They may hate the rigidity of this new life and feel ruled by some mysterious demon. But many of us have to live out the bad parts of a strong and conflicted identification before we can incorporate the good ones.

In the process Blair acted like one possessed. While her husband was being buffeted about by a normal crisis of midlife that he didn't understand, Blair kept accumulating fat. It ran into all her corners and hardened like aspic and covered everything, her looks, her sexual desire, her dreams. "I had a feeling all was not well. I wasn't in charge of me. Something felt binding, but I couldn't put my finger on what. I put it all down to my weight."

At 30, Blair told her husband, "All I want to do is go away and get rid of this abominable fat!"

For all her accelerations, it took Blair until the age of 35 to begin bringing her warring parts into alignment. Like so many people, she thought, "All the bad things will go away if I get divorced."

At the base of that thought is a common magical belief. One can get rid of the unresolved problems of self by getting rid of the person onto whom one has been projecting them. In Blair's case, the projected problem was her own conflict between being an indulged wife like her mother and a high-powered business whiz, as her father wanted her to be. It wasn't her husband who insisted she give up her career; it was Blair who had to "live out my fantasies of what a wife was." But she found herself no less impoverished as a self-made charge account wife than she had been as a bloodless success machine.

Unfortunately, before Blair could see the couple lock her own contradictions had created, she helped to provoke her husband into a dismal faithlessness, then into throwing plates, until the marriage was brought to convulsion.

"When I finally did leave," she says, "it was with three years of thinking in my head. Given a choice, I would never have walked through the ugly doors of those three years, but I was compelled. For the first time, now, I'm being honest about my feelings. I can't be anybody's appendage anymore. And I won't let men just walk through my life either, the way I did in the old days when I made myself a hotel. All my problems weren't with my father, as I'd thought. The unresolved problems were with my mother and how to identify with being a woman. What I might be now is a whole person who is not afraid of loving someone or having him love me. Let's hope so."

Ordinarily, I would stop here, where the Age 30 passage is resolved. But the shift in Blair's attitude at 35 gives us a preview of changes to come.

On her 35th birthday Blair bought a little house. She seems as comfortably rooted here as the tubbed tuberous plants that climb toward the skylight. Homeowner—the very act of making that commitment to and by herself has begun a centering. When she invites someone to dinner now, she invites them *home*, and very selectively. When she cooks, she can let herself enjoy it rather than feeling robotized into the "bad mother" role. Her new job is impressive and demanding, but rocketing to the top is no longer a goal.

"I've seen the hotshots as grown-ups by now and said to myself, This is the top? They can have it! What interests me more is trying to do work of higher quality. I can do it now without a hot coal in my stomach and the fear I used to have—that any minute now, they'll find out I didn't go to college and I can't spell."

There is about her an expectancy, as if she is waiting to put the major missing piece into her life. The children she never had are uppermost in her mind. "Yet I'm aware that the children I'm going to have may always be someone else's children, my sister's children or the children of a man I marry." She smiles and swallows the last of a brandy. "On balance, I have so much more than I expected. And that may be what life is. Maybe you get the box and not the ribbon."

The Rebound

Not everyone is in command of the decisions that change their lives, of course. What happens to people who are quite content to remain in the chair provided by their twenties when that chair is pulled out from under them? Many reactions are possible. Rosalyn's story illustrates a response that might appear weak but one that is potentially a way to catch up on undone developmental tasks.

Rosalyn's girlhood was over, but it didn't make sense to become an adult. The Trying Twenties hadn't added substance to her dream; they had destroyed it. And that dream was typical of the girl who makes a jailbreak marriage.

"When I left home to go to college, I thought, 'That's it, I've done my time, I'm out! My mother can't touch me anymore!' But when I finished school, I had to go back home. No marriage proposals. Back to Brooklyn and my whole repulsive background. I was about to take a job that paid $65 a week. Instead I met Borden and married him. You didn't have to think about the choice for ten minutes."

The only prospect more odious to Rosalyn than remaining in Brooklyn had been the possibility that, to be sprung, she might have to marry some complex-laden geek from her Hillel Club. But now here was

Borden Rayburn from Clayton, Missouri, as Wasp as they come.

"I just loved that. He came from the life I'd read about. I never wanted to work. I was not who women's liberation was aiming at. Dependent on my husband? Oh yes, totally, for money, for companionship. I knew nothing at all about reality. And I was very content with my life. It consisted mostly of shopping."

On being happy or miserable the couple never seemed able to coordinate. One season in their twenties all Rosalyn's friends were separating, and she flirted with the idea too. No, Borden said, we're very happy. They decided to have a second child. When the child was a year old, Borden came home from his office one night and said, "Are you happy?"

"Yes, aren't you?" Rosalyn said. Later she wished she had just said, "Let's watch TV."

"I have another lady," Borden said. "Who I love."

"How long?" she asked.

"Since you got pregnant."

She had been happy all that time.

"I know," he said, "that made me all the more miserable." Borden thought of himself as an ethical person.

"Okay," his wife droned. "I'll go."

"No! You can't take the children away."

Borden assured Rosalyn he could be happy again now that he had unburdened himself of his secret. He could have a wonderful marriage *and* an exciting girl friend. "It's a bonus," he explained.

Rosalyn thought for a year and a half: These people holding me down, they are all like my mother. Borden has taken the place of my mother. That's no way to run a life. I married him to escape my mother and Brooklyn and that whole vulgar background. The trouble is, I don't know enough freaks. That's where the real fun is. Borden won't even drop acid with me. I want an inner spiritual existence.

At 30 she decided she did not want to be Rosalyn the shopping cart married to Borden the adulterer. She wanted to take off her life uniform and go for radical change. At heart she was an unusual person, an artist or an astral spirit, something like that. In Big Sur she would be sitting around getting high with Joan Baez.

"I'm going to California," she told her husband.

"Why?" he asked.

"I don't want to do this anymore."

"Your going won't make me happy," he said.

She met a sculptor who was in a dormant period. He was on his third incarnation from the advertising business. "I want to further myself spiritually," he said.

"Oh yes, oh yes," Ros said.

Borden's going-away gift was his Exxon gas card. She set out on New Year's Day in a Rover TC2000 with the sculptor and her leather coat from Afghanistan. Her kids had the back seat. They were seven and two and loved tearing up the beds in Howard Johnson's motel rooms while the grown-ups smoked something they held with a hair clip. Howard Johnson fed them all their meals because Rosalyn could charge it on her gas card. They followed the weather map as if they were on a treasure hunt, going from cool to warm, from Chicago down Route 66 to Texas, getting warmer across Arizona, and then splashing down in Laguna Beach, California. Full-color freeze-frame freedom.

The sculptor expressed interest in Marin County. Ros said she was tight with some gays in Big Sur. That was where the artistic people were really getting it off.

Ros thought: I have no idea what is going to happen to me. That has definite appeal. I always used to know exactly what was going to happen to me.

Once Rosalyn had gone, Borden put off reporting his availability to his other lady. She had become, he decided, a grasping person.

Here is yet another response to Catch-30: the rebound. If it makes no sense to go forward because the transfer of dependency from parents to husband has not worked out, the pull may be back to where a girl left off before her romantic illusions were contaminated by reality. Back to adolescence. She will try Pulling Up Roots all over again, seeking immunity from her background and immunity from choosing her course while she looks for new people and groups to emulate. This biography happens to be of a woman, but of course there are men who rebound too.[1]

Shortly after joining the dropout Sur culture, Ros got the feeling that if a nuclear accident were to befall the eastern seaboard, these people wouldn't hear about it. There was no television, no printed matter in evidence. Conversation, as that term is understood in the east, did not exist. The whole idea was to have a truck, cut wood, and play music. At first Ros thought it was her fault that she felt so out of place. She tried going to parties given by the nearest commune, tried to transcend the noisome world by listening to their bamboo flutes and conga drums. What she heard was a lot of talentless people playing uncomplicated instruments, badly. None of these people seemed to have heard of governments, wars, the newsmakers of the day. Oh no, it's not my fault, she decided, these people are *dull*.

She began living for her trips to the Safeway in Carmel. It was her reentry zone to the civilized world. She would never "shop up," so that it was necessary to drive to the Safeway once, maybe twice every day. By the check-out counters, in luxuriant rows, waited a host of golden periodicals. She would make a dive for *Time* first and tear through the pages to the "People" section. Yes! they were still out there: fascinating, vigorous people. And she, Rosalyn, was a shopping cart again. Upon this one thin tie line to her old life she became wholly reliant.

By this time it had become clear that her glorified sculptor was a deadhead. Neither of them worked, but it didn't bother her lover. He was perfectly in tune with the tail end of the California immunity dream and content to live in the unilluminated immediate. More distressing for Ros was the realization that he was financially dependent on her small alimony checks. He was better at being dependent than Rosalyn ever was, infuriating! The call of the Safeway became stronger, so strong finally, she picked up and moved him and the two kids to Carmel. At least Carmel had a television cable.

I went to visit Ros after she had become one of the free-floating women of Carmel, most of whom are in their early thirties and fugitives from "perfect" marriages gone bad. I was met at the airport by a vivacious divorcée who acts as something of a den mother to them. Her car was a wreck. One of her free-floating friends had crashed into it. "She just got back into her car and said, 'Nice running into you today.'" The den mother laughs. There is only one rule here: Nothing must be taken too seriously. And the surroundings encourage it.

In this Kingdom of Narnia that is Carmel, twisting roads trespass the imagination, breaking open when one least expects it into glimpses of a cold sea where otters play with abalone shells like babies with rattles. There are no ordinary flowers, rather, aberrant patches of wild lilac and rare red-wattled lilies. Rosalyn lives in a small rented house. Jutting beyond her view of the sea is Point Lobos, an isolated outcropping rumored to be a prime site for UFO's. Most everyone here is like that, a creature from somewhere else, destination unknown. Carmel is a condition of the mind. A leap back from growing old or growing up.

Most of the people Rosalyn knows are old enough to have gathered the cash from a former incarnation (wife or job holder) that allows them now to stop the momentum. Want ads are rarely answered. Up and down these hills people choose to remain in glass houses with long ivy hair, temporarily encapsulated in a private experiment with life. "The way we look at things around here," the den mother says, "whatever works, go with it."

Rosalyn had given two years to Carmel by now, three years' commitment all told to the go-with-it

California Way. The vapor sheathing her adolescent illusions had thinned, and she faced an ineradicable suspicion.

"I find that I'm exactly the person I used to be. There was no other poetic inner *me* waiting for me."

Her basic activity since the California transplantation had been getting stoned and flipping channels on color TV and reading magazine articles and eating sweet food, all at the same time. She didn't think any one of these sensations worthy of concentration. The point was simply to maximize the input. It was second choice, of course, to being connected with other people.

Other people. Somewhere in the very way she speaks of them, in her promiscuous respect, lies the key to her predicament. That she knows now. She is running out of do-nothing Siddharthas and joy-peddling Arica people to believe in. "They all disappoint me." At 32, Rosalyn has begun at last to back into the adult world in small, painful steps.

She sat one afternoon, that idyllic seabed at her back, and let the tears run out of her lost green eyes.

"I'm heavily dependent on other people and other things. Because, well, I'm not creating much inside of me. I have no work. I have my kids; there hasn't been much in my life besides mothering. I market as well as anybody. That's it."

Admitting her cumbersome dependency was progress. Although it might have looked as though Rosalyn rebelled mightily against her parents, she had left the conflict entirely unresolved. She simply transferred her dependence onto an idealized husband, then onto a pedestalized lover, then onto the Safeway, and for the last year in Carmel she had tried to fill the gathering void with random input.

In the course of fighting their dependency, as Edith Jacobson describes in her monograph for the Journal of the American Psychoanalytic Association, such people may derogate their parents and turn away from them in disgust during adolescence. But as "adults" they continue to emulate and pin their hopes on other persons and groups, unduly admiring them until again they rebel, abandoning these substitutes in rage and disappointment and looking for the next object to be glorified and emulated. So long as they keep this up, they will remain fixated at the adolescent level of insoluble conflicts.[2]

"I'm very anxious to rejoin the world again," Rosalyn is saying now. "I think it's been slow stages. Next summer I'm going to try moving to Los Angeles. At the moment I have a very basic lack of confidence in my ability to get a job and be interesting. I don't think I'd get out and do it if I didn't have to."

Having to is probably a gift.

Some months later Rosalyn did make the move to Los Angeles. Her children whined in the back seat: "We want to go back to Daddy." Rosalyn kept up a banter. "Kids, it's going to be palm trees and Holly-wood and stars."

When I visited Rosalyn in her rented house in Hollywood Hills, she had made another step. There was a résumé in her typewriter, and we talked about a job as a script reader, but I don't mean that. I mean Rosalyn was finding the part of her authenticity that she had been fleeing for fifteen years and was making friends with it.

"Everybody here is Jewish, from Brooklyn, like me!" She looked tickled, not repulsed. "I find them intensely interesting because they're the people I would never touch before. It's like coming home."

Having gone the full circle, Rosalyn did come home to New York. She auditioned for a major publishing house that was looking for freelance writers to do books on careers for their school division. A year later —she was now 35—Ros phoned me from Fire Island. "I'm out here with the kids and a man we all love and my writing, which is going like wildfire."

She had just finished her third book.

Back when Catch-30 was first explained, it might have seemed there was no way out. By now we have met a couple of people who prefer to let the tangle of inconsistencies gather tension and a couple of people who have managed to work their way out. We have also seen what Catch-30 is not. It is not strictly a career problem; people solve it by going out of careers as well as into them. It's not necessarily a dilemma that requires more independence; some people solve it by letting their dependencies come through. And it won't go away by running away from it, although sometimes a great deal can be learned from the escape attempt. Ros, for example, found out by experimenting with an alternative life pattern that she is comfortable with a more conventional course. Had she remained a shopping cart, she might well have turned to her husband in midlife and raged, "It's all because of you that I never found the artistic inner me."

The Catch at 30 requires a personal solution. One part of that solution remains constant: the willingness to change.

Part Five

BUT
I'M
UNIQUE

Probably a crab would be
filled with a sense of personal
outrage if it could hear us
class it without ado or
apology as a crustacean, and
thus dispose of it. "I am no
such thing," it would say; "I
am myself, myself alone."

—WILLIAM JAMES

By now there should be a healthy chorus of readers protesting, "What about me? I'm nothing like these people you've been talking about. They're made of conventional stuff. I'm unique."

To be sure, people distinguish themselves by following very different patterns, *depending on how they make the choices of their twenties*. Because we have only one life to work with, each of these choices means restricting some possible line of growth in order to develop another line more fully. It is against the backdrop of such differing life patterns that each of us plays out the mystery story of the acts to come.

These differences intrigued me, troubled me at first. Although there are many patterns for passing through each period, there is only one sequence. It was Levinson who stated categorically that each period of development must follow as A to B. One cannot jump from A to C, and the only path to D is through engaging the tasks of C; there are no alternative routes. When I explained my concept of Catch-30 to Levinson, framing the predicament in the terms he uses for each period, it made even more sense. That is to say, it was an even crueler inconsistency.

"If it's true that one must Get Into The Adult World between the ages of 22 and 28, before moving through the Age Thirty Transition (28 to 32), before being ready to engage in Settling Down (32 to 39), then what happens to the woman who is left behind? All of a sudden, husband, skimming through his Age Thirty Transition, turns to wife and says, in effect: 'Skip getting into the adult world. Now I want a companion-peer to go into settling down.' Wouldn't that drive both of them mad?"

"That's nice," he said, "that fits." Levinson's conclusion was that it is probably not possible for a woman to work out a combination of the two careers (domestic and extrafamilial) until 30 or 35. "The chances are that by the time she has begun to arrive at the integration necessary to do it, so many other things have gone haywire that she is probably divorced or the family has been impaired in ways that can't be fully remedied."

I asked Levinson to depart from theory and apply his own marriage to my Catch-30 idea. Although they chose a different pattern, the outcome was the same. Maria Levinson spent the married years of her twenties being a graduate student, childless, and working on research with her husband, which intertwined their lives in every way. "For her, the Age 30 thing was a strong wish to change, but from career to family," he explained. For the next six years Maria was deeply involved in being more domestic. When he pushed her to work with him on a book, as she had done in the past, she was interested but doubtful.

"I thought she was getting narrow," Levinson admitted. "So that's part of the complexity of women's development." He left it stewing.

Part of that complexity I was certain could be sorted out for both sexes by distinguishing among the different life patterns people set in motion in their twenties. In what direction were these early choices likely to take them? Which patterns might be more tolerant of self-expansion, which more suffocating? Some would be more likely to depend on the exploitation of a mate; others would depend on dependency. Placing people within their patterns is another way to slice the cake, the better to see the filling. The important thing to remember is that these are not fixed slots. If you don't like your pattern, you can change it. People commonly move from one track to another one as they accumulate experience and self-knowledge. Indeed, in some of the examples used, the people did not remain true to their pattern.

You won't necessarily warm to the person whose story has been used to illustrate a life pattern. Particularly if it's too close to your own. We'd all like to be represented by the most inspiring standard-bearer. So let me add a disclaimer. The book didn't bring these patterns to the people; the people brought their lives to the book. It wasn't a talent search or a popularity contest. Only after I had collected all 115 biographies and compared them did distinctions in the patterns of people's choices and expectations begin to suggest themselves. Therefore, these patterns are descriptive, not prescriptive.

Each of the life stories in this section describes a person in passage from the twenties to the thirties and sometimes beyond. Even if no overt action is taken during the Age 30 passage, there is almost always an unseen shift, a change in the way a person *feels* about his or her way of living that will most likely lead to external changes later on. It is not as important as it was in the twenties to prove oneself unique. The equilibrium regained by reaching the other side of 30 makes it easier for people to examine their origins and gradually to acknowledge the parts of themselves that were left out by earlier choices.

Examining these unadmitted parts is the central phenomenon that now begins to occupy our internal life.

15
MEN'S LIFE PATTERNS

Three patterns emerged as most prevalent among the men interviewed.

Transients: Unwilling or unable to make any firm commitments in their twenties, they prolong the experiments of youth.

Locked In: They make solid commitments in their twenties, but without crisis or much self-examination.

Wunderkind: They create risks and play to win, often believing that once they reach the top their personal insecurities will vanish.

Three other patterns were far less common.

Never-Married Men: Since only five percent of American men over 40 are unmarried, it is difficult to make a valid statement about so small a group.

Paranurturers: They elect by their occupational commitment to care for the family of man (clergymen, medical missionaries) or devote the kind of nurturing to a mate customarily provided by wives.

Latency Boys: They avoid the process of adolescence altogether and remain bound to their mothers through the adult years.

One more pattern deserves attention. Not too many have yet figured out how to follow it. But with the relaxation of sex role stereotypes, the intuition released by mind-expanding experiences, and the gentling of ego encouraged by Eastern thought, men of all ages are thinking about how to loosen their competitive straitjackets. They want to be connected to life at many levels. Those few who make a pattern of it would correspond to the woman who attempts to combine an individual pursuit with being a wife and mother. I call these people:

Integrators: Male integrators try to balance their ambitions with a genuine commitment to their families, including shared child care, and consciously work toward combining economic comfort with being ethical and beneficial to society.

With this outline in mind, let us examine the most common patterns.

THE TRANSIENT

The urge is to explore and experiment, to keep any structure tentative and therefore easily reversible. Taken to the extreme, these are people who are unwilling or unable to have anything more than limited emotional involvements, just as they have trial jobs but no clear and chosen occupation. Permanence is not a goal. At least, not in the twenties.

Some transients prolong the experiments of youth in a positive way. Even though each experiment is only a tryout, they plunge into it with zest and sincerity. This young man might spend a year working on a political campaign, then drive a taxi while he tries writing poetry, then take off on a personal odyssey through strange countries and mysterious drug trips, returning filled with notable experiences (although flat broke) and eager to get some business experience so he can manage a rock group. The explorations of the transient are positive if they help to form a basis for later choice.

Other transients operate in a drifting and destructive way. Think of the rich vagrant antihero of *Five Easy Pieces* or of Rizzo in *Midnight Cowboy*. They may also become hitchhikers along the road of life's causes, unable to invest much in any one crusade because they cannot permit themselves to know how they really feel. Although the inner experience of the period is chaotic, the outer structure of transiency is still likely to be maintained for at least six or seven years.

Transients were the superstars of the counterculture in the 1960s. And then they turned 30. Was Rennie Davis moving from political activism with the Chicago Seven to the search for inner spiritual truth as a devotee of Maharaj Ji? Or was he moving from his twenties to his thirties and emblemizing in up-to-the-minute form a transition we all make?

Another celebrated transient of modern times was Jerry Rubin, and one of the germinal statements he made in his twenties was: "Amerikan youth is looking for a reason to die." At that time in his life Jerry Rubin was about as highly developed as a Mattel war toy.

Some of the hundreds of thousands of kids Jerry Rubin reached did die. But not Jerry. Passing 30: "I saw myself being moved by fate into a martyr's role. Martyrs die. . . . I wanted to live—and love. Do the things I never had time to do in the demonstration-packed '60s. Like discover myself."[1]

Reporting that he is now in touch with the repressed female in himself, Jerry Rubin concludes: "In the 1960s I spent a lot of time living in my head—ego and image . . . People were not aware of their own need for personal growth. In the 1970s we are going inward and discovering that we are the creators of our experience."

He is still at pains to explain himself as part of a political movement, rather than as part of the humbler process of growing up.

A not-so-famous transient may be the white ethnic. By that I mean Middle Americans of southern and eastern European descent, but the term may also include Irish, Jews, French Canadians, and others who arrived from Europe during the last hundred years of immigration. Depending on how broad your definition, it takes in from 40 to 70 million Americans.

In more than half of all ethnic families, both husband and wife have jobs. But their economic status is marginal; the median income is somewhere around $11,000 or $12,000. They feel left out culturally as well as economically. And the man's work is ambiguous. Well into his twenties he may live with his parents or in-laws (as Archie Bunker's son-in-law did). Having missed out on the experimental round trips that help middle-class youth to pull up roots, he maintains dependent ties to his family. He often has no vision of himself. Drifting from one job to the next, he may give little thought to organizing his work into a career direction. There is no one around to tell him how. He isn't about to run into a mentor on the assembly line or in a truck stop. When he marries, it is mainly to comply with what he believes he should do.

Superficially, it may look like this man has made adult commitments, but it's likely that very little of his gut-level self may be involved in any one of them. Some life accident could snap him out of his drift: a recession that shuts down the assembly line, the death of a parent, maybe a run-in with the law. But it is also likely that no coherent career pattern will ever take shape. He may do his time on earth making a living, rather than committed to a lifework, and seek his satisfactions from other sources—hunting and fishing, perhaps, building his own home, betting on horses, becoming a tavern orator.

How long can one delay adult commitments before becoming a failure? Judging by George Bernard Shaw, it is possible to be a no-count, disagreeable wanderer, inwardly tormented by cowardice and personal shortcomings, at least until the age of 30. GBS granted himself that prolonged a moratorium to avoid being roped in by success. "I made good in spite of myself, and found, to my dismay, that business, instead of expelling me as the worthless imposter I was, was fastening upon me with no intention of letting me go."[2] To elude an occupation he detested, GBS broke loose at 20 and left his homeland, let himself be drawn into the Socialist movement, and eventually homed in on his own remarkable gifts by studying and writing about what interested him. He produced five novels in his twenties, in the obedient manner of a schoolboy filling his tablet; and although they weren't published until fifty years later, the effort did teach Shaw how to write. More important, this long period of unfettered exploration allowed for the filling out of a personality that then burst forth to take its place among the world's great aristocrats of idiosyncrasy.

Popular wisdom assumes today that the limited-commitment route is best in the twenties. Too many young men have seen the price their fathers paid for obediently sitting out their youths at the bottom of a big bureaucracy. "That's not the place to be when you're in your twenties and wondering, 'Who am I?'" says a famous political columnist, who has all his life been trying to build the high-profile identity that was drubbed out of him when he worked under the corporate stamp of a giant news organization. "The answer is 'You're a worm.'"

On the other hand, people who do not invest much of themselves in their early choices may not get much in return that will allow them to change or grow. Taken to the extreme, the unwillingness to commit leaves no quarter for expression of the merger self. If no school, organization or love match can be trusted (or if, as in the case of Eldridge Cleaver, the only way the individual sees fit to redress the wrongs of society is to smash it or choose exile from it), the path leads to isolation. The perpetually rebellious transient is in danger of becoming locked up, or *locked out*.

Generally speaking, people who begin with a transient pattern will feel around 30 an urgent push to establish personal goals and attachments (although not necessarily to marry).[3] Some men remain in moratorium, still groping for a personal identity and strongly felt values straight through to middle life.

Tony's girl friend has spent the night again and left her makeup out on his sink. Her hairs are in his hairbrush. Her jeans are on his floor and also her panties. He steps into the shower and fills the room with steam as fast as he can, flushing out her scent, nullifying the invasion. Things have gone too far, he decides. He will have to call it quits.

At the office his desk is a tower of unopened mail, and somebody else is using it. People are surprised to see him. Tony is a free-lancer; he comes in as seldom as possible. His latest assignment is to edit a special issue on couples, which is funny, given the fact that since leaving home he has never spent more than three consecutive nights with another mammal excepting a cat. Tony's only goal in his twenties has been to have at least three different jobs and no wives at all.

"I have no interest in 'running for president,'" he will tell you. "Half my contemporaries, in the first few years after we graduated from college, gave up on that and withdrew from seeing life as a series of hurdles in the race with other men. Drugs made many of them less aggressive. But after the drug phase, most of them jumped back into the Brooks Brothers suits and picked up where they left off."

Not Tony. The whole idea has been to avoid becoming part of any structure. He remains truly a child of the 1960s, he says. But as his story comes out—guardedly, spaced with holes—it would seem to have less to do with his generation than with his father.

"Smart is the man who makes the most money in the shortest period of time without being an out-and-out criminal." That was the father's philosophy. He worshiped the buck but he wasn't about to come by it easily, not as a TV repairman with a high school education. He used what he had, which was a presence. In the eyes of his son he was handsome as a movie star and muscular as a thug, a coarse man but charming, a charming con. He wanted his Tony to grow up to be a killer in the corporate world.

Tony's genes had done a different dance, a sort of do-si-do that caused him to come out short-legged and porky and also cursed with the kind of skin suitable for illustration in medical texts of the permanent ill effects of acne vulgaris. He was in no position to compete with his father's physical attributes. But he was smart.

Very early Tony began to marshal this talent into his main line of defense. He would be the one thing his father couldn't hope to be: an intellectual. In high school he hung around with the wizards of the debating team. But all the while he was teaching himself how to put on an impressive mental fireworks display, he wasn't certain of his intelligence. Secretly he felt like an intellectual hanger-on, a doubt that his father worked hard to cultivate. "You don't belong with those eggheads," was the standard taunt. Nevertheless, the smarties acted as allies who helped Tony to repudiate his father's materialistic world view. His mother's input was: "Be a good boy. Be a priest." It took one year in the seminary to mobilize him into turning away from her Catholicism, but he had to lay back a year, one more year at home, before he could begin to move on this radical program of his.

Tony's father might rather have seen the boy become a loan shark than some Ivy League smartmouth. It amounted, therefore, to a *coup d'état* when Tony began pulling up roots by winning himself a scholarship to a fine men's college.

Yet despite leaving the family, Tony still did not feel anything like a separated entity until his junior year. Certification was the key. The actual key was a Phi Beta Kappa. Now that the adult world had certified his brain power, he believed it to be real. It became his engine. It would take him anywhere, stun his detractors; why, he was certain at one point, he'd be a great nuclear physicist.

He scratched the physicist idea after all because that would have violated his code of noncommitment. Like any coup-maker after the overthrow, Tony had to hold for some years to doctrinaire practices (that is, antithetical to his father's doctrine) before he dared hope the opposition had been subdued. And so rather than becoming part of an institution, which a career in physics would have required, he wrote a book about the nuclear arms race. It was all about things. At that time he didn't think in terms of people. The book concerned death in the abstract. Personal death had no meaning for Tony at 25. "While on the one hand I was intellectualizing about the holocaust, I was doing a lot of reckless things." He would cycle the Boston-Washington corridor without a crash helmet, for instance.

He thought about women in abstract categories, too. "If the last girl was Barbarella, I'd treat this one like Barbarella. If she couldn't go through *grand mal* seizures of pretense more than twice, then it was up to her to let me know she was somewhere between Barbarella and the Flying Nun." Intimacy, by Tony's definition, was the kind of communication that occurs in the third and usually terminal stage of a relationship.

All of which sounds very advanced and compatible with a dehumanized era. Tony might even have gone on believing himself. He certainly was not expecting to have his hand tipped by a young heiress.

She called him up one evening for dinner. Exactly the sort of move that attracted him. Any girl with the confidence to ask him out was probably not stalking. On the other hand, as he was quick to warn himself, any girl who reminded him of his mother turned him off. "I know I would be bad at being half of a couple," he would explain. "I guess I believe in prolonged adolescence."

No sooner was this ideal dinner date under way than the wealthy young beauty, dispensing with any emotional foreplay, made Tony a purely impersonal proposal. She was ready to have a baby. He was the smartest man she knew. Would he consent to making the genetic contribution to her offspring? With the guarantee, of course, that she would take full responsibility after conception?

Of course he was disarmed by the compliment, confirming as it did that his mental pyrotechnics could indeed blind people to his physical limitations. On second thought he froze.

"Jesus Christ, I thought, how could I be sure a child wouldn't awaken all kinds of possessive father feelings in me? It might bring down my whole self-image as a cool, detached character. I couldn't do it."

At 28 Tony had the life structure of a transient, and he said no to anything that violated it. He couldn't father a child for fear it might produce a commitment. And worse, there was a chance it would set loose the old man in all his physicality and coarseness—you never know! He might begin to behave just as his father had behaved. The girl who reminded Tony of his mother was the one who threatened to expose the part of him that still wanted mothering. Very little human warmth could get in so long as Tony had to freeze out any awareness of his parents' influence.

He was unique all right, but at a price that could eventually impoverish his development. At some point he would have to admit those influences if he were going to work out his own authentic response to his father's business ethics and his mother's strong Catholic family values. As he moved into the next passage, it remained to be seen whether, having gained some confidence in his own attributes, he might be surprised to find a side of himself that was not so freewheeling and that called out for human closeness.

I visited Tony a few months before he turned 30. He was a man with an apartment and a lease and place mats and a woman to whom he was pledged. The same woman could cause him panic a couple of years before simply by leaving her makeup in the same bathroom. We all sat down to a meal, and Tony talked about the joy he got out of cooking their first Thanksgiving dinner this year "with everything that Mother made and some things Mother never made." We also talked about Tony's new book. This time it's a book about people, about people in white-collar crime. It is no coincidence that the figures Tony is now so interested in examining believe, like his father, that the smart man is the one who makes the most amount of money in the shortest period of time.

LOCKED IN

Safe but stifled, these are the most familiar men. They do make solid commitments in their twenties, but without a crisis of identity or much self-examination. The goal is to be set. In the reach for early stability, they often do not seriously question the value system underlying their goals. Approaching 30, they may regret not having made use of the earlier years for exploration.

Those with the courage of their insights may use the Age 30 passage to break out of the "should" mold if the career they've tried on doesn't fit. This early and dramatic turnaround in career direction is becoming more attractive. As that happens, more models are created, and the anticipated dangers of making a change are minimized still further.

Any such change will be painful. A crisis. But not nearly so painful as it is for the man who waits until his forties and bumps into the midlife crisis like a submarine into a reef that wasn't on the charts. The fact that he is locked in only compounds the crisis. Because the forties, as writer Barbara Fried so succinctly captures them, are a time when it seems no matter what course one has pursued, "everything is turning grey, drying up or leaving home."[4]

Men with "father's footsteps" disease are the most

obvious of the long-term locked-in cases, but there are far more commonplace routes into this pattern. All those men who lock into civil service jobs for lack of the resources that would allow them to shop around— before they know it they have become the contents of one small drawer of the bureaucracy, and in private life, Dear Occupant, Dear Charge Customer. Sons too of the upper class, upper-middle, middle-middle, are all represented here. Basically, these are the men who continue to do what's expected of them. Reluctant to take risks or to be too different, they are also the ones most eager to thrust themselves into the pipeline leading to executive titles or academic tenure. Titles, tenure . . . something to hold on to.

A whole generation of such men is reflected in the Grant Study of Adult Development.[5] These 268 Harvard students drawn largely from the classes of 1942 to 1944 were selected for their psychological health and, with an irony surely unanticipated, for their high level of independence.

Almost all served in World War II. The careers that most attracted them were law, medicine, business, and college teaching, in that order.

Two of the blunt conclusions drawn after this favored group had been studied from their freshman year to the age of 48 were: Over time, a person's psychological health is quite *in*consistent. Secondly, even the men in this group, chosen for their well-being, were still busy weaning themselves from their parents at 40. The Grant Study has been analyzed by psychiatrist George Vaillant of Harvard Medical School, who offers the following highlights:

Between 25 and 35 these men worked hard at their careers and "devoted themselves to the nuclear family. Poor at self-reflection, they were not unlike 'latency children'—good at tasks, careful to follow the rules, anxious for promotion, and accepting of many aspects of the 'system.'" By 30, their potential excellence was, Dr. Vaillant writes, "lost to conformity." They were the hangers inside the gray flannel suits.

In order to preserve the illusion that their marriages and career choices were adequate, most of these men became masters of self-deception. They did their share of diapering and avoided looking too closely at the wives who were with them inside the well-built lockups. Almost all their juice went into scaling career pyramids. The early thirties were a particularly crass and shallow stage for them, little or no expansion having taken place in the previous transition. By 35 they couldn't wait to take over the wheel.

At 40 their compulsively calm exteriors ruptured. Most of the men found themselves in a tumult more punishing than anything they remembered in adolescence. Forty to fifty was a troubled decade in every area of their lives. Yet, however marred by depression and doubts, the men who faced up to the agonizing self-reappraisal of midlife came out renewed, and looked back on the period from 35 to 49 as the happiest in their lives. The saddest outcomes were those who ignored the rising sap of the forties. Most of these men were lawyers. Paradoxically, they had been among the most adventuresome in their twenties. But by midlife, serving as guardians of the establishment and protectors of their own large incomes, they resisted fresh growth. Compared with their classmates, they seemed prematurely old.

The best outcomes, as Dr. Vaillant describes them, were the men who faced up to the mortality issue in midlife and whose preoccupation in their fifties shifted away from themselves and their own advancement. Their emphasis changed dramatically from making money and winning awards to caring about other people, which included concern for their children, teaching and consulting, and often becoming mentors for younger men. So far this is a description that holds precisely to Erikson's view of the central crisis of the middle years: defeating stagnation through generativity (a subject discussed at length in Chapter Twenty). But Dr. Vaillant confuses me when he explains how the men who received the highest scores in overall adult adjustment mastered intimacy in their twenties. "Of the best adapted men," he writes, "93 percent had achieved a stable marriage before 30 and had stayed married until 50." He would seem to define intimacy as staying married. One wonders how many of those wives enjoyed full adult development.

The Grant Study begun at Harvard in 1938 ranks in distinction with the Oakland Growth and Development Study (comparing personality development of men and women, as described in Chapter Eleven) that was undertaken at Berkeley in 1929. They are the longest prospective studies of adult development in the world. The impressive similarity in both was the way the men ran that fast track between 25 and 35, gaining confidence and consolidating their careers, but just as swiftly losing touch with their feelings and learning to block change by massive self-deception. Except to deepen their professional commitments, most of the men in both studies appear to have ignored the Age 30 passage and to have remained locked into the "I should" behavior appropriate to the twenties, at least until they turned 35. It's no wonder there is today such urgent interest in the male midlife crisis. These are the locked-in men who are currently suffering from it.

Dwight is of more recent vintage, a graduate of the 1950s, but of course that was an era remorseless in its efforts to turn young men into latency children. It was further incumbent on Dwight to reflect well on his flinty New England heritage. Father hadn't much style, but Grandfather, whom Dwight idolized, started as a runner on Wall Street and ended up running a railroad. Just to look at Dwight was to assume he had been born with a smashing backhand and a set of glands that could sweat only in a herringbone pattern.

Beneath appearances, though, ran a vein of loneliness. The only child, Dwight had lived alone with his mother while his father went off to war, until one day she disappeared, too. The boy came up from playing at the pond and puzzled at the cars filling the driveway. His mother was dead. Pneumonia was the official explanation, and after that the subject was never discussed. The boy was taken in by his grandparents. A few years later he was looking for scratch paper in Grandfather's desk to do fifth grade fractions when he came across the *New York Times* notice of his mother's suicide. Father came home and took a new wife. The boy's legs barely reached the first step of the train when he began carrying suitcases back and forth to prep school. He liked prep school. He had company there. He never caused trouble, never went through a turn-against period. In fact, by the sound of his early twenties, Dwight seemed ready to shut himself up inside one big safety-deposit box.

It wasn't a case of financial need. So moved was Grandfather by seeing his only heir graduate college, he gave Dwight a handsome sum to do with what he wished. The lucky graduate might have used it to go excavating in Crete or bawdy-housing across the Continent or simply for adventuring in capitalism. "I guess the old Protestant ethic in me said, 'Invest it.'" He safed it all away in blue chip stocks. Lock!

Vanessa went to Vassar. Vanessa was a shipboard romance. Vanessa skied. Based largely on those qualifications, Dwight set about convincing himself he loved her. He had to go into the army. He felt lonely again. He wasted not a moment between finishing basic training and starting married life with Vanessa. Lock!

Dwight had no grand plan for himself when he got out of the service. And of course neither did Vanessa; she just went along, having babies and keeping her hair curled, the way wives were supposed to do. All his peers were filing into Wall Street or executive training programs. Dwight knew what he didn't want to do, and that was it. Father had been an executive, and Father held sour associations for him. It was Dwight's commanding officer who suggested teaching, and perhaps because school had been his surrogate home for so long, Dwight decided to try it. He took a job in a boy's prep school in California.

"Vanessa was in no way involved in my decision, not even to the point of volunteering where she wanted to go. But once I started teaching I had no reservations about it. I just poured in an immense amount of energy. I loved the idea of becoming a scholar." With almost no experimentation Dwight had found his one true course in life. Lock!

Bits of plaster began chipping off this glossy marriage as the pair edged toward the end of their twenties. For want of excitement, Dwight took a mild turn off his course and went to Washington for a year as administrative aide to a congressman. It tickled him to make contacts with celebrities. Vanessa began to voice minor complaints, nothing he could put his finger on. "I didn't feel any real support behind me. But I didn't feel any pure antagonism either."

Fifteen years later Dwight can speculate on what was going wrong, but even today it somewhat bewilders him. "I suspect one of our real problems was that her sense of herself was so much me. She was constantly looking for something 'to do' to make her time useful. She was a good mother. She still is a superb mother." And she is still, to this day, searching for her own identity.

At 30, the outlines of his life in the academic world seemed to fall into place as clearly as the stone geometry of an old land-grant college. His alma mater, a New England college, lured him away from Washington with a position as assistant to the president. Heady stuff! All at once Dwight was looking down the line at a future in administration, seeing himself in the dean's chair, then the president's chair, wielding influence, being in charge. Like Grandfather.

As Dwight galvanized, his wife panicked. Growing more fearful as she narrowed and narrower the more she feared to try expanding, Vanessa began to lash out. She reminded Dwight of his lapsed commitment to teaching. What had happened to all his high-minded talk about becoming a scholar who would attract grants and do field research and write books that would be appreciated by learned societies? She reserved her respect for faculty members. Her considered opinion of the people she had to invite to administrator's teas for her husband was: "These people are a super pain in the ass."

Dwight could not admit the extent to which he agreed. Vanessa, damn her, was implying all the things he refused to face: Was he compromising his talents for security? Deserting pure scholarship to chase the power of the presidency? Instead of grappling with the demon inside himself, he made Vanessa the demon. "She was putting me down." He responded by dishing out the same sort of harsh but deadly accurate criticism of his wife.

"You take art lessons and paint a picture, to hell with the quality. Tomorrow it's a new enthusiasm. You never finish anything you start; what's the matter with you! It bugs me. There's no standard of—of what I would call excellence. Why don't you go back and finish college?"

Later Dwight claimed, "I did encourage her. To her credit, she did go back and finish. By then our marriage had already gone sour." In hindsight, Dwight was also the one who said (as quoted in Chapter Thirteen), "I think there might have been some envy on my wife's part that I had a vision of myself. She stopped being supportive. Well, she still participated, but without showing much enthusiasm for the responsibilities of being my wife, such as entertaining. She still had nothing of her own. She was feeling frenzied." Snap!

The couple decided to separate for a year. Vanessa took the children to a city; Dwight remained in the college town, where he soon became attached to the dean's young secretary. Her marriage too was tottering. In the pale light of late wintry afternoons they warmed one another, coaxed one another to become someone new. "How can I go back to being a student again, at 32?" he would ask rhetorically, for this is what he now wanted to do. She laughed away his doubts. "So you'll get rheumatism before you get tenure, so what." In turn, he took great pleasure in being a Pygmalion figure. He convinced her to give up the stifling security of her marriage and go back for her master's degree. When Vanessa returned, hoping to patch up their marriage, she found a man in high rebellion, so highly charged, in fact, that he couldn't hear his wife saying, "But that's exactly what *I'd* hoped you would do!"

Dwight ripped up just about everything he had built in his twenties: the marriage, the home, the career as an administrator. He was sprung. Except for missing his children, he had no regrets.

"It was very much the infatuation of a new mate, a new sexual adventure, and most of all, this girl was very supportive of what I wanted to do. At that time in my life I took an occupational gamble. I missed teaching, and I wanted to be a college professor. The only way to do that was to get a Ph.D. I quit the good job as assistant to the president to come to New York and drop back into graduate school. She believed in me. Both of us were coming to this cold, impersonal city alone. We gathered together; I was very close to her. I was ready to put together a whole new life with her."

Do you hear the echoes Dwight could not?

Wife says: *Be faithful to your own values. You value scholarship over power. You should therefore be a professor, not an administrator.* This was a truth, however unpleasantly packaged. But when Dwight was still in his twenties and Vanessa carried this message, it was unwanted. He translated it as an external demand and a criticism. He projected it back onto his mate: "She was putting me down."

During the passage into his thirties, an imperative rises within Dwight himself that says: *The pursuit of scholarship is of greater value than power. I should be*

269

a professor, not an administrator. The message is the same. Except that now it is acknowledged as part of him, so he can work on it. At the same time, a new buoyancy is overtaking him. *Never mind safety for a change; take a gamble!*

The same message communicated at different stages puts an utterly different complexion on the bearers, who might otherwise be interchangeable. There was little difference between the wife and the Testimonial Woman in Dwight's life except where they came in. Before Dwight was ready to give up the safety of his administrative job, the woman who coaxed him to go back to his faculty dream was a detractor. When he had reached the stage of internal preparedness, the woman who encouraged him to make the change was a supporter. The new woman also viewed him as a man voluntarily going backward, willing to risk a secure position to be a student again. She was privy to none of the vacillation and self-deception that had gone before. Where his wife saw a coward, the Testimonial Woman saw a man struggling to become. And perhaps most important, he now *wanted* her help.

Dwight, in turn, cloaked the two women in very different expectations. Both had been academic sparklers until they married and turned their attention to baby- and husband-tending. Both were becoming dulled and desperate as they backed up the hill toward 30.

To his wife Dwight was saying: "Enjoy the duties of an administrator's wife; be a hostess; get in gear on my career. Be a fine mother, too, of course. And incidentally, why don't you finish college so you'll feel more confident and sound more polished? It would be nice for the guests."

To the Testimonial Woman, however, he was extending exactly the sort of magic carpet that might have rescued his wife. He was saying to the new woman: "Come fly with me, back to student life; we'll pick up the dreams of our youth and believe in each other and build it all together this time, beginning with good-bye to our funny old sexual hang-ups."

And fly they did. Three years later Dwight crashed. The Testimonial Woman pushed him out in midair without warning, for another man. "It was sudden and brutal. I'd had no regrets whatsoever about breaking up with my wife. But this—I was totally devastated. I don't know, maybe I was beginning to take her for granted."

All of which goes to show, one can break the lock and still not evade the Catch at 30. As Dwight discovered by the time he was 35, a change of mates was not the key. A change in *him* was. And that change only began to take place in earnest when he stopped expecting his partner to be the support (either by exploiting her, as he did his wife, or by leaning on her, as he did with his Testimonial Woman). As he began to assume the authority for his own support, Dwight stretched on all levels. He spent several years working independently on a scholarly research project and dating an assortment of women with their own irons in the fire. He loosened up. Grew a mustache. Learned a thing or two from a lusty married woman. Mixed around in antiwar politics. Eventually he remarried and wrote a book. She was a film producer. On the brow of 40, brimming with vitality and more daring than he had ever before displayed, Dwight whisked off with his new wife to the last wilderness in the West to make a documentary: in his field, using her medium.

THE WUNDERKIND

"I've always played to win, rather than playing not to lose," is how the son of an Irish laborer explained his own ascent to the presidency of a lavish conglomerate. "They sound alike, but there's a tremendous difference."

So there is. It is represented here as the distinction between the locked-in pattern and the wunderkind.

Both kinds of men may have dreams of high achievement. The difference is in the degree of risk they are willing to take. The man who starts out "running for president" or playing to win goes to bat for himself at every opportunity, steals bases, takes the credit, and along the way usually shows fidelity to any team or principle only so long as it's a winning showcase for him. He not only takes risks, he creates them. The very uncertainty of the outcome is what sustains his excitement. Almost invariably he has a coach (the mentor or nonparental career model described by Levinson), and this coach grooms him early. He'll win a few just for the Gipper. But the first chance he gets he will move on to a bigger and better team or take the Gipper's job.

The wunderkind usually enjoys career success early. One tip-off to a man of this pattern is his reaction to the whole foreign notion of adult development. He will buy it only if he is allowed to be ahead. "You may be right about that stage," he will say, "but I went through it five years earlier." And he does go through the vocational hoops sooner than his peers— although he doesn't always reach the top or stay there if he does. Work is what he thinks about. Work is his fix. The dividing line between work and private life is blurred early. He works at parties, in the shower, in his fitful early-waking dreams; he works even at play. The point of the vacation is to recharge his batteries for more work; the point of the golf game is to sew up a business friendship, unless the point of the game is even more basic: to win the championship.

The sports world is chockablock with young prodigies. Perhaps more than any other professional group, champion athletes need a concept of the total life cycle. Too many of them rise to the limelight in their agile years only to drop into punishing obscurity before they've prepared a second career, and that means something more vigorous than signing cereal boxes. The smart ones extend their celebrity status into related fields, becoming media personalities, columnists, restaurateurs. And every once in a while a wunderkind who begins as a winning athlete goes on to harness his will to win in the service of mankind.

Einstein produced the theory of relativity at 25. Napoleon and Alexander carved empires before they were 30. The legacy of such dazzling displays of precocity, together with America's only enduring religion—Productivity—help to perpetuate the lure of the wunderkind position. Not without some unfortunate consequences.

Scientists, as a group, are massively infected with the belief that they will burn out after 30. The emphasis is on early productivity rather than on broadly arched achievement over the long run. Harriet Zuckerman's work on Nobel laureates is sobering as it traces the work cycle based on this belief. Nobel Prize winners begin publishing earlier than their colleagues (at an average age of 25) and continue publishing at a furious rate (a median of four papers a year from the start of their careers) until they reach a peak of productivity in their forties. Their prodigious effort is rewarded, but the reward itself, intended as an incentive for further contributions to science, acts instead as a deterrent. In the five years following receipt of the Nobel Prize, the productivity of laureates declines sharply. Their collaboration with associates is strained, usually to the breaking point. Suddenly they are stars. Drafted for administrative advice, dinner speeches, policy decisions, talk shows, government service, they are left no time to go back to the lab and get on with their work. They become victims of the bias in favor of precocity that is built into many of our institutions.[6]

The circle is completed by less distinguished scientists who leave the laboratory early (before they supposedly burn out) to take on administrative posts. Believing in the magic link between youth and productivity, they make the belief a reality in the way they then organize the occupation itself.

A mythology has also grown up around other professions which says that one must pass a high-water mark by a certain age or one can forget the race. And a good deal of that mythology is malarkey.

The wunderkind often seems to possess a boundless capacity to bounce back from career failures. Business losses, power struggles, lost elections, even criminal charges are viewed as temporary setbacks; they merely stiffen his resolve to come out a winner. But as the biographies of such men unfold, they are often revealed to be retarded in the personal sphere, poor at mutuality, and sometimes without the capacity for empathy at all. You might say a full-dress superachiever is all seek and no merge.

Classically, the wunderkind makes a utilitarian marriage, attracts an "office wife," and accumulates mistresses who seldom tire of waiting for him not to leave his wife. It's no surprise that most of these men marry caregivers, particularly those caregivers who come with pedigrees, trust funds, or important fathers. They are also attracted to models and actresses who can be displayed as prestige possessions. It would be difficult to exaggerate the importance such men place on maintaining the traditional marriage structure. Among the studies that have documented this, one adds pointedly: "Their wives form a sanctuary which psychologically and literally frees the men to work. [But though] the existence of a family may be crucial, their wives and children could be interchangeable."[7]

The office wife is another matter. She knows where everything is: his papers, his quirks, his dirty professional linen, his timetable for winning. Their relationship may or may not extend into the sexual area, but a mutuality of purpose evolves. She is not easily replaced. Because the wunderkind is a complicated man, and seldom introspective, he yearns for someone who will understand him without challenging him. If not the woman he works with, then an adoring girl friend, student, or protégée. Wrung out from an evening of romancing clients, he may drag back to the bed of his knowing lady and confess, "I feel like a prostitute." But he rarely shares with his wife the private thoughts, fears, and hopes invested in his work. One book-length study of such men says the reason is that even when the man would like to share this world with his wife, he can't bridge the chasm of specialized language and, most of all, the value system accepted in the corridors of power which is altogether strange to her.[8] (And apt to be repugnant?)

My subjects revealed a deeper reason. They were afraid to admit they were not all-knowing. Afraid to let anyone come too close. Afraid to stop filling their time with external challenges they could probably surmount, for fear of glimpsing that vast and treacherous interior which seems insurmountable. Afraid that the moment they let down their guard, someone might ridicule them, expose them, move in on their weaknesses, and reduce them again to the powerlessness of a little boy. It is not their wives they are afraid of. It is themselves. That part of themselves I have called the inner custodian, which is derivative of parents and other figures from childhood.

Somewhere, back in the dark recesses of boyhood, each wunderkind I studied recollected a figure who made him feel helpless or insecure. An overbearing mother, a father who wouldn't give his blessing, an alcoholic father, an absent father. In some cases the force was more global: grinding poverty or prejudice. One man, who is today a wizard of the financial community, had a particularly memorable Jewish boyhood. He was accosted by a party of Germans in jackboots. They left him with one testicle. But that, of course, is the extreme. The inner custodian may also derive from a parent who meant to be of goodwill: "You have the chance I never had to become a doctor," or "You must enhance the family name by running for high public office." But the most important legacy of such dictates is the last and implied part . . . *or you'll be nothing*.

Money is often a secondary motive in the whirlwind life of the wunderkind. The main thrust is to enter the inner circle. They make this happen by subordinating everything else to the drive to be Number One, whereupon, they expect, their insecurities will vanish, they will be loved and admired, and nobody can humiliate them or denigrate them or make them feel dependent ever again.

The wunderkind can go many ways in midlife. A stage, incidentally, that most are loathe to admit they have entered. The great crisis for these men is triggered by the *achievement* of their success.[9] The unconscious assumption is that once they reach the top, the inner custodian—that sinister dictator or detractor —will be disempowered once and for all.

Occasionally, the subscribers to this life view end up in jail. But many of the others wind up running the nation's top corporations, if not the nation itself. They may be an elite few, but their impact is multiplied by the hundreds of thousands of people they pass on their way to pinnacles of influence. It is for this reason we must be concerned with them. And also because we put them up there.

In a competitive culture such as ours, which celebrates killers and outlaws and whores, the wunderkind is goaded on in his give-em-hell goals. His most cynical manipulations of others are willingly overlooked so long as he keeps on winning. He is a staple American screen hero and a magnet for women. Think of Gable in *Gone With the Wind*. Think of Bogart in *Casablanca*. The wunderkind is the fantasy outlet for millions of weaker-kneed men who get off on Billy the Kid, James Bond, Michael Corleone; who idealized John F. Kennedy's courage during the Cuban Missile Crisis until, in retrospect, even a television documentary offers the chilling interpretation that he risked the extermination of mankind in order to prove that Khrushchev was no match for him. Multitudes got off on Richard Nixon, until he got caught. As social observer Shana Alexander has pointed out, Mr. Nixon's fall is important in a way none of us much care to face. The archetype of the American Dream, the poor boy who made good, Nixon adhered to the gospel of winning for winning's sake. "The gospel . . . leaves you in spiritual wreckage when the game is over and lost."[10]

Sociopaths and paranoid personalities are heavily represented in the wunderkind pattern. Psychiatrist Willard Gaylin of Columbia University has warned it is precisely these traits, the most dangerous in people of power, that are best suited for attainment of power in our culture. These are the men, he says, most likely to succeed as corporate chiefs and most likely to be elected as our leaders.

First, the sociopath. Sociopaths are not mentally ill, merely oblivious to the needs of others and unencumbered by the capacity to feel guilt or empathy. "The capacity to be ruthless, driving and immoral, if also combined with intelligence and imagination, can be a winning combination in politics as well as commerce," writes Gaylin.[11]

It is easy to recognize some degree of paranoia in the profile of another kind of wunderkind. As Gaylin explains:

> The paranoid personality with his conspiratorial mind, his tendency to personalize, his readiness to see policy challenges as personal attacks, his preoccupation with pride and humiliation, his endless tendency to create power struggles where none need to exist, his constant reassertion of his courage which is not being questioned and his masculinity which is not being threatened, his exaggerated sense of humiliation and his terror of exposing his deep-felt sense of impotence and inadequacy, is a particular threat in a position of power.

There are other superachievers, of course, who surmount their own success and find refreshment and renewal by extending their talents to benefit society or by guiding the next generation.

Every one of the twenty subjects in a University of Michigan study of outstanding successful men had made radical career switches or had become social activists in middle life. One physician had left a middle-class practice to establish a clinic for the poor. A venerated academician was working to change national social policy. The men, interviewed in depth by Professor of Psychology Judith Bardwick, lived in Boston, New York, and Ann Arbor, Michigan. Although it is a selected study, it reveals important consistencies in the lives of such men.[12]

Characteristically, all twenty of these dynamos insisted they never had a middle-aged crisis, do not expect one, and do not feel they are moving toward their own death. They were not introspective. With a few exceptions, such as the doctor and professor, the work these men were doing was not socially beneficial, but they rewarded themselves by perceiving their jobs or institutions as valuable. However, the importance of an ethical self was a secondary line of development, of concern only after these men had achieved power.

Because most of their wives do not work at all, and none full time, the men in the Bardwick study do feel apprehensive about their children growing older. Soon their wives will be out of a role, and they know it. But a glaring discrepancy showed up between the men's initial declarations that their wives were wonderful women (meaning wonderful wives and mothers) and their true judgment as it ultimately came out. About three-quarters of the group did not respect their wives as people.

Unless their spouses precipitated a showdown, the egocentric behavior of these men went unchecked. A failure in career only spurred them on to greater efforts, but for dealing with a marital crisis they were altogether unequipped. The men who faced such a blowup were the luckier ones. Only they were led in midlife to an honest reappraisal of themselves.

All the wunderkinder I studied had a midlife crisis. Not an observable career crisis necessarily, but a screeching inner halt that forced them to take stock. Once the loneliness gap had grown too wide to ignore or their wives had walked out or ended up as alcoholics, some tried to write off their emotional losses: "But she was a superior mother," or "She was the basic ingredient in any success I had." Occasionally, in the squalor of recent abandonment, with tears worming down his face, such a man would confess, "I must have been almost criminally insensitive to her."

The specific travails of the wunderkind in the midlife passage will be discussed later in the book, but the pattern leading to it is graphically demonstrated by a man I'll call Barry Bernstein.

In the magical deeps of the third row of the Quickway Cinema, he passed his minority dreaming of the day when he would be Mr. Movie. When that day came he would be leaving messages for John Wayne and negotiating for rights to the Bible. The name on the picture wouldn't be Zanuck or Preminger or Louis B. Mayer. It would be Barry Bernstein. His parents had to drag him out of the movie house to eat.

At 17 he went to work in the mail room of a major film studio. Apart from an interruption known as the Korean War, he pressed steadily up through the ranks of a major talent agency to the point where, at 30, he had a sweet expense account and many other perqs attendant to a show biz bachelorhood. No dependents. No distractions. He lived in a semipalatial apartment in the five-star section of Manhattan and had a maid to pick up his socks, as well as numerous interchangeable models to date when he cared to make the party scene. Which was not very often. They didn't mind if Barry liked working better than he liked them, so long as he mentioned their names to casting directors.

His parents were the only dark cloud. They were salaried people with little inclination to improve their lot. They had no concept of their son's success. It was treated like the cripple one passes in the street, as if it didn't exist.

In the absence of a mentor, Bernstein relied heavily on a distant model. Jack Kennedy was his idol. He worked in the campaign to make him President. The reason he idolized Kennedy was this: "He proved that a young man could move quickly and do the job just as well as any older man." Belief in this premise was vital to Bernstein's program.

The only evidence of change during his passage from the twenties to the thirties was a nebulous feeling that something inside was not fulfilled. As Bernstein diagnosed it, the trouble was that he still lacked a personal identity in the movie business. He was a spoke. All the wheels were in Los Angeles. He didn't brood about it, however, nor was he moved to change any of the terms or conditions of his life. The emptiness was easily concealed by a physical move, this time to an "Oh baby, what a view!" perch overlooking the East River, more befitting his $35,000 income. He was 32.

One day Bernstein's maid awakened him suddenly. He was at home in bed, recuperating from bronchial pneumonia.

"The news is bad," she said. "They shot the President right in his head."

In his weakened condition, Bernstein could not take in this information. He looked at the maid as if at a wall. Soon a model he had been dating came by to comfort him. They stared together at the television set for three days.

"It gave me a different perspective of what life was all about," he remembers. "I mean, I saw a man sliced up at the pinnacle of his career. All my running around and tumulting and materialistic attitudes made no sense. It was a very emotional period. Nothing seemed important anymore. And here was this lovely girl whose entire center of attention was me, who didn't want to do anything but take care of me.

"My whole attitude toward her changed. We started going steady like two kids. Shortly after the assassination I asked her to marry me. It was that simple. I told her she could stop work the moment she became pregnant. So the first time she thought she was pregnant, she stopped. I never made her go back to work again. We were the perfect couple. I mean, everyone thought this was the perfect marriage."

At 37, Barry Bernstein was the head of production for one of Hollywood's top film companies. And ecstatic.

"All of a sudden I thought, Jesus, little me, I'm a mogul! Everybody has to come to me, everybody."

Except his wife. "She couldn't have cared less."

The first two years of their marriage had been blissful. She took care of him, and eventually he took care of making her pregnant. As an exhibition of their bliss, they even arranged a little party at home on the night of the Academy Awards. The guests were encouraged to touch Lorna's belly; she was starting to show. Lorna was very young and proud of the sexuality that would allow her to push babies into the world. The rest of her universe was Barry, the protective walls.

Late that night a stretcher took Lorna away. The surgeon said there was a good chance she wouldn't make it. Her baby had grown in the wrong place and ruptured one of her body's most important tubes.

She survived, but something else had ruptured that was not so easily repaired. Both she and Barry were now frightened people. Lorna's fear was all twisted up with an impotent rage. Two grand illusions of her twenties—that her body worked perfectly and that her safety was her husband—had been shattered simultaneously. She was not ready to accept the dark side of life as part of herself. She projected it onto her husband. How could he, her protector, have allowed this evil force to invade? It was up to him to make the nightmare go away. In the years that followed she tested Bernstein, dragging herself again and again to the precipice of destruction in the hope that her husband would save her and take the terrible fear away.

Bernstein chose to flee his fears by grabbing on to the fastest trolley car marked Success. A year before, two of the slickest new theatrical agents in the business had approached him to join their team. A great mystique surrounded them, as well as a reputation for being cutthroats. He had decided with Lorna, before her tubal pregnancy, not to be wooed away from his respected company by these dubious hotshots. Now he couldn't wait. The worm of mortality had been glimpsed in the apple.

Lorna was six months into her next pregnancy when Bernstein's new partners told him the time was ripe for his move to Los Angeles.

"How can I leave my obstetrician?" she pleaded. "My family, all my friends?"

"You've got me," he said, "and California has good doctors. I've already made the arrangements, you'll see. It's a beautiful furnished house in Benedict Canyon."

There was no one to ask to the circumcision ceremony. Both families were too poor to fly out. Bernstein papered the house with business associates. His wife never came out of her room.

"I was losing myself in business, working seven days a week like a madman," is the way he recalls his late thirties. "I paid little or no attention to my family. Everybody said, 'If you want to make sure your wife feels content, buy her a house, give her something to hold onto.' So I bought a house. But she wouldn't be part of my business. She hated going to parties and screenings, so I went alone. I don't know what she did. I never really bothered to think about it. We were still sleeping in the same bed, but I had no desire for her. I still cared for her but—nothing in bed. I didn't understand it. The only way to cope was to hide in more work. Build my own relationships in the company. I was starting to feel a sense of power. LA is a very fickle town. When you're in a position of power, everybody loves you. They cater to you."

The fever, they call it in the movie business. And Bernstein had it bad.

At the first trace of depression he would make

them cater harder. Sweeping into Mateo's, *yes sir!*, they would show him to the best table. Sunday afternoon he could call up his vassals and throw a tantrum. *You're god, you're god,* they would dutifully say, and his depression would go away. The harder he worked, the more people catered to him, the higher he levitated. Can it be grasped by ordinary folk, this tremendous seduction of being above humanity and making grown men jump?

Barry Bernstein was now a mogul all right, the magical Mr. Movie of his dream. And completely anesthetized from inner sensations. He was living out the illusion that leads many a wunderkind into a dead end: *I must hurry up and fulfill my dream because success will make me the final authority—over my own life, over others, over time, over death.* In reality, success accomplished exactly the opposite. Bernstein had regressed back to the narcissism of a very little boy playing king of the mountain. He was an infant god. There was only one person left in his world who expected him to be human. His wife, in bed. He left her.

The call came a few weeks later, on a Saturday in 1970. A cruel recession had hit the movie industry. His company, among others, was floundering. Bernstein had every reason to believe he would be made president of the company. The current head, he was assured, fancied Bernstein as his protégé. This call was probably the pivotal one—the emergency had forced them to turn to Bernstein prematurely. He would slash the budget, carry the company through.

The caller said he would be paid off. The company was closing down within the week.

"I remember the headline. 'XYZ Closes, Bernstein Exits.' It was like reading my own obituary."

It was like reading his obituary because Bernstein no longer saw any distinction between the business and himself. If the company was dead, the infant god was dead. What's more, it became abruptly difficult to prove that he had ever existed. The company president to whom Bernstein thought he was so close would not take his calls. The down success syndrome of the movie business had already gone into effect: Failures disappear into the walls.

He hid out. A friend who was leaving town to make a picture offered to let Bernstein baby-sit for his Beverly Hills mansion. For the first few weeks he rose, dressed, drove each morning through the home of the stars, and tried calling on people. Then the panic hit. He couldn't look another lying secretary in her vinyl face while she said, "I'm sure he'll be in touch with you." He stopped dressing. He pulled the shades so he wouldn't have to see the gaudy sun lifting leaves the size of elephant ears effortlessly out of the shrubs. He stayed inside in the dark. Weeks went by and then months, like waves in a winter ocean, unmarked, undifferentiated one from another.

"In my kind of work you can't just go looking for a job. I mean, I'd had a position. Either somebody picks you up or—nothing. I got to the point where I couldn't even go out to the swimming pool. I'd be cheating. I became a recluse."

True to his step-style, at a time when the task was to confront the demon inside himself Bernstein found instead an adoring little girl who would deny the dark sea at his back, romance it away. "I became very much involved with her during this period. She took care of me." But Bernstein did have time now to hear what the old neighbors had been telling him. His wife had become a drunk. She was signaling: *Save me!* He didn't respond. She became gravely ill. This time the surgeon would have to disfigure her body to remove the tumor, and even then they weren't sure. Bernstein convinced her to gamble with her life. Lorna came through, but the plastic surgery didn't take. Her rage was reborn, redoubled; Bernstein had betrayed her again. He filed for divorce.

One Saturday morning his new girl friend called him to the phone. The old neighbors again. Lorna had taken an overdose, and his children were out running in the street in their pajamas like mad things. In his underwear Bernstein drove to the old house. A bloated bluish growth, rather like one of those segmented balloons sold at the circus, slumped half off the bed. It was his wife. He heaved his own breath into her mouth. When the coma lifted, he signed her into Neuropsychiatric.

Bernstein is 43 now. The job he has is respectable. Some of the people he works for used to be the vassals who catered to him. Once upon a time, when he measured his worth solely by the barbarous values of the movie business, the humiliation of this turn-around would have been unbearable. He can live now with such unpredictable losses. He has had a lot of practice. One by one all the people who formerly took care of him, including his girl friend, his wife, his mother and father, have either removed their support, deteriorated, or died. He has had to meet each loss with its mountain of anxiety, and in doing so, he has learned something about where his real worth lies. When he looks in the mirror now, the infant god is not there. He accepts his face as it truly is.

"I'll tell you something very important. I know I can survive. At this stage of my life I don't panic any-more. You learn the difference between self-imposed problems and external pressures you can't control. I'm never going to be president, but I enjoy my kids. I still feel like I'm 22. But I have gray in my beard and lines that only life can put in your face. There's no way I can hide from it. Now I look less for material-istic rewards and more for inside satisfactions. I had this childlike, almost neurotic attitude. To me a man was a stud, a guy who was fantastic in bed with a woman and could go out and punch another guy in the mouth. I have since learned what a man is. What a human being is. I don't want to say I'm pleased with myself. God knows, I still have shortcomings. But I know what I am."

Success didn't prod Bernstein toward growing up. Surviving failure and embracing his own humanity did.

NEVER-MARRIED MEN, PARANURTURERS,
AND LATENCY BOYS

Less often seen are these three patterns.

By all accounts of statistics and studies, men need marriage more than women do. Only five percent of American men over 40 are unmarried. Divorced men remarry sooner than divorced women do. Widowed men remarry much sooner than bereaved women do. And while the number of men choosing to remain single is on the increase among the under-35 population, the ranks of bachelor men beyond that age continue the traditional trend toward thinning out fast.[13]

Older men, in particular, are at a loss to find within themselves a renewal of purpose once the external world has devalued them. Or, as Margaret Mead succinctly puts it, "Men are much more likely to die when they retire, while women just keep on cooking."

The supportive aspects of marriage for men received a high vote in the Harvard Grant Study. (Remember, when Vaillant scored his subjects for overall adult adjustment, a stout 93 percent of the "best adapted men" had made a stable marriage before 30 and stayed with it until 50.)

The myth that marriage offers an equally supportive structure for the development of men and women is dealt a blow, however, when husbands and wives are compared. As everyone knows, women enjoy physical health equal to that of men and better health beyond age 65. But as everyone doesn't know, the mental health hazards suffered by married women are far greater than those of married men. Sociologist Jessie Bernard has brought to light startling evidence on this score. More married women than married men have felt they were about to have a nervous breakdown; more have experienced psychological and physical anxiety; more have had feelings of inadequacy in their marriages and blamed themselves for their own lack of adjustment. More wives show phobic reactions, depression, passivity, and mental health impairment. It is not just a sex difference. For when the mental health profile of wives is compared with that of single women, the married group shows up just as unfavorably.[14]

This leads to the most stunning myth crusher of all. Women without husbands are the frustrated incipient alcoholics washed up by our culture on the island of despair, whereas the free-swinging bachelor is to be envied by all. Correct? Absolutely false.

Psychologists Gurin, Veroff, and Feld report that single women in this country experience less discomfort and greater happiness and appear in most ways stronger in meeting the challenges of their positions than single men. Unmarried men suffer far more from neurotic and antisocial tendencies and are more often depressed and passive. Age only widens the distance between the two.

Between the ages of 25 and 34, there is not a great deal of difference in education, occupation, or income between the single men and single women. But by the time they reach middle age, 46 to 54, the distance between them has stretched to a gulf. The single women are more educated, have higher average incomes, and work in more prestigious occupations. And it is not the old maid but the old bachelor who suffers from the poorest showing of psychological distress.[15]

Occasionally society is the beneficiary of extraordinary gifts from the unmarried man who brings all his talent and energy to bear on a worthy cause. A man like Arthur Mitchell,* whose single absorbing purpose has been to introduce children of his race to classical ballet, is exemplary.

Mitchell left the New York City Ballet Company at the peak of his career to start a ballet school in Harlem for black children, the first of its kind in the country. "Six years ago I was just a dancer. Now I've become an administrator, a moderator, a teacher, a

---

* Mr. Mitchell gave permission to use his real name.

director, a businessman, and most of all, a more aware human being. I am stronger in my conviction that the more you give, the more you get. Most people exist, but they don't live."

It is stretching a point to put Arthur Mitchell in the Never-Married category; he is only 42. But it is interesting to hear how he has become a paranurturer through his work. "I've almost gotten married three times. But it never worked out. When people get married so many things change. People become possessive. All three of the ladies were dancers. It's not fair if you're on the road and consumed with your career, because you can't devote the necessary effort to a home life. With Dance Theater I've gotten so involved, I'm almost a father figure to the kids. Right now, there's just no time to get married. Eventually I know I will. Yes, I would like to have children of my own. But I couldn't have accomplished all this if I had been married. This is a twenty-five-hour-a-day job."

Other men who are paranurturers, such as clergymen and medical missionaries who choose by occupation to care for the family of man, face quite a different crossroad at midlife. Like most women, they have spent their early energies in being responsive to others. What they need now is time for attending to themselves, and time out from being the man with all the answers to become the pilgrim with questions.

The man who devotes the same nurturing and succoring that wives customarily provide their aspiring husbands is a rare bird. But there have been some. Edna St. Vincent Millay's husband gave his time to caring for his emotionally fragile wife so that her talents could be realized. Janet Travell, who was John Kennedy's physician, had a stockbroker-husband who retired at 50. He devoted the rest of his life to driving her on long professional trips and reading to her at night when she was exhausted from overwork.

Some of the most impoverished male lives observed by Vaillant were those who avoided the crisis of identity altogether. Their adolescence was placid, and the *Sturm und Drang* was not engaged at a later stage. The cycle never got under way. They lived out their existences like "latency boys," remaining bound to their mothers, underperforming in careers, and spending little if any time living with a spouse.

INTEGRATORS

If his wife is fretting out a precarious pregnancy, he doesn't wrench her away from all support systems in order to chase a distant career opportunity for himself. He considers the human costs. If his wife is elected town supervisor, he might work part of the time at home so that he can share being there for the kids. If the sweet upward swing of his career requires that he cover for the boss by committing a little white crime, he doesn't tough it out. He resigns. The integrator is a man who tries to balance his ambitions with a genuine commitment to his family and who consciously works toward combining economic comfort with being ethical and beneficial to society.

This is obviously no easy pattern to follow. Not in a country that continually promotes the dangerous fiction that all rewards will come from an external, impersonal acclaim. It usually takes a man some living time to discover that Sunday ethics don't rate bonuses in the Monday-to-Friday world, that no bureaucratic structure will return his loyalty, that the zoom of success exacts its pound of flesh in a cruel professionalism.

Remember Jeb Carter from the One True Couple chapter? At 25, he has the hopes of an integrator: "At one level, I'd like to be the next Edward Bennett Williams. But at another level, I don't have the need to achieve to the extent that I'd overwork myself to get there. More than anything I'm worried about my relationship with Serena, maintaining that at a full level. At the same time I certainly don't want to be an incompetent lawyer." But his choices are naturally still in the conditional tense. And there are no children. It remains to be seen what pattern Jeb will actually follow.

A 29-year-old professional counselor admitted that "I'm still struggling with the Big S and the little s," meaning public success versus private success. "There's a moving tension inside me that I haven't satisfied," he explained. "I worry that I'll get so far into achieving, I'll lost the intimate, feeling side of myself that I'm just getting in touch with. But at the expense of achieving, will I be left behind?"

When I talk to such earnest young men who want to be integrators *now* (but *how*?), I tell them not to flog themselves. It's appropriate in the Age 30 passage to be struggling with the Big S and the little s. It is probably fair to say that a truly integrated life is not possible to achieve before the middle thirties. If this is the pattern desired, it is one to be seeking.

There are many counterforces, however, over which the would-be integrator has little control. By the time the typical man begins wishing for the satisfactions of a more broadly built inner life, he has a great deal of old baggage to unpack. The trip from earliest childhood has prepared him for solving problems based on the math-test model. He has been outfitted for a culture in which feelings are demeaned in favor of fact. In which competitiveness is valued over human interconnectedness. In which rules and systems are to be followed and thinking inventively on one's feet is discouraged. He is desensitized. He is rational. And if the technocracy has succeeded in training him as one of its favorite sons, most of the plugs to his intuition have been pulled.

It is not only the marketplace that militates against a kinetic integration of all one's human capacities. A body of research is evolving that describes a dramatic distinction between the functions of the two hemispheres of the brain.

The left cerebral hemisphere works like a computer. By stringing together linear messages into a logical chain of thought and filtering out sensory messages that don't directly apply to solving the problem at hand, it acts as an abstract deduction center.

The right cerebral hemisphere operates intuitively. It allows a person to link external and internal qualities so that the self can be experienced as interrelated to nature, to others, to the chain of existence. It has the capacity to fantasize, which makes possible leaps of imagination and invention.

All our conventional teaching methods exercise the left side of the brain. Modern management techniques and systems analysis rely on it. The kind of foreign policy that gave us the Bay of Pigs and the Vietnamization strategy is a global extension of it.

The right side is what allows a child to anticipate how a ball would feel when struck by a bat. It is the basis of the intuitive powers we call "street smarts" or "wise in the ways of the land," which allow people to survive in their special ecological medium. The right hemisphere is fluent in using visual imagery and opens the mind's eye to aspects of our surroundings that our linear mind selectively ignores. And it probably is part of what allows the artist to communicate a sense of the universe that would never come out of the best computations of the intellectual.

Suppose a man has surrendered some of his linear thought walls to the mystical awareness of Eastern philosophy. There is still a powerful prejudice against using anything other than the rational half of his brain. Dazzling as are the functions of the right hemisphere, they are ridiculed by our society. As educator and researcher Robert E. Samples points out, they are lumped under the demeaning references to "women's intuition."[16]

"We have found that very often when groups of people do not work well together, the reason is that individuals within the groups do not feel as if they are allowed to communicate ideas that are intuitively and metaphorically meaningful to them," writes Samples. "It does not matter whether we're dealing with corporate vice-presidents and management, teachers and students, husbands and wives or parents and children. Intuition is cast in a lesser role than logic. . . . With such an emphasis on the rational and logical, it is no wonder that levels of 'normal neurosis' are so high."

After a dozen years of working with children whose natural metaphorical thinking strategies have not been weaned out, Samples draws a conclusion very close to one reached by Abraham Maslow shortly before his death: "Human beings reach the highest expressions of their existence when their entire essence as a being is blended into the synergic involvement of all their capacities at once."[17]

Things are changing. Every day swells the tide of men who are trying to shake the habit of competitive climbing up through the narrow grid of the technocracy. They are branching out into endeavors that allow them to be connected to life at many more levels. And the young ones are choosing their partners out of a radically different pool of women. These new pairs will try almost anything to make possible the pursuit of an independent intention by each of them. You find them living in separate apartments, living in different cities, facing realistically the fact that the same place may not be right for both at the same time. It is only those of an older era who are still stunned.

16

WOMEN'S LIFE PATTERNS

"If you could pick any woman of this century as your model, the one whose life you'd most like to have, who would it be?"

The question popped out of a group of people who had gathered together at an ecumenical retreat center to reflect on where they were in midlife. I was supposed to be the expert. It was a few weeks before I finished this book. My mind raced over names— brilliant women, remarkable women, beautiful women —but stopped nowhere.

"Margaret Mead!" one woman declared.

"Oh, no!" This flashed out from an ordinarily quiet minister's wife. A controversy ensued over what was good, what was bad, and what had been left out of Margaret Mead's life.

"Well," I said, "her biography is in the book. I'd love to know what you think after you look it over."

"Who else?"

There wasn't a single reply.

Names like Eleanor Roosevelt, Katharine Hepburn, Coretta King, Rachel Carson, Doris Lessing, Anne Morrow Lindbergh, Georgia O'Keefe, and lots of other names that wouldn't be famous in anybody else's book but are esteemed in mine flitted through my thoughts. Still, I was stumped for an answer. Perhaps I knew too much. None of these women had pursued their dreams or satisfied their heartsongs without giving something else up or without having something cherished taken away.

No one can tell a woman how to make the choice that is best for her. There is no one *right* choice. But today there are more choices and more support for trying them out than ever before in American history. Which also leaves women with the burden of choice.

Think of it this way. Although the Great Depression was an economic disaster that forced many young men into the locked-in position, it also became for other, unmotivated men the great American alibi: "If I hadn't started in the Depression, I wouldn't be stuck where I am today." Similarly, although the confinement of patriarchy kept many women second-class citizens, it also provided airtight excuses: "My husband won't let me; my place is in the home; they wouldn't give me a decent job even if I tried—I'm a woman." (Today, unfortunately, many women feel obliged to explain or defend the decision to be "just a housewife.")

This thing called women's drive for equality cuts across all age, class, and color lines. It has stimulated a flux in all the old patterns. And from out of that flux is emerging a new breed of women. Their guiding commitment is to autonomy. The chief thing is not to *lean*, not to let themselves become dependent. This heartfelt commitment informs all their choices.

But the only women who came fresh upon this idea, who haven't the old baggage of a preliberated era to unpack, are those now in their twenties. We don't know yet where they will come out, what novel patterns may evolve from their declared intentions. I wouldn't be at all surprised, for instance, if the young women of today who are declaring, "No children for me—ever!" will, when they reach 30, produce a minor baby boom.

Three out of five women *under 30*, surveyed by the Roper Organization for Virginia Slims in 1974, spoke up in favor of combining marriage, children, and careers. The same majority preferred divorce to staying with a rocky marriage. They no longer expected to have their cake and eat it too. A majority rejects the idea of alimony in cases where the woman can earn a reasonable income. And only one in four of all the women questioned claims the right of custody should be automatically granted to the mother.[1]

Those are the current attitudes of the middle class. What about the working class? In a recent study of blue-collar wives, the new dream described by the younger woman included returning to work when her two (and only two) children are in school. By then she wants a career more personally rewarding than the utilitarian job she had before marrying. The "capstone of life" as she foresees it will be when her children leave home and so do she and her husband, embarking on a succession of trips to other parts of the world and the pursuit of favorite interests and hobbies.

"This is one of the most significant changes in attitude we have witnessed in more than a quarter of a century," says Burleigh B. Gardner, whose organization, Social Research Inc., has been conducting these studies since the 1940s. "The working class woman will never go back."[2]

One comforting thought to keep in mind is that you can always change your mind, and your pattern. Women have long lives with many seasons.

The most one can do in describing women's life patterns is to report on where various choices have led in the past. All we have to draw upon are the patterns that do have a history. I will try to introduce those patterns in a chronological way, beginning with the most traditional and ending with the more experimental.

Caregiver: A woman who marries in her early twenties or before and who at that time is of no mind to go beyond the domestic role.

Either-Or: Women who feel required in their twenties to choose between love and children *or* work and accomplishment. There are two types:

Nurturer Who Defers Achievement: She postpones any strenuous career efforts to marry and start a family. But unlike the caregiver, she *intends* to pick up on an extrafamilial pursuit at a later point. *Achiever Who Defers Nurturing:* She postpones motherhood and often marriage, too, in order to spend at least six or seven years completing her professional preparation.

Integrators: Women who try to combine it all in the twenties—to integrate marriage, career, and motherhood.

Never-Married Women: Including paranurturers and office wives.

Transients: Women who choose impermanence in their twenties and wander sexually, occupationally, geographically.

Again, the patterns that follow are meant to describe, not prescribe. And again, they are intended to view people dynamically, from the priorities they set when young to the incorporation of other vital aspects of themselves as they move across time.*

THE CAREGIVER

Of all the life patterns possible to set in motion by the choices of the twenties, most women have elected to be caregivers. Theirs is the life of cherishing, succoring, listening to, and believing in other people. They live for human relations and work out any personal ambitions through others.

Rather than pursue her own dream, the caregiver carries the dream of the most promising husband she

---

* Readers will note that this chapter is longer than the one that preceded it. My experience echoed that of U. of Syracuse's Irwin Deutscher in his study of postparental life: "Interviews with husbands were characterized by a lack of emotional quality—of expressiveness. They were not nearly as communicative as their wives. This does not mean that their tendency toward neutral responses was an artifact of the methodology; the impression of the writer (and interviewer) is that it is more likely an artifact of the culture."

can find. That is the signal characteristic of her pattern. She may get on fine this way by being always the compliant one. Many thousands of caregivers will work in a part-time, supplemental way to help along their husbands' careers, or to make enough money to remodel the kitchen. It has nothing to do with "realizing one's full potential in work."

What the caregiver is seldom prepared for is a marker event or life accident that may bump her out into the world in a sink-or-swim way. Husbands, after all, do go off to fight, become prisoners of war, lose jobs, take mistresses, have heart attacks, and leave their caregiving wives in midlife with dismal regularity. Children grow up. All other circumstances remaining felicitous, she will have a difficult time not outliving her husband. Such eventualities seldom figure into the youthful illusions of the caregiver. If someone says, "You really should take your bead-stringing seriously, you might need to support yourself someday," she won't listen.

Just as the caregiver lives for her attachments, she is dependent on her attachments' continuing need for her.

Most of us have mothers who were caregivers. Some of them had full and satisfying lives and then at 50 bopped on out to become hotshot real estate ladies. And some of them, caught unprepared in the momentous sea change wrought by the women's movement, retreated to entrenched positions and made a virtue of defending non-equal rights for women. Most of them did neither—but simply went on as before, cleaning up after the rest of us.

The emergence of a Marabel Morgan was probably inevitable. Once a beauty queen, then a 36-year-old Miami housewife and mother, Marabel Morgan wrote the number-one nonfiction seller of 1974: *The Total Woman*. Although virtually ignored by critics and unknown to most urban women, it found its way through religious bookstores into the hearts and minds of Middle America. In it, Marabel described the age-old problem. After marrying Charlie and expecting the Cinderella story to last forever, she felt helpless when things began to change.

Marabel studied the Bible, Ann Landers, Dr. David Reuben, and collected a set of principles that she applied to her marriage "with stunning results." Here are some quotes from the book:

> It is only when a woman surrenders her life to her husband, reveres and worships him, and is willing to serve him, that she becomes really beautiful to him.

> God ordained man to be the head of the family, its president, and his wife to be the executive vice-president. Every organization has a leader and the family unit is no exception. There is no way you can alter or improve this arrangement.

> Tell him you love his body. . . . Give him one good compliment a day and watch him blossom right before your eyes.

> Adapt to his way of life. Accept his friends, food and life-style as your own.

> Thrill him at the front door in your costume. [Mrs. Morgan's first and "more conservative" costume was pink baby-doll pajamas and white boots.]

> Eat by candlelight, you'll light his candle!

> Be prepared mentally and physically for intercourse every night this week. . . . Be the seducer, rather than the seducee.

> Read the Bible to your children every day.[3]

The results of applying such principles to her marriage were revolutionary, Marabel writes. "Charlie began bringing me gifts at night. . . . A truck pulled up with a new refrigerator-freezer. . . . Now, without being nagged, he was beginning to give me what I yearned for."[4] Marabel was moved to pass on her principles in the Total Woman course (sometimes referred to as the "totaled woman"), which she and her hundreds of alumnae now teach across the country.

Allowing for my own bias, I will make only a brief comment. If there is anything "total" about adhering to these principles, it would be total personal dishonesty. The woman is never told to do or say what she feels or believes, only what she thinks will bring her safety and fabulous kisses and improved kitchen appliances. It insults a man's intelligence. It trains a woman to remain a manipulative child. That may work acceptably for the first half of life. But playacting bodes ill for any truth knowing, and people must be willing to know their own truth if they are to pass into midlife as adults.

Certainly there are caregivers who stay within the pattern but manage to develop as individuals, too. One would think educated women have the best chance. While compiling statistics from a Radcliffe twentieth reunion booklet, I was fascinated to discover that even women who had graduated in 1954 from one of the most prestigious colleges in the country had elected in droves to become caregivers.[5*]

Now 41, many of the caregivers had been brilliant beginners: a world figure-skating champion, a concert pianist, an aide to a setter of foreign policy. But all that was in the brief period known as "Before I Married Your Father," before they were 25. In the act of marrying, most of these brilliant beginners piggybacked their dreams or tried to live them out through their progeny.

The ice-skating champion recites the sports triumphs and golf handicaps of her children, although she has recently taken a job teaching figure skating.

The concert pianist married a violinist and produced babies while he took advanced degrees. "With

---

* Of the 127 respondents who wrote about themselves in any detail, the breakdown of patterns went like this: 70% had chosen to be caregivers, 10% were deferred nurturers, and 8% were achievers who deferred nurturing. Only 6% had tried to be integrators in their twenties, and another 6% had never married.

two infants and limited choice, I didn't have to dwell on whither or what. I gave away my private students, put playpen near the piano, started work on Kirchner Sonata Concertante." At 41 she is now back to a full-time practice schedule.

The foreign policy aide piggybacked her dream by marrying a foreign service officer. She has been traveling in the Middle East as his wife for sixteen years and writes: "If I had it to do over I would have picked the Far East or Southeast Asia—but that would have meant another husband." (And a different piggyback?)

The majority of caregivers found that even though their marriages may have been good, it wasn't enough. Nearly two-thirds of them have by now gone back to school or sought jobs.* The fields toward which most have been drawn are teaching and library and social work, and many of that two-thirds are still looking for jobs. A few of the caregivers came up with imaginative ways to turn their talents into their own businesses (an art gallery, an architectural office) but only a few. The overwhelming majority felt it necessary to go back to school, to train in areas that are extensions of their caregiving skills and in which competition is swelling while the job market is shrinking. The hard data on career opportunities for women returning to work are given in Chapter Nineteen.

But there is another 36 percent of the caregivers who have remained full-time homemakers to the present. They say things like this:

"I've never regretted majoring in history and not having specific training for a job. It remains to be seen if I can convert. . . . Can a 40-year-old woman with a fabulous education and no other specific credentials find a job in a small mid-western city? A meaningful job?"

"I'm lucky I've got a good husband, 2 healthy

---

* Of that two-thirds, seven made the move at age 30, fourteen at age 35, and the largest number, thirty-five, at the age of 40.

children, and through Bob's work I've been to Hawaii and Far West. We visited my folks in Spain last summer. Next year I'd like to learn Spanish since my folks might invite us back."

"Now wish I had devoted some of my energies after graduation to developing a career base. At 40 I discovered I had a well-trained mind, a lot of executive level volunteer experience, and no marketable skills. . . . Acquiring professional credentials should have been part of my goals 20 years ago."

"That's what I've been saying to myself this past year, what are my special interests?"

"The best thing that happened to me at Radcliffe was meeting John at the Freshman Orientation Dance. . . . The thing I'd most like to be when I grow up is a Nader's Raider."

The achievers who deferred nurturing for at least six or seven years, on the other hand, include a pediatrician, a psychiatrist who practices with her husband, a U.S. naval officer who is about to retire and who looks forward to picking up on the friends and community activities she had to put aside, the regional director of an insurance company, a writer of children's books, and a recovered alcoholic who has dedicated her life since 35 to helping others with the same illness.

For all their foment, the most impressive things about these Radcliffe women are their willingness to disclose themselves and their openness to change. Harvard men of the same class, asked to respond to a similar questionnaire, wrote mostly about how they had moved the sales curve forward at Owens-Corning or the like.

Probably the caregiver's greatest fear is of being dumped. But there is also the fear of progressive vegetation. Frequently, the conflict between safety and autonomy does not come to a head until midlife. And then there is a difficult distinction to be made. Has she jockeyed her partner into being the blockade to her growth? Or is he truly an unsatisfactory partner? If that is the case, is a woman in her forties better off with an incompatible, insensitive, or philandering husband, or on her own?

One of the Radcliffe women who has faced all these questions offered to reconstruct her biography with me. By following her through each passage, perhaps we can get a better feel for how the caregiver in particular faces common developmental issues.

Kate's dream all through childhood was to have somebody to talk to at night. Her parents were old. They liked peace and quiet. It was only the three of them in the stillness of Maine. Mother and Father came home from their jobs and had dinner with their only child and retired early. Kate prayed for it to be summer again so she could go away to camp and snuggle down under the covers with other little girls her age and whisper.

In her fifteenth year she invented a big brother out of the boy next door. They talked through their windows in sign language for hours and hours. He knew everything. He went to Harvard. He was Kate's window on the world, without whom she might not have known there were Trotskyites, a Tolstoy, an off-Broadway theater, a place called Radcliffe. When he came home that summer they sat on Kate's porch and put their arms around each other while they talked. Kate's mother called her inside. "You can't see him anymore," she said. "He's too old for you; it doesn't look right." Kate shrieked. It was as if her arms were being ripped out. "You can't do this! He's the best friend I've ever had, and it's perfectly innocent." Mother was adamant. "You must do what I ask," her mother said, "because I'm sick."

It was true. Something was giving way in her mother. Kate had no one to talk to about it. And so she assumed that any day now the woman she knew, who had always been a strong-backed nurse, would be herself again.

Before, they had done things together. Amateur

302

theater and horseback riding and art classes, cherished things of which her father disapproved. Father had been a crusty old bachelor lawyer for hundreds of years before their marriage. It was Mother, having borne Kate at the age of 38, who had taken the girl's upbringing into her own hands. But now Mother's hands felt different when they touched Kate's shoulders. They were thin and dry and meatless.

So Kate gave up her big brother next door. Sitting on the porch alone she brooded and at the same time regretted not having been kinder to her mother. Yet even then Kate still wished she had young, handsome parents and a father who played baseball in the street. Wished so hard, she nearly retched with guilt.

The day her mother died Kate insisted on going to school. She showed no grief; in fact, she performed in a school play. Midterm report cards were passed out. This was a triumph. In the attempt to please her big brother from Harvard, after years of dreary grades, she had pulled five As and a B. She carried the precious card home to her grieving father. He said, "Why did you get a B?" It was not his way to praise Kate to her face.

Filling the loneliness caused by the loss of her mother with an immediate and desperate love, Kate fed on letters from a boy who was away in boarding school. She blew him up into a towering figure. At the time she was also waiting to hear about college. One day she rode her bicycle home from school and found two letters. The first was from Radcliffe; she had been accepted. In a splurge of joy she was ready to jump on her bike and go back to tell the English teacher who was waiting to hear. She stopped just long enough to read the daily letter from her boyfriend. He had met another girl he liked better. She flew back to school and threw herself across the teacher's desk. Thinking the girl had been rejected by Radcliffe, the teacher comforted her with great tenderness. Mute in her displaced grief, Kate handed her the letters.

Not until ten years later, when she saw him again,

did Kate notice that her great love was a small and vapid man. But to this day she has not done the grieving for Mother.

Mother's death did not bring Kate and her father any closer together. He married again a year later, a woman Kate did not like. They moved away from her childhood home to South Portland, where she had no ties at all. From that time on Kate did not consider home as a place she went, except for ceremonial visits. Her search for a surrogate family became more fervent than ever.

At the drama camp where she taught in the summer, a couple almost as dazzling as Lunt and Fontanne came into her life. They were both actors, young, bright, childless, in their early thirties. Campers and counselors alike sat at their feet worshipfully. To Kate, the most wonderful thing about this couple was the way they finished each other's sentences. She worked for them devotedly all through college. The woman was strong. She told Kate, "You must learn to cope and fend." The man encouraged heart-to-heart talks. Hope surged through Kate for a marriage just like theirs. Plus twenty-four children.

One might think, given her history of interest in the theater, that Kate excelled in stagecrafts by now, which she did. And that Kate would aspire to being an actress, which she did not. She was trying to find Mr. Right, a man who would finish her sentences. She wanted a houseful of children so that she would never again be without someone to talk to at night. And so the choices of her twenties were the choices of the caregiver.

In her senior year of college she threw herself madly into love. Shepherd Wells Southby, I shall call him. He was two years older, and he came over from Harvard to join her acting group. Shakespeare himself couldn't have created a more beautiful face to play Hamlet. He took her home to meet his father, who was also dashing, and his family, who formed an unbroken chain of distinguished actors.

This is what I ought to do, she thought, marry into this marvelous family and settle down. Shepherd did not exactly finish her sentences. He corrected her pronunciation. He read to her from Beowulf and from Chekhov—in the Russian. She quit acting. She wanted to be loyal to this man she wanted for a husband, and it was he who saw his destiny on the classical stage. When he performed at Radcliffe, Kate told him he was superb. She was lying. His acting was abysmal.

Many years later, to confess that she knew this makes her feel naked. At the time, she had cast Mr. Southby as perfection, as her safety and protector. Everything had to fit in, she says, and this was the one thing that didn't. She willed it out of her mind. They became engaged.

A year followed during which Shepherd went off to army duty in Europe, leaving Kate to luck into a job with the Garry Moore TV show. She lived in New York exuberantly. There were two engaged roommates and endless friends to share the cooking of endless spaghetti dinners. It was a whole year off from the man-woman focus. She was at last free to have fun.

When Shepherd came home and she had to give it all up, an awkward thought barged through her mind: *That year on my own may have been the happiest point of my life*. But Kate believed in molds. She should be the perfect whatever-my-husband-wants-me-to-be. They went back to Europe together. She became the army wife who always has the cocktail tray ready.

Upon their return to the States, the first people Kate looked up were her surrogate family, the acting couple. She found the wife, depressed and distraught, running the camp alone.

"You don't mean to tell me you didn't know all those years," the wife said. It seems that her husband's custom was to give most female counselors a full sexual initiation and that he had impregnated a dull and witless bunkmate of Kate's. He had left his wife, married the girl, and moved to Scarsdale to nest. The irony was, his first wife had yearned in vain for children. During that earlier season of his life he had told her no, they were actors and they must be free; children tie you down.

The story shattered Kate. It was a moment worse than when her mother died. She remained friends with the actress, and the actress remains for her a powerful and frightening model. She is in her fifties now and directs the whole camp by herself. But as Kate sees it, this "damaged woman" wouldn't notice if a prince fell at her feet. The actress sounds like a woman who is beyond thinking about men, a state of mind Kate cannot fathom.

Kate was only 23 when she heard about the breakup of this perfect couple. The notion that people can change without apparent rhyme or reason was then abhorrent. She erased it from her mind and redoubled her efforts to wear whatever persona her husband desired. But now a confusion began.

Kate was Shepherd's one pass at rebellion. By marrying his idea of a scruffy, wrong-side-of-the-tracks person, he had made an antiestablishment statement to his family. Yet no sooner did he bring Kate back to New York than he set to work upon her metamorphosis. She was to wear hats and carry handbags that matched her shoes. He gave her tiny seed pearls, though she was large of bone like her mother. And there was nothing to hide her broad-toothed country grin. "You must belong to the Colony Club and do charity work," he said. People sometimes mistook her for the help. Her husband left no string unpulled in the effort to get Mrs. Southby into the social register. Kate was humiliated by having her credentials measured against the standards of the social register, which incidentally she had never heard of.

Meanwhile Shepherd went each day to the American Academy of Dramatic Arts, where they crawled around on the floor pretending to be lions. Later he joined a repertory company of unemployed actors who performed Shakespeare to empty houses.

Kate got pregnant on schedule. Two babies came. She adored them and wanted to take care of them herself. Shepherd insisted on nannies in uniform who would push the prams. Dinner had to be at seven sharp. They sat like andirons astride his family's antique chairs. There had to be a dessert. It was a Southby tradition. The Southbys, however, were congenital skeletons, while Kate was forever trying to slim down after some pregnancy or other. But she faithfully made dessert. Everything was as it should be on the surface. About her feelings, Kate held her tongue.

"I always had the feeling I was tagging along. It wasn't true. I don't know why I felt like that. My ego went way down, from the time of having tremendous confidence in myself in college. I slipped too deeply into my husband's frame. It certainly wasn't his fault.

"Then came a moment of epiphany. I was 29 and beginning to have feelings of 'not enough.' I was restless. When I walked into a grammar school to vote—it was so lively and familiar—a wonderful excitement came over me. I said, 'This is something I could do!' I couldn't wait to go to Columbia the next morning and register for a master's program in education."

This is where Kate Southby diverges from the classical response of the caregiver at Catch-30. When she felt the impetus to broaden, she didn't retreat from it to the security of an earlier stage and try to reel her husband back in with her. She acted on it.* Coming out of this passage, after three years of school and the birth of her third and fourth children, Kate was blissfully happy.

"I'd come upon myself as if I were in a dark corner. I can remember looking at myself in the mirror the year I was student teaching. I began to *like* the way I looked. Straight hair and short skirts were in, and I felt

---

* It is important not to confuse Kate's divergence from the classical response with the pattern of the Deferred Achiever who, unlike Kate, *intends* when she marries to pick up on a career.

attractive for the first time in years. I had loved being pregnant, but now that was over. Here I had the husband of my dreams and four gorgeous, healthy, intelligent children. We'd just bought a brownstone. I had a brand new job I was in love with and students who adored me. 'I've made it,' I thought."

Shortly after Kate started the new job teaching at a tough public high school, Shepherd's sister-in-law came to visit. He had been home all day working on a play in verse. The three of them were finishing dinner.

"Where's dessert?" Shepherd demanded.

"I didn't have time to make any," Kate said.

He leaped up and rampaged through the kitchen opening cabinets and banging them shut. "Now that you're teaching, you don't care about me or your family! There's never any butter, there's never any dessert."

His sister-in-law sat at the table saying, "Look, I never eat dessert, I want to get thin. Nobody wants dessert."

Shepherd stormed off to the bedroom.

Their guest, who was in the process of getting a divorce, gave Kate a piece of advice, "You know, he's going to leave you. You'd better quit teaching." Kate thought she was crazy.

During the next couple of years Kate's husband threw other fits. She made ever-ascending efforts to keep the fridge glutted with butter and the Bavarian cream gelling while she went to school; it blew over. Nonetheless, at 35 she began to have odd but persistent apprehensions. Whenever Shepherd took a plane trip, she was afraid it would crash; an ambulance siren meant that one of her children had been run over. Guilt weighed particularly heavy because she didn't *have* to work. Shepherd never earned a dime, but he did have a trust fund.

During a bitter New York City school strike, Kate, being one of the dedicated teachers who continued without salary to hold classes, introduced what she thought was her best innovation. A group of black seniors was having trouble reading Shakespeare, and they had to pass an exam on the subject in order to enter the practical nursing program. Kate translated *Macbeth* into street prose.

"You shouldn't be *allowed* to be a teacher," Shepherd shouted. He gave her a scalding lecture and left the house in disgust, to perform one of the classics with a church group. There was no mistaking his open hostility to Kate's job by now. It soon hardened into a stone wall. And then Shepherd turned 40.

Out of the blue, he changed. He grew a ponytail and began wearing Indian *kurtas*. He turned against his charm, his good looks, the classics. He switched to open theater and became a resident actor with a radical SoHo group. At home he sat cross-legged and meditated. He told Kate she could be reborn, too, if she would sit cross-legged with him and stare at the flame. She sat and stared and thought about running out of butter.

Even then, she wanted to make herself over into an image that would please her husband. He was saying, in effect, "You can only be reborn by my methods." But the notion that she could change her personality at will, which seemed quite possible in the twenties, no longer worked. She had to tell her husband, "I'm sorry, but you can't fake something like this." He began spending nights with a "spiritual partner," a woman who told him he was Gielgud, Burton, and Brando rolled into one. His absences became more frequent and lengthy.

Kate became pregnant. Shortly thereafter, her husband left for good. She had an abortion. She felt a total failure.

Kate lost herself for two years. "I was in very bad shape, and no one knew it. I tried to tell people but they wouldn't believe me because there I was—coping. I felt like an amputee. I would look at the little creatures without arms and legs who roll themselves down Madison Avenue on carts, and I'd say, 'Sure, they're functioning. But their arms and legs are not going to grow back. Neither are mine. What's left is going to be brave and strong, but I will always be a cripple.'"

She took in a housemate, a man who loved family outings and had little ambition. They lived together for two years as if they had been married for a hundred. One night an old friend of Kate's in publishing came for dinner. "It's wonderful to see you so happy," he said. Her rage boiled up: *Doesn't he see that I'm in limbo, that this is not me?* The next thought was more sinister. If she was making it appear it was good this way to everyone else, maybe she was making herself believe the lie.

But the two years had not been fraudulent; they were a gathering-in time. That night (Kate was 40) she decided to give up teaching. She told her housemate, "What I want to do is go to work in publishing. And it's probably going to take me five years to become an editor." He was intimidated by her decision to join the rat race. She knew it meant they would go separate ways. But all these changes, to her amazement, put virtually no strain on Kate. Unconsciously, she had been doing the inner preparatory work for two years.

Going back to work as a 40-year-old woman was hard, she says. (She didn't consider teaching "work" because it was an extension of her mothering role.) She knew nothing about publishing and became an assistant in the contracts department. But Kate was revved up, in another gear altogether. At night she read manuscripts for as many editors as would let her. She trained herself to read a 300-page book in a night, learned how to judge a manuscript and write a tight report. After only one year, she was made an editor.

The intense concentration on learning a new lifework and stabilizing around it has relaxed now. Kate is a cheerful, skillful, pretty, and unpretentious woman, a grown-up, although she doesn't quite believe it yet. There is still the lingering sense that a woman is not quite whole without her attachments.

"I can't use the children as an excuse anymore. It doesn't matter now if I come home for dinner or not. They're perfectly able to take care of themselves. They're 17, 15, 11, and 9. They come and go; they don't need Mommy, which scares me a little. I've always had that.

"What frightens me now is that I could just get out of the habit of being with a man. Because I'm not crying in my pillow the way I was two or three years ago. I'm not in despair. And I really like going home to the children a whole lot better than when I was teaching. The evenings go by quickly. A friend now and then, I practice the piano, I cook dinner, I talk to the kids, read manuscripts, go to bed. And I could just go on doing that for years."

Kate would still rather be with Mr. Right. But no matter what she had done, her husband's midlife crisis could not have been prevented. He was a man who never challenged his family destiny or confronted his own identity until he felt pronounced a failure at 40. If she had quit teaching, she would have been around all the time to watch her husband being a failure. And if she hadn't followed her own impulse to expand at 30, she would probably have ended up not only dumped but bitter and disabled in seeking any function beyond the domestic one.

At some point, every caregiver must learn to care a little more for herself.

Either-Or

When studies are conducted on women's early choice patterns, about half of the respondents usually fall into the either-or camp. These are the women who believe they can implement only one aspect of their self-concept at a time: Either I put off any strenuous career efforts while I marry and start a family, in exchange for the dependable affection of a mate. Or I stick faithfully to outfitting myself for a career, postpone marriage and motherhood, and resign myself for the time being to scraps for affection. At some point most women feel required to choose either love and children *or* work and accomplishment. If a man were presented with such a choice, would there be any husbands?

THE NURTURER WHO DEFERS ACHIEVEMENT

Her way of coping with the either-or dilemma is to defer or suppress the part of herself that yearns to seek a professional place in the world. But if she is one of the women who follows this pattern, eventually it will come back into play. Because of the identity diffusion that so often characterizes the early part of this pattern, the nurturer has a great deal of inner preparation to do before she can pinpoint her outer goals. Vagueness and apprehension are to be expected at that time.

Betty Friedan demonstrates this pattern in spades. She had an exquisite education at one of the top institutions, distinguished herself by graduating *summa cum laude,* then got married and moved to the suburbs to have babies. Although she had genuine feeling for her four children, she found that a large part of herself was frozen out of existence, but she couldn't imagine even at 35 how to put it into effect.

If anyone doubts the difficulty of bringing a suppressed aspect of the self back into play, Friedan makes an astounding confession:

"It was easier for me to start the women's movement than to change my own personal life."[6]

An unforgivable disservice was done to women who were promised pie in the sky later if they were good little role fillers now, meaning for fifteen or twenty years. The hypocrisy was that most of the articles in the housewives' magazines which made such vague promises, telling the deferred achiever she could always "pick up" on her schooling or career later, were written by women who had not dropped out. It is not hard to imagine why some of the angriest middle-aged women around today were the intellectual girls of the 1940s.

Charlotte was such a woman, and this was the set of directions she bought: She should finish college, marry, but postpone children while she finished graduate school. Toward the end of her twenties, she should begin having her children and take ten years out. Around 40, she would be ready to reenter her field.

The catch was this: By the time *she* was ready, the field had moved light years beyond her grasp. Theories and methods in any academic discipline change too fast in a decade for anyone to refresh himself quickly. She found she could only reenter her field at a demeaning level, as an assistant instructor with a teaching load of seven hours a day. It was too late to launch any serious research project from which she might have published the work that gains one entrance into the academic hierarchy. Not only did she face a punishing ego loss, she wasn't earning much more than her housekeeper. While her contemporaries who did remain current are now being given chairs at universities, in their fifties, Charlotte is still trying to catch up.

If only she had had a wife.

How about volunteer work? Not appreciated. Running a home and raising wonderful children? Not considered a contribution. A woman can't collect unemployment insurance for losing her job as a wife (hence, the continuing campaign to save the right to alimony). If she rides it through to widowhood without taking an outside job as well, the wife will be told she made no contribution to her husband's estate. It will be taxed at the highest level. If the Internal Revenue Service were to tally up, say, twenty-five years of her in-home service at the current rate of comparable services on the open market ($793 a week) that would come to a contribution of $1,124,500.[7]

Did we multiply right? A wife worth over a million dollars? It couldn't be. Our tax structure tells us what we really value. And it isn't the social contribution of being a lovely wife and mother.

Does housework, then, have any redeeming psychological value? Nervousness, insomnia, heart palpitations, headaches, dizziness, fainting, nightmares, trembling and perspiring hands, and above all, inertia. Housewives suffered more from every one of these symptoms of psychological distress than did working women, according to data collected by the Department of Health, Education, and Welfare in 1970. Only in having felt an impending nervous breakdown did women with outside jobs suffer more than women who did housework. But more of the housewives had actually experienced nervous breakdowns.[8]

Some of the injustices done the nurturing woman are now being corrected by continuing education programs that give credit for life experience, by reforms in the pension law, and by affirmative action programs. And just in time, because now it is not just middle-class women demanding a fuller life. Blue-collar wives and welfare mothers are, too.

When all the family life cycle statistics are put into the hopper, the message that comes out is that motherhood is a phase. A contemporary mother can expect to bring her last child into the world well before she has grazed the surface of adulthood: by the age of 30. And with some private mixture of heartache and relief, she will watch that last babe board the school bus when she is 35.[9]

Then what? Invigoration? Panic stations? Procrastination?

Melissa gave up her work fifteen months after the wedding ceremony. Not forever, it was understood, but for now. She had decided to stay home and have a baby to "make the marriage work." She felt her full attention was required to smooth out any problems. Particularly since, in Melissa's life, there was little precedent for facing problems.

Orange groves, peach orchards, mimosa and boysenberries . . . she had been raised in a small fruited Eden near the Pacific where she had her parents all to herself. (Except for her brother, who rebelled.) She went on trips and to sophisticated parties with her parents. Mother said she was the perfect child. The change was abrupt, then, when Melissa took herself across the country to a college in New England. "It was small and quaint and beautiful and I adored the college itself. But I was a wreck. I cried. After a year and a half I couldn't stand it any longer. I came back." She enrolled at UCLA, a trade-off for the voluptuous comforts of living at home again. She had no desire to strike out on her own until the standard fantasies culminated in her wish, at 22, to "play house."

Her parents were too generous to say they disapproved of the husband Melissa chose to complete her fantasy. He was a television actor who did soaps and series. In them he played support to the supporting actors or else a Mexican who gets shot off his horse. The rest of the time he stayed home and drank. He was not secure.

Their first child became the focus of intense competition. Armed with the latest books and implements, each of them attacked the child's thumb-sucking and head banging, determined to prove competency as the best parent. After five years together the word *divorce* had to be deliberately kept out of their conversations.

"Let's keep on trying," she always said.

"You're scared to do it, and I'm scared to do it," he pointed out.

"That's right." She tried to will herself into loving him. Anything was better than the uncertainty of the unknown.

They made other arrangements: first-name-only liaisons with tennis instructors and the like. Melissa had a second baby. This reinforced still further the "impossibility" of their splitting up. Was the ruse obvious? Of course.

Even Melissa's mother saw it. "Why, lots of women with children get remarried," she told Melissa. "The right man wouldn't mind."

After seven years the situation came to a head, although the couple never openly discussed it. In private, Melissa felt a dramatic change of tone: "Why remain? I'm itchy to get back to work. And I really do want my independence. I'll never get married again."

The couple moved down from the isolated hills to a small rented house not six blocks from Melissa's mother. Here the children easily found playmates, and Melissa cultivated a network of single friends. The moment she received word that her husband had found himself a serious remarriage prospect, she staged the showdown: "Out! Good-bye!"

Only then did Melissa realize that she had been a solid year in preparation for this moment. She was 29, and feeling all the expansiveness of the Age 30 passage.

"His leaving was like a lifting off of weights. I never had a tear about it after that day. A tremendous change took place. I went out and bought books, enrolled in classes at UCLA, had my hair cut, had my first smoke. I began dating like crazy. My mother was always coming around to help me out, transferring meat from her freezer to mine. She didn't want me to spend my savings. It was the happiest time of my life. I felt so promising. No, more than that, I felt reborn."

One has to wait to seek Jake. He is a deliriously busy man, a movie agent. We are supposed to be talking about his second marriage. The speaker box on his desk keeps drawing him into the daily round of deal making, which if you want to know the truth, he finds more exciting. He smokes a tightly held cigar and talks in blurts.

"I sent the script over. It's terrific, terrific. They want Paul for that? Who's talking to who? Shit. I was talking to Antonioni about it. Chances? Fifty against ten. Listen, I'm going to be in Cannes too. Can I call Paul?"

Jake explains he is like a doctor, in demand twenty-four hours a day. "Someone always wants more time. My clients or my wife or kids. I've been thinking a lot lately about the balance." He is disquieted too about his wife's being—how to say it?—in a rut. "She doesn't work. And I'm sure she's frustrated. She spends a lot of time with her children."

At home, Melissa sounds confused. Wasn't she the one who felt reborn after her divorce? The one who declared, "I'll never get married again. I really do want my independence." She might have taken up horticulture at UCLA or opened a car wash or packed the kids into a van to explore the Mayan ruins.

Six months after her swan dive into the world she had married Jake.

"After our third date I knew we were in love. I stopped calling all my old friends. I moved totally into Jake's life, his friends, his places. My whole personality changed. I became more and more like him. He gave me a lot of strength. I was so weak and frightened. All I wanted to do was learn how to be Mrs. Jake Pomeroy."

If her husband mentioned the Civil War, she rushed to the library for an illustrated history. If he talked about a deal, she read the contract; a movie, she read the script. "Whatever he wanted me to be, that was the way I was going to be."

It was so much easier. It finished off for the next five years any unreliable notions she might have had about the independent life.

Melissa's step-style has been consistent. Each time she breaks out of dormancy at home, she feels vitalized. It happened when she crossed the country and found the college quaint and beautiful. No sooner did she experience the first hot spurts of independence than the pull back to home became overpowering. After seven more years of dormancy, she vacated the marriage that she saw as what was restricting her.

There was a gush of animation, a few tremors, and she ducked back into the first hopeful safety zone. This time, she "took over" her husband's life, moving into his dream so completely that she excused herself from the tasks of development which are her own.

Now she is 34, and the pinch has returned. This time, it is beginning to take on the character of a major crisis. "I feel totally bombarded. By children, housekeepers, husbands, friends, telephones, televisions. I'd give anything in the world to have my privacy again. Just to be alone. The way I was after my divorce, that was the happiest time of my life."

This is not to suggest that Melissa has any desire to undo her present marriage. What she is longing for is the courage to loosen up on the strings that tie her security to her husband and children.

"I can start now," she says doubtfully. "Yes, a crucial time is coming up in my life. This summer my children will be going away for a month with their father. It's a big test for me, whether I'm going to sit home and weep about that separation or start thinking about what direction to take when I go back to work. If I can get through that month, then I'll be completely happy."

A car honks outside. The children's Sunday afternoon father is here. "Good-bye, my angels," Melissa sighs. The children march out the door like prisoners of war.

She is alone now with the suitcases and the phones. The suitcases make her feel guilty because she has packed them to go to Cannes with her husband. This will be their first trip together. Jake had to battle her into it. "I know logically I'm supposed to be with my husband," she says. "My kids are going to leave me one day anyway, and you only have one husband. But emotionally, I've never been able to take myself away from those children. I keep thinking, *What if they don't want to come back to me?*"

The phones arouse a different response. Frustration. They are all over the house. His phones. In the den, the bedrooms, the kitchen. An endless orgy of extension cords that wind their white arms around her husband the moment he comes home, embrace him at three in the morning with calls from overseas, stroke him all weekend with pleas for help from his clients—the important people. There are times when she thinks she would have more communication with him if she were a telephone operator.

The burning question at the center of Melissa's life has turned up again, but now the flame is high. She is almost 35. "How does a woman find her own identity outside of marriage without jeopardizing it or her children? I really don't know a woman my age who isn't going through this right now."

This is the central question for all nurturing women who postpone their own expansion. Each passage raises the issue anew, and if it is not resolved, eventually the pilot light goes out, and something begins to foul the air.

Melissa is typically vague about where to begin. "Just this year I've decided," she says brightly, "now it's my turn. I want so much to go back to work. I'm still trying to get to that point. I'm going to a therapist now because of it."

Without pause or notice, Melissa slips in another postponement. "*Next* year, I'm going to go out on my own."

One of the compelling features of sharing one's days with a growing child is that at every step, the adult is vividly reliving his or her own childhood experiences. The unsatisfied wishes, rivalries, unrequited love, fears, and frustrations that the adult knew as a child and never completely put to rest are revivified through the new child. This is a process commonly known and accepted by psychiatrists. But since many couples are unaware of it, they can be led into blind fights with each other that are in reality duels with their own phantom parents. At the same time, though, this ventilation process of reliving childhood experiences through their own child gives the parents an

319

opportunity to work through old angers and wounds, to "make it better."

With such a convenient and comforting outlet at hand, many mothers are reluctant to leave their children's side. The explanation they give will sound maternal, even sacrificial. "I intended to go back to work this year, but now I see my children just aren't ready to give me up yet."

A 40-year-old woman I know has been saying this for years, and her choice seems to bring her great contentment. Her own childhood was a nightmarish vigil of waiting for her alcoholic mother to die, which she did, gruesomely. It would seem that the daily catharsis of experiencing her own children's secure existence plays a large part in keeping her at home.

It is not only the mother with a traumatic background who finds comfort in reliving her experiences through her children. When Melissa says, unconvincingly, "I really want to go back to work, just this year I've decided," and then immediately gives herself an extension, "*Next* year I'm going to go out on my own," what really comes through is her wish to prolong the beatific unity of her own childhood. Melissa's parents made themselves such an enveloping sanctuary that she had little motive for striking out after independence. Each time she did, Mother was there filling up her freezer or her bank account. How could she possibly improve on this cloistering, or even retain it, if she claimed her place as an adult? Melissa's step-style was shaped by the attentiveness of her parents. Her wish is always to go back to that, bask in it, to remain the indulged and never difficult child.

And so the cycle may repeat itself. Lavished with attention as the center of a close nuclear family, the indulged child grows up and recreates the sanctuary, becoming a parent who finds it unbearable to leave the children and who may bequeath those children the very same burden of dependency.

When the twice-married Melissa extemporizes on how she would design her life if she had it to do over, what comes out is her envy for the opposite choice. "The lucky ones are the women who already had their careers established when they got married and had a child later in life. That's what I would do. Have a career, absolutely. And get married at 28."

As it happens, Melissa hit the magic age right on the nose.

THE ACHIEVER WHO DEFERS NURTURING

Among 1,500 achievers randomly selected from several editions of *Who's Who of American Women,* slightly more than half have married. But first, once they had their bachelor's degrees, they devoted an average of seven years' undivided attention to their careers.[10] The seven-year cycle reveals itself again.

What body of research into life experience can we offer such women as they grope toward their totality? Lamentably little. Biographers have always been eager to dig up the personal remains of imperial queens and movie queens, as well as of women of accomplishment in the arts and sciences, to present us with the aberration. But the achieving woman who defers nurturing has not been included in developmental studies of the adult years, and the models are few.[11]

Women holding executive-level positions are about as hard to find as men at home with chicken-poxed children. Of the 27.8 million Americans who in 1973 earned $10,000 or more, fewer than ten percent were women.[12]

In 1975 a New York consulting firm reported the results of a nationwide search in 2,000 industrial concerns for women who had two years of experience as managers and were earning a minimum of $20,000 a year. They found forty women answering such a description.[13]

The only thorough examination of female achievers in the commercial world, as far as I know, was undertaken by a professor of business administration as the subject of her doctoral dissertation at Harvard (1970). Margaret Hennig combed *Who's Who in America, Who's Who of American Women,* and the annual reports of the top 500 corporations. She found 100 women who hold positions as presidents or vice-presidents of large business and financial corporations. She traced the lives of twenty-five of them, and her findings are fascinating.[14]

All these women saw marriage and career as an either-or choice. They chose to reach for more than the traditional woman's role would allow and in their twenties put aside most of their romantic yearnings. Hennig set out to learn whether that was a fixed character type, the stock figure of woman as male copy, or a developmental stage that might lead to a resolution later on.

Every one of her subjects enjoyed the position of being the firstborn child. They liked being girls and objected only to people saying there were certain things girls didn't do. Their fathers, however, encouraged them to resist such constraints. This clear and early conflict between the culture's instructions and the freedom encouraged at home, Hennig observed, figured largely in the formula that brought these women to success.

In early adolescence they resisted the Oedipal loop that would have sent them back to identification with their mothers. They envied the more active and exciting existence of men. Hennig observes that the envy phenomenon here did not seem fraught with any murky Freudian fears. It was the straightforward desire of human beings who had enjoyed early experiences of freedom and wanted to retain that freedom all their lives.

None of their mothers had particularly magnetic personalities. They were classic caregivers who tried to teach their daughters to be the same. When those daughters entered the crucial period between 11 and 14, they resisted being turned into "young ladies," moved away from their mothers, and found their fathers to be the port in the storm. But there is no evidence that the fathers treated their little girls *as* boys. Instead, a unique element was described by all the subjects in the dynamic between father and daughter. The relationship transcended both of their sexes.

The fathers did not in any way reject the femininity of these girls. They did emphasize skills and abilities rather than any sex role. It was common for the two to play tennis or sail together and to talk about Dad's business. One has the feeling these men were seeking in their daughters the comradeship they couldn't have with their more limited wives. The Bardwick study of successful men (described in Chapter Fifteen) might explain it. Although their wives were definitely expected to be noncompetitive and nonachieving, the men took pride in a competitively successful daughter. Such a daughter is often the favorite because she, unlike a son, can reflect well on him without becoming a rival. And encouraging her will not mean losing the services of a wife.

When Hennig's outstandingly successful women were questioned about the family romance, the very notion that they might have had to rival their mothers for their fathers' attentions struck them as foreign. Their mothers were felt to be no threat at all. Dad had been won over years before.

The relationship between father and daughter remained constant throughout the tempest of adolescence: Their fathers confirmed the girls' self-worth and became their chief source of rewards.

All Hennig's subjects went to college, and all but one chose a coeducational university, preferring to be educated in a profession-oriented environment and in the company of men. Half majored in business or economics, presumably influenced by their fathers as occupational role models; only a few chose liberal arts. They excelled academically. Three years after graduation, they were secretaries or administrative assistants either in manufacturing, retailing, banking, public relations, or service companies. Most of these positions were created as favors to their fathers.

As distinct from the male wunderkind, these women did not company-hop with a roving eye toward maximizing opportunities. It was clear to them that a woman could advance only by proving herself more skilled than any man available for the job above hers. And since it took enormous effort to establish good working relationships in one company, they felt it would be wasteful to move to another. So they were impressively loyal. Over the next thirty years, every one of them remained with the same firm until they were rewarded with a top management position.

It never occurred to them as young women that marriage and children might have to be forfeited forever. But around the age of 25, Hennig observes, all of them "stored their femininity away for future consideration." Although most of them had dated regularly up to that time, they now took care to limit themselves to married or unattainable men, and allowed little or no room for expression of their sexual desires.

One deep and vital attachment was formed by all these women in their twenties: to the boss, who took over where their fathers left off. Once in the protective custody of this mentor, each of the subjects subordinated all other relationships to it. The repetition of earlier experiences was plain. The mentor was one person she could dare to reveal all her sides to, and he, like the father, supported her and cheered her on. When he was promoted, she was promoted along with him at his request.

All these women remained dependent upon their mentors until they reached middle management and the watershed age of 35.

Thirty-five! Time had suddenly caught up with them. Exceptional as their accomplishments were, they realized they had little else in life but the job. The edge of challenge had worn off. At the same time, they felt more secure in their professional stature than they had ever dared imagine. When they took a close look at the Big Mentor-Little Me relationship, many of the women were astounded to discover it had evolved into an association of peers. The carpet beneath them was kicking up in every corner. Those sticky feminine questions that had been previously swept under it would no longer be ignored. An accounting was imperative, for now the issue had come to crisis.

Their explanations of the crisis always had to do with biological age: "I suddenly realized that if I was going to have children, I had a limited period of time to do it." The biological boundary line did not turn out to be the real issue, however. It was simply the motivator. The real issue was, "What happened to that piece of me I left behind and intended to pick up in five or seven years? It's now 15 years."

The consistency with which these women chose to handle their midlife crisis is truly remarkable. All twenty-five took a moratorium for a year or two. They continued to work, but much less strenuously. With devil-may-care exuberance they all did things like buying flirtatious new wardrobes and having their hair restyled. They let themselves have fun again and freed time to enjoy the sexual part of their beings.

Almost half the women married a professional man they met during this period. Their nurturing side came into play too. Though none had natural children, all those who married became stepmothers.

The other half apparently did not meet anyone they could marry; when this momentous change caught them by surprise, they had literally no social life. But the fact of marrying or not marrying proved to make little difference. The women who remained single, no less than the others, realized they could not go on without making a basic shift in emphasis. They, too, became more outgoing, more responsive to people, and often, for the first time, were willing to become mentors themselves.

Two years or so after their moratoria, all the women recommitted to a goal of working toward top management. But their behavior and sense of self had undergone a profound change. They weren't acting a stock part in some early Joan Crawford film anymore. Their exchanges with people had become more honest and spontaneous. Where formerly they had felt segmented, they now began to feel more nearly integrated. And instead of describing themselves as they did in earlier stages, as "satisfied" or "rewarded," for the first time they all added the word "happy."

"It was never a simple case of what others did to them which made so much conflict in their lives," Hennig concludes, "but very much a case of what they did with the duality within themselves. Clearly, this process was made more difficult . . . because of societal and cultural attitudes about women who seek executive careers. Yet it was much easier for them to find ways to avoid those external conflicts than to overcome their internal ones."

A not-so-happy ending awaited a control group of women who got frozen in middle management. When Dr. Hennig compared them to the major research group, she found that the parental situation had been very different: These fathers had treated their daughters not *like* they might have treated a son, but as sons. Their femininity was virtually denied; some were even called by boys' names. As they moved up in occupational life, these women formed only "buddy" relationships at work. Perhaps most important, they never allowed themselves a crisis, not even in midlife. Whatever gates had been latched inside they left latched. None married. This group tended to remain dependent on their mentors until the mentors dropped them. They did not proceed to the top, but arrived in their fifties lonely as women, second-best as executives, feeling bitter and cheated as people. It was the businesswomen who did bring to the surface in midlife an emotional, sexual, and nurturing side that had been left behind who easily outgrew their mentors shortly thereafter, broke out of middle management, and went on to the president's or vice-president's chair and a triumph of personal integration.

A more promising variation of this pattern is being chosen by some young deferred nurturers of today, Margaret Mead's daughter among them. Such women make every effort to gain a confident professional footing first, although they are not exclusively career-oriented. Next they try riding the seesaw of marriage until both partners learn something about balancing mutuality with individuality. Only then do they have a child, which usually means waiting until they are around 30. They are young women who know something about what has happened to people in life.

Obviously, the bright young achievers of today face fewer inner and outer obstacles than did women who tried to launch careers in darker decades and who were often misshapen by ridicule for being unmarried. They were confined almost entirely to male models and male mentors. Whatever fresh inspiration their femaleness might have brought to business and politics was for the most part lost, lest they be backed into the female stereotype and labeled "too emotional."

The fervent sisterhood abroad in the land today has committed many already successful women to being mentors for their eager juniors. Only equality will tell us what values women leaders might bring to bear on the shape of civilization. "And we will have equality," as president of the Association of Women in Science Estelle Ramey says, "when a female schlemiel moves ahead as fast as a male schlemiel."[15]

Now about the deferred side: What happens when the achiever lets her suppressed desire to nurture come through? It produces some of the most ecstatic moms to be found in the female population.

The publicist I've mentioned before, who traveled around the country in her twenties glowing with proofs of her skillfulness, found herself "bowled over" at 29 when an older man proposed. "In the past ten years I've packed in six children, including twins," she says with a broad smile. "It hasn't buried my identity; it's brought a lovely balance to it. Now I'm beginning to get itchy to do my own thing again. Having a business background makes me empathize with the career pressures on my husband. Frankly, I can't see how marriages survive where the wife hasn't worked." There is a noticeably unhurried self-assurance about this woman. When she talks about what she intends to do with the next season of her life (work part-time until the baby enters school and then take over client relations for her husband's firm) one has no doubt she will do it.

Another achiever who waited even longer to give birth, says with gusto, "It's a great joy to have your first baby in the mid-thirties. I will never have to look at a child and say, 'If it weren't for you.'"

And that brings us to an even more rarified group of women within this pattern, those we will call:

LATE-BABY SUPERACHIEVERS

Among women who are remarkably and visibly accomplished, a significant number did not become mothers until they were 35 or over, Margaret Mead, Barbara Walters, Shana Alexander, and Sophia Loren among them. Some chose postponement. Others had problems conceiving, physical, psychological, or a mysterious combination of both. In any case this places them in a very special position within the chain of generations. The woman whose own menopause will coincide with her daughter's puberty will have a strikingly different self-concept from the woman whose nest is emptying at that time.

If I must select one biography to illustrate the quintessential woman achiever, it must be the one that first comes to almost every American mind: Margaret Mead.

She has done it all. Sought high adventure in Samoa in her twenties, endured malaria and miscarriages and found enlightenment on the Sepik River in her thirties, cooperated in three marriages and an extraordinary joint household before she turned 45. She has studied seven cultures and written nineteen books, preserved fifty years of field notes on primitive cultures before their missionization, taught 2,500 students, needled conventional wisdom at hundreds of conferences, and mastered the four-minute attention span of TV talk-show fans. She has had a child, had a grandchild, had three husbands, written her autobiography.

At five in the morning, curly head bobbing, she is already pounding the portable typewriter on her dining room table. Getting the job done. She needs less sleep these days. She is only 74.

Mead is the General among the foot soldiers of modern feminism. Among all of us who have paid a price for liberation—those who lost or left husbands, those who gave birth to themselves as professional women at the cost of not having children, the runaway wives who did not find their latent genius baking clay in Big Sur, and certain celebrity feminists who from time to time, bored and spent with their sexual athleticism, confess to craving one night of zest with an unregenerate male chauvinist pig—among these minions there is still no one quite as self-liberated as Mead. In her general's role she is a prophet in her own country. As a woman she was a deviant in her own culture. She had it all figured out more than fifty years ago.

A first and wanted child, Margaret Mead tells us in her autobiography, *Blackberry Winter*, that it was her father who defined her place in the world. He was a conservative professor at the University of Pennsylvania who held the conviction that the most important thing any person could do was add to the world's store of knowledge. Mead also observed as a girl that her mother's career as a sociologist was limited by the number of children she had, a decision she left up to the Lord and which left her filled with passionate resentment about the situation of women.

Given such classically fertile soil for the germination of an achiever, Mead's own gift for assessing the lay of her culture's land guided her to break new ground once "it became perfectly clear both that bright girls could do better than bright boys and that they would suffer for it."[16] She extended this insight into her anthropological field choices and decided not to compete head on with men in male fields. She uncovered instead two areas in which women can do field projects better than men. One, which she accomplished by twice marrying anthropologists, was to work as a male-female pair, her area the study of women and children. The other was to work with both sexes as an older woman, "using a woman's postmenopausal high status." Thus Mead designed a life that would not make a woman a prisoner of her sex or of her age.

I asked the woman who is now mythologized how she had fit together her many lives. "You certainly had to make some sacrifices and compromises along the way," I suggested.

"Yes. For my generation, to have even one child and a career took a tremendous amount of energy. Which I had. Or a tremendous amount of money or a tremendous amount of luck. I have enough energy to do two jobs. And I understand the culture well enough to study and, in a sense, to outwit it."

She went on to talk about the cheapest schooled labor in the world: a wife. It stirred a recollection of Dr. Mead on the lecture circuit tossing off the line: "American women are good mothers, but they make poor wives." I later asked her why.

"Americans are very poor at being attentive to anybody else," she began. "American women have been strong, fair, taken the rough with the smooth. But a good wife, if you make a career of it, is anticipating the needs of another, being ready to take care of him when he comes home. Any man who has something important to do, an educator or a political figure, for instance, needs a full-time wife to make it possible."

How could so traditional a view possibly relate to her own experience?

"We ought to cultivate people who enjoy devoting their lives to other people—to husband or children—and who really enjoy it." It was the General speaking again.

There is no doubt that Margaret Mead is deeply moved by children. Her lectures are peppered with an angry concern for the abandoned victims of deserting middle-aged husbands and the newer runaway wives. The responsibility for the children is shifting to society, she warns, which isn't accepting it.

Yet in seven years of knowing Dr. Mead, I have puzzled over what educates her emphatic pronouncements on American family life. Up front we hear the General. With the highest purpose and a scorching humor, she surveys the follies of our ways of loving, housing, working, birthing, and driving fatal wedges between the generations. Her mind is intent upon moving the human battalions around and regrouping them in a healthier configuration: in multigenerational communities where the aged and childless would have access to children and all her legions would feel a stake in the future. Why don't her legions follow?

Mead has very little patience with people whose capacities are impaired by wrestling with their private hells. She has conquered her own or ignored them. Why can't the minions march briskly out of their barbarous suburbs over the bones of their charred marriages, gather up their freaked-out children, admit the nuclear family was an experiment in disaster, and get on with the job done right? What is holding them back? Not being Margaret Mead, of course. But clear as the answer is to an admiring observer, it is ever a mystery to Mead herself. An incident several years ago struck me with how great is the distance between the General and the grunts.

Our paths crossed one evening in the living room

of an educator who seemed less than content with her lot as a woman. She told me the story of her marriage to an eccentric. I knew him, a creative man both charming and infantile. The educator had invested twenty years in being "the complex auxiliary" to her husband. He left her on the brink of middle age. She staggered about in disbelief for a few years, then listlessly brought her schoolgirl credentials up to date, and by this time held an important position in a university.

Nevertheless, I sensed that the woman had been not so much liberated into her new career as stunned into it. Dr. Mead had known the couple for many years. Her perception of the situation, I discovered, was very different from mine.

On the way home with Margaret Mead, I remarked, "It's sad, but I think she still feels incomplete without a man."

"What does she need a man for!" Margaret Mead turned to me, stiffening with incredulity. "She works with men. They all respect her. She has established her own university department and is busy all the time. And don't forget, she's still a mother."

I said I didn't know if the woman was aware of her husband's mistress, and that skirting around the subject had been delicate. Mead dismissed any such thought; everyone knew about the mistress.

Tentatively, I suggested that the woman still seemed to be waiting for her husband to come back.

"Not for one minute." And that, for the General, was the end of that.

The woman and I spoke later that evening by phone. "Oh, no, Dan and I have never acknowledged that he lives with another woman," she insisted. "It's a deception we carry on. The only way I know about her is through Margaret. I'm convinced I will be taking care of Dan when the day comes that he needs nursing. That's the way I feel about commitment. This is what Margaret can't understand because her life has been so different from mine."

This placed Mead in perspective as the General. She surveys the world from a distant peak, while her friend, one among the multitudes of foot soldiers, is simply trying not to get shot.

Margaret Mead's father once told her, "It's a pity you aren't a boy; you'd have gone far." By never allowing him too much power over her, she went literally to the ends of the earth.

Their wills were matched over her determination to go to college and to marry a student minister before she graduated. Money was sparse; it was 1919. Her father took the position that as a married woman she would not need a college education. Margaret pointed out that he had married a woman who was still working for her doctorate when Margaret was born. He sent her to college.

In her twenties she was a beauty, full-lipped and sloe-eyed. Someone was always falling in love with her. For one with such firm ambitions, this was an occupational hazard. A five-year engagement to the student minister, Luther Cressman, freed her from the trivialities of mate seeking. But she felt an exile in the dozing, small-town atmosphere of DePauw University in Indiana. New York City seemed the fount of intellectual life; what's more, Luther was there, and so she persuaded her father to let her transfer to Barnard College. There she belonged to an avant-garde set as intensely involved in Freudian psychology as they were in writing poetry and exploring nascent fields of science. Above all, she was determined to bring about a change in the world.

To head off the marriage when she graduated, Margaret's father offered her a trip around the world. She turned him down flat. Two years later, by playing off her father against her mentor, anthropologist Franz Boas, Margaret negotiated the trip on her terms. By then she had finally married the undemanding seminarian, who sometimes joked about having to make an appointment to see her. Mead believed she had what she wanted: a marriage with no obstacles to being herself.

In her mentor, Professor Boas, one can see the silhouette of a latter-day Mead. He presided in 1924 over only four graduate students in anthropology at Columbia. "He had to plan—much as if he were a general," she describes, "with only a handful of troops available to save a whole country." Each piece of work had to count. Boas directed her to work among the American Indians. Young Margaret was determined to explore Polynesia.

"So I did what I had learned to do when I had to work things out with my father," she candidly admits, though she later learned to repudiate this kind of manipulation. Intuition told her that the one thing her mentor valued above the direction of anthropological research was his posture as a liberal man. She implied that if Boas insisted, he would be bullying her. Simultaneously, she appealed to her father's sense of male rivalry: Boas was trying to control his daughter. It did the job. Her mentor give in, her father backed her with the money for that trip around the world, her husband left with his own grant for another hemisphere, and the married Margaret set sail for Samoa. On her own terms. Retaining her maiden name.

She weathered a shipboard infatuation with a New Zealand anthropologist, Reo Fortune by name, a handsome and brooding ascetic by his pictures. But he was not her match professionally. Nor did she approve of him as a father. She returned to her husband, Luther, and visions of life in a country rectory filled with their children.

When a gynecologist erroneously declared that she could never have children, the 25-year-old Margaret fully redesigned her future. Here is the way her mind worked: ". . . if there was to be no motherhood, then a professional partnership of field work with Reo . . . made more sense than cooperation with Luther in his [changed] career of teaching sociology."[17] Her choice, as always, was educated by Margaret Mead's vision of Margaret Mead. She married Reo.

Her next and most exotic imbroglio occurred in New Guinea. Mead was in her early thirties and just released from nightmarish months in hostile Mundugumor country, where babies of unwanted sex were routinely drowned. She and Reo were starved for intellectual company. The rivalry between them had grown dangerously tense. When their launch pulled in at a friendly Iatmul village, they were thrown together with a handsome British anthropologist, equally parched for companionship. He was Gregory Bateson, and he was different. He carried himself with the loose-kneed assurance of a Cambridge education. Next to the diminutive Margaret he stood tall and detached. Next to Margaret's husband, his nonaggressiveness gave sharp contrast to Reo's dark jealousies and tiresome competition. Reo wanted to write his own books; he resented sharing the work with Margaret.

Again, intimate feelings were sublimated in ever more intense fieldwork. She and Gregory were falling in love. The potentially explosive triangle was turned to long nights of debate in a tiny, mosquito-proof room, debates on the relationship between sex and temperament, which became the subject of Margaret Mead's next book.

One night the three were quartered on the floor of a guesthouse in a village expecting a raid from unfriendly neighbors. While Gregory charmed the villagers by chatting with them in pidgin Iatmul, Reo covered the scene with a revolver. The raid never came, but the personal crisis heightened. Reo later woke to hear Margaret and Gregory talking privately.

Three years later, she married Gregory. The early Bateson years were probably the richest of her life. The perfect partners in mind and temperament, they shared in Bali a field experience of feverish effort and unprecedented accomplishment. They worked through the night developing film and refreshed their faces at dawn in whatever water remained. Having planned to take 2,000 photographs, they came home with 25,000.

The recollections in her book of the fieldwork with Bateson are both stirring and wistful. "I think it is a good thing to have such a model, once . . . even if the model includes the kind of extra intensity in which a lifetime is condensed into a few short years."[18] She has tried yet never succeeded in duplicating the Balinese experience, but vivid it remains.

Even in the mother's domain, her experience as a woman was exceptional. Safe to say, it would be unimaginable to most within the human platoons who continue to look to her for guidance.

When finally a child was born into the well-ordered world of Margaret Mead, the General was already sheltered by age and reputation from the havoc such an event can play with a career. She was 38. Benjamin Spock himself attended the birth. She took the baby home to her father's house in Philadelphia and the ready laps of a young nurse and a warm housekeeper. When Gregory Bateson returned from war work in England during his daughter's episode of infant colic, Mead writes, "We let the nurse go and took care of her ourselves for a whole weekend."[19]

The grammar of the American nurse was not good enough, insisted the British father. And so the couple parked the baby in the padded bureau drawer of a friend while they found an apartment in Manhattan and a proper nanny from one of the great English country houses. Mead returned to part-time work at the Museum of Natural History and taught between breast-feedings. She delighted in her daughter, Catherine. A late child who is brought to its parents freshly bathed for a romp in the morning sunlight and again for a couple of hours after their return from work could be nothing less than a joy. The common American family experience? Hardly.

Mead soon found an even more pleasant and efficient way of getting the job done. She joined a cooperative household. Again, the solution was exceptional. It depended on Mead's close professional kinship with an entrepreneur in the social sciences, Larry Frank; upon his gracious compound in Holderness, New Hampshire; and upon the extraordinary services of an old-fashioned caregiver, Frank's third wife. Mary Frank had married a widower with five children. She was young and beautiful, and to her fell the role of the housekeeper-mother.

After two summers of experimenting in the country compound, the two families decided to merge full time. The Franks' spacious house in Greenwich Village became home throughout the war years. Mead was immediately released to commute to Washington with Larry Frank, who included her in a series of interdisciplinary efforts. They returned home for weekends. Mary Frank welcomed Mead's daughter into her active nursery. And Bateson began spending more time in war work overseas.

I was curious about Mary Frank's attitude because this was the pivot around which the three highpowered social scientists freely spun their wheels. Was she content being the mother?

"Yes," Dr. Mead replied flatly. "Everybody doesn't need to work." Mead hastened to add that she could afford to pay half the expenses for a cook and a cleaning man, leaving Mary freer to pay attention to the children. And the older children baby-sat.

Did envy develop?

"Well, I think Mary had no idea during that whole period that I knew how to boil an egg," Mead explained. Over her smile flickered the grace notes of pride in silent strategies past. "I acted very much as a hus—, an extra man in the house. I just thought it was easier to leave her in charge. I was terribly busy."

The next most obvious subject that comes up with any change in the basic scheme of marriage is fidelity. But Dr. Mead does not think the two are closely related.

"You can handle group living with a general incest

taboo for everybody in it. With everybody's lives being so dependent on each other, nobody wants to rock the boat. Marriage is difficult enough, just plain monogamy. Polygamy is more difficult; it requires more institutionalization. And group marriage is just too difficult for anybody. It's never been practiced, therefore. Nowhere in the world. That's just a fantasy."

So bountiful was the fruit of her two-year professional partnership with Bateson, they had to wait nearly twenty-five years for the work to make its impact on the anthropological field. By then their love match had been dissolved for over a decade.

This critical juncture in Mead's personal road, when she was 43, is obscured in her autobiography. One stumbles over this quick stroke:

> The atomic bomb exploded over Hiroshima in the summer of 1945. At that point I tore up every page of a book I had nearly finished. Every sentence was out of date. We had entered a new age. My years as a collaborating wife, trying to combine intensive field work and an intense personal life, also came to an end.

I later inquired why the bomb had brought her lifetime of collaboration as wife and scientist to an end. "Because I got divorced," she said. "Otherwise, I wouldn't have made that decision." The words had no boots. I guessed that the victor in that battle (if there was one) marched away barefoot.

During midlife passage, then, Mead tore up much of the personal and professional structure that had sustained the first half of her life and began building a new support system. Her intellectual life took a new direction, involving her in a long series of activities in mental health. She learned to work alone or in collaboration with a female anthropologist. She learned to live alone or share her apartment with a woman colleague. Still an active teacher-mentor, she keeps a card file on the thousands of students she continues to counsel, scold, and recommend for grants.

And as intended, she uses her postmenopausal high status to travel constantly as a citizen of the world, whose contributions are always in demand. The design of the second half of her life has rewarded Mead's vigor well beyond the compulsory retirement that dooms so many to premature obsolescence.

One has had the feeling in recent years—watching her propped and dozing on yet another panel while a colleague rhapsodizes about restoring zest to the post-menopausal woman by getting her back into the labor force ("rubbish"), watching her field questions on test-tube babies ("They can do it with goats, but stay out of human life")—that the General is running short of patience with the persistent refusal of Americans to learn from their experiments.

Yet tomorrow she will rise again at five, as Augustus rose to review his legions, forehead curls clipped, vast distances in the eyes, a cape furling over her sturdy frame, and go forth with forked staff to claim her dominions.

Foot soldiers, can you keep up?

INTEGRATORS

With what wildly racing private engines we struck out in our twenties, we wanted to do it all and do it all at once! Learn. Love. Explore. Excel. Escape the suburbs or the Midwest or wherever retrograde ideas of femininity prevailed. Achieve. Find a mate. Have a child.

Such a program was still considered insurrectionary in the late 1950s and early 1960s. Women like me were the mutants of our generation. Marriage did not stop us from working toward accomplishment, nor did childbirth, although it usually caused us to slow down. The guilty rub at the center of our twenties was, "How will I integrate the baby with my life so it won't cut me off from the world?" Sometimes we took our toddlers to the office or the school library and gave them grease pencils to break. More often we hoarded the ghostly hours between midnight and dawn, gathered up the shavings of our unproven talents and ran, ran in place, in isolation, like the caged pets of our children, round the treadmills of our chosen crafts.

We were determined not to end up as the hard-boiled career woman stereotype, or as the forgotten drunks at the other end of our husbands' commuter line, like the misguided and miserable women we knew even before Betty Friedan gave their problem a name. And most of us didn't. We found ourselves coming out somewhere else and passed into our thirties with a different crisis. Something had to go.

Most integrators subtracted the marriage, or gave up on the career, or let the children go to hell.

Some who attempted to do it all were overwhelmed by their tasks and found they could complete none of them. They sought refuge by subtracting their sanity. Psychiatrists tried to "reeducate" them to their proper role. They had little choice but to acquiesce or be institutionalized.

One husband I know well told his wife, who was trying to do it all at 25: "The *optimum* thing is for the wife to want to give up her career after the first child and stay home. Failing that, she should do it anyway."

It is rarely possible for a woman to integrate marriage, career, and motherhood in her twenties, and it's about time some of us who have tried said so. It is quite possible to do so at 30 and decidedly possible at 35, but before then, the *personal* integration necessary as a ballast simply hasn't had a chance to develop. In discussions with Margaret Mead and Daniel Levinson, I found both agreed. Levinson holds that

> when the tasks of one period remain largely unmet, they will complicate or interfere with the work on the tasks of the next period. In the extreme case, development may be impaired to such a degree that the person cannot truly enter the new period: feeling

overwhelmed by the burdens of the new tasks while he is still struggling desperately with the old, he may seek death or become psychotic or lose his way; or he may find some protected niche that frees him temporarily from pressing external demands and gives him space in which to do the internal preparatory work for the new period.[20]

No one can tell you what it's like to have a human being, helpless as a beached flounder, in a crib in the middle of your own life. An interviewer once faced Gloria Steinem with the key question: Could she have a child and still be the amazing activist journalist? Gloria was certain of it. She would just write when the baby was asleep.

The thing is, babies only sleep for half an hour, and then they're into your sewing box and wrapping thread around your typewriter.

Consuelo Saer Bahr, in a book she is trying to write at the age of 33, gives a far truer answer to her small son. "After supper my child comes slipping and sliding in his 'feet' pajamas to bid me goodnight. . . . What's your pleasure, my darling? . . . To have me to yourself for thirty whole minutes and not hear me say, 'OK, now you play by yourself until Mommy's finished'? We all certainly know by now that Mommy is never going to be finished."[21]

From time to time newspaper stories appear about integrators who have decided to subtract their careers. In their late twenties and early thirties, well-educated, married to business or professional men, and mothers of primary schoolers, these are women who have worked for five or ten years and now can afford not to. They talk of having run out of psychic energy to cope with it all. What they seem to seek in this transition is a loosening of the rigid schedules of the past, a gathering in of time to enjoy rambles with their children, browsing in shops and museums, and perhaps doing some volunteer work. It would seem an idyllic refreshment for anyone who can afford it, including men. And it is likely to be only temporary. As people begin to ask them, "What are you doing now?," these women generally speak of feeling the pressure to return to work.

The thirties, for the integrator, are a time for additions. By then she may be practiced and confident enough to dovetail all her competing priorities.

One new life structure that has evolved over the last decade in response to this problem is the single mother and the every-other-weekend father. Although we give it little recognition as a new support structure, it is not in each case a spontaneous event. It has become a common way of coping with the predictable couple crisis.

Divorced parents are truly put to the test of treating each other with tolerance, courtesy, and a realistic acknowledgment of the time and financial pressures on both because now it must be done for the child's sake. The father who alternates parenting on weekends and school vacations makes it possible for a woman to balance mothering and a serious career and have some time left over to revive herself as a loving, sexual woman. Had the same fathers been that available and attentive while in the marriage, it might have allowed the woman to integrate all her aspects.

Somehow, full-custody fathers manage a full parenting load along with their careers, usually by hiring top-notch help and pitching in enthusiastically on nights and weekends. Some of them demand more flexible hours from their employers. Young widowers do the same. In fact, to watch some of the more popular television series of recent years, "Bonanza," "Courtship of Eddie's Father," "My Three Sons," "Bachelor Father," one would think a man alone raising children is uniquely blessed. And perhaps, by being concerned daily with details of feeling, he is.

Why must such resourceful solutions wait for divorce or death?

NEVER-MARRIED WOMEN

Our society is stingy about acknowledging this as a legitimate pattern for women. But the evidence is that at every age level (in education, occupation, and income) the average single woman surpasses the average single man.[22] Roughly ten percent of women never marry. As she ages, the unmarried woman also appears to bring stronger psychological reserves to bear on the challenges of her position than those demonstrated by bachelor men.

In the history of women artists, the unmarried are liberally represented. Often it was the benevolent quiet of their parents' home that sustained them. Jane Austen read her chapters aloud to her lively family and enjoyed the confidence of a warm reception from them. Louisa May Alcott, educated by her father's intellectual circle which included Thoreau and Emerson, turned to writing at 30 and cared financially for her parents. Numerous women poets, most of whose work went unmarked until after they died, resisted the division of energy that domestic life would demand. Their male biographers, however, assumed that to retreat from marriage with a man was to retreat from the world, and routinely described them in terms of their "withdrawal." Finding this to be the case, Louise Bernikow reconstructed the lives of four centuries of women poets and observed in the introduction to her anthology:

> Women who do not love men, and women who do not have sex with men, in the eyes of men, have loveless and sexless lives. . . . the truth seems to be that most of these women poets have loved women, sometimes along with loving men. Women have found in other women exactly that companionship, encouragement, and understanding that they did not find in men.[23]

Today we have many vigorous models among unmarried women who are the cutting edge of new forms. Some are among the most heterosexually prolific women of our time, some are lesbians, and some are pretty average.

Others of the unmarried become paranurturers, along the Jane Addams model. As social workers, teaching nuns, custodians of the orphaned and re-tarded, they bend their creativity to caring for the children of the world.

And still others become office wives. Cities like Washington are magnets for women who devote their lives to caring for public men and politicians, and who, like Rose Mary Woods, do so to the exclusion of any other deep personal tie.

TRANSIENTS

These are the women who choose in their twenties to keep their options open. Yet by the very choice of impermanence, like the transient men described in the last chapter, they do follow a pattern—the pattern of prolonged wandering without commitments.

Young, single, healthy women can gain rich experience by prolonging their seeking experiments. By refusing to trade self-determination for the security of marriage, they have more freedom. They can initiate sexual relationships. They can try out various counter-culture life-styles, some of which may sound more promising as part of radical rhetoric than they turn out to be in the nitty-gritty of daily living. Communal farms, for instance, are mostly male-oriented setups that return women to the kitchen to bake bread. It is also an enlightening challenge for counterculture women to find a way to support themselves. Because they have few marketable skills and little job training, they must survive by their wits and talents. Many support themselves by weaving, potting, jewelry mak-ing, and other cottage industry crafts. Some travel the rodeo circuit or take jobs in factories; others try to outwit the system by inventing welfare ripoffs or selling pot or simply by wanting less.

To be a rolling stone makes a very different demand on the two sexes, however. Roughly 400 times in her life a woman must make a sober choice. Either she will leave herself open to pregnancy, or she will deny her uterus its animating powers. For a woman there is no such thing as casual noncommitment. If she wants to wander free, it requires an act of negation every month. And a good deal of psychic energy is involved in that denial. She can never simply not think about it because that in itself is a way of tipping her destiny.

Counterculture men often cannot find jobs of any sort. And as part of the bargain of mutual noncommitment, transient men feel justified in rejecting family responsibilities. Child raising is still considered, even in the most radical outposts of our society, women's work.

And so for a woman, even transiency may not remain exclusive of all obligations. I am thinking here of the bachelor mothers I first met and wrote about in 1969. They had existed before, of course, unusual young women determined to defy convention and to raise a child without the accoutrements of marriage, but this was the first time they had announced themselves.

Lorna comes most vividly to mind. She was a member of the first graduating class of hippies. As she told me, "Growing up when I did, with the roles so vague, it was much harder making the one choice out of so many." Instead, she followed the nomadic pattern that was the should of her time. It took her from classical studies to a crash pad in the East Village to a commune in the Haight.

For all the talk about loving everybody, the slap-dash commune life offered not a single, sustaining human connection. Lorna stopped taking the pill.

"The circumstances weren't right. But I was 24. It's the right time to have a baby."

While her wish was only an embryo, Lorna continued as before, minibusing between California and

New York. It was only in the last two months of pregnancy that an inner change began to register. Seeing her silhouette in store windows she was astounded. There was something here beyond a misty reflection of her own need for love. Something heavy and felt. An idea that would soon become a reality.

Even after the birth of her daughter Lorna continued in the vagabond pattern, although her days came to have a beginning, middle, and end. She moved to a closed commune where everyone had jobs. Bedded down on a mat with her babe, in a tiny space between two curtains, Lorna sounded happier. "I have to plan my life now because of her."

A few moves more and Lorna became terminally disenchanted with communes. She might have drifted off into drugs. The child gave her reason to be intentional. Lorna rented a tiny house and discovered she had the mettle to live alone. That's the funny thing about bachelor motherhood. It has a way of galvanizing stumblers into functioning adults. Time goes by; the child grows; the life takes shape and finds purpose.

News of Lorna recently came to me from her mother. Lorna is a transient no longer. She is settled on a farm. Her life is rich with working at her potter's wheel and sharing the rambunctious years of her daughter with the artist she married. He does carpentry to make a living. About the only time that Lorna travels now is to deliver her ceramics into the city. And hurry home. Home is something not to miss another moment of.

She was exactly 30 when she stopped wandering.

I'm going to give Margaret Mead the last word. After listening to the patterns I have outlined, she projected that the only way we will make any headway toward integrated lives in the future is to forget role playing. We must give leeway to all kinds of patterns.

"Some men are more interested in human relations than they are in public achievement. Some men would much rather manage a house and children than go to the office every day. There are some women who are just no good at all at houses and children. If we had a notion of every possible combination—man older, woman older, man goes out to work, woman goes out to work, both of them go out to work halftime, one of them works one year and the other works the next year—then no one pattern would be regarded as peculiar. We would remark on them in the way we say: 'These people go to Europe every year,' and 'Those people never go to the country in the summer.' They would just be interesting differences."

Part Six

DEADLINE DECADE

Whatever you can do, or dream you can, begin it. Boldness has genius, power and magic in it.

—GOETHE

17

SETTING OFF
ON THE
MIDLIFE PASSAGE

The middle of the thirties is literally the midpoint of life. The halfway mark. No gong rings, of course. But twinges begin. Deep down a change begins to register in those gut-level perceptions of safety and danger, time and no time, aliveness and stagnation, self and others. It starts with a vague feeling . . .

I have reached some sort of meridian in my life. I had better take a survey, reexamine where I have been, and reevaluate how I am going to spend my resources from now on. Why am I doing all this? What do I really believe in?

Underneath this vague feeling is the fact, as yet unacknowledged, that there is a down side to life, a back of the mountain, and that *I have only so much time before the dark to find my own truth.*

As such thoughts gather thunder, the continuity of the life cycle is interrupted. They usher in a decade that can be called, in the deepest sense, the Deadline Decade. Somewhere between 35 and 45 if we let ourselves, most of us will have a full-out authenticity crisis.

We see the dark at the end of the tunnel first. The apprehension is often sudden and sharp. We don't know what to do with it or even what "it" is; no young person really believes his end will come. The first time that idea breaks through, no matter how sound the state of our health and how substantial our position, most of us become intensely preoccupied with signs of aging and premature doom.

Does this make sense? Not rationally, no. If our apprehensions were logical, then the fear should mount as we grow older and come closer to dying. Usually, it doesn't. As people restabilize on the other side of the midlife passage, the specter of death moves farther back in their minds. They talk about it a lot and compare protective strategies, but by then "it" is real, not a private, unmentionable gargoyle.

This chapter will explore some of the predictable inner changes most of us can expect to feel in the Deadline Decade as we move through it: seeing the dark first, disassembling ourselves, then glimpsing the light, and gathering our parts into a renewal. The remainder of the book will describe men and women actually groping toward authenticity, each in his or her own pattern, trying to find his or her own truth. Or running away from it, or blocking it until something explodes.

This is not to suggest that people who suffer the most severe crisis always come through with the most inspired rebirth. But people who allow themselves to be stopped, seized by the real issues, shaken into a reexamination—these are the people who find their validity and thrive.

Seeing the Dark at the End of the Tunnel

The sudden change in the proportion of safety and danger we feel in our lives is seldom anticipated, which is why people often feel depressed at the start of this passage. When we were buoyed by the optimism of the early years, we could easily steer clear of the dark side by sailing from one channel of vigorous activity to another. Our juices were running full. Ordinarily, our potency was building in every sphere—stronger bodies, better sex, bigger accomplishments, more friends, higher salaries—and oh, how we loved to exhibit our powers! It seemed they could do nothing but increase. They defended us well against the inadmissible truth that no one has forever.

Ask anyone over 35, when did you first begin to feel old? Was it when you looked at yourself in the buff and realized that everything was half an inch lower?

"Hold your stomach in, Mom."

"It's in."

Most of us notice first the cracks in our physical shells and see them in distortion, as if in a funny-house mirror. A comedian gave as ridiculous an answer as any. "I knew I was middle-aged when I woke up one morning to find a twenty-three-inch hair growing out of my ear."

What we turn away from in the mirror, we can't escape seeing in our friends, our children, our parents. These are the "others" who register the fact that "you" are soon going to be different.

You go to a reunion. Your classmates now have titles. You listen to the accounts of their achievements and you can hear they are impressive, but you are not impressed. What you are obsessed with is the pink glacier pushing back the class president's hairline. You hear about Harry; he dropped like a fly while dancing the bump.

In the locker room you, a woman recently past 35, find yourself staring at the women well into their forties, at the purple bull's-eyes in their thighs where it looks as though a BB gun went off under the skin. You wonder if they still undress in front of their husbands.

Your mood swings up and down by sheer caprice. Madcap optimism in the morning, in the doldrums by lunch. You make a joke to yourself about acting like "some nutty menopausal woman." But you don't believe it, of course. You are a woman still menstruating regularly, and women of 38 are at the sexual *peak*. Or you are a man, and after all, Charlie Chaplin was making babies at 81.

It is a paradox that as we reach our prime, we also see there is a place where it finishes.

Change In Time Sense

Going into this crisis decade, every one of us can expect a distortion in our sense of time. We have stumbled onto that apostrophe in time between the end of growing up and the beginning of growing old. Like the apprehensions associated with death, this disruption in time sense is most unsettling at the start of the passage. The jolt as felt by men and career women sounds something like this:

"Time is running out. Time must be beaten. Can I accomplish all that I'd hoped before it's too late?"

To women who have been at home, time is suddenly seen as long:

"Look at all the time ahead! After the children are gone, what will I do with it?"

Social psychologist Bernice Neugarten in an interview confirmed this broad difference in change of time sense for the two sexes. Career position is significantly involved in the personality changes for men, and health is more of an age marker for them than for women.[1] Women are much more likely to see a realm of unimagined opportunities opening up in the middle years. An initial sense of danger and timidity may give way to invigoration. For most of them there are still so many firsts ahead.

The change in time sense forces each of us to a major task of midlife. All our notions of the future need to be rebalanced around the idea of time left to live.

Change In Sense of Aliveness versus Stagnation

Before we are able to do this rebalancing, thē time problem will have most of us feeling stalled. Our

353

distorted perspective foreshortens the future so falsely we are likely to create our own inertia, saying, "It's too late to start something new." Boredom is what it *feels* like, but as author Barbara Fried explains so nicely, we have boredom mixed up with time diffusion.[2] They are different. Routine boredom can be cured by seeking out simple novelties of experience. Time diffusion is a deeper malaise that stems from our sudden, drastic lack of trust in the future and an unwillingness to believe there is anything to look forward to.

Trust is the foundation of hope formed in earliest childhood. Now we are back to "go," reckoning all over again the balance we can expect between our needs and when, or if, they will be met. Except that now there is no caregiver. *We* are our hope. And we can't very well trust in our own resources for enlivening the future until we find out who we want to be on the other side of the meridian. That's the circle. It's not vicious; it's the runaround that leads to revitalization. We have to go all around it, stagnate in it, before we are spurred to break out and make use of the time left. "Yes, I can change. It's not too late to start what I put aside!"

It is a paradox that as we come out of the crisis, although we have less actual time left, the depression and ennui lift. The future is again seen in truer perspective because we infuse it then with the faith of our redefined purpose.

Change In Sense of Self and Others

About now, your son beats you at tennis for the first time. Or he asks if he and his girl friend can take their sleeping bags out in the backyard. You stew all night, wondering how do they *do* it? The next morning you ask a few oblique questions. But by his expression, it is clear that your son knows your interest is less parental than lascivious.

Your daughter wants to go shopping. You stare

at the store windows and see yourself in the same clothes. Inside the store your daughter looks shocked when you try on a supersexy dress. "Oh Mom, that's disgusting."

It is a paradox that teenage children are totally intolerant of midlife parents for having much the same romantic fantasies they have.

You look to your parents for comfort and find they have weakened. Their eyes aren't so good. They would rather you drive. When a parent contracts a terminal illness, who is next? You, the 40-year-old, are abruptly flung to the front of the generational train, followed only by your own children.

With your own role as child to your parents intact, you still felt secure. With the death of your father or mother, you are exposed. "Today there are a tremendous number of people who experience death for the first time with a parent's passing when they themselves are 35 to 40," as Margaret Mead observes. "This is altogether new in the world." The death of the remaining parent has been documented as one of the most constant crisis points in the individual's evolving image of self.

Your curiosity at looking into the funny-house mirror mounts to morbidity. You never read the obituaries before; now you note age and disease. For the first time in what might have been a spectacularly healthy life, you become a minor-league hypochondriac.

People in the middle years will often say, "All my friends are dying of cancer." *All* their friends aren't, but if even one or two are, it comes as a shock. We hear so much about our increased longevity, how is it so many people become seriously ill in their late forties? Because infant mortality has been sharply reduced in recent years, more people who would have died at birth survive infancy but are not as physically strong as our grandparents had to be to survive. Consequently, as indicated by government analysis of lifespan statistics, there is an ever-increasing population of middle-aged people and hence a larger pool susceptible to death in the middle years.[3]

Had any such sudden tragedy struck a friend or relation when you were 25, your sympathetic reaction would have been of a safely distant kind. The pestilence would have been theirs, a life accident. Now it is a red alert to make more of your own life before it is too late. And that is all to the good.

It is a paradox that as death becomes personalized, a life force becomes energized. In the very jaws of this danger is opportunity, the chance for no less than a second christening.

De-Illusioning the Dream

The changes in perception are most vividly reflected in the way the dream is now seen. Whatever your occupation, you cannot help but face up to the gap between your vision of yourself in the twenties and the actuality of your arrival at 40. If you are a 40-year-old mother, your purpose will soon slip from your arms. If you are a chief executive officer, the business psychologists who proclaim "no man over 45 should be in a line position" will soon be talking about *you*. Saying that you should be put out to pasture in a staff job. Saying that all they want are young hustlers whose whole focus is the bottom line. Never mind these philosophical middle-agers who want to make a social contribution.

The affirmation you have or have not accrued by 40 will tell you in what league you can expect to play out your life. No matter what your position you will wonder, "Is this all there is?"

The same disillusionment seizes everybody, steam fitter or top brass, and that is crucial to remember if you are to save yourself from wallowing in self-pity. Studs Terkel collected the stories of Americans in over a hundred occupations for his extraordinary book *Working*, and the one common denominator he found was concern with age. "Perhaps it is this spectre that most haunts working men and women: the planned obsolescence of people that is of a piece with the planned obsolescence of the things they make."[4]

You must give up believing that all the riches of life will come from reaching the goals of your idealized self. If your ideal self is evidently not going to be attainable and you refuse to adjust down, you will go the route of chronic depression. On the other hand, if you recognize that you will never be president of the big-city bank, you can get on with becoming branch manager in your favorite community and maybe find your greatest pleasure in becoming a Little League coach or starting a choir.

If your ideal self *has* been achieved, what happens after the dream comes true? If you don't replace it with a new dream, there may be no zeal left for the future, although there may be plenty to fear. On the other hand, you are freed by your success to take old passions off the shelf, to open that funny little restaurant you always had a yen to cook for, to throw yourself into song writing or helping minorities or landscape gardening for your friends. I know people in midlife who have turned to all these things. They are far more ebullient people than their counterparts who stay with the old, achieved dream and find themselves in their fifties literally squeezing it for lifeblood.

It is a paradox that while medical science has increased our longevity, business psychology seeks to shrink our work span.

Groping Toward Authenticity

As our distorted glimpses of the dark side grow into convictions and the dream disappoints our magical hopes, *any* role we have chosen seems too narrow, *any* life structure too confining. *Any* husband or wife, mother, father, child, mentor, or divinity to whom we have given faith can be felt as part of the clasped circle hemming us in.

The loss of youth, the faltering of physical powers

we have always taken for granted, the fading purpose of stereotyped roles by which we have thus far identified ourselves, the spiritual dilemma of having no absolute answers—any or all of these shocks can throw us into crisis. But in all of us, before this decade is out, the crisis makes sweeping changes in personality possible. And some degree of personality change is probably inevitable.[5]

These changes may permit a woman to assert herself, a man to allow his emotions, and any one of us to let our narrow occupational and economic definitions fall away. When that happens, we are ready to look for a sense of purpose truly our own. The very act of striking out on that path can pave the way to a new, freestanding intimacy between us and the ones we love.

But first, letting the dark side open up will release a cast of demons. Every loose end not resolved in previous passages will resurface to haunt us. Even chips off the archaic totem pole of childhood will come to the surface. Buried parts of ourselves will demand incorporation or at least that we make the effort of seeing and discarding them.

These demons may lead us into private hells of depression, sexual promiscuity, power chasing, hypochondria, self-destructive acts (alcoholism, drug taking, car accidents, suicide), and violent swings of mood. All are well documented as rising during the middle years. The midlife crisis has also been used by psychiatrists as an explanation for why so many highly creative and industrious people burn out by their mid-thirties. Even more dramatic is the evidence that they can die from it.[6]

If we do admit the dark side, what are we likely to see?

We are selfish.

We are greedy.

We are competitive.

We are fearful.

We are dependent.

We are jealous.

We are possessive.

We have a destructive side.

Who's afraid of growing up? Who isn't? For if and when we do begin the process of reexamining all that we think and feel and stand for, in the effort to forge an identity that is authentically ours and ours alone, we run into our own resistance. There is a moment—an immense and precarious moment—of stark terror. And in that moment most of us want to retreat as fast as possible because to go forward means facing a truth we have suspected all along:

We stand alone.

We are the only ones with our own set of thoughts and bundle of feelings. Another person can *taste* them, through shared experience or conversation, but no other person can ever really *digest* them. Not wives or husbands, although they may be able to finish our sentences; not mentors or bosses, although they may be of goodwill in working out their own ambitions through us; not even our parents.

From the childhood identifications with our parents we carry along the most primitive layer of imaginary protection: the protection of that dictator-guardian I have called the inner custodian. It is this internalized protection that gives us a sense of insulation, and even into the middle years, shields us from coming face to face with our own absolute separateness. We look to our mates, to our children, to money or success, hoping they will extend the protection of the caregivers from our childhood. The illusory power of the inner custodian has made us believe that if we don't stick our necks out, if we don't test our full potential, we are somehow insulated from danger, failure, getting sick, dying. But it is an illusion.

Trying to keep that illusion alive by maintaining what psychiatrists call an "incomplete identification" only soothes us against the *idea of* separation. It does nothing actually to protect us from being separate.[7]

We push and strain against all of these truths.

Retreat and tremble. Chase after the sweet birds of our youth. Stop. Stagnate. And finally we come to know the unthinkable: The dark side is within us. So powerful becomes the sense of internal collapse that many of us are no longer willing to prevent it.

People whose biographies I have taken can say at 44 or 45, "I really went through hell for a few years, and I'm just coming out of it," but their capacity to describe what "it" felt like is often limited. People right in the middle of midlife passage may be so panicky that the only descriptions they can summon are of "living in a state of suspended animation" or "I sometimes wonder in the morning if life is worth getting up for." To be any more introspective seems dangerous.

A 43-year-old designer was able to articulate the feelings that bring on the emotional vertigo of this period. "What I've discovered over the last year is how much of what is inadmissible to myself I have suppressed. Feelings that I've always refused to admit are surfacing in a way *I am no longer willing to prevent.* I'm willing to accept the responsibility for what *I really feel.* I don't have to pretend those feelings don't exist in order to accommodate a model of what I should be."

By his own admissions, this man is engaging the midlife crisis. "I'm really shocked now at the range and the quality of those feelings—feelings of fear, of envy, of greed, of competition. All these so-called bad feelings are really rising where I can see them and feel them. I'm amazed at the incredible energy we all spend suppressing them and not admitting pain."

The consensus of current research is that the transition into middle life is as critical as adolescence and in some ways more harrowing. Can it possibly be worth it to ride with this chaos and see it all? Is it worth it to become real?

I'm rather partial to the answer given in a children's book, *The Velveteen Rabbit.* One day the young rabbit asks the Skin Horse, who has been around the nursery quite some time, what is real? And does it hurt?

"Sometimes," said the Skin Horse, for he was always truthful. "When you are REAL you don't mind being hurt."

"Does it happen all at once, like being wound up," he asked, "or bit by bit?"

"It doesn't happen all at once," said the Skin Horse. "You become. It takes a long time. That's why it doesn't often happen to people who break easily, or have sharp edges, or who have to be carefully kept. Generally, by the time you are REAL, most of your hair has been loved off, and your eyes drop out and you get loose in the joints and very shabby. But these things don't matter at all, because once you are REAL you can't be ugly, except to people who don't understand."[8]

From Disassembling to Renewal

While the dilemma of this decade is the search for authenticity, the work is to move through a disassembling to a renewal. What is disassembling is that narrow self we have thus far put together in a form tailored to please the culture and other people.

It is the form we hurried through our twenties to find, the identity we developed in order to stabilize ourselves, and around which we built the life system of the early thirties: the ambitious executive, the supermom who always copes, the fearless politician, the wife who asks permission. We could not afford then to act on our own *internal* authority. The unspoken promise was, if we did a good job and stayed within that straight and narrow form, we would be liked and rewarded and live forever.

The shock of this turning point is to discover that the promise was an illusion. That narrow, innocent self is indeed dying, must die, in order to make room for the fully expanded self who will take in all our parts, the selfish, scared, and cruel along with the expansive and tender—the "bad" along with the "good." No matter how shattering is this collision with our suppressed and destructive impulses, the capacity for renewal within each human spirit is nothing short of amazing.

It is not *either* disassembling *or* renewal. It is both. By allowing this dis-integration, by taking in our suppressed and even our unwanted parts, each of us prepares at the gut level for the reintegration of an identity that is truly our own. We are free to seek the truth about ourselves more vigorously and thus to see the world in truer perspective.

Along the way to that freedom, we must do some grieving for the old "dying self" and take up a conscious stance with regard to our own inevitable mortality.[9] It is this mature insight that will protect us from slavishly following what the culture wants us to do and from squandering our time in seeking the approval of others by conforming to their rules. Moreover, when we act on this knowledge, we can be less defensive toward others.

"Take back your silly rules!" we can shout at last. "No one can dictate what is right for me. I have glimpsed the worst, and now I can afford to know whatever there is to know. I am my own and only protection. For the fact is, this is my one and only journey through life."

Through the process of disassembling, then, we provide for the grandest expansion. By the end of this period we can include inside our boundaries all that we are and have experienced—and *re*value it. That is renewal.

Riding Out the Down Side

One solution is to go into the darkness and explore it. Stick in the mire for a while. Take a sabbatical and become a midlife delinquent, or pit oneself against nature on a backwoods canoe trip. It is one way to know our own depths and possibly to be reinvigorated by that knowledge toward making the most of our lives.

Others appear to wing it past this midstation without pause. Their solution is to continue denying the down side. To play more tennis and run more laps, give bigger parties, seek better hair transplants and higher face lifts, find younger partners to take to bed. That is not to suggest that jogging isn't worthwhile or that younger partners can't help to revitalize a stagnant sex life, but people who rely on only these outlets may be losing in the bargain even more than a critical chance for personal development. To disallow the momentous changes underneath forces a skimming of all experience. The eventual price is superficiality.

Still others block this passage in a razzle-dazzle of compulsive activity. Whiz-kid businessmen or hyperactive hostesses or politicians, for example, seem to have no time for a midlife crisis. They are too busy starting a new business that year or giving dinner parties or running for higher office. They consume themselves with externals for the very reason that they fear dipping into what might be the poverty of meaning inside.

The catch is, inner issues pushed down in one period tend to swing up in the next one with an added wallop. To face a midlife crisis for the first time at fifty is horrifying (although people can get through it). Or development may simply be halted for the person who continues to wear blinders. He becomes more narrow in view, self-indulgent, and finally juiceless and bitter.

"If a man goes through a relatively bland period when midlife transition is going on," Levinson asserts, "it will limit his growth. Many men who don't have a crisis at 40 become weighted and lose the vitality they need to continue developing in the rest of the adult stages."[10]

The only way, finally, to make fear of the down side go away is to allow it entry. The sooner we allow the truths of this period to fill our container, the sooner they can be integrated with our youthful optimism and reground us with true strength.

The most important words in midlife are—Let Go. Let it happen to you. Let it happen to your partner. Let the feelings. Let the changes.

You can't take everything with you when you leave on the midlife journey. You are moving away. Away from institutional claims and other people's agenda. Away from external valuations and accreditations, in search of an inner validation. You are moving out of roles and into the self. If I could give everyone a gift for the send-off on this journey, it would be a tent. A tent for tentativeness. The gift of portable roots.

To reach the clearing beyond, we must stay with the weightless journey through uncertainty. Whatever counterfeit safety we hold from overinvestments in people and institutions must be given up. The inner custodian must be unseated from the controls. No foreign power can direct our journey from now on. It is for each of us to find a course that is valid by our own reckoning. And for each of us there is the opportunity to emerge reborn, *authentically* unique, with an enlarged capacity to love ourselves and embrace others.

18

YOU ARE
IN GOOD
COMPANY

Let's look at two creative men who have written about themselves during exactly the same years. The similarity of their turmoil will be obvious. What is striking is that their lives are more than six centuries apart.

The first is the poet Dante Alighieri. His words in the opening stanzas of *Divine Comedy* express powerfully the psychological impact of this period:

> In the middle of the journey of our life, I came to myself within a dark wood where the straight way was lost. Ah, how hard it is to tell of that wood, savage and harsh and dense, the thought of which renews my fear. So bitter is it that death is hardly more.

Dante not only wrote those words in his 42nd year, he had been experiencing them in his own life since the age of 37. Only two years before, a passionate idealist of 35 with a propertied wife and several children, he had been elected one of the chief magistrates of Florence. He attempted to rule justly in the midst of violent political struggles. But in 1302, Dante was convicted *in absentia* of refusing to recognize the Pope's authority in civil matters. It was an offense of which he was proud and would not repent. He rejected "their" rules in favor of his own authority. As a consequence he was dispossessed and banished from his native city.

So it was that Dante began wandering through the villages and woods of Italy, the "dark wood" of which he wrote. In that wood, face to face with demons that confront us all in this period, he wrestled with the fearsome divisions inside himself.

Essayist George P. Elliott describes Dante's task in terms that are universal. "If he was to become himself, he must find a way to assemble the parts of his dreams into one whole."[1] Being both a man of ideas and a man of passion, Dante could not content himself with a life system that was exclusively intellectual, nor could his political nature allow him to confine all his parts in the construct of theology. He yearned to help set the church in order and to bring order to the state, apparently with equal desire. From a holy infatuation with the idealized girl child of his boyhood, he had moved on to loves that were profane. When he took the part of the pilgrim in *Divine Comedy* he was Everyman. And he chose not a saint but a pagan to lead him through hell.

"For him to renounce the world, as a religious does, would be to deny a great deal of himself, and this he was far too proud a poet to do," Elliott points out. "He wanted to get it all in, even his own evil."

The second man belongs to our own time. He wrote the book that precipitated the war on poverty in the 1960s, *The Other America.* A socialist and an intellectually honest man, he, like Dante, had been living an active, cosmopolitan life predicated on the idea that reason leads to truth. His name is Michael Harrington, and his loss of balance on the precipice of midlife caught him totally unprepared. He was giving a routine speech on the subject of poverty that he later described in his autobiography:

As I reached the podium I suddenly felt faint and had to grip the sides of the lectern in order to keep my balance. Then the sense of being on the very edge of losing consciousness became so intense that I had to sit down and explain to the audience that I was indisposed and could only go on if I were seated. . . . I cut the question period short and went back to my motel. By the time I reached the room I was sweating profusely and there were tremors in my back and chest. I wondered if I were having a heart attack. The next day I flew back to New York in a daze and went to bed. The doctor who came and examined me, like several others I went to see during the next few weeks, could find nothing physically wrong with me. But why, then, did I feel worse than I ever had in my 37 years?[2]

Like most of us, Harrington seized on external factors to convince himself this was just an isolated episode. He was overworked and tired out. But even while chatting pleasantly about art at a party, the terrifying sensation of losing his balance pushed through: ". . . the floor of the house seemed to sway slightly under my feet, and I drank quickly to blot out that seasick sensation."

Plunging ahead as if nothing had changed, as if he were still the pure and narrow civil rights militant of his own image, he joined Martin Luther King's march from Selma. One activist was murdered, and another collapsed at the airport. Harrington kept his equilibrium in the face of these unsettling events. The terrifying sense of losing his balance, he decided, was a fluke that had passed. "I was wrong . . . as soon as I got back to New York I had to confront once again some powerful, and repressed, antagonisms within myself. These forces were to dominate my life for the next year or so and profoundly influence it for still another three years."

The years between 37 and 42 are the ones Michael Harrington was writing about. These are peak years of anxiety for practically everyone. But Harrington, like most of us, knew nothing of this thing we now call midlife crisis. And so Harrington, like many of us, believed he was cracking up.

"I had never met my own id," he writes, "at least not face to face. Now—and it was months before I realized this was the case—my unconscious had seized me by the scruff of the neck in a surge of pent-up destructive fury. It was, quite literally, an id, an 'it,' an alien thing that took over my life and dictated frenetically and imperiously to my rational, daylight self."

He began cohabiting with anxiety, a free-floating fear that could not, would not, be conveniently attached to anything at all in the world of specific events. His body, his work, his wife, the whole outer structure of his life was intact. Yet the most trivial matters, a key sticking in a door or having to stand on line, could trigger an outburst of rage or panic. Every second in an airplane seemed a threat to his equilibrium.

"What was it that had turned my life upside down?" He turned for help to a psychoanalyst. For the next four years, as the symptoms gradually decreased, he groped toward an answer to that question. "My world had been transformed in an extraordinary number of ways in the period of a year or so and I could not, or would not, admit to myself what was happening. I pretended to be the person I had been; I refused to recognize who, or what, I was becoming."

It was a process he could no longer prevent: the disassembling of his smoothly functioning, sophisticated "daylight self" into separate and warring, but all authentic, parts of the same Michael Harrington. As he began to sort out those parts, he could recognize one as the itinerant radical of his Antioch College youth who "still lived in spiritual blue jeans," undefiled by the bourgeois markings of money, power, and success. This was the good segment, as he saw it. But since his mid-thirties another part of himself had been gaining territory. It had led him out of acceptable poverty and the glorification of communal living. It had drawn him into marriage, wanting children, a grudging embrace of the nuclear family and, worse, into advising men of power, accepting middle-class fees for his speeches, and even enjoying his sudden elevation as a celebrated author.

This was the part he considered impure, soft on success, an alien and unallowable "it." Yet the fact remained: It had forced entry. It demanded incorporation. It, too, was he.

The Creative Crisis

The most startling evidence that we reach a major crossroads at this age comes from London psychoanalyst Elliott Jaques. His first insights came from observing that the artistic giants of Western history have been consistently beset by a crisis in creative work in their middle and late thirties. Among the artists he considered (to give you an idea of their span) were Beethoven, Goethe, Ibsen, and Voltaire. From this proceeded Jaques's theory that we all reach a critical stage of development at this point. Although his first examples came from a very special group, he went on to analyze other case histories from his practice. In a paper published in 1965 he postulated that a critical transition begins around 35, not only in creative geniuses; it manifests itself in some form in everyone. Jaques called it the "Mid-Life Crisis" (probably coining the term, although at least one competitor challenges that). Jaques was careful to point out that the process of transition runs on for some years and that the exact period will vary among individuals.[8]

This creative crisis may express itself in three different forms.

The creative capacity may emerge and assert itself for the first time. The most familiar example is Gauguin, who at 35 left his outraged wife and his career in banking, and became a leading post-impressionist painter by the age of 41.

Second, the artist may burn out creatively or literally die. The age of 37 kept coming up as a prominent death line among artistic and highly industrious people. Jaques verified his observation by taking a random sample of some 310 painters, writers, composers, sculptors, and poets of superior gifts. "The death rate shows a sudden jump between 35 and 39, at which period it is much above the normal death rate," he writes. "The group includes Mozart, Raphael, Chopin, Rimbaud, Purcell, Baudelaire, Watteau. . . . There is then a big drop below the normal death rate between the ages of 40 and 44, followed by a return to the normal death pattern in the late forties."[4]

Third, of those artists who physically and creatively survive this unanticipated crucible, there are few whose work does not undergo a decisive change. The reactions vary from an agonizing eruption to a smoother transition, just as they do in the general population. It is useful to follow Jaques's analysis of the change in creative process that marks the artist as having passed through a midlife crisis. It is a strong metaphor for the change in quality and content we can all begin to feel in our chosen enterprise at this time.

The spontaneous, intense, hot-from-the-fire creativity that uses every experience as kindling, that combusts unselfconsciously and spews out work in whole ingots as if ready-made, belongs to the twenties and early thirties. Keats, Shelley, and Mozart are Jaques's prototypes. Jaques offers Robert Gitting's biography of Keats as a telling description of this feverish creativity characteristic of young adulthood:

> Keats all this year had been living on spiritual capital. He had used and spent every experience almost as soon as it had come into his possession, every sight, person, book, emotion or thought had been converted spontaneously into poetry. Could he or any other poet have lasted at such a rate?[5]

The artistic person who tries to force this style of combustion beyond its spontaneous point is the one most likely to burn out. To Keats's biography I would add the revelation of F. Scott Fitzgerald in *The Crack-Up*: "I began to realize that for two years of my life I had been drawing on resources that I did not possess, that I had been mortgaging myself physically and spiritually up to the hilt."[6] Fitzgerald wrote those words at the age of 39. Five years later he was dead.

If the artist is to endure, a change from the fevered pattern generally emerges. Jaques calls this new method a "sculpted creativity." From the late thirties on,

> the inspiration may be hot and intense . . . but there is a big step between the first effusion of inspiration and the finished creative product. The inspiration may come more slowly. Even if there are sudden bursts of inspiration, they are only the beginning of the work process [and] must first be externalized in the elemental state.[7]

Working then with the raw materials of his imagination, the matured artist begins the more considered creativity Jaques describes. The canvas, the score, the play that initially emerges is not the end product but the starting point, and it may be modified over a period of years.

A tragic sense begins to infuse the creative work of mature adulthood with new philosophical content. Shakespeare's comedies were the product of his twenties. His tragedies began with *Romeo and Juliet*, at 31, and are believed to have flowed in their triumphant series between the ages of 35 and 40.

Ruminating on a shaky Shakespeare or a depressed Dante may help to rebalance our perspective on the private travails of midlife crisis. Humanistic psychology is always talking about our "personal evolution." So often, focused egocentrically on the tribulations of our own meager seventy-year span on the earth, we dismiss evidence of the same themes throughout the evolution of Western man. Even in the thirteenth century, Dante lived on to a ripe 56 and Shakespeare, three hundred years later, to the age of 52. From their first encounters with the Deadline Decade and its savage fears, each of them went on to enjoy about fifteen years more of astoundingly prodigious creation.

The Spiritual Crisis

While religion yields less comfort to fewer people in this world of vanished certainties, it is a world view that has given many people a framework to make some sense out of the chaos. In Dante's time the Christian universe was ordered and meaningful; there was an earthly existence and an inferno of evil to be passed through on the way to a permanent state of joy reachable with transcendence to the next life. Dante the poet and Dante the pilgrim of *Divine Comedy* were lost at the beginning of the passage, but they both knew where they should be going. The divine intention was everywhere, pointing the way.

It took the philosophy of existentialism to say, in the words of Nietzsche, "This is my way; what is your way? *The* way doesn't exist."

The modern journeyer, Harrington, despite having been a highly vocal Catholic in his youth, spoke not of God as his shepherd through the valley of the shadow of death. He turned instead to psychoanalysis, where both guide and journeyer are constantly beset by shifting interpretations of sex roles, value and belief systems, and healthy behavior. Over a few short years it can turn out that gay is "good," CIA is "bad," and the only "healthy" defense system is to let it all hang out.

It was quite different in Freud's time. All his patients belonged to a cohesive class within Viennese society. When a person cried out, "I'm drowning!," Freud was able to bring the patient back to a consistent, if rigid, world. Today's psychiatrist is in a different position. He too paddles out to his drowning patient and tries to ferry him gently back to the float. But when they return, the float may be gone.

Many people locked in early to a tight religious tradition find themselves struggling by midlife against absolutist positions that no longer correspond to their experience.

Such a man came to see me not long ago about my writing in this field. He was a 46-year-old minister. "I'm glad to meet you, Reverend Raines," I said. (In this case, the name is real.)

"I don't like to be addressed as Reverend Raines anymore," he replied. "Call me Bob." He had taken off his clerical collar and was obviously enjoying it. His was a classic story of the young man who follows the family destiny and winds up in the corner I have described as a foreclosed identity. In this instance, his father was a retired bishop.

"All three boys in our family went into the seminary," Bob Raines explained, chuckling, "which indicates there was a quiet but very pervasive pressure on us. I bought it all. It was like carrying the family mantle. I never did disestablish myself from my father in adolescence, so I've had to do it in middlescence. He was a very powerful role model in ways that I've only been able to recognize in the past few years."

At 40, Reverend Raines felt as though his person had collapsed inside his profession. He was the one who was supposed to have all the answers, and he was not in touch with the answer machine. He wanted room to admit his own fallibility, his anger, his need to be stroked, and all his other blocked feelings. Convinced there must be others going through this profound personality change in midlife, he took the post of director of a nondenominational retreat center called Kirkridge in the Pennsylvania hills. The isolation in nature suits his need right now for reflection. He is experimenting with the group process in a varied program of retreats and workshops. Bob Raines's solution is to find his humanity by sharing his uncertainties with men and women, ministers, researchers, and writers, people like himself who seek a refreshment of purpose in midlife.

The Difference Between Midlife and Middle Age

In almost every way, the person who is *in the passage* of midlife is dramatically different from the person who has restabilized around middle age. And that goes for doctors who do the delving into our minds as much as for the rest of us. Indeed, the best brief illustration I can give is from a research project that compared junior analysts with senior analysts at the William Alanson White Institute of Psychiatry.[8]

The junior analysts, aged 37 to 39, share an orientation distinctly different from that of their seniors. Virtually every issue for the junior analysts is tied to their relationship to others. Midlife is defined in terms of the marriage partner. Career and status is connected to competition with younger people. Physical attractiveness is seen as a battle to hold their own against the inexorable march of others more youthful. The junior analysts believe that they are happiest right now, at the very age they are, and they all see themselves as just below the limit they set for middle age.

The senior analysts, having reached an average age of 53, view the midlife crisis as an individual matter. The middle years are seen as offering a new stage in the ongoing life cycle in which the person is defining himself in contrast to his parents, in contrast to his spouse, in contrast to his children. He is engaged in reevaluating his own life. The senior therapists are less likely to blame the marital partner for problems; whereas the junior therapists believe they can assign blame to one partner or the other and do *not* see marriage as a process that follows different stages. For the older people the terrific competitiveness with the other, all others, has relaxed, and more personalized enjoyments can be sought. As distinct from their juniors, they stress that the middle years are a release from pressures of involvement. The greatest freedom of all has opened up: the freedom to be independent and self-sufficient within any relationship.

The researchers sum up all these changes as the movement from "us-ness" to "me-ness."

How to put an age label on true middle age is a hot potato. Working-class men describe themselves as middle-aged at 40 and old by 60. Business executives and professionals, by contrast, do not see themselves as reaching middle age until 50, and old age means 70 to them.[9]

It is all very well for Neugarten to point out that middle-aged men and women are the "norm-bearers and decision-makers" and that while "they live in a society . . . oriented toward youth," it is "controlled by the middle-aged."[10] But trying to tell that to a 40-year-old is like trying to convince a teen-ager who has just lost a first love that the sky hasn't fallen. Possessed as most of us are in the midlife passage by thoughts of aging and imminent death, we are unwilling to identify ourselves with the stage beyond and therefore unable to believe in middle-aged power.[11]

After 45, most people who have allowed themselves the authenticity crisis are ready to accept entry to middle age and to enjoy its many prerogatives. The wrenching reexamination of the past is set largely to rest, and grisly fantasies of the future fade into almost comic perspective. The present once again absorbs them in living the now.

With this overview in mind, let's examine the specific responses of women and men and the predictable changes for the couple as they move through the midlife passage into middle age.

19

THE
AGE 35
SURVEY

Eleanor Roosevelt, a woman who was afraid of being alone, wrote in her diary at the age of 35, "I do not think I have ever felt so strangely as in the past year . . . all my self-confidence is gone and I am on the edge, though I never was better physically I feel sure."[1]

Her husband had taken a younger, prettier, gayer companion. She saw herself suddenly as older, discarded, a failed woman. The disassembling process began.

"Tightly, desperately, Eleanor clung to the old familiar ties and attachments—family, friends and duties—yet she could not shut off the moods of black despair that seized her when she felt that no one belonged to her and she was of no use to anyone," writes Joseph P. Lash in *Eleanor and Franklin.* "It was a time for her of harsh self-reproach and depreciation . . . there were moments when her belief that life had meaning slipped away from her." Painfully, the mold of her young adulthood crumbled. Inside the stereotype of the puritanical political wife she was no longer safe.

Her refuge was a place of death, Washington's Rock Creek Cemetery, where she often passed hours contemplating the bronze figure of Mrs. Henry Adams, who had committed suicide. It was a fitting place for Mrs. Roosevelt to grieve for her own dying self. She envied the peace reflected in the tranquil face of the statue, Lash tells us, and often wondered whether such peace could be achieved while one lived, through self-mastery. She buried herself in work. Work, she later wrote, is almost the best way to pull oneself out of the depths.

Bitter though her confrontation with midlife was, she did not die from this period of disassembling, nor did she vent her pain in divorce. She carried on through four decades of marriage and eight of the most significant decades of our political history, leaving her own indelible mark. The renewal process eventually did reward Eleanor Roosevelt with self-mastery, but only after years of exertion and a fierce display of self-discipline. Through her dedication to doing her own work in the world, she was able to master the most difficult task of all for a dependent wife in midlife.

The crux of it is to see, to feel, and finally to *know* that none of us can aspire to fulfillment through someone else.

From the age of 57 Eleanor Roosevelt looked back to write, "Somewhere along the line of development we discover what we really are, and then we make our real decision for which we are responsible. Make that decision primarily for yourself because you can never really live anyone else's life, not even your own child's. The influence you exert is through your own life and what you become yourself."

The Crossroads for Women

To each of us, our own crossing into midlife is the most dramatic. Women come upon the crossroads earlier than men do. The time pinch around 35 sets off a "my last chance" urgency. What a woman feels it is her "last chance" to do depends on the pattern she has followed so far. But every woman—the caregiver, the deferred achiever, the deferred nurturer, the integrator—finds unanticipated questions knocking at the back door of her mind around 35, urging her to review those roles and options she has already tried against those she has set aside, and those that aging and biology will close off in the *now foreseeable* future:

"What am I giving up for this marriage?" *or* "Is this career depriving me of personal happiness?"

"Why did I have all these children?" *or* "Is there still time to have a child?"

"Why didn't I finish my education?" *or* "What good will my degree do me now after all these years out of circulation?"

"Shall I take a job?" *or* "Why didn't anyone tell me I would *have* to go back to work?"

"Am I in a rut because I'm afraid to break out?" *or* "Is my husband the one holding me back?"

"Am I still single because I'm unappealing?" *or* "Have I cut myself off from love for fear it would end my career?"

"Am I really uninterested in remarrying?" *or* "Am I just afraid to risk another try?"

A half-dozen facts of female life combine to bring the sense of deadline to the fore at this particular age.

Thirty-five is when the average mother sends her last child off to school.

Thirty-five begins the dangerous age of infidelity. Kinsey's figures showed that a wife is most likely to be unfaithful, if ever, in her late thirties. The desire for a torrid experience coincides with her sexual peak, which for most women is reached at about 38. And just like men, women are likely to flirt with, fantasize about, and not infrequently launch into a promiscuous phase in midlife, hoping to cure the fears, "boredom," and sudden sense of bodily decline. Several recent books and studies have reported this, and the interviews conducted for this book confirmed it.[2]

Falling in love or finding a new husband is not usually the point. The idea is: "This is my last chance to have a fling before I lose my looks." Feelings that many women will confess to but not say aloud to their husbands were bluntly expressed by one suburban Westchester wife. After twenty years of faithful marriage and four children, she decided to take her first vacation alone and told her shocked husband: "Look, pigeon pie, you've been out in the world all these years, and I've been home. I'd like to have some more sexual experiences. I have the feeling this is not the way it's done."

Most women I have talked to, like most men caught up in the panic of midlife, do not want to give up the comforts of their marriage or risk being left alone. What they really want is to be saved from the jaws of bodily rot and delivered from the threat of death through the magic of a narcissistic experience, that is, by seeing their youthful self-image restored in the untainted eyes of a new lover. Beyond the apparent universality of that wish, women in particular are often seeking a replacement for the children who no longer preoccupy them but who are still dependent, a filler for the time suddenly available, and an outlet for rising sexual energies no longer met by a husband who is working harder and coming home with less sexual ardor. Most of all, they are looking for a diversion now that their lives lack direction.

Thirty-five is when the average married American woman reenters the working world. Census figures show she can then expect to be part of the work force for the next twenty-four years or more.[3] Few homemakers are prepared for that thunderbolt. There is no mention in high school of what comes after the proper selection of a husband, household appliances, and schools for the children: *twenty-four years* of using the skills she had the good sense or accidental fortune to acquire before she got married—or—twenty-four years of being a sales fixture or operator 47. No one tells girls that motherhood is only half a lifework.

As of 1970, seven-eighths of all women who held jobs were working "to help make ends meet."[4] The necessity factor is often overlooked in the zeal of the women's movement to explain, correctly, that many wives also want to work at something they like doing, around which they can build an individual identity. Furthermore, the necessity factor extends into very high income brackets. The wife of a senator goes to work because her husband's $42,500 salary is not enough to maintain a second residence in Washington and still fly her and four children home for Christmas to the west coast. Women in all social classes define making ends meet by whatever style of life their family would like to become accustomed to: moving up from a housing project to a middle-income apartment, being able to escape from a city apartment to a summer house, moving the children from public to private schools.

If the deferred achiever faced with the midlife reentry crisis is one of those fortunates pictured in the hair-coloring ads—college-educated, cashmere-sweatered, undirected, and mildly depressed—she has only her internal timidity to overcome. And her addiction to the luxury of *not having to work,* which cannot be stressed enough as a powerful counterforce.

For a vastly larger group of women, reentry to the labor market has nothing to do with the thrill of getting paid for selling whale-tooth pendants in one's own boutique. It is a matter of being bumped out of their homes by necessity and shunted off to the dead ends of the nation's marketplace. Waitress, typist, telephone operator, seamstress, hospital worker, sales help, office temporary, or back to the assembly line—these are the kinds of reentry jobs available to most wives, who were neither educated nor counseled to meet the task that will claim a quarter century of their lives.[5]

Ninety percent of women between the ages of 30 and 44 have no college degree.[6] Most of them expected to be caregivers forever.

Three-quarters of all the women who work either have no husband or a mate whose income falls below $7,000 a year.[7] The previous sentence is meant to be read twice.

Such a woman is often raised in an ethnic working-class community to believe in togetherness, home-cooked cabbage, and venturing outside only to sponsor church suppers. At the entrance to midlife, a Baltimore community organizer of this background spoke for many like herself:

> We dreamed of marrying white collar organization men and moving up and out. [Later] we looked at our husbands' paychecks and found that with incomes between five and ten thousand dollars we weren't making it anymore. We were the near-poor. So for many it was back to work. It was a shock to be 34 years old and out of the labor force for 14 years.[8]

The most severe penalties in pay are connected not with a woman's educational level but with the number of years she has been out of the labor force as a homemaker. Women over 30 have a rough time, and the prospects are even drearier after 40. Many married women with children (according to a Labor Department study) actually moved backward in occupational status from the jobs they held before they married. And nearly a third of the women reentering the work force between the ages of 30 and 44 were unable to progress beyond the jobs of their youth. After 40, the unemployment rate is more than one-third higher for women than for men the same age.[9] To top off all these depressing statistics, in a recession, women along with blacks are the first to be fired.

These are the realities into which the young blue-collar wife will run, despite her new dream. If you recall, she has been found in the most recent study to envision returning to work when her two children are in school. By then, she wants a career more personally rewarding than the utilitarian job she had before marrying. She has moved into the pattern of the deferred achiever. This may be one of the most significant changes in *attitude* in the past quarter century, but it is still far removed from the factual possibilities.

Thirty-four is the average age at which the divorced woman takes a new husband. By this time an average of thirteen years has elapsed since her first wedding day.[10] She will have another try at building a partnership to fulfill her need for intimacy.

Thirty-five is the most common age of the runaway wife. And the runaway wife is one of today's fastest-growing phenomena. In the last twelve years, the ratio of bolted wives to runaway husbands has gone from one in 300 to one in two. The typical profile of the runaway wife, as described by President Ed Goldfader of Tracer's Company of America in an interview, is a 35-year-old woman who was married at 19 and had her first child within eleven months. "Since then, she has devoted her life to child-rearing and housekeeping and is now at an age when she feels she no longer has time to make a meaningful change in her life-style. Often, her husband has almost stopped thinking of her as an individual."

The tracer's firm sends the husband a questionnaire. He is to fill in the blanks of his wife's personal history. The common responses are revealing.

EYE COLOR: can't remember
HAIR COLOR: dishwater blonde
HOBBY: none

Under "Habits" the husband also leaves a blank.

Under "Mental condition" he almost always writes "emotionally disturbed."

The startling aspect of the runaways is that they are economically well off. It is not the deprivation of things that drives them to break out. It is the loss of feeling valued or even noticed by their husbands and the anticipated deprivation of meaning in life.

Margaret Mead said in one of our interviews: "I think the principal rebellion today, following the rebellion of men in their forties, is the tremendous number of women who are leaving their husbands *before* they're deserted. These are women under middle age, the women of 35 who feel, 'This is my last chance.' "

Thirty-five brings the biological boundary into sight. Probably for the first time a woman glimpses that vague, uncharted realm ahead leading to what demographers so aridly call the end of her "fecund and bearing years." The deferred nurturer is running out of time to defer. The unmarried achiever must face the motherhood issue squarely. The greatest number of single-mother adoptions are made by women between 35 and 39. And some of the most high-powered, late-boozing, unmarried, and unsentimental career women simply stop in their tracks and fall in love with the new experience of being pregnant.

Irma Kurtz is a free-lance journalist who made exactly that decision at the age of 37. An unmarried, witty, and egocentric American who had reached the top of her profession in England, she'd never had time to have a child before. "This was my last chance," she has written. She loved being pregnant. "It was my first act of devotion." There were also moments of panic when she could see only endings: "an end to vanity and adventure, an end to freedom, an end to my own egocentric childhood." But there is a certain seemingly universal comfort in pregnancy once the baby begins to kick. One is on an express train. One can settle back and enjoy going to the end of the line. "It was delicious to enter an entirely new area of information and interest," this journalist wrote, "at just about the age when one feels all feasible experiences have been explored."[11]

Irma Kurtz's baby had to be delivered by Caesarean section, but she was prepared for that possible consequence of her choice. The surprises that lay in store concerned the completely altered perception of time, and of self and others, common to the older mother. Rather soon after the birth of her son, her social cupboard emptied out.

> Broken sleep, which probably affects me more than it would a younger woman, and a hectic daily schedule, mean that hangovers are out, at least for the time being; it is surprising how an unwillingness to drink a great deal limits a social life in my age group and it is even more surprising how very boring I now find the alcoholic conversations and boozy enthusiasms I used to enjoy. . . . Looking back, it seems to me that before my baby was born I rarely talked about anything but myself anyway. . . . I now know for sure that I am mortal and I know that I am growing older. . . . My God, I think sometimes, when he is 13, which is so very young, I'll be 50, which is no mother chicken! . . . but I have not found this knowledge alarming.[12]

The conventional wisdom has been that having a baby after 35 is risky and not to be recommended. In gynecology textbooks the woman who becomes pregnant for the first time at 35 or over is still termed an *elderly primagravida*. And when the interval between births has been ten years or more, it is said that labor may simulate that in an elderly primagravida.[13] But there is mounting evidence that the dangers have been very much overplayed.

Just what are the risks? After consulting a dozen sources, the only age-related risk I can report on with certainty is Down's syndrome (mongolism). In mothers of 20 the chance of bearing a mongoloid child is one in 2,000. At 35 the risk is no more than one in 1,000. But by the time a woman is 40, the chance increases to one in 100, and the incidence of mongolism doubles almost every year after the age of 40.

Amniocentesis, a procedure in which a small amount of amniotic fluid is withdrawn by needle from the uterus, is now 100 percent accurate for detecting Down's syndrome and other chromosomal abnormalities.

Other factors found by a March of Dimes study to correlate with high risk in having babies in the thirties were low socioeconomic status and inadequate medical care. That is because the mother's general health and nutrition contribute so significantly to the infant's birth weight. And low birth weight was found to be the most important factor in fetal deaths.

Beyond these risks, which can be ascertained in advance, some of the most experienced specialists in the country tell me that all the rest of the warnings about late pregnancies, such as a rigid birth canal or inelastic tissues, have been overdone. "With good obstetrical care, there should be no difference between women who are 40 and women who are less than 40," said Dr. Raymond L. Vande Wiele, professor and chairman of the Department of Obstetrics and Gynecology at Columbia Presbyterian Medical Center, in an interview. He also noted that the most frequent elderly primagravida is the divorced woman who is childless and remarries at 38 or 39.

"These women are usually willing to go through anything to have a baby. If there's anything abnormal about their pregnancy or labor, they ask to be put on the operating table without batting an eyelash." The obstetrician, too, is much more likely to terminate a long labor with a Caesarean section in the older first-birth mother. There are other possible complications connected with her age, but the hard facts are few. Hypertension and diabetes are more common with age, and 40-year-old women who have never been pregnant are much more likely to have fibroids, which can cause hemorrhaging. Whether or not any of these conditions is present can be determined by examination before the woman tries to become pregnant. The one common complication that cannot be predetermined is a *placenta previa*, or low-lying placenta, which exposes the mother to serious bleeding either near the end of her term or during delivery.

Most obstetricians do not like to see women get pregnant after 40, which is rare anyway. But all the evidence on this question of late motherhood is not in. So if you are a woman of 35 or over, be advised not to take the first opinion you hear in answer to the question: "Is there still time to have a child?"

A different phenomenon is noticeable among caregivers faced with the biological boundary line. They may return to school or pick up on a latent talent or prepare themselves to reenter the working world. But just short of completing the degree or taking the actual plunge into the career world, what they often do instead is become pregnant again. "This is no mistake," I was told by Dr. Ruth Moulton, an assistant professor of psychiatry at Columbia University. "By having another child, they let the baby make the ultimate decision by default."

Even if a mother has already made one of the most definitive decisions of her life—"I have had my last child"—and is happy with her resolve, she senses that a momentous period in her life is about to close: "My time will be freer as the children grow older, and though the prospect is exciting, I wonder if I'll find something important enough to replace them."

When all the converging factors are toted up, it is no wonder that a woman begins to feel the change to a midlife perspective at 35. Whether or not she *acts* on her life survey at that time and what part her husband might play are other matters. The expansion of Eleanor Roosevelt, a caregiver who might otherwise have remained in the background, was precipitated by a painful marker event. Such an outer event often speeds up the process of disassembling and renewal. The process may just as well begin with an inner pull that has no explanation but won't let go. Let's step now into the life of a contemporary Washington wife and feel the pull as she experienced it.

The Re-potting of Priscilla Blum

In the midst of an evidently splendid existence, with all her girlhood wishes apparently fulfilled, a baffling symptom appeared. Crying.

She found herself weeping in the bathtub of her second husband's charming Georgetown town house. The wife of one of the fastest-rising comets in political journalism, she was in her own fullest bloom, ginger-haired and lithe and vivacious. But there it was again, a little spill of tears before her ritual morning phone calls to the various secretaries and ambassadors. Another spill *after* they had accepted the invitation, which would extend her husband's contacts and later be reciprocated with a loftier invitation, raising her husband's professional stature yet another notch.

The weeping spells lasted for six months. It made no sense.

Priscilla had been with Don Blum for two years. (Their names are fictitious.) Together, in a happy remarriage, they had fused into something like a new delta-winged aircraft. He was the body of it, the breadth of his information backed up by a blunt ambition. She was the sensitive radar, aligning their social life from day to day with the shifting winds of Washington power. "I was totally involved in balancing everything," she says. "I didn't want to bother Don with my problems. He was working furiously."

Washington is a company town. The line between public and private life is seldom discernible. Priscilla had come to this town a new bride at 33. Her two children had a new stepfather. The Kennedys were starting the New Frontier. "It was terribly heady stuff, wondering if Don would be happy with me, wondering if he would 'make it' in Washington. I was very much impressed with Don and very much in love—with that pragmatic driving force of his, yes, the *force* of his dream and the restlessness of his ambition. It was so seductive."

Perhaps, it was suggested, Don was just as ambitious as she could not permit herself to be?

"Oh, he was nothing like me."

Priscilla had been raised in the Wasp tradition to balance all things graciously but never to step into the foreground herself. Projecting her own wish to "make it" and her own unallowable "driving force" onto Don, she became the backseat driver of his career. She says as much, but doesn't hear what she is saying. "Don was a worrier, filled with anxieties about whether this was going to work or that person was mad at him. He asked my opinion again and again and again, talked over every problem with me. He really ended up a columnist because I made him send off his stories."

Priscilla was victorious at 35 in helping Don make it, yet something always rings hollow in vicarious success. She busied herself with the Washington wives who play tennis and meet at the White House for classes with the curator. Everybody laughs and swims and there is always the pretense of friendship, but it is only their husbands who have something in common, whose conversations have content. The husbands are trading information for power, to which only the men of Washington can nakedly aspire.

"Why was I crying? It seemed to be almost a physiological thing. I couldn't go into it very deeply; that came much later. I had to be calmer to ask myself any questions."

The answer that might have come up from below, from her inner custodian, would probably have been: *You have no right to want something for yourself. You are supposed to be your husband's support system.* Priscilla was not ready to do battle on that level. She still had to be the "good" girl, raised by her mother never to be evidently assertive. When something began tugging at her to be "bad," she cried.

"Finally in a desperate moment, I told Don, 'You've just got to take me out to dinner alone!'" She confessed to him that she was constantly weepy and depressed. "The only reason I can think of is, it's Washington. You go out five nights a week, and every night you see Arthur Schlesinger. After nine months of seeing Arthur Schlesinger five nights a week, you discover you don't know him any better than you did in the beginning."

Don Blum did not see his wife as a blank, nor did he see only the single dimension of her that fitted comfortably into his dream. He saw through her symptom to Priscilla, a woman literally crying for separate self-expression. It was never going to be met in the ritual minuets of Washington dinner parties.

"My advice to you is, don't entertain anymore," he told her. "The hell with it. Don't be careful of your tongue; you can say anything you want. Why don't you try going back to art?"

It took Priscilla two years more to believe what her husband had said. She rearranged her life structure first, going back to school to study art and trying to fit her entertaining around it. "But it took two years before I really believed that Don didn't need me to help him see the people in power and that I could take my painting seriously. To get that discipline back takes a long time and tremendous confidence. One of my teachers thought I was fantastic. That helped. Who else was important in that period—? Oh, Jesus, Don almost died!"

She was 37 when Don had a heart attack. He spent three weeks in the hospital reading Shakespeare's tragedies. Returning home, he announced, "I'm not going to live like a vegetable. I can't change my habits even if they do bring on another heart attack." He was only 41.

"I thought about nothing but death," Priscilla

remembers. She fretted over the body-monitoring of her husband while he, though subdued with tranquilizers, plunged again into work. But he did cut back their social schedule to nothing. The funny thing was, after some months, they became devoted to this splendid seclusion. Priscilla began to devise better ways to coax out Don's anxieties and defuse his angers. Nights were not allowed to pass with a "What's wrong?" and "Oh, nothing."

"We were constantly reassessing everything," Priscilla says. "Then the Kennedy assassination. I got pretty morbid on the subject of death. We both gave up smoking. I wouldn't fly for two years. To the point where I took the children to Florida for spring vacation by train, twenty-seven endless hours! That's how vulnerable I felt. I also had the feeling that I was going to be punished for some unfathomable thing. But the more I got into my painting, the less and less I thought about death."

Change of action so often precedes and stimulates change in gut perception. For the next two years, Priscilla was absorbed in developing a gift that enlivened all her senses. She had a discipline, a new community of friends, and a dream that couldn't be confused with Don's. To come home from the university paint-stained and spent, no less happily spent than a woman after love—this is when Priscilla can say her outlook began to change.

And so did Don's. Like so many men who encourage their wives to stay at some individual endeavor, he became bewildered when she actually did. "In the beginning he didn't really notice it. He was too involved in his own problems. He wanted me to be happy. I went back to school and stopped crying, and he said, 'That's great.' As it lasted longer and longer, depending on his mood, he was just annoyed. 'If you'd get your head out of your studio, maybe the dishwasher would get fixed!' Yet now, when I sell a painting or have a very successful show, he struts like a peacock. He doesn't understand what I do, but he appreciates the praise of people who matter."

Her fortieth birthday passed over like a brief summer shower; Priscilla had already come through the thunderhead. The inner change continued to evolve and took shape around the country house they bought. In time this has become Priscilla's world, her creation. "I'm allowed my reclusive nature there," she says. She retreats to the country for six weeks at a time to work on her annual show while Don, ever the peripatetic journalist, travels the world.

"Are you all right, Pris, out there in the country all alone?" come the calls from certain Washington acquaintances. For the past few years, with mounting frustration, these gossips have been waiting like jackals to comfort themselves with the carcass of yet another dead marriage. But the Blums' marriage has never been better.

Every now and again when the phone calls give Priscilla guilt tremors, she goes to Don. "Am I being a bad wife? Should I postpone my show and stay with you in Washington?"

"You're mad," he will say. "You know me, I've got my nose in my work night and day. And when you're preparing a show, you're *thinking* the show. My great antidote is taking rest weekends in the country with you. Don't let other people make you unsure. You'd be letting yourself down."

Priscilla is 45 now, and much that was extraneous has been cut away. What remains is the deepening bond with Don, a few lovingly cultivated friendships, the quiet of her country world and her painting. "It's a minor talent," she can say, because self-honesty comes more easily, "but it doesn't matter. I give people pleasure, and to be engaged is life-giving. I couldn't live now without the seriousness of my painting."

She no longer enters rooms expecting to attract men, although she is a perennial beauty. There is something stronger in her soil now, and she is determined to preserve it.

"I want to be able to grow older with all my female toughness intact. Serenity, yes, but with a certain sharp edge to it. Accepting that, goddamit, being 45 has some pretty great things about it, and being 50, and 55. I tell myself in the mirror, 'If you're going to paint, you can't drain your energy fighting the inevitable! You're going to get older, so face it; master the fear.' I'm also not going to compete for attention in an arena that is going to give me pain, with a lot of younger women. I'm going to get attention because I'm somebody *in my own right*."

What we have seen here is a woman signaled by a symptom, at 35, that she could not dare to interpret. She was changing but afraid to change, wanting more than her role allowed her but not allowing this new aspect. And it was new. There was nothing dishonest about her earlier choices. She was a caregiver who piggybacked her dream and happily followed the dictates of that pattern. She had simply arrived at another turning point. All she knew was that the container she had chosen and found satisfying up to that time didn't quite fit anymore. Where it used to be filled with the excitement of feeling needed at every moment to help launch her husband's career, now that he was moving up, she felt a looseness around the edges. She was an incidental dinner guest in a company town.

Suppose her husband had been less perceptive or more selfish or simply alarmed, as so many of us are in midlife when our partners suddenly become unpredictable. He might have denied the crisis. Told her she was being childish, she ought to keep busy, stick to her promise to promote his career, and so on. That would have reinforced her feeling of "badness." From crying, she might have moved on to drinking, swallowing pills, divorce, or running away in desperation. Instead, he let his partner have her crisis and suggested a moratorium on her former activities. Even then, she was afraid to give up her old role. So strong was the direc-

tive of her inner custodian that she felt she was going
to be "punished for some unfathomable thing."

It took the event of her husband's heart attack to
force them both to a complete reassessment. Letting
go of the other-directed activities that were now life-
wasting, each became more selective of purpose and
more tolerant of the other's separateness. He is a man
who thrives on the scattershot stimulation of global
contacts and involvement. She is a woman whose
sensibilities have grown more private. Her creative
energies are drained by overexposure to people; she
thrives on being alone. Gradually, over the course of
the Deadline Decade, they have worked out a way of
being both more intimate and more individual. If it
flies in the face of Washington's codes or causes people
to gossip, they say to hell with all that. They have
found a way suited uniquely to Priscilla and Don, at
their time in life.

20

THE
AGE 40
CRUCIBLE

Men feel the time push around 35 as well. Yet it seldom prompts them to stop and take an all-points survey as women so often do at this age. Most men respond with a burst of speed in the race for career position. It's "my last chance" to pull away from the pack.

Whatever the field . . . the middle manager can't wait to take the driver's seat . . . the idea man, tired of accommodating others, may begin scrambling for the capital to start his own business . . . the skilled worker considers quitting to buy his own cab . . . the corporate lawyer who has been content to do a little public-service work on the side wants to pull real weight in the political arena. It is no longer enough to be competent and promising; a man wants now to be recognized and respected. As an established writer with his own style. Or a scientist with his own research specialty. Or an academic who is published. Notwithstanding the deprivations in personal life and disregarding the legions of others with the same idea, many white-collar men dart ahead over the next five years in a double-time run to "become president."

The career acceleration that for so many men precedes any inner survey also serves to delay it. By the time the true and sobering issues that are driving them forward begin to insist on acknowledgment, the impact may be more cruel. A crucible rather than a survey.

Jung was the first to propose that between 35 and 40 "an important change in the human psyche is in preparation. At first it is not a conscious and striking change. It is rather a matter of indirect signs. . . ." But Jung was clear about pointing out that the change of perspective generally begins earlier in women, while men show a rise in frequency of depression at about age 40.[1]

In our society, turning 40 for a man is a marker event in itself. By custom, as if he were merchandise on a rack, he will be looked over by his employers and silently marked up or down, recategorized by his insurers, labeled by his competitors. Pyramids being what they are in the professional world, most men will have to adjust their dream downward to some degree. That doesn't mean they have to flog themselves for being second-rate. In fact, it may save them from running into blighted hopes much later, prod them into finding refreshment in a second career or another way of working within the original occupation that provides more meaning.

The startling observation here is that the wunderkinder and workaholics who *do* come close to realizing their dream often have a more rugged transition to make than those who miss the mark. These recognized successes have the problem of following their own act, an act that rarely brings the sweeping fulfillment they anticipated. If they are to avoid stagnation, they must generate a new set of aspirations and listen to the other voices in themselves that have been neglected up to now.

One puzzlement about all this midlife momentum is the different directions it takes in men and women. Most women pause to reconsider both the inner and the outer aspects of their lives and then try to rebalance whatever distortions they feel between personal contentment and worldly aspirations. Why is it that the same sudden change in time perspective so often urges men to run harder in an even narrower track?

Corporate life in particular encourages a man to slight all other aspects of his personality to fit the narrow role of organization man. If he has learned well the lessons of conformity, he will believe that his work performance is the only criterion of his worth.

The Middle Manager

Ed Dilworth, never what you would call a driven man, is the manufacturing manager of a General Motors components plant. He was raised along lower-middle-class lines in a midwestern farm community. If it weren't for an executive officer on his submarine who influenced Dilworth to "step up a plateau," he wouldn't have made the effort to go to college. Three years into service with GM, he was still working seven days a week as a night foreman on the third shift and thinking, "I went to college for *this?*" It was the promotion to quality control foreman, he says, that really started his career. He was 30. Since then his promotions have been regular, although not remarkable. With bonuses as the incentive, he has been content to concern himself with the care and feeding of a hydraulic brake press the size of the Loch Ness monster.

Today Dilworth is 36, and what he wants to be is president of General Motors.

"Age is starting to be a factor," he told me. "Right now, it's to my advantage. But if you look at the people driving to the top, you have to move fast, or usually you die before you get there."

I asked this unpretentious man, whose personal style runs to black shirts and white ties, if he had always had the idea of "running for president" in the back of his mind.

"Absolutely not."

"And now?"

"Now, yes, I want to be Number One. The bonus

potential is what makes any executive perform—up to a certain level. Then, they tell me, they're motivated by just wanting to be Number One. President or chairman of the board. It's not because of the money; it's because they want to try running the show. So I think there are stages of it. I figure if you're going to be in here, giving it all you've got, you might as well try to go to the top. Once people have got all the money they want, they become philanthropic. The older guy who's all for the good of humanity has already made his million."

Like many men at this stage, Dilworth is now in competition with his mentor and touchy about being told by his wife to hang up his coat or any other vestige of being treated like a little boy. He keeps the phone plugged in on the patio during dinner. The problems he is having with absenteeism or alcoholism at the plant are not so easily diluted by a couple of drinks. He doesn't care to talk them over with his wife the way he used to. Although Dilworth still thinks his wife has a "fantastic personality," his idea of her role in the life plan has changed.

"If you want to carve it up in cold, hard facts, what she was supposed to do before the children came was provide the main means of support while I tried to get an education. We just thought about having a nice family and a nice home."

Today he relies heavily on his wife to manage the money and the children, but there are little stabs of doubt that her lack of a college education might hurt their movement into more exclusive corporate circles. They have more fun, more financial freedom, but at the same time, Dilworth's accelerated career goals are becoming a self-imposed curb on that freedom.

"I'm not the best father; that bugs me a little bit. I try to do things to make up for that. Like this year, I contemplated a four-week vacation. But I only took one week because I'm limited as to how long I can be away from the plant. It's probably not true, but I feel that way."

The change in time perspective is still hooked entirely onto external issues. And like many men seeking to cope with the hurry-up feeling, Dilworth has set a clear timetable for his goals. What is unusual about this middle manager—and propitious—is that he has two alternatives mapped out.

"The next thing is to get to general manager level. It's got to happen in six years if I'm going to get all the way to the top. If it doesn't happen by the time I'm 44 [giving himself two years grace], rather than getting into a mess with my family or giving up, I would try self-employment. I've always thought farming was rewarding. That's what I come from. It would be a secondary choice, but that's better than letting GM make an old man out of me. If I don't think I can get all the way, I don't want to go any farther than general manager. Because after that, there's about four VP steps you have to go through, and you lose all your notoriety in the process.

"An example is this John DeLorean. When he was general manager of Chevrolet his picture was always in the papers. Then he was promoted to executive VP over all the assembly divisions, and he started to lose the limelight. Those jobs are not glamorous. You make a lot of money, but you lose the power you had on the step below. If you could interview DeLorean, I think you'd really get a story."

The Corporate Wunderkind

John DeLorean is one of the legendary mystery stories of the auto industry.* In his entry years, he offered exactly the profile General Motors prefers for its executives. He came from the same lower-middle-class background that most of them did, went to the same brand of small technical college, and was never exposed to Harvard Business School, where minds are

---

* This subject, a public figure, gave permission to use his real name.

developed that are apt to be dangerously receptive to change. He owned one suit.

Even at 32, when the man who was to become his mentor made him head of research and development for the Pontiac division, DeLorean was still "the squarest guy in the world," married to a secretary and rapidly becoming too flabby to fit into his suit. All of which tells General Motors this is a man to be trusted. A technically trained man with a narrow focus will concentrate on making a bumper better by using less steel and increasing the profit margin. He can easily be polished up with a Dale Carnegie course and a trip to Brooks Brothers.

If such an eager young beaver performs excellently and conforms personally, he can become boss of a whole division at 40. Before reaching 50, he might even be making three-quarters of a million dollars a year and rolling toward the presidency.

All these things John DeLorean did. Had he continued to comport with the profile, he was a shoo-in for president of the largest manufacturing company in the world. But DeLorean got religion. What are the dislocations in store for such a man? Big business does not want people with a "broad vision," people who talk (even before the Arab oil embargo) about giving the public smaller cars because that's what the public wants. The auto industry wants to give the public what they're making. John DeLorean resigned from General Motors at 48.

"I'll tell you what really happened," he said halfway through our first interview. "When I got into the car business, I couldn't tell you the name of the president of General Motors. I had my engineering project, whatever the hell it was, and I was totally consumed by it. As I moved up, I slowly started to recognize the gigantic impact of the automobile business on America—unbelievable!"

Raring to become a giant himself but not knowing the first thing about how to behave like brass, DeLorean came under the wing of Bunky Knudsen. His boss was a most unusually stylish man for a GM general manager and a revelation to DeLorean. "My dad was a factory worker. He had very little interest; he was an alcoholic. No person had the influence on my life that Bunky Knudsen did. It was like exposing a ghetto kid to the finer things of life."

At 35, looking directly into the mirror of his dream, DeLorean was shaken by the first dark reflection. The occasion was a trip to Palm Springs for a dealers' conference. There he met a man he idolized as "almost a god," the retired president of GM, Harlow Curtice. The next day DeLorean dropped in on the golf pro to find out more about his idol.

"That's the loneliest human being who ever lived," he was told. "He comes into my golf shop for a couple of hours a day and talks to me and my assistant about the automobile business. We don't know anything about the automobile business, but we listen to him. He just seems to want to talk so badly."

The shock of this premonition unleashed painful questions. "What's it all about?" DeLorean asked himself. "Why are you doing all this? You're just like one of the machines. Suddenly you'll get obsolete and worn out, and they'll scrap you. Does that make sense?"

But rather than stay with this painful survey, DeLorean drummed it out by driving ahead to become, at 40, the youngest general manager in Pontiac's history.

As the midlife crisis closed in, DeLorean grew more frenzied about making external changes. He tightened the pressure on dealers and drove up sales, hoisted heavier weights, raced more motorcycles, divested himself of a wife his own age, lifted his face, dyed his hair, turned up in discotheques with bosomy film stars, turned around the failing Chevrolet division in a virtuoso performance, and took a wife younger than most GM officers' daughters. Having retooled the whole package, he adopted a son, his first child. Still he ran, pausing only for a few moments at dawn to see the boy before he left for marathon days of work.

Soon enough, lonely and shunned by the older wives of Detroit, his beautiful child bride fled back home to California.

DeLorean was 46 before he let those painful subjective questions break to the surface again. He was at the Detroit Automobile Show. "It just struck me. Here I was spending my life bending the fenders a little differently to try to convince the public they were getting a new and dramatically different product. What gross excesses! It was ridiculous. I thought, There's got to be more to life than this. Am I doing the thing God would have me do here on earth?" Even then, he was projecting the discontent with his own superficial body changes onto the equally superficial changes in chassis styling that made his work in the auto industry feel, at bottom, a sham.

Another two years passed. DeLorean's restlessness was intensified by his promotion to corporate vice-president. Deprived of his showcase as a star division manager, where he had run his own show, he found himself in a decompression chamber, an isolated group executive on the fourteenth floor a few seats behind the control panel. If he couldn't be seen, what else was there to recommend his position? More influence for the social good? The company had ignored his earlier predictions of the demand for smaller cars. It seemed that now at least he was in a position to convince his fellow officers to take a more realistic approach on federal emission standards. His arguments were shot down. Prestige? The price was conforming to the good gray visage and narrow social life of the GM inner circle.

Perhaps the most unsettling part was the view of the presidency from up close. The man currently occupying the chair was the same kind of hands-bound evanescent god he had first glimpsed at 35. Breathing down the neck of his dream, DeLorean knew at last that it would not be deliverance.

Plunging deep into his second adolescence, he entered a sexual olympics of dating and discarding name beauties. In December 1972 he called up the Max Factor cover girl, a model half his age, and by May had taken her for his third wife. Three weeks later, he walked out on GM. In what would seem another projection of fears he was fighting in himself, he announced, "The automobile business has lost its masculinity."

Explaining this explosive rearrangement of his life, DeLorean says, "The hard thing is always to give up the structure. Corporate life is a security blanket. Sure, I could have coasted for seventeen more years at $750,000 a year without trying too hard, but coasting along is not my style. I live on adrenalin. And I wanted to make a contribution. Most people wait until retirement age, and all of a sudden they don't have the drive and zest left. I thought, as long as I'm going to change the direction of my life, this would be a good time to stake out a year and do some of the things I've been talking about."

With zeal approaching the evangelical, DeLorean threw himself into a year's nonpaying tour for the National Alliance of Businessmen. He was doing in a committed way what had only been possible as a sideline at GM, where he had pioneered some of the first hiring programs for ex-convicts and hard-core poor.

"I really want to give the rest of my life to working in areas that are important to the country," DeLorean told me, "but still for profit. I don't mean I'm going to be a social worker. I want to be an important part of the solution to the energy problem. I must be working twice as hard as I did before. But no amount of money or success remotely approaches the feeling you get inside from doing a good thing for somebody."

Letting Go of the Impossible Dream

"There are two tragedies in life. One is not to get your heart's desire. The other is to get it."[2] Even though a bon mot typical of George Bernard Shaw, perhaps this is a truth that applies to all. No matter how close a person comes to achieving his dream, it will not fulfill all his wishes. The loss of magic that he feels—that everyone feels to some degree in mid-life—is the loss of magical hopes attached to the dream when it originally took shape. Out of the bushel-ful of factors peculiar to a man's occupation and personal background, I noticed one that seems to predict more generally whether a man's midlife crisis might be mild or severe. That is the degree to which he still sees his dream primarily as a solution to per-sonal problems or has converted that dream into more realistic goals.

Although DeLorean is genuine in describing his rising need to make a social contribution, this is still overshadowed by the one issue he dared not mention: his terror of advancing age and powerlessness. He had a father who made him feel powerless, who left the family floundering financially and emotionally when the boy was young. Once DeLorean saw the power wielded by giants of the auto industry, his dream took shape. Everything about it was predicated on the image of himself as physically strong, mentally fleet, emotionally fearless, and on his way to becoming all-powerful.

Today he cannot admit one stroke of the terror that would bring down the whole masculine mystique. Instead, he banishes all physical reminders of his advancing age: the fat, the same-aged wife, his own sagging face and graying hair. Like a sorcerer with a magic wand he has recreated for himself the face, the body, the wife, and the child that belong to the heroic dream of the 25-year-old man, for in this private king-dom all reflecting pools give back the image of per-petual youth and idealized masculinity.

Whatever life pattern a man has followed up to this point, he is not immune to wanting the magic of his youthful dream revived (although he may play out the wish in fantasy only and find enough of an outlet that way not to endanger the life structure he does value). Particularly vulnerable are those strivers and superachievers I call wunderkinder: men, like De-Lorean, who are spurred on by the hazy but deeply ingrained belief that full gratification and complete liberation await them upon attainment of their success.

The gratification fantasy, boiled down from my discussions with wunderkinder, goes like this: Once I become president, or full professor, or create the building, the book, the automobile, the film that captures the imagination of our times, people will recognize me, admire me, defer to me. I will be raised aloft like the hero of Saturday's game and allowed to indulge all the desires I have denied myself.

The liberation fantasy would go rather like this: Once I become powerful or rich, no one can criticize or order me around anymore or try to make me feel guilty. I won't have to stand ever again for being treated like a little boy.

The gratification they are really seeking is derivative of the childhood desire to center the world on ourselves and to have all our demands appeased. The liberation they are looking for is freedom from the influence, censorship, and guilt-provoking love of the inner custodian. Above all, there is the vague promise that by becoming masters of their own destiny they will beat even the grim reaper.

What a brutal letdown to discover that this is not so. Success, no matter how grand, does not bring omnipotence. There is always someone who can make us jump. The chairman of the board, the stockholders, the constituency, the advertisers, or someone closer to home, perhaps the aloof adolescent daughter who rules the powerful man with her disdain: "You're an elitist patsy of a corrupt system."

Not only that, colleagues are seldom altogether charitable about a man's success. As Karen Horney noted, "Even the winners in American life feel insecure because they are aware of the mixed admiration and hostility directed at them." Even if the winner's colleagues are not better qualified, many will believe they are, but due to luck or his manipulation of connections or his unsavory tactics or the aesthetic crimes he is willing to commit in the name of commercial success or whatever, he is on top instead of them. They wait for any chance to expose the winner's weaknesses. Many a man who has come a long road to success is deeply saddened by the critical attacks from those very colleagues he expected would recognize and respect him at last.

Nor is it automatic that once a person becomes acclaimed or powerful, the voice of the inner tyrant will be stilled. The work of individuation is internal. We all have to do it unless we prefer to remain very old children. Even when we do finally claim the authority formerly wielded by that inner custodian, we are not only freed but also bereft. We have lost the inner companion who for so many years also made us feel watched over and safe.

The Joys of Caring

Once we run into this inevitable disparity between the dream and whatever it leaves wanting, what incentive do we have for continued growth?

Erikson says it comes from moving through the crisis to *generativity*. Generativity means feeling a voluntary obligation to care for others in the broadest sense. Having children does not ensure generativity, nor does being childless necessarily prevent it. Erikson's definition also includes becoming more productive and creative. Adults who miss out on the enrichment of generativity, he warns, will lapse into prolonged stagnation. Often they will begin to indulge themselves as if they were their own only child.

Many men in their forties do experience a major shift of emphasis away from pouring all their energies into their own advancement. They begin taking pleasure in teaching other people or correcting social injustices. Some, like DeLorean, make a dramatic shift away from purely materialistic goals. Some become consultants. A stockbroker I know is still busy making money but has turned in his free time to helping rescue Jewish refugees around the world. Quieter men who have always seen their work in terms of doing their duty and being responsible may take a job in government or the community that nobody else wants but that needs to be done. Still other men may not register a change in job title or recognize the shift, but although they stay in the corporation, they gradually commit more of their time to training younger men or improving the quality of product or services for the public good.

The Problems of Generativity

For every tycoon who turns philanthropist and every executive who moves into the role of mentor, there are dozens of middle managers who believe that unless they can hang on to their percentage of the mouthwash market, they are no good. Having measured their worth for so long by profit and loss sheets, they have internalized all the values of the corporate system. And few American corporations have been accused of being in the generativity business. The midlife manager who wants to take the cancer-producing agents out of the fertilizer or to introduce a new and truly useful product that doesn't promise the same profitability as mouthwash will be told in so many words: "Tell it to the stockholders!"

Behind their protective fenders, their collapsed rebellions, most middle managers know they are a dime a dozen. By the time they are 40 they also know their ceiling. Younger men are not a joy to teach; they are a threat. Along with this conflict of generativity goes the fear of taking further risks and the loathed lack of heroism that every day leaves behind further evidence of that fear.

One night at a banquet I sat between two bearded men, both 40, who were treading water somewhere in the 400-man middle-management pool of a California cosmetics company. Gray beard mentioned to black beard that he had recently seen an old college class-mate of theirs. "He was the high-diving champion, remember?"

"Well, not *the* high-diving champion," black beard corrected. "When they sent him to the Olympics he was only an alternate."

Undeterred, gray beard went on to relate that what their classmate does now is fly around the country appearing at the openings of shopping centers. He dives off the roof onto a mat. He has become a human champagne bottle. Twice he has missed the mat and injured himself badly, spending many months in the hospital. Straightaway he goes back to jumping off roofs again.

"Can you imagine what it's like to get on a plane for Des Moines knowing you might die in a shopping center parking lot?" gray beard speculated.

Black beard replied, "I'm not sure I wouldn't rather tell my kids what I do is dive off buildings than what I really do. Which is to go around in circles talking bullshit and trying to hang on to a job I hate."

A man in this familiar state, feeling unappreciated and unutterably valueless, often keeps the tears inside; they are shunted into ulcers and covered by accumulations of overweight. He sits in restaurants eating and swelling, saying he shouldn't, "but just this time," and slowly committing suicide. Anyone who challenges him to reconsider his priorities—a wife, a friend, a management consultant—becomes the enemy. He may try every form of self-delusion, retreat into drinking or hypochondria, cast his wife as a monster, abandon his family, almost anything to forestall looking into the mess inside. For if he were to examine one-tenth of what is making him miserable, he would know too much to ignore the other nine-tenths. And that would mean changing so many circumstances of his old life structure, he might prefer not to look at all.

The ideal response would be to consider lightening his load of cars and mortgages and sixty-hour executive workweeks so that his spirit could be freed for exploring other endeavors that might be satisfying in a deeper sense, activities or intimacy for which he had no time when he was riveted on "making it." There's no telling where a man might find a revival of purpose. I know several men who joined their volunteer fire departments and feel good about working in this physical way as caretakers of their communities. Others go to cooking school, study Gaelic poetry, spend one whole weekend getting to know their wives again in a motel room. Among other nice things that can come out of a long weekend of love and talk is the "Let's try it!" decision to begin some joint enterprise they long ago set aside.

The Courage for a Career Change

Yet for many executives there is so much in this kind of adjustment that implies failure and obsolescence. They may want to get out, but they often find it harder to move to a less prestigious job than a skilled worker does.

I tested this observation on a Harvard-trained management consultant, James Kelly, who works actively with executive officers of large companies. He agreed. "One clear stage," he described from many experiences, "is a man who has been in a large company for twenty years and has achieved high levels of status and compensation, but not quite enough to make it to the top echelons of power and prestige. He's over his head in business. He is earning too much money for his own good. The corporation is not getting its money's worth. He knows it; they know it. But to settle for anything less, he would consider demeaning."

The consultant has two ways of handling middle managers in this kind of midlife occupational crisis. He may try to convince the executive that the role he is playing is an appropriate one for him, that he's good at it, and that to think about being president of his company is not a wise aspiration for him. To others he would say, "Get out! You have a lot of money and time. Do something else." How long it actually takes for a middle manager to make such a change is another story.

"It requires a couple of years, easily," says Kelly. "The fears are of stopping and flopping. These men are workaholics. They have something they know very well and have worked at. To stop and move to something else is very tough."

Is there still any need to question, "Why a second career?" The simple fact that people are living longer in better physical condition than ever before makes commitment to a single, forty-year career almost predestinate stagnation. Added to that is the accelerated rate of technological change that makes almost any set of skills subject to obsolescence. We are becoming accustomed to the idea of serial marriages. It will be progress when we come to think of serial careers, not as signifying failure, but as a realistic way to prolong vitality.

Many executives are beginning to think this way. The American Management Association found in 1973 that 70 percent of middle managers surveyed did expect to search for a way to make a career change in the foreseeable future. It is not dissatisfaction with their original occupation that motivates them. Rather, they are "actively searching for new interests which they had not previously entertained as career possibilities."[3]

The man who has already obligated himself to support a wife and children cannot consider such a felicitous midlife readjustment. Or can he?

The Turnaround

After thirty years of conscientious service with a big oil company, Mr. Gifford had asked for a transfer to Maine and been told, fine, he could take care of Maine operations. The next paycheck he received was for exactly half the salary he had been making in Boston; no warning.

His son, young Gif, having watched all this, turned heel after college and went to work for a small local theater company. It was a transient's life, with no truly solid commitments (he couldn't tell you why he'd married his wife, for instance), but nonetheless a pleasant life for seven years. Then he began to grow jumpy about being at a dead end, a little too comfortable; this coincided with a divorce. The next thing he knew, Gif had talked himself into being the public relations man for a senator. He was 29.

In the highest of spirits he moved to Washington. Soon after, he persuaded a woman for whom he had always had a yen to give up her footloose, Europe-roving, bachelor career life and marry him. A child followed.

"The sense of power, Jesus Christ, little kid from Maine and suddenly you're down there in the nation's capital, getting to know leading journalists on a first-name basis. They're courting you, and you're courting them. There's also the growing sense of having an *influence*. If you read the paper and something strikes you as correctable, by Jesus, you've got a senator to bitch to! I was well paid. We could afford to eat out. The whole setup was secure and comfortable."

Rooting and Extending in personal life and professional influence—by all measurements Gif's early thirties were good years.

The pace changed when the senator he worked for decided to run for President. The men around him began to levitate on the rising heat of attention. Following some natural law of Washington, where so many people identify with men of ephemeral power, the vicarious importance felt by the senator's staff members turned some of them greedy and others vicious.

"I'd come home at night and have three stiff ones. I didn't play with the kids anymore; I could hardly speak. After another drink the fatigue would break, and I'd tell Annie the story of the day. She's basically optimistic. But I had the increasing feeling of being a captive. The senator could call at three in the morning. Then the traveling began to bother us. I don't like a night away; I feel very strongly about home and family. Above all, I was troubled that I was not my own man."

This last is virtually a motto of men in their mid-thirties. Keen to stake out their own turf, impatient to cut restrictive ties so their own worth can be appreciated, many of them begin sprinting faster up that mountain.

Gifford's reaction was different. He halted in place at 35 and surveyed the territory both before and behind him. "The prospect of working for a president is very heady stuff, but if that didn't happen, what the hell was I going to do? I was getting to be 35, and I had no real profession, no independence. I could have gone back to theater management, but where? I couldn't see myself starting all over again. So what are the options? I had the idea I had to get back to reality. To me, reality was Maine. From the moment I told the senator I was leaving, I couldn't wait, just couldn't wait."

Gif had just as many family obligations as your average man, perhaps more: five children by now from the two marriages. Nevertheless, his instincts said, "Go back to Maine before it's too late," and he followed them. The next two years were breathcatchers. He worked for the governor of Maine while scratching around for a commitment that fit, took a course in real estate, and started his own realty business.

On the lip of 40, Gif is an independent man. The housing business is terrible, but he waves that off with admirable élan. If he and Annie have to live on their savings for a while, that's all right, too. They would just as soon take the winter off and go skiing.

But the result of Gif's early midlife reappraisal extends further. Unlike many men who feel the first stirrings of a more nurturing, expressive, feminine side around 40, Gif is not terrified about admitting this aspect. Indeed, he relishes letting go to it. "I told

Annie, any time she wants to go back to work, by
Jesus, if she can earn enough, I'll stay home and take
care of the kids. I really mean it. I adore children. And
to tell you the truth, at this time in my life, I would
just love to paint houses and build cabins."

It costs money to have a midlife crisis. It costs
even more in security waived. If a man insists upon
maintaining, or accepts without a whimper, the status
quo of roles that says all economic burdens should be
on his shoulders (and many do), then he must face up
to the fact that there is no light at the end of his tunnel. He is locked in for good. The last breath he draws
will be to say, "The insurance is paid up, honey,"
because he will be taking care of his wife even after he
is dead.

If the average couple is to find refreshment in midlife, the earlier division of roles between breadwinning
husband and caregiving wife needs renegotiating. It
is much easier said than done, of course. Realistically,
whether or not a wife has marketable skills depends
on the life pattern she has followed up to now. Sub-
jectively, the questions are: Does she want, or dare, to
try them out? Is he willing to watch his wife go into
independent orbit, or does he fear the competition?
She has to face the female's inner timidity problem.
He has to contend with the male's Atlas complex.

21

SWITCH-40s
AND
THE COUPLE

A cry tries to rise to his lips. This is no pipe-smoking evening where the public man rests briefly from doing the work of the world, to be revived in the effulgent circle of family pride and love. When the firelight dims and the dogs have been walked, there will be no cradle of expertly working wifely hips to draw off his tensions. He is stretched out on the floor of a friend's den, for there isn't any more a familiar bed for the politician to go home to. His wife has left.

"I notice for twenty years I never wept a tear," Kilpatrick is saying. "In the Marine Corps the important thing was not to show fear, don't let your emotions reach the surface. Now I can't go to a happy movie without getting red and weepy."

Fiercely, he contracts his stomach muscles, ten times, fifteen—as if only by the repetition of this old soldiering exercise can he hope to maintain control—twenty times, stops. He seems to be climbing alone, terminally alone, up and up into the regions of primal dark.

"I've never seen grief of this magnitude," he whispers. "How long will it take to get over it? A psychiatrist told me to expect two years. I suppose I worshiped my wife. I feel she was the basic ingredient in any success I've had. I don't know quite what to do without her. It's a somewhat selfish attitude, I guess, thinking of my own capability and not of what her needs are. She's selling real estate now, and I think she's completely happy. She's pleased with her own ability to do something she never thought she could do. I'm knocked out by her performance."

The last linking illusions to his old dream seem to give way. Dry sobs are torn from so deep. . . . It is a while before he speaks again.

"I think a man trains himself to make great decisions on issues about the world. But to become tough enough to survive in the political competition, you also become a consummate asshole. All I know is, a year later, in retrospect, I'd drop out of this phony business tomorrow if I could get her back to work on this *human thing*. As you get older, the great things become family and friends and children."

My own throat is choked with sympathy for this man, for the necessity of his painful confessions. I have heard them before from men of his age, whatever dominions they have conquered. What signal didn't he see? What switch didn't he make?

Put together the mounting strong-mindedness of the midlife wife and the strange stirrings of emotional vulnerability in the midlife husband, and what have we got? A mystery story at the peak of its suspense. A chase of highest excitement after our missing personality parts. And an almost predictable couple crisis.

Many of those personality parts will be hidden right under our noses—in our partners—for most of us choose a mate who represents the unknown or un-allowable aspects of our own psyche: "I was in love with his driving force," or "I called her a year-round fireplace." We also project on that partner all sorts of magical ideas: "My wife was the basic ingredient in any success I've had," or "All my security has to be attributed to my husband." Furthermore, over the years we manage to fob off many of our own faults and defaults on this man or woman: "She brings out the meanness and jealousy in me," or "If it weren't for him, *I'd* be the artist in the family."

It is only now, in this mysterious passage leading to our second season, that we confront the sexually opposite side of our own nature. It is a strange and frightening side, not yet made fully conscious.* All suppressed parts of the self are not linked to sex roles. As has been repeatedly stressed, no matter what we have been doing, there will be some aspects of ourselves that have been neglected and now need to find an expression. In the case of the woman who has put achieving first, midlife may be a time to relax that effort and put more of herself into cultivating friendships, being a companion to a man, being more active in her community, letting a spiritual side come into play.

It is virtually impossible to bring the mystery to resolution without a struggle. The intimacy balance will almost surely be upset. Being open to intimacy depends on a strong identity, including a firm sense of our sexual identity. Any time our self-image becomes shaky, as it does during every passage, but particularly in the passage to midlife, we can expect our capacity for intimacy to be disrupted too. If we are to emerge from the struggle as whole beings, our sexually opposite side must be made conscious. The magical powers assigned to our partners must be given up, the projections withdrawn. And if we do this enormous work, what then do we have left?

Jung offers the best explanation:

> Above all we have achieved a real independence and with it, to be sure, a certain isolation. In a sense we

---

* Among others to observe this exchange of characteristics is Dr. Bernice L. Neugarten, who writes: "Important differences exist between men and women as they age. Men seem to become more receptive to affiliative and nurturant promptings; women, more responsive toward and less guilty about aggressive and egocentric impulses" (From *Middle Age and Aging*, 1968).

are alone, for our "inner freedom" means that a love relation can no longer fetter us; the other sex has lost its magic power over us, for we have come to know its essential traits in the depths of our own psyche. We shall not easily "fall in love," for we can no longer lose ourselves in someone else, but we shall be capable of a deeper love, a conscious devotion to the other.[1]

It isn't easy to grasp the connection but it is one of the central points of this book: How is it that accepting our essential aloneness allows us to become more loving and devoted? It is because the dismay of realizing that our safety does not reside in anyone else emboldens us to find security within ourselves. And once our individuality is no longer endangered, we can be more magnanimous in giving to another. It is possible, at last, to compose the dividedness between our Seeker and Merger selves.

"To be sure," says Jung, "it takes half a lifetime to arrive at this stage."

Correcting Disparities in the Dream

There is also the possibility, of course, that the couple will collide, crack up, or simply fall into that haphazard, slow-motion lapse known as the twenty-year marriage slump. It isn't the weight of twenty years of marriage that makes people miserable, so much as it is entering midlife in a youth-worshiping culture with the false expectation that the roles and rules, the dreams and ideals that may have served well in the first half of life will carry over into the second. They do not; they cannot. The second half of life must have its own significance. Else it shall be little more than a stunted and pathetic imitation of the first.

Much has been said earlier in the book about couples who have already taken the divorce route and in the process may have corrected their course in some way. In this chapter we are dealing mainly with those couples who have remained together. It may not yet have occurred to them that change is essential, that change is good.

Whatever unvoiced disparity persists between the husband's and the wife's expectations of the dream, it will now be forced into the open.

A 43-year-old writer confided, "I was absolutely horrified to discover that in the back of June's head— she admitted it one night—she had always expected I would become Scott Fitzgerald or Gay Talese, that at some point I would have the half-million-dollar book. She only admitted it after I'd had two bad failures in a row. I realized that what she'd had all these years was the white middle-class dream that you marry the romantic writer. It threw me into deep depression. I didn't write for six months. I went to the track every day, and everything began to slide. Our sex life went to pieces. June saw what was happening. I was retreating from her, retreating from intimacy. I felt rotten, and I began to shove off some blame on her. I began to dread going to bed, and it was horrible for June. She let herself go physically."

Of course this man had wanted to be a famous writer. When that began to look impossible, he transferred to his wife the blame for unrealized hopes they had once upon a time shared. June reacted like so many women who live through their men. She admitted aloud to a disillusionment that her husband couldn't bear to look at as his own. If a man who loses his dream feels like nothing, the dependent wife feels doubly nothing. She loses even this bootlegged identity, which may be the only one she had. Perhaps June would not have been so brutal and accusing with her husband if she'd had a sustaining importance of her own. She might have helped him enjoy the liberties of time and talent that can follow from letting go of the stereotyped famous-writer dream.

What happens when the wife piggybacks her dream and it does come true? For fifteen or twenty years she has been living off the vicarious fruits of her husband's slowly ripening success, very often acting as his inspiration, intuiting for him how to treat the people he works with, insulating him from the humdrum of how to get the roast thawed in time for unexpected guests, and sparing him the million and one details of feeling that have gone into cultivating the children. The fruits of expectation may have been fine to savor, but when it comes time for the awards to be passed out, he is the one who walks to the podium to bask in recognition. She is known only as Mrs. Brown, as in "Find Mrs. Brown a chair," an uncomfortable appendage no one quite knows what to do with.

Coming into their forties, many such women find themselves no longer satisfied to be silent carriers of the dream that formerly made them feel safe. "I feel this reemergence of competitiveness," the wife of one admired man explained. "I think the reason I'm so shaky now is, I don't know what to do with it."

The Envied Wife

The most striking contrast between husband and caregiver wife in the midlife couple is his sense of staleness compared with her usual feeling of unboundedness. For all her qualms and confusion about where to start looking for a new future, she is free. Up from the years of having small stumblers affixed to her hand, able now to walk at an adult pace, better at organizing her time and integrating her priorities, she is released to soar into realms undared on wings untested, and while seeking her originality, to sing with the unaccustomedness of all that she attempts.

Approaching the same stage in life's journey, her husband finds his sense of self in quite another condition. Whatever rung of achievement he has reached, from his feet hangs a ladder of endlessly repetitive acts. And above him, are there any surprises? Not unless he creates them. "There are no second acts in American lives," was the attitude of Scott Fitzgerald.[2]

418

And although everything in this book and most of adult developmental theory contradicts him, many men of 40 would agree, if only until they have floundered through this passage and left the depression and ennui behind.

In the meantime, most of the men I talked with expressed envy of their wives.

"Oh Christ, she's unbelievable now," is how one businessman portrayed his spouse. "She looks marvelous, she's found out she is still attractive to men, and it's all because she has found a whole new purpose in the world. I can't help feeling envious of her. Life seems so hard to me now; it's just the constant effort of keeping up. All I have to look forward to is writing another annual report and then another report—"

Now, the complaints of boredom with a narrow, preoccupied spouse are more likely to come from the woman.

The switch is painful, if predictable, for here is an almost exact reversal of the husband and wife positions at Catch-30. Back then, she was the envious one. Feeling stagnant and formless in the wash of domesticity, she looked covetously upon her husband's nice, tight career container. He had a form, a solid identity. Little did she anticipate the terrifying staleness that could build up inside that container over twenty years—making her own unshaped yeastiness in the middle years seem to him the very elixir of life!

Just as she is brought up short by seeing the *actual man* behind whatever masks of strength and heroism she might have projected onto "my husband," he, too, must reckon with the *emerging woman* who will no longer be contained by his fantasies of "my wife." The descriptions men give of "my wife" as they have seen her up to now fall into quite repetitive clichés.

"She provided a continuing peace of mind."

"She has been my Rock of Gibraltar."

"Judy was kind of an anchor, not dragging me down, but making it possible for me to wander around a lot without feeling I had to confide my troubles in anyone else. I could be the self-contained, cool character. I think I used Judy in lieu of other people."

What happens now, when the docile wife and dutiful hostess, on whom he has always counted to be the absorber of anxieties, begins to feel her own oats? She is ready to strike out, go back to school, get a job, kick up her heels, just as he is drawing back, gasping for breath, feeling futile about where he has been and uncertain about simply holding his own on the job and in bed? How is he likely to react to her sudden surge of independence?

A moderately successful man in his early forties, after several hours of grousing about his wife's recent thrust into the world, admitted, "It would be simple to distill all my complaints into, *Where is she going when I might need her?* It's as ugly as that."

The time-honored advice to wives of forlorn 40-year-old husbands is, "You must build a man's ego." Wives obediently pour out a heaping dose of mothering, only to feel betrayed when it backfires. And it will almost certainly backfire. Exactly what a man cannot accept as he attempts the midlife transition into full adulthood is a wife acting conspicuously like mother.

The word *conspicuously* is the key, for what we are talking about is very like the push-pull felt by the adolescent boy: He wants to know his safety figure is still there to back him up, but he'd rather die than have her hover oppressively over his private wounds, asking, "What's wrong?" "Where are you going?" "Why won't you talk to me anymore?"

The same wifely qualities he idealized in the marriage of his twenties, when they benevolently provided for his nourishment, he now rejects as maliciously designed for his entrapment. There is probably always an undercurrent of ambivalence in the way a man feels about his home, but it seems to peak during the midlife passage. However stable his line of development has been up to now, he may begin oscillating from one extreme of behavior to another in a way that looks, and often feels, mercurial, capricious, "crazy."

A saint could not beat this ambivalence. For if his wife reacts like a saint, he will see her as trying to seduce him back into the trap of being the little boy.

That is his side. What of her side? She is trying to muster the courage to market her skills or acquire new ones or simply to sort out the odd bag of capacities she has accumulated over the years into something that connects. Autonomy is not so frightening because by now there have been repeated experiences with separation and loss. But the excitement a woman finds in her new self-expression often makes her husband feel, incorrectly, that he is devalued. "What was Nancy looking for that her family—primarily I—wasn't able to supply?" fretted one man whose wife began making serious work of her pottery. "I felt dislocated. I no longer had the same claim on Nancy's time and attention. Her pot-making was a competition."

Cutting through all the fear-ridden bickering that accompanies this emergence of a person from a role, one woman wisely extracted this insight: "Ed calls me 'tough' now, but it's not nearly so frightening as he pretends it is."

If a formerly dependent wife is determined to take the next developmental step, she must at this stage withdraw the parental authority she has assigned to her spouse. She must give *herself* permission.

Suppose she does make some bold external changes. Suppose, for instance, she pulls together her tattered self-confidence and runs for president of the League of Women Voters and wins? She sees her husband becoming more anxious. He would have become anxious at this stage in any case, but a wife is likely to believe that she is the cause. This idea pushes her back. Guilt creeps into the picture. And then anger.

She is thinking: *Why can't he hold together like a strong husband, so that I can go out and grow without feeling so guilty?*

While he is thinking: *What in hell is she doing running off in the other direction when I'm falling apart?*

This is a common lock (though not the full stock and barrel) that challenges the couple on approaching the Switch-40s.

No couple contract is forever. Just as surely as he must give up the confining idealization of mother-wife, she must let go of the magical notion that she has a father-lover who should never show self-doubt or vacillate in his commitments. The couple contract *must* be renegotiated in midlife. That doesn't mean that two people sit down as if in a board room and hammer out a new deal overnight. It means that a series of readjustments must be made over a period of years. If this isn't done, she may well turn into just the domineering harridan he dreads—Big Mom, sworn somehow to even the score by becoming house bursar and the curator of her husband's every weakness—while he perhaps slips into the passive and effeminized role of a Dagwood Bumstead. One way or another, if her mounting assertiveness and his set-aside feelingness are not made conscious and allowed healthy expression, they will come out in some other, disagreeable form.

Where Have All the Children Gone?

Another, and most poignant, aspect of the Switch-40s concerns the children who are slipping away.

She is only eleven, my daughter, and she is going, almost gone from leaf to flower to fruit. Two faint strawberries are sweetly filling on her chest but the dressing room curtain must be drawn tightly, tightly, Mother! The very *idea* of easy privilege that comes with being a beautiful young woman is already working on her, modifying the zeal she had only a moment ago for being an undercover agent. Although there is still enough careless child to pack her fingernails with play dirt, she is in awe of the big ladies who buff and paint their nails until they become ten perfect plastic spoons. I regard as precious every night she still calls for me to tell her secrets to.

But forests of prose have recorded the bittersweet experience of mothers letting go their children, as if we were the only ones moved by this profound shift of purpose. What struck me in the interviews was the unsalvageable loss suffered by so many men. Their own tenderness comes into flow just when their children are demanding distance. It comes too late.

After all the years spent (or misspent) on building his career, the midlife man so often turns back to the nest to recapture "this human thing" at just the time when his children are in high revolt. The vignette that follows speaks for thousands of similar situations.

"He started from nothing and built his own company, which now has worldwide offices," recounted Nora, the puzzled wife of a young president, "but in the past year he's been in some kind of personal agony. [The young president has turned 40.] More and more he thinks less and less of himself and what his work means. He needs to know he matters to the children. I think he's feeling that all his past absences have to be made up for. Suddenly he wants to do things like family outings. I've done all that. I'm feeling like a teen-ager! Everything's flowing again and I'd rather go off on a wild weekend for two. We're out of sync. And the children think it's positively claustrophobic to be with the whole family."

Fathers hang on to children too, asking the utterly impossible, which is not, "Give me the present with you" but rather, "Give me the past with you."

As often as we are reminded that the adolescent must be allowed to give his allegiance to another or devote himself to an idea in order to pull up roots, those roots are being torn out of our hearts. Father is called upon to give up the embrace of a son or daughter who formerly saw him as the repository of all the world's wisdom and to give it up to the embrace of dubious heroes, opposite causes, other and probably transient messiahs. It feels to the parent like a kidnap, of course. Shall just any stranger, clever enough to manipulate this need for a new and glorified model, be permitted to poison a child it has taken so long to grow? Or if not to poison, to lead him into suspending any subtleties of judgment? But sensible debate is out of the question. This is a battle for emotional authority.

"But shall I tell the truth?" confesses William Gibson the playwright, or rather, William Gibson the father of a doubting 16-year-old son. "For years I've been in mourning and not for my dead, it's for this boy, or for whatever corner in my heart died when his childhood slid out of my arms."[3]

Having feared for his son's dissolution in the numbness of drugs and nonbelief, Gibson demurred when the boy took up residence in Spain under the tutelage of the Maharishi. The Indian guru points the way to bliss consciousness through clean living and meditation. Gibson himself was raised a Catholic and is married to a psychoanalyst. But these gaping distinctions in dogma were not allowed to blind the father. Gibson went with it wisely. He traveled to Spain and saw that the boy had found healing by his own methods. Waiving judgment on the virtue of his son's hero, he encouraged the quest. "I don't enjoy the veneration of his master," Gibson writes in his book about the experience, "but I know how significant it is in his growth."

Envy Gibson the capacity to write out the pain. Most men haven't that outlet while they negotiate their end of the father-child shift.

And so the 40-year-old man is likely to be challenged on three fronts at once. He allows his emotions just as his wife is distinguishing herself from him. He reaches out for his children just as they are repudiating him. He gropes for some way to be generative exactly when he is feeling at his most stagnant ebb in work. Perhaps it wouldn't be so hard if he knew all this was predictable. And temporary. And that it is a necessary preparation for the period of easement that follows.

Roughly at 45, a man will generally restabilize. Having come through the worst of the tempest, he will probably tie up to whatever set of living conditions and priorities he has arrived at. If he has reordered those conditions and priorities while in turmoil, it augurs well for his growth and good cheer. He can't be positive this restructuring will work out in a satisfying way, of course. No one can; that remains to be seen in yet another season. But equilibrium does return, and that is certainly welcome. The man's inner attitude toward this restabilization, however, runs a gamut of variations. His spirit may be charged with the vibrancy of renewal. Or it can be marred by resignation or the ache of incompleteness, in which case midlife issues will resurface again at the half-century mark.

At 50 there is a mellowing and a new warmth. The competitiveness that gave so many relationships an abrasive edge in the past is tempered by greater self-knowledge. If a man has come to terms with his essential aloneness, parents can be forgiven. If his individuality is no longer threatened, he can be more relaxed with his colleagues and enjoy a new kind of fellowship with his former mentor. If he has stopped measuring his worth by job status alone, he can better enjoy whatever part of his work holds most meaning for him. And if he has allowed his sexually opposite side free expression, he may find a true friend in his mate.

Provided he has granted her the same license.

Mother's Release from the Nest

Generativity is a fine concept as far as it goes. All the male researchers into adult development agree with Erikson that the path to replenishment in midlife is through nurturing, teaching, and serving others. Yet once again, the male life cycle is presented as the adult life cycle.

Overlooked is the fact that serving others is what most women have been doing all along. What is the first half of the female life cycle about for the majority of women if not nurturing children, serving husbands, and caring for others in volunteer work? If a young wife has any extrafamilial career at all, it is most likely to be in teaching or nursing.

It is not through more caregiving that a woman looks for a replenishment of purpose in the second half of her life. It is through cultivating talents left half finished, permitting ambitions once piggybacked, becoming aggressive in the service of her own convictions rather than a passive-aggressive party to someone else's.

But the difference between men and women with regard to generativity is even more basic. Losing her powers of procreation forces a woman to redirect her energies. At whatever age a woman knows incontrovertibly that she will never have another child, an intriguing phenomenon has been observed. A new kind of creativity is released. Whatever pursuit a woman decides to follow, she pours more of herself into it than she ever did when the option of reproducing was still available.[4]

That is not to imply that a woman will or should give up caring about others. On the contrary, the emptying nest frees many mothers to extend their concern for future generations into local political reform, national movements, international congresses, even protection of the species. Society becomes the beneficiary of a creativity formerly reserved for serving Papa and 2.9 Baby Bears their porridge.

If a struggle for men in midlife comes down to having to defeat stagnation through generativity, I submit that the comparable task for women is to transcend dependency through self-declaration.

Why does a cultivated and intelligent couple like the Kilpatricks, who began this chapter, so often miss

426

the switch? Let's go back over their story, beginning where the first signal of midlife beckoned one person to change before the other had registered any inner shift. For as always, the tempo of development is different for each partner.

The Second Wind of the Citizen-Soldier

They were sending the marines into Vietnam, but he, of course, would not be called. Korea was his war. No one calls up a 37-year-old reservist with five dependents and a law practice fat as sirloin.

The sun lay in the valley like liquid silver that spring: he had so much time. The poverty years were over. There had been ten of them, then five more of holding a vacant lot in a lush southwestern valley until they came out of debt. Now their dream house was going up. The workmen saw to that, each with his guarded expertise. Kilpatrick had time to coach Little League and take the boys rock-climbing. And if he was lucky, the rocks would be wet. There might be a slip in his footing—a call again for cool savagery, a feeble spurt of adrenalin, a split-second chance to pit body against nature before he went home to lie beside his tanned wife and watch the war by pressing effortlessly on a remote control box. Things were as fine as they could be. That was what bothered him. It's a terrible thing when a marine hero goes soft.

His wife happened to open the letter from the Marine Corps denying his request for active duty. That was the first she knew. She cried, and then the hurt turned to cold anger. How could he even consider it! she demanded when Kilpatrick came home.

"I'm restless. It would be a great challenge to go to Vietnam," he said. "I want to serve the country."

"Your obligation to family comes first!" She said it, believed it, as if this truth had been set down incontrovertibly in the Justinian Code. Peggy's idea of what a lawyer should do was what her father had done: build a financially successful practice and fill a

safe full of wills and come home every night to romp
with his children and work in the garden. She thought
she had married exactly that man. Kilpatrick, however,
had elected to go to Korea right in the middle of
law school, although he could easily have gotten out
of it. She had been pregnant at the time. One does
not easily forget.

By now he could argue, "My practice is in the
kind of shape now where I can turn it over. I have ten
lawyers working for me and ten secretaries—"

"And you pay your secretaries too much as it is."

"Are you going to tell me what I should earn?" he
lashed back. "You've never worked. You're not in
touch with the real world."

She told him she was in touch with raising children and being a good wife and that was more important than any damn war.

The next year Kilpatrick tried again to go to
Vietnam, this time as a civilian with a government
agency. He and Peggy had their ritual argument about
obligation to familia versus patria. But then she came
around. She and the children would only be happy,
she told him, if he was happy. Kilpatrick was stunned.
He had already decided not to go.

They built a pool that year and sat around it
drinking gin and tonics.

One day Peggy pulled a drowning child out of
the pool and calmly brought him back from blueness
while everyone else, including Kilpatrick, lost their
heads. He remembers thinking how strong she was.
Hell yes, he made all the decisions, and she believed
that dependency on a man was a woman's lot in life;
thank God for that. But he had begun to see in her a
toughness, an enduringness plain as that of a sound
tree and thus taken for granted. "In a lot of ways she's
stronger than I," he thought. The switch made him
very uneasy.

At 40, out of the blue, Kilpatrick announced he
was going to run for office. Brick-chinned, feisty, un-
guarded, and unbought—this was the thrust of the

man as he charged into politics for what he called "the glorious fight." All the odds were against him; that was the best part.

It is important to know that Kilpatrick recalls having no changes before this. None at all. When asked if he had any reservations about how his life had worked out at 40 as compared with what he had projected: "I never thought about it. I had exactly the same ideal I'd had since I was 20. An American who becomes a good lawyer, serves his country in peace, and serves the military in time of war—this was my whole ideal of what a citizen ought to be. A citizen-soldier in the Greek concept."

And his wife, did she have a goal? "Her life has been built entirely around my life."

What was his idea of Peggy when he married her? "I honestly don't know. She was just basically a very happy person. I suppose I idealized my wife. I feel she's so important to any success I've had. She was the heart and soul of my campaign effort. A really enthusiastic effort."

Peggy hated politics.

Winning a seat in Congress was for Kilpatrick like taking Pork Chop Hill with a platoon. Recharged, he made his trip to Southeast Asia at last. What he found were refugees maimed by U.S. bombs and living in caves and beggars roaming the scorched fields of Cambodia. Shaken and disgusted, he returned a zealous convert to the antiwar effort.

The 43rd year of Kilpatrick's life takes on the quality of the present tense. It is a year of presidential primaries, and he is appearing at an enormous rally. His voice crackles as he calls for a national dialogue on the "administration's policy of deliberate deception in Southeast Asia." The fire comes up from his belly. In the lineup of deft and purring professional politicians he stands out, once more the lone grenade pitcher and hero of his youthful dream. For a man of no clubhouse credentials representing a conservative state, it is a fleeting luxury to put his own convictions on the line.

He is racing with time. For the past ninety-seven days Kilpatrick hasn't been home long enough for more than a frozen pizza.

On the plane back to Washington he is writing a letter to the Pentagon. He writes straight through the landing. The plane empties. All except the fiery politician, an aide, and me. We are pinned three across. Kilpatrick is still burning up the page. With a knowing smile, his aide suggests that others might like to go home now.

"What? Oh. Sorry." The citizen-soldier lost in the oblivion of duty, Kilpatrick blurts, "If you can wait one more minute, we may end this war one day earlier."

Peggy is waiting at the end of the campaign trail, slim, blonde, barefoot, shirttails out over her corduroy pants. At first glance she is a dead ringer for Doris Day.

The politician clinches her waist and plants on Mrs. Kilpatrick a genuine Keepsake Diamond kiss.

"How were you?" she asks.

"Not so good, honey. Low key, scared of all those people."

Kilpatrick slips on a cassette and draws his second wind from *The Sound of Music*. "You know what?" he turns back to Peggy with unabashed delight. "Talking to eight thousand people, that was a new experience!"

Peggy is beginning a new experience, too; she is 40. Books and papers for her course in real estate are stacked all over the dining room table. They will have to eat in the den. She brings in the frozen pizza and French wine.

Kilpatrick makes a few jokes about his wife's new project, but there isn't a great deal of punch in them. The previous year, labeling himself an intractable sexist, he had voted against the Equal Rights Amendment. When he came home, Peggy was sitting demurely on the sofa. He ran down all his arguments.

430

She gave her verdict in a word—indeed, a word she had never used before.

"Bullshit."

Kilpatrick says she has been that way ever since.

While the couple discusses strategies for the politician's future public appearances, Kilpatrick browses through the *Washington Star*.

"Half the couples in Washington will be single by next year," he quotes idly.

Peggy says this is a tough town on couples.

"Widows live longer," he reads from another article.

Peggy says, "When women get equal job opportunity, we will start dying as young as men." She pokes the politician, "And *you're* going to help legislate that opportunity, aren't you, darling?"

The head of the intractable sexist jolts up. The instant freezes. This is the look mixed of shock, envy, pride, and fear that says the couple switch has begun to register. Peggy will never again be the same woman, and they both seem to know it.

Kilpatrick drops back into his newspaper, muttering, "God, a pushy real estate lady. Just the image scares me."

For the next year Kilpatrick was away three weekends out of every four, wrapped up in primary campaigning. Peggy rarely joined him. Something had gone out of her since he'd pulled up the family and moved them to Washington; the senator didn't know why. He supposed it was a blow to her security when their income was cut in half. But ever since Peggy had mopped up the details of closing his law practice and draped the contents of their dream house in shrouds of white sheeting, she couldn't be budged. He resented it.

"You get so goddamned tired of staying alone in hotel rooms. There's a great desire to have another human being who's sympathetic to what you're trying to do."

The girl was 26 and said "right on" to everything Kilpatrick did. For the six months he was in love with her, he couldn't touch his wife. That came as a shock. It was women who were supposed to be skewered to their emotions. Men, it is said, can fuck a chicken. "Well maybe some can, but most of my friends around 40 found themselves in the same boat. They started affairs and stopped being able to make love to their wives."

The girl soon grew restless with sharing only the senator's political commitment. She wanted more than his urgent need for restoration on rough hotel sheets.

"You're a lovely, sensitive girl," he had to tell her, "but compared with the family and the home, there's no contest." Peggy, he said, was still his idea of what a girl ought to be.

Just before the New Hampshire primary, Peggy did join the politician. He reached for her hungrily in the motel room. She lay forbiddingly still.

"What's wrong?" Two words—like a book so immensely overdue, when one thinks to return it, the library has been bulldozed.

"I'll keep on with you until the primaries are over," Peggy said. "But after that I'd like a divorce."

It was February. She carried off the appearance of loyal wife and campaign supporter until May.

One night the politician's 21-year-old daughter found him alone and distraught. "You'd understand, Dad," she said, "if you knew there was another man."

The next time I saw Kilpatrick he was not at home because there was no home. We met at a mutual friend's house and after dinner went into the den to talk. That was when Kilpatrick lay on the floor, working his stomach muscles.

"You catch me a year later, and sometimes now I wonder if it's worth being alive."

His reddened eyes were nailed down tight.

"I think the man's reexamination of himself in his forties is completely understandable. What isn't understandable is the woman reexamining herself after the children grow up. I never gave much thought to it. And I never would have if it hadn't been for the shock with Peggy. The one great quality my wife had was enthusiasm. Earlier in our marriage she had commitment in the world too. But as a woman gets older, that fades. Most of my friends in their late thirties or early forties found a younger girl who shared their commitment to a cause. It's a male chauvinist world in that this same man will look to his wife to support his commitment and lick his wounds, but he doesn't recognize *her* needs."

Kilpatrick clenched and unclenched his fists in a disciplined rhythm. While feelings ran loose in him that had never before been allowed, you could almost see the handgrip, see him reaching for something solid to hang the disorder of his life upon.

"Hell, I pulled Peggy and the children out of one of the safest, loveliest—I think now had we stayed in the valley, our friends and environment would have kept our marriage together."

What else, I asked, did he think had pried their marriage apart? "I think the combination of my accelerating commitment outside the home, plus Peggy's beginning awareness of the women's movement and the courage it gave her; it must have made her wonder if she wanted to spend the rest of her life married to someone like me, who was almost criminally insensitive to her needs."

We tried to talk about those needs, but all that Kilpatrick could summon was the Peggy he had married, the Peggy who wanted a father.

"When do you think your wife began to change?"

"I honestly don't know."

It is all so complicated. The rights can still come out wrong. Kilpatrick was right on schedule in his mid-thirties career acceleration. Caring more for his country than his own comfort, he took the risk of a wrenching change. Not only did it reeducate and revitalize him; he was moved to act from heartfelt conviction, rather than being seduced into the selfish reelection strategies that turn so many politicians into cotton-mouthed cynics. And yet, more than halfway across this Deadline Decade so boldly entered, he is left with only pain for a companion.

Kilpatrick's behavior at the crossing into midlife reminds me of the Lion in *The Wizard of Oz*. When the travelers came to a ravine that divided the forest as far as they could see, the Lion asserted that he could probably jump it, and the Scarecrow volunteered to be carried across astride the Lion. But as the nervous beast crouched at the edge of the ravine for one great, death-defying spring, the Scarecrow coaxed him to step back first and survey the whole problem.

"Why don't you run and jump?" the Scarecrow asked.

"Because that isn't the way we Lions do these things," he replied.

When a former military hero like Kilpatrick comes to a treacherous crossing, he doesn't step back to take a full survey of his feelings because that isn't the way marines do these things. The heroic dream of Kilpatrick's youth, to be a citizen-soldier, has undergone no remodeling. Neither has the idealization of his wife as handmaiden to his dream, even to this day. Unless he can be the roaring warrior out front and charging in all things, he feels disgraced—a lion without courage.

The pull of Kilpatrick's commitment to duty and the counterpull of Peggy's demands that family come first were usual enough in the couple's younger years. But neither of them was willing to take back the parental projections until forced to do so.

Had the Kilpatrick of 39 capitulated to his wife's demands, had he remained the larded lawyer sitting on his hide in their lush southwestern valley, the odds are great that he would have felt submissive and become a baked-out conservative, unconvinced of his own beliefs but doomed to uphold them as his only flag in the parade of perpetuity. That wouldn't have been much help to his wife's development either.

But although he acted vigorously on his own re-examination, he neither noticed nor imagined that the woman he lived with would need to do the same. He never would have, he says, if she hadn't left him (though I would doubt that).

Peggy appears to have given up the wish that her husband be a replica of her father only when she became convinced that her wish would never come true. Turning to an independent pursuit out of exasperation, the good feelings it gave her nonetheless bumped her out of the old dependency pattern.

Although Kilpatrick's sense of loss is surely sincere, he continues to overestimate his wife as some sort of amulet that wards off dangers and charms his successes. He still has not marked the change in his wife. When he yearns to solve the new problem, it is only the old methods that occur to him. When he says that he would drop out of this phony political business tomorrow to work on "this human thing," he means that to get his wife back he would now be willing to play the father. Unless Peggy has some unlikely relapse, that is not where she is anymore.

The big question left hanging is: Does the movement from one stage to another *require* that one discard the old partner in order to proceed with one's own growth?

Suppose, instead of Kilpatrick looking for a pretty Testimonial Woman who would understudy for the girl Peggy; suppose, instead of Peggy returning the insults of his absences by turning to another man and eventually punishing his insensitivity by flight—what if this couple had faced each other squarely at some earlier point and talked about the door between them?

SHE: Your life is building toward something. You've always counted on me to help, and I have helped. Now I have to find something of my own. It makes me angry that you won't take my needs seriously.

HE: The fact is, I really think you're becoming the stronger one, and it scares the hell out of me.

SHE: But all these years, *I've* been the one who resented the power you had over *me*.

HE: My power is in your mind because you don't have enough self-confidence.

SHE: I think you have cost me my self-confidence.

HE: How? Don't I earn enough to keep you secure?

SHE: Be a little nicer to the maid if it looks like she might quit. That's what you're really saying. That's how you see me.

HE: You're the one who's always wanted a safe and sound family life. You don't see me as *I* am either; I'm just some flawed edition of your father.

SHE: Well, that's beginning to change. I'm rather drawn to your flaws. Especially as I find my own sea legs. It's funny, the less I feel you're the only lifeline to my safety, the more I can cheer you on even in your outlandish causes.

HE: Suppose I flop?

SHE: It isn't going to be the end of the world.

HE: Oh, so once you turn into a pushy real estate lady, you won't need me anymore.

SHE: I won't need you like a golden passbook savings account. But I will need you to love.

And so on, a little at a time, with lots of laughter and lovemaking in between, until perhaps one day they get down to discussing the real lock.

From there, each of them might proceed to locate the gate inside, the gate presided over by the inner custodian. For whether we know it or not, and usually we don't, it is this dictator-guardian from whom we all are struggling at last to be free. In midlife, all the old wars with the inner custodian flare up again. And eventually, if we let it happen, they will culminate in a final, decisive battle. The object of that battle is to overtake the last of the ground held by the other and end up with the authority for ourselves in our own command.

But then, alas, we will be confronted with our own absolute separateness.

So staggering a loss is this to accept that most of us shrink from the final confrontation until we have exhausted other, apparently easier possibilities.

If we can fob off the blame for our disunity onto a spouse, a boss, the society, the aggrieved state of our gender, we can hold back the sense of isolation that comes with the breakthrough to full independence. The deepest layer of imaginery protection, carried along from our childhood identifications with our parents, can be maintained. But by giving up the illusion, what is to be gained is no less than the full release of our freely authentic selves.[5] This fullness of being is ours only when we are ready to face the final truth of the midlife period:

There is no protective other with you inside the dark room of your mind. There is no one who will always take care of you, no one who won't ever leave you alone.

The "Who's Crazy?" Argument

Fighting against this truth does make people act crazy. The simplest punishment, one that can be exercized by either mate at any time, is withdrawal. One can stop hearing, touching, talking, caring, or even being there. This hovering threat makes each partner feel controlled by, and at the mercy of, the other. It is critical to know that self-absorption at this stage is *natural*. Some breakdown of communications and disruption of intimacy is *predictable*, which leaves any action open for misinterpretation.

A punishment with even more potential for damage is the "Who's Crazy?" argument. This seems to be a staple among midlife couples. The two people go round and round the accusation tree until one of them says, "You really need some help. I think you should see a psychiatrist." (Or a marriage counselor, or some other substitute for the old tradition of consulting a clergyman or going home to mother.) The trouble with this suggestion is the motive. What the mate

437

usually wants is a judgment that the other is the guilty party. Sensing this, the partner who has been told to go to a psychiatrist often digs in his or her heels and refuses because to set foot inside this arbiter's office would be an admission that "I'm the sick one."

The whole "Who's Crazy?" argument is usually about who has "it," the demon, the unfinished business with the dictator-guardian from childhood, which everybody has and which everybody is trying to exorcise in midlife. The demon is passed back and forth. You project it onto me; I project it onto you: *"You're* the crazy one because this unsettlement can't be mine; it's your problem that is bouncing back on me, thereby making me upset."

But suppose a couple resists the "you're crazy" route. Each of them patiently goes through the work of inner growth. They no longer need to use the partner and misuse the relationship. They take back the projections. Is the next scene guaranteed to be a passionate clinch?

Not necessarily. What you may find is that the person you now see clearly, for the whole of his or her qualities, is not compatible as a partner. It's a good thing to find that out too, and if there must be a parting, it might be done with the mercy and respect that preserves your friendship.

For one thing is certain as we grow older: The few people who have truly passed through us and us through them, until the dreams, images, memories are past sorting out, these people become precious links to our continuity. That includes our parents, our children, our loves, even fetuses never brought into the world and incompletely mourned (old women wake in the night seeing their tiny fingernails). If we try to bury the images of others who meant so much, part of us dies with them. How much greater our aliveness if we can come to a freestanding friendship with those who have shared us.

In any case, middle age is not the time when marriages characteristically break up.[6] The teen years

438

and Catch-30 are the high-water marks for divorce, and from then on the rates drop steadily with age and duration of marriage. What middle-aged couples are more likely to do is separate. Sometimes this is a way (either conscious or unconscious) of immunizing themselves against a precipitous remarriage. It can also serve well to stimulate individual growth, as if two mature plants were transplanted with more room between them, until each has flourished to the point where they touch again, in a way that is no longer forced but now natural.

Whodunit?

Who then *is* the villain and who the victim in the couple? While we were distracted by all the action, the two major suspects were moving away from the opposite poles of their twenties. But by some mysterious exchange, they have come out to a different set of opposites in their forties. We can hear the same villain-versus-victim argument in midlife, but now the accusers have changed sides.

Confound it, will this mystery never be solved?

The answer is no. The whole idea behind developmental change is that *things can never be settled once and for all.* Life is a thriller all right, but not one we can solve with the right set of clues, nor a puzzle with one correct fit. Getting it right at 30 will still require taking apart all the pieces and refitting them in the forties. And most of us will need several years simply to see that the second half of life is a whole new puzzle.

22

THE
SEXUAL
DIAMOND

I have deliberately left the discussion of sexual changes and exchanges within the midlife man and woman until last. That is because of the old chicken-and-egg argument. There is little doubt that upheavals in the hormone levels of both sexes stimulate at least some of the psychological changes of the middle years. On the other hand, when the 40-year-old married man says, "Our sex life went to pieces," or the same-age wife says she has taken a lover "to shore up our marriage," it usually turns out that the change in sexual circumstances is not the cause of but the accompaniment to all of the other shifts in perspective already described.

Many modern women exhibit their erotic potential most boldly at just about the time their husbands' sexual incentive is diminishing. For men, the very *thought* of this can be disastrous.

Midlife "impotence" results, in over 90 percent of cases, from a devastating combination of ignorance and male sexual anxiety. Many researchers and studies confirm this. Masters and Johnson lay it flat out: "The susceptibility of the human male to the power of suggestion with regard to his sexual prowess is almost unbelievable."[1] More than any fluctuation in hormone level, it is anxiety, the free-floating fear of losing his male powers as he has known them, that can so often make the first time he can't get an erection crippling. Even the slightest suggestion that his sexual prowess is diminishing can psych the midlife man into a repeat of what too often seems to him to be a humiliating failure.

He notes that it takes more time to become aroused. Where it used to be a matter of seconds and a mere glance at the orbs of flesh colliding beneath a pair of tennis shorts, he may take minutes or more to reach erection as he gets older. He also notices, correctly, that he is slower on the comeback. In the sweet agonies of teen age he may have walked about with an erection all day, seldom completely losing it even after he made love or masturbated—a virtual prisoner of his hormones and tight-fitting pants. But now each sexual act has a definite beginning and end, and it may be a matter of hours or all day before he can reach erection again. Comparisons, stinging comparisons . . . he is not the boy he once was.

The accumulating effect of such comparisons may soon have him believing that he is heading into terminal sexual aridity. In trying to will or force an erection that he thinks may soon be completely unattainable, he becomes a candidate for secondary impotence. That means, having enjoyed a perfectly healthy sexual history, he is now unable to get hard at least a quarter if not half the time. Or, if this episodic failure becomes a pattern to which he resigns himself, not at all.

The facts are these: Masters and Johnson assert that all but the tiniest percentage of impotence cases are psychological in origin. However, one-quarter of men are impotent by the age of 65 and one-half by 75.[2]

What's normal? How well should the man over 35 be able to perform? (The very emphasis on performance has been the single greatest cause of sexual dysfunction over the ages.) Something is happening and there is no one to tell him how to interpret it. Most men won't ask other men, nor would they be likely to

441

get a straight answer if they did; the level of lying in sexual matters is very early raised to the incorrigible. Hence each man thinks that his failure is in some way exceptional.

There are considerable advantages for the midlife man who lets himself enjoy his sexual maturity. Prolonged lovemaking comes naturally to him. And he is capable of a deepening intimacy. (Intimacy does not flourish in the presence of need to prove machismo.)

One man described to me how threatening some of these changes appeared to him and how he fought them for almost five years. He had been quite a stud during his thirties as a divorced man about town. When he was close to 40 and quite happily remarried, a ripe and willful beauty from his past invited him to a party. His second wife was out of town on business. "I felt I had to try. I'd always been successful before." As he led the temptress to bed, he was feeling not only guilty but—something else—used. There was no emotion here, his feelings were all tied up with his wife. In fact he wasn't leading at all. This other woman (like so many older women, he later observed) was the aggressor.

"After the first few times when I couldn't get hard with another woman, I began to realize it was because I was being forced into something I didn't want to do."

He could not perform on demand, but as time went on he began to resent being demanded of. All the while he was becoming more attached to, more vulnerable to, and more involved with his wife. It wasn't easy to get used to this switch from using sex for dominance to wanting affection and exclusivity. Gradually he saw an advantage to it all.

"It's the freedom not to feel you have to chase after women." But even when the change was positive, this man resisted it.

A recurring theme in the biographies of men describing midlife is their escapades with younger women who were supposed to restore their waning sexual powers. Sometimes, this does help to dispel the anxiety that is the real culprit. And sometimes, to their chagrin, they find themselves suddenly flat champagne in the presence of the sexual feast, or that the affair reduces them to flaccidity with their wives. In any case, they are baffled. And ashamed. And scared.

When Joe declares at a party, "I wouldn't consider sleeping with a woman over 40," or Sam announces to his friends, "I'm bunking with a 17-year-old girl this weekend," they are revealing more than anything else their own middle-aged fears of inadequacy. The 40-year-old woman is not evaluated as an individual; the 17-year-old girl is given no name, no personal characteristics. In both instances the female is narrowed to one dimension: she is an age.

It stands to reason that as a man begins to sense his own feminine side in this period, he will also feel somewhat threatened by the initiating behavior now showing up in his partner. The shifting characteristics that become evident in both sexes during the Switch-40s cannot be fitted together, not for at least several years. But if a man doesn't understand or can't accept this process, it can cause a locking of feeling. Sexual apprehensions only aggravate the situation. From his perspective, as nature is narrowing his own sexual potential, an eager and experienced woman of his own age knows too much, expects too much. The most obvious defense is to find a way to miniaturize women.

Seeking younger and more superficial partners is not the only device by which women can be miniaturized. The entire sexual experience can be reduced in scope by dehumanizing women, by seeing them as an assortment of only slightly varying objects to be used and discarded. Prostitutes can be paid for. Massage-parlor models can be activated like coin-operated machines. Some men make a contest of trying to seduce other men's wives or women friends, a form of male rivalry in which the female can be discounted for having cooperated in the infidelity. Sexual fetishism also holds great appeal. Most of the readers of *The Fet-*

ishist Times are men in their forties and fifties. A man may insist on sex in odd combinations. Feet suddenly become an obsession, or dark nipples or whatever. Perhaps the real motive is not to attract but to disqualify as many women as possible.

The basis for the ignorance problem is that until recently the American man has had almost no reliable source of information about sex. First he was a little boy being told by the big boys, "When you're older, you'll know." Next he was an older boy telling another ignorant youth he'd know. Then he graduated from being a son into being a husband and father, rarely asking the girls along the way specific questions because that would have meant admitting he still didn't know.

A bent penis at midlife throws him into a panic.

The least likely action a man will take, according to Dr. David Marcotte at the Kinsey Institute, is to describe his real dilemma to a doctor. To reveal to anyone a real or imagined weakness in living up to our society's standards of virility is repugnant. Furthermore, men don't have doctors for middle age. What man has a long-standing confidential relationship with his urologist the way women do with their gynecologists? Men find unimaginable the idea of opening their legs at the word of any doctor the way women do to have their privates probed, Pap-smeared, episiotomied, scraped, fitted with rubber disks, clamped with metal coils; the male role in the reproductive years doesn't require it. Beyond keeping up a solid virility front, then, most men are also squeamish about baring their sexual problems before a physician.

Even if they do, the general practitioner is untrained in sexual problems as a rule. He won't take a sexual history or inquire about the situational impotence that is the real problem. The patient will usually disguise his real concern by describing other physical symptoms ("I'm rundown, over-tired, overweight"), or he'll invent an organic factor. If the doctor does ask him direct sexual questions, he will probably lie. As a consequence of all this dodging, the doctor usually ends up by telling him, "Don't worry about it; it's just a natural part of the aging process." The implication being: "You won't need it much longer."

Meanwhile, his female counterpart is often, literally, on the prowl. The "delayed blooming" of sexual desire and orgasmic capacity in women over 30 has been paid profuse attention, of which he is only too uncomfortably aware. Masters and Johnson matter-of-factly state, "A woman will usually be satisfied with 3–5 orgasms."[3]

This leaves us with what would seem a vicious circle: the midlife woman actively seeking satisfaction of her now uninhibited sexual desires from a man who, wary in the presence of any naked demand, goes into involuntary retreat. How, we wonder, could nature be so perverse?

Facing the Facts of Male and Female Sexual Life Cycles

Males and females are most alike before they are born, at 18, and over 60. In between 18 and 60 they move toward opposite poles that reach an extreme about 40.

The whole configuration can be seen in the shape of a diamond. That is, males and females at the age of emancipation start out quite alike. In the twenties they begin moving apart in every way: in sexual capacity and availability for sex (especially once the woman's reproductive potential is tapped), in social roles that are massively different and that also favor different personality characteristics, and in the overall sense of themselves. By the late thirties and early forties, the distance across the diamond is at its greatest. Males and females are exhibiting the most strikingly dissimilar aspects of their sexual capacities. At the same time, they are called upon to admit the sexually opposite sides of their nature, which are so frighteningly unfamiliar. In the fifties, they both go into a sexual involution, which eventually brings them back together in the unisex of old age.

Now, to go back and fill in the details . . . In our first five weeks after conception we are all females. The genetic instructions for which sex we shall turn out to be are given at conception, but all mammalian embryos are female until, in some, the growth of ovaries is suppressed. It takes the stimulation of male sex hormones to begin the differentiation of the sexes in the fifth week. But no matter what the genetic instructions were, if the fetal sex organs are removed before this differentiation, the fetus will develop as an otherwise anatomically normal female (without ovaries).[4]

Both sexes continually produce some of the opposite sex hormone. A female who is experimentally injected with testosterone will easily accept the male hormone, and although it often increases her sex drive and enlarges her clitoris, little or no added estrogen is required before the innate human femaleness reasserts itself. The reverse is true for men. The liver closely monitors the estrogen supply in the male and rids his body of any excess. He is also strongly resistant to injected estrogen and its refeminizing effects. As the years go by, however, his liver becomes less efficient. And so in middle age his female-hormone level begins to climb or at least remains stable. Meanwhile his production of male hormone, which has been declining since the late teens, is inexorably dropping off.

As he moves into the fifties, the contours of his body gradually regain some of the femaleness that was anatomically natural to the original embryo. Although the postmenopausal woman does not find herself in a parallel situation (that is, her male-hormone level is not climbing in the same ratio) her estrogen level does fall off once her reproductive cycling ends. The two sexes again become more alike. Or, to be more precise, by exchanging many characteristics they become less different.

But what about the likeness at 18? What was once

only shaky and secretive personal experience is now supported by recent sex research and the new honesty among women.

It is widely known that a male reaches his peak sexual capacity at about 18. Sexual capacity is defined as the ability to respond quickly and repeatedly, and the young man lives up to it as indefatigably as the tollgate at the entrance to a superhighway. Not only does a young man erect in seconds, he is capable of having a chain of ejaculations without fully losing his erection. Ten minutes after the first orgasm, he can be restimulated from a state of swollen excitement to full erection again *within the same sex act.* That is to say, the resolution phase is not fully completed for minutes or even hours, and he is potentially able to have multiple orgasms by reentering his partner again and again.

But the true sexual potential of the 18-year-old girl is as yet unrecorded. Suppression of the young female's sex drive has been fundamental in stabilizing cultures around settled family life. That doesn't mean it hasn't always been there.

The shock wave caused by evidence that even nice girls are just as interested in sex as boys has only recently begun to register in our own society. Few can fail to notice that something has been left out in our long-prevailing notion of women's sexuality as a lethargic and quiescent thing, a tight little bud that opens only after ten or fifteen years of prying, prying, prying.

In fact, the vagina is a highly elastic space that enlarges with sexual arousal. Even a small or very young female can receive an exceptionally large penis, just as she can give birth to a ten-pound baby at the ripe age of 18. The more sexual experience she has, the more quickly excitable and repetitively orgasmic she becomes except that no time at all is required for her to return to readiness.

Societies have always suspected this about women, hence the efforts to suppress female sexuality. The ever-ready simplification seems to me to be just the other side of the tight-little-bud extreme. The truth is much more complex. We are touched by our emotions as well as being creatures of our physical capacities.

Having guiltily enjoyed a rather hot-blooded adolescence myself, I always wondered how much truth there was in the "delayed blooming" idea of female sexuality. I put the question to a friend.

"I remember an adolescence of absolute frenzy," she groaned. "Not getting through a day without seventy-five percent of it being occupied with sexual dreaming, wishing, watching, touching if possible."

Many young women "went all the way" with their steadies expecting them to be, of course, future husbands. Still others sought to please. Whatever other motives they had at the time, what now comes out in consciousness-raising groups is that they felt guilty about enjoying it so much. They didn't know if it was normal, and they didn't talk about it.

Even when it ran contrary to our own experience, women of my generation accepted the mythological profile of the 18-year-old boy who is a prisoner of his hormones and the young girl who is reproductively ready but won't sexually arrive for ten or fifteen more years. Indeed, many of us *willed* ourselves back into sexual dormancy. It was common for nice girls who had "gone too far" to do penance for their erotic irresponsibility by entering a period of revirgination.

That explains the kind of letter one man remembers getting over the summer from his girl friend: "What we've done is wrong. When we get back together in the fall, things will have to be different." He was baffled. All they had done was pet.

The last five years or so have prodded women of my generation to talk and laugh about the sexual intensity we felt when we were very young. And the risks we were willing to run for it. Much of this honesty was stimulated by the abortion issue. Calls went out for all notable women who had had an abortion to speak up. The necessity for abortion on demand could not be ignored if a solid block of celebrities and important men's wives, even wives of legislators, stood up to be counted. Some of them had sought abortions back when they were 18, or 19 or 20.

This is not to say that most 18-year-old girls in the pre-pill era did act in a way that would awaken their sexual energies, only to suggest that a responsiveness close to the male's was there if they had. But religious prohibitions and the double standard, not to mention the legions of premature ejaculators, all together were remarkably effective in cooling the young woman's attitude toward sex.

Boys, too, were given a double message: "Don't do it, but we expect you will." Instead of emphasizing the likeness in his and her desires and capacities, the double standard had an opposite effect that is well known. His part was to play the attacker while she struck the pose of unwilling prey. Any feelings to the contrary had to be falsified or apologized for, and nothing in this ritualized contest allowed for mutuality. It cast a long shadow of mistrust into the adult years for men who continued to believe "Women always give you a hard time," and for women who were convinced, "Men only want one thing."

The Diverging Sexual Life Cycles

The similarity of males and females at 18 extends into many areas other than sexual capacity. At that age they are more alike or allied in the need to break away from their parents than they are unalike as male and female. They need one another to find out how they *are* different. Both he and she are insecure, inexperienced, and as yet undistinguished by the carapace of firm social and vocational roles. Enthralled as much by what they are learning about themselves as by the other one, young lovers gladly lose their egos in each other as if in a warm whirlpool bath. That's why the first love is so hard to give up.

Once into the twenties, the social sorting system

begins segregating them by domestic duties and career opportunities, and the massive distinction in sexual roles takes effect. They begin moving apart in every way, including sexually. An overwhelming proportion of the babies born are produced by women in their twenties.[5] Pregnancies cause sexual interruptions, and small children are distracting. Men have already experienced "the sexual acme of their lives . . . and will never again attain higher levels of total sexual outlet."[6]

After completing her baby-bearing at the statistical age of about 30 or 31, the woman is at her fullest sexual availability. Although a slow physical decline begins in the thirties for everyone, this decline is more than offset in the American female by her gradual loss of sexual inhibition. Psychiatrist Mary Jane Sherfey particularly emphasizes the effects of pregnancy.[7] The capacity for repetitive orgasms (orgasms that continue in a series uninterrupted by a full resolution phase), she says, most often occurs during the last fourteen days of the menstrual cycle in women who have already borne children. This is because of the high levels of vasocongestion reached by the woman who has already reproduced. The female erectile chambers have the capacity to refill immediately after every climax, and this recreates the sexual tension by engorging the entire pelvis with an inexhaustible supply of blood and fluid. It is one of the most striking differences between men and women and between women and other primate females.

And the man? What changes when, and what remains forever? After 30, it is widely agreed that the man loses his capacity for multiple orgasms. That is, he loses the ten-minute boy power to re-erect by entering his partner again and again. A full resolution follows each ejaculation, and at least a half hour is required before he can have another erection. Nonetheless, the quality of his sex life usually improves as he gains more social skills and higher status. His status not only makes him more desirable in the eyes of women, it makes him more potent in his own eyes. The effect of self-confidence on male-hormone level cannot be stressed enough.

It is a biological fact of life that as the years pile up, the male erection capacity goes down, and he must have longer and longer rest periods between sexual acts. The gradual physical slowing noticed by everybody is not so easily offset for a man by a new sexual experience, the way it often is for a woman, because ordinarily he has fewer inhibitions to give up. On the contrary, midlife is when serious inhibitions are likely to trouble him for the first time.

With unsettling changes in his sense of self going on in every other area, obviously a man's sexual confidence will be affected. He may try to conceal a flagging libido from his partner by picking a fight with her and then retreating into a self-righteous sulk. Or he overworks to the point of exhaustion or gets psychosomatically sick, all to explain why he can't make love on the weekend. There are easily hundreds of ways to avoid the real issue. Although his partner probably senses the real reason, she would be risking annihilation to say so.

In America and all over Western Europe we place a premium on the vertical penis. As anthropologist Ray Birdwhistell says, "Unless the male can get up this hyper-erect vertical penis and not ejaculate prematurely, he thinks he's incapacitated."[8] And then, too often, he is.

Some societies accept the fact that sex is quite possible with a nonrigid penis. This requires cooperation between the man and the woman. She prepares her tissues for reception of the partially erect penis, using added lubrication if necessary. In a society that assumes only bad girls cooperate, a taboo is created against such helpful efforts. The nearest thing we have had to a sexual revolution, claims the professor, is that women are now allowed to admit what they know about sex without being regarded as bad girls. And to teach men. But a big blind tank of ignorance still rolls through midlife, and I would suggest we have a long way to go to reduce the sexual casualties.

The bright side of the male sexual life cycle is this: A man in generally good health need *never* lose his erective capacity. The sexually educated and experienced middle-aged man can be a most satisfying lover. Once he overcomes the anxiety of no longer being a boy, he can begin to appreciate his matured powers to give tenderness and receive love, and to prolong his own state of excitement by withholding ejaculation while he brings his partner to ecstasy again and again. That's power. But he should also know this: Women don't like to feel they *have* to come again and again, in order to compliment a man's masculinity. As with erection, any rigid expectation of a standard of performance is incompatible with good sex.

Looking at ourselves in cold, hard evolutionary terms, we are all relatively useless after 30. All a species needs to survive is to reproduce itself, which is easily possible at the age of 15, and fifteen years more to raise the next generation to reproductive age. Certainly by 40, when both the male testes and the female ovaries begin to show the changes of age, we are, from an evolutionary point of view, thoroughly disposable.

But we don't want to go! We're doing everything in our scientific powers to prolong our years of health and vigor. Today, an American boy baby who has survived his first year can expect to live to 69 and a girl to 76.[9] Most child-bearing is over by the time we reach 30. What do we do with all those years of fulminating eroticism and undirected potential we have left? Lamenting the apparent upsurge in male impotence that seems to coincide with the lifting of age-old restrictions on female sexuality, writer Phillip Nobile expressed in *Esquire* a common viewpoint: "Indeed, the design appears badly botched."[10]

Botched by us, I would suggest. Botched only

because we continue to set the adolescent ideal into cement and then crab about it when the next fifty years will not reciprocate our wishes for adolescent love, adolescent sex, adolescent male strength and female beauty. We remain wholly unprepared for the long stretch of the life cycle we will spend as nonproductive sexual beings.

The Educated Male Orgasm

One reason we have come to believe that men enjoy sex less as they grow older while women enjoy it more is the Kinsey hangover. Kinsey measured the sexual experience solely in terms of the number of "outlets." Reflecting in his research design the bias of his culture at the time (1943), Kinsey's definition of male satisfaction was ejaculation—nothing more, nothing less. Kinsey wouldn't put up with any talk about "premature." If primates do it fast, he argued, then men should go them one better:

> It would be difficult to find another situation in which an individual who was quick and intense in his responses was labeled anything but superior and that in most instances is exactly what the rapidly ejaculatory male probably is, however inconvenient or unfortunate his qualities may be from the standpoint of the wife of the relationship.[11]

So, to some degree, we have Kinsey to thank for several generations of premature ejaculators.

The male orgasm does not happen naturally. As Birdwhistell states, far more often than Americans and most Western Europeans like to admit, a full male orgasm, unlike ejaculation, does not happen at all without learning or training. Ejaculation is composed of a two- or three-second sensation that coming is inevitable, followed by three or four strong muscle contractions that expel the semen and produce the most pleasure, then several minor contractions, and it's over.

What's more, the man over 50 may feel only one or two contractions before expulsion or may lose the subjective feeling of inevitability altogether and be reduced to a one-stage ejaculation.

The full male orgasm is an exercise in exquisite delay. By training himself to slow down every time he approaches the margin of ejaculatory demand, the man can luxuriate in being stroked, savor the waves of hot swollen tension, fantasize, and delight in bringing his partner through an ascending chain of orgasms until she reaches a moment of climax comparable to his.

Because young men of today generally recognize the pleasure of prolonged lovemaking, they make efforts and experiment with different methods to cause this delay. The problem for the older man is different. Although he is much more easily able to be a mature ejaculator, that unfortunately was not the ideal conveyed by "making it" American style when he was a boy. The ideal assumed that the man must come if he is to give a good performance. The woman was also led to believe she had failed if she didn't "make" him come.

Very recently in America, Masters and Johnson have indicated that the man of 60 will find greater sexual contentment if on two out of three occasions, he reserves his ejaculation altogether. In that way, sexual tension will accumulate to a climax worthy of his expectations. Although this notion is only now being gingerly advanced in this country, in Oriental culture it has been the ideal. The ancient teaching in Chinese sex manuals is that the young man must be trained not to ejaculate, for his own as well as his partner's pleasure. In old Chinese wisdom, the deepest mutual joy in sex derives from stimulating the woman's orgasms. The man is urged to improve upon this pattern all through life: to hold back as long as he can and, if he does succumb, to do so as infrequently as possible so that on those occasions he will be primed for satisfying release. It all dovetails so gracefully with the changing human capabilities as we grow older. But then, Chinese culture has always venerated age; whereas our own celebrates only a youth we all lose.

As the most sober researchers attest, if sex were the only criterion, the best match would be the adolescent boy with the woman twice his age.[12]

The Curious Ups and Downs of Testosterone

In some ways, the burden of aging put upon American men is more nearly intolerable than it is for the women. Our men must be something that no living creature has ever been able to achieve: They must be eternally strong. We have prepared them for nothing less by ignoring possible evidence to the contrary.

We do know that the male hormone, testosterone, is intimately connected with aggressive behavior, as it is with sexual behavior. And we are just beginning to find out that male hormone level varies enormously with the man's emotional state. Dr. Estelle Ramey, a physiologist at Georgetown University School of Medicine who is actively studying variations in testosterone with particular attention to its role in male heart attacks, called to my attention a fascinating study by Dr. Robert Rose, a professor at Boston University School of Medicine.

When a rhesus monkey is number one in the hierarchy of a primate colony, his testosterone level measures higher than that of any of the other monkeys. One might conclude that testosterone is the take-charge hormone and that the one who has the most gets to the top. But take this primate who is at the top of the pyramid and put him in a colony where he is unknown, where he has to reestablish himself, and his hormone level plummets. It all depends on his sense of security.[13]

A testosterone level is not something that an individual "has," regardless of the social situation; it is an open system. Two more studies by Rose show how very susceptible this system can be. After an animal is defeated in a fight, his hormone level drops and remains low. But put a low-status male in a cage with a female he can dominate and with whom he can have an active sex life, and up soars his hormone level along with his spirits.

Although similar patterns can be seen in humans, there has been an inexcusable lack of scientific research in this area. Only now are new techniques in chemistry being developed to measure sex steroids in human blood accurately. Data are just beginning to come out:

The older the man, the more readily anxiety will cause a drop in his testicular hormone.

From the age of 18, when the male's testosterone secretion reaches a peak per day, there is a slow fall-off until he dies.

Not all men are so gradual. More commonly than was anticipated, men show a substantial drop in hormone level beginning between the ages of 40 to 55. And then they have all the signs and symptoms of the menopausal woman.

Mysteries of the Climacteric

Up to now this has been a male problem with no name. Well, there is the vague term *climacteric,* but there is nothing visibly markable that changes; he has no menstrual period to stop. People don't expect him to have hot flashes and dizzy spells, memory lapses and irritability. He may withdraw into obsessive work, but other common symptoms such as waking anxiously for hours in the middle of the night, lassitude, chronic fatigue, and headaches are sure to cut back on the energy and quality he once counted on taking to the office. His co-workers will eventually notice something is wrong, even if he refuses to admit to it himself and especially if his moodiness prompts him to lash out at them. Colleagues begin to be concerned about how well he can uphold his end of the enterprise. Competitors may use any of this odd behavior as ammunition against him.

A nasty downward spiral can ensue. Feeling his

security on the pyramid slipping, he becomes more apprehensive. He is anxious about getting older. And the older he gets, the more that anxiety will suppress the production of male hormone he needs to take charge with confidence. Eventually the spiral will come back home to play havoc with his sex life. For as we already know, the relationship between sexual capacity and testosterone level is a highly synergistic one. But before going any further, I hasten to add Dr. Ramey's reassurance: "Potency is really not a function of how much hormone you're secreting as long as you have enough."[14] Most men have enough for moderate sexual activity deep into old age.

That question aside, the next two concerns everyone has are: How many men undergo severe disruptions in their physical, emotional, and sexual equilibrium as a result of the climacteric? And what is the age of dread?

A current estimate is that about 15 percent of men suffer from the rapid, sharp decline of testosterone associated with disruptive symptoms of the climacteric. For the other 85 percent of men the hormonal change is slow and gradual, although there is considerable variation. Most hardly notice it; some experience no symptoms at all; and some are buffeted by wide swings in hormone level over a period of a few years, causing equally unpredictable swings of mood, and then the symptoms disappear without treatment. The symptoms of menopause also "affect almost all women to some degree, but only about 10 percent of them are obviously inconvenienced by these problems."[15] There are important reasons that percentage has dropped so low. Menopause has been studied for many years. A woman knows what to expect. Volumes of information are now available to educate her further. Hormone replacement therapy, although controversial because of the uncertain cancer connection, is nonetheless well along in clinical use. Most of all, menopausal women have a specific event to complain about and adjust to and everyone knows it; they can expect a little sympathy. For men it's all so undefined and unexpected.

Reporting conclusive results from a study of impotence in 100 climacteric patients, Boston urologist Thomas Jakobovits gives this picture:

> Beyond the age of 40, a man may manifest symptoms of the strains and stresses peculiar to this particular time of life. An individual may suffer from irritability, nervousness, and a decrease or a loss of sexual function. . . . this decline of gonadal function with associated symptoms of the male climacteric can begin at any age, but most commonly begins between the ages of 40 and 55.

Referring to three other studies, he reports that the average age of the climacteric patient is 53.7.[16]

Dr. Helmut J. Ruebsaat, whose practice in British Columbia has become increasingly involved with men experiencing the climacteric, puts more weight on the forties decade. Three-quarters of the cases that have come to his attention began between the ages of 41 and 50 and the remainder sometime before 60. The tricky part of assigning an average age is that many cases are not reported until long after symptoms begin, and many other cases are never presented to doctors at all.[17]

Symptoms of the climacteric come in clusters, and they are elusive. A man doesn't wake up one morning feeling suddenly sick all over, as he does with the flu. One or two symptoms may come on for a period of days, followed by a spell of more ominous symptoms; then it all passes, and he feels fine. Until a few weeks or months later when another spell begins. With all this confusion, it's no wonder that a man might think he is suffering a series of illnesses with no connection. In summary, here are the complaints most often associated with the climacteric:

Morning fatigue, lassitude, and vague pains are the most common.

Nervousness, irritability, depressive phases, crying spells, insomnia, memory lapses, apprehensiveness, and frustration are the cerebral symptoms.

Diminished sexual potency and loss of self-confidence are particularly subject to the reciprocal effect of his situation at home and at work.

And then there may be any one of a mixed bag of circulatory signs: dizzy spells, hot flashes, chills, sweating, headaches, numbness and tingling, cold hands and feet, plus an increased pulse rate and heart palpitations. The last one scares the hell out of a man; he thinks he's having a heart attack.

But the most bothersome symptom, as Jakobovits calls it, is the "decline in psychologic stability."

This is what got to Raymond Hull, a successful author in first-class physical condition who began having spells of night fears and drenching sweats alternating with chills, along with a few days of feeling stupefied at the typewriter where he ordinarily writes 2,000 words a day. When an attractive woman friend turned up at his home eager to spend the weekend and he had to let her sleep alone, he knew he had lost his sex drive. But most unnerving was the topsy-turvy change of temperament. After several weeks of normally good spirits, being ordinarily a placid man, he would fall into an unfathomable depression. For a few days he would be down on himself, his work, his friends, the whole human race—and a fear-ridden spectator of his own volatile behavior.

"I'm wondering how such mood changes affect other men," Hull noted in the journal he began to keep. "This depression is unpleasant; but there is another emotional effect that is dangerous. On any trivial provocation I may switch from the depressed, apathetic mood, to one of near-insane rage."[18] Within a couple of weeks he would be soaring with unaccustomed exhilaration. And then another spell would come on until he began to think he was going mad.

The oddest part of it all was that the symptoms

coincided with what was by far the most successful and satisfying period of his life. In two years he found himself just about back to normal. Ultimately the collaboration between Hull and Dr. Ruebsaat produced *The Male Climacteric*, a 1975 book and apparently the first full-length treatment of this subject.

Undiagnosed, the climacteric can have a pretty dreadful ripple effect. "The spells of bad temper that are a common symptom of the climacteric will obviously cause problems for the man at work and with his friends," says Ruebsaat. "In extreme cases they may lead to quarrels, fights, even murders."[19] He also describes the fallout to be expected from the ambitious man who has achieved some success; he commonly reacts with panicky defenses against nonexistent threats to his prestige and livelihood.

> An employer who begins to exhibit the emotional symptoms of the climacteric can become a terror to his staff—unpredictable, unfair, the most-hated man in the firm. He may be rash in his judgment of business affairs, slow to take necessary action, or wildly changeable in his decisions, as his moods alternate between the optimistic and pessimistic.

That such havoc can descend on an otherwise well-adjusted man is not a pleasant revelation. Indeed, in my experience, men will often dismiss any mention of the climacteric as a misery-loves-company idea cooked up by menopausal women. There is truth in the assumption that the menopausal sex resents having taken most of the blame for their husbands' middle-aged problems. Eccentric behavior due to a change of life has been traditionally ascribed only to women. The terror and fury felt by dumped "old" wives and anticipated by married women upon approaching the age of abandonment, does seem to find a common voice when the climacteric is mentioned. Thus when the *New York Times* ran an article in 1973 asking "Is There a Male Menopause?" letters flooded in from women whose marriages were already among the midlife body count. Their scars showed big as life:

> Unfortunately doctors, psychiatrists, men in general, have kept it all under the rug, where they have swept it themselves. They are in terror of acknowledging a condition which affects their behavior beyond control, but which they readily ascribe to women without mercy. They cannot even talk about it among themselves.[20]

The "Name Withheld" who authored that letter also wrote that had she read about the symptoms when her husband was going through vivid climacteric changes at 46, she would not have turned in hopelessness to divorce.

What can be done? The quest for potions of sexual rejuvenescence is as old as the Bible. Rich men have been braving an icy trail to Switzerland for years to imbibe monkey glands, which may have boosted their sexual morale but otherwise had no physical effect on their gonads. Even when pure male hormone is given, mind seems to be as important as matter.

The results of Dr. Jakobovits's double-blind study are optimistic. He treated 100 men, most of whom were in their seventies and eighties, for impotence. Half were given oral hormone tablets (methyltestosterone) and half placebos. After a month, a favorable response was seen in 78 percent of the cases treated with active medication. Even among those who had been soothed with sugar pills, 40 percent regained their libido. The urologist concludes that hormone treatment provides an uplift both physical and psychological for a complex problem that may involve both influences. "Once successful sexual ability is again reestablished and once the patient is thoroughly convinced of his own virility, then medication is usually no longer needed."[21]

To replace or not to replace hormones is nonetheless a controversial question. The flaw in prescription of testosterone for older men is that cancer cells are thought by some to grow well in its presence. One-quarter of all men over 40 have latent cancer of the prostate, although it generally remains dormant and is discovered only on autopsy. It is therefore imperative that any man about to embark on testosterone therapy have a thorough physical and chemical examination first to rule out the presence of any incipient prostate cancer.

Obviously it would be a bum rap to point the finger at every jumpy middle-aged man and say, "Aha, male menopause!" More often than not the poor guy will be struggling through a garden-variety midlife crisis. So far as we know—and we don't know very much—only 15 percent of men are candidates for a riotous change in hormone levels. Given the new laboratory techniques, we shall soon know more about the mysteries of the male climacteric.

Sex and Menopause

The onset of vaginal lubrication for a woman corresponds to an erection for a man. After 40, as the aging process sets in, vaginal lubrication will diminish to a degree. But it need not impair her pleasure or receptivity. Sexologists offer a very direct piece of advice: Use it or lose it.[22] Indeed, it is the woman who continues to exercise an active sexual life, even without hormone replacement, who shows the least evidence of this physical change. However, there is for her as big a "but" as for her mate. If she senses this delay of moistening as a loss of womanhood, it *can* impair her spontaneity.

Menopause creeps up on women. Most women think that as long as they are menstruating regularly, they are not in the menopause. But even though their flow may be normal in the forties, a chemical measurement will usually show wide swings in sex hormones. That can bring on all the symptomatology of the menopause, even though the woman has monthly evidence that she is still fertile and may even become pregnant.

Because we have not been aware that these wide hormonal fluctuations commonly occur throughout the forties in both sexes, even the best-known symptoms can be misunderstood. What is happening when waves of heat spread over the upper body, often followed by chills? The medical term is *vasomotor instability*. The vasomotor nerves are responsible for enlarging or decreasing the diameter of the blood vessels. Ordinarily, these nerves will take their cue from the body temperature; if hard exercise heats us up, more blood is sent to the dilated capillaries at the skin's surface so that excess heat can be ventilated out of the body. The same process holds true in reverse; in severe cold, the capillaries constrict and blood is drawn deep into the trunk of the body where the heat can be better conserved and important organs maintained. But when hormones become unstable, they disturb the signals going to the vasomotor nerves. Dizziness, too, in the middle-aged woman or man, is usually caused by some disturbance of blood flow caused by the agitated vasomotor nerves. The palpitating heart can have the same cause.

As I have said, 90 percent of women today are not overwhelmed by problems of the menopause period, and the actual cessation of menses appears later. The severe depression experienced by roughly 10 percent of women, which was once widespread, has been offset by the increasing opportunities and options available to the middle-aged woman and by a profound change in consciousness. All the experts talk about "the world is opening up" attitude that has replaced the closed-book uselessness women once felt when their children left home.

Many women today emerge with a burst of "postmenopausal zest." Once the worries of pregnancy are thrown out along with the tampons and contraceptives, women in good health will often experience a reawakening of sexual desire, as well as great enthusiasm for directing their creativity into new channels.[23]

We often wonder, "Who is that woman? She must be 55, and yet her skin is terrific, and her breasts don't sag. What's her secret?" Chances are, she is the woman with especially vigorous adrenal glands. Estrogen is produced by the adrenals, which are not affected by menopause, as well as by the ovaries. Some women then compensate for the estrogen loss from this other source; they age well, remain strong and energetic, and enjoy much the same vaginal lubrication and elasticity they have had all along. Although this defense against sexual aging is out of a woman's control, the other most important counteractive factor cited by Masters and Johnson is not. And that is regular intercourse, once or twice a week over a period of years.

The same can be said for both men and women. Consistency of sexual relations is the key to continuously vigorous sexual expression.

23

LIVING OUT
THE
FANTASY

In California I looked up a girlhood idol of mine who was for years. prima ballerina of a major American dance company. I remembered the beauty of her features, the black chignon, the way her tense, muscular body commanded the most difficult roles. She danced all over the world and was still dancing in her forties. People told me she was happily married now, and when I phoned she invited me over without the slightest hesitation.

A thickset woman with tinted red hair answered the door. Her loose shirt lapped out over wide-legged trousers. I gave the dancer's name. She held out her hand, amusement playing over the ample contours of her face. It was she.

Leading the way into a solarium flooded with sunlight, she served me a sandwich. Presently her husband joined us. He was an infectiously buoyant and handsome man, clearly ten years her junior. The two of them came together like fragments of a picture being mended. It was apparent that they complemented each other remarkably, and when I asked about this, the dancer smiled her amused and contented smile while her husband said, "It's inconceivable to me now to imagine life without being married to Irina."

They told me their story. Unorthodox as it is, both of these people found ways to expand beyond the narrow lines that had confined and contented them earlier in life but that if extended, would have left them unhappy. The dancer provides an example of how the Switch-40s might be made manifest in an achieving woman who never had children.

The body was her instrument. Before she could read she was working that body muscle by muscle. As the bones grew, it was necessary to bend and torture them over the barre, to keep after the muscles by forcing that turnout, stretching that extension. It was also the way to please her Russian-born parents. Friends and fun were for later, when she was finished. Irina submitted to the discipline. Her lover was her talent and she followed it monogamously, followed it through an eternity of morning barres, afternoon rehearsals, evening performances. Few others know the narcissistic intensity shared by dancers and professional athletes.

"Part of me was happy with it, and part of me not at all," she says. "I was always at war with my career and what I thought I should have as a woman."

Two husbands passed briefly through her early life. One when she was very young and concerned with proprieties, the other a great artist and good friend whose admiration matched hers but whose itinerary did not. He toured; she toured; they never saw each other. To call these two intersections marriage was a gross overstatement. But she did hanker for some stability, a stop that could be called home. This nebulous idea of home would not, could not come into focus while there were still dramatic roles she had not yet danced. Ambition remained her consort for more than forty years.

"It wasn't until I began to achieve a certain maturity, I guess, that I realized there must be something else, something besides just going from role to role."

They were on tour together, the venerated prima

ballerina and the brooding young choreographer. He was a flippy sort of character, only 32, given to creating deeply ideological ballets that didn't interest Irina. But on this tour they fell in love. They closed at the Opera House in Cologne and squeezed into his tiny MGA for the all-night trip to Rome.

As they drove through the Black Forest she began tossing her toe shoes out the window. Laughing, lightening with every toss, she scattered seventy pairs of toe slippers to the moss and aphids. "This is it!" she thought. "Now, the end of it all!" He was jubilant.

In Rome she stopped dancing and started eating. She got fat. Blew up in a matter of weeks. It was amazing; it was sublime. He went off every morning to work on a show, and she did nothing. She was intensely happy. He marveled at how well they got along. "Forgetting love and all that," he decided, "I really liked her, and she liked me." They wired friends they had married. Terrible jokes came back: "Hope you enjoy dancing your way through life together." And what of her career? The age difference? Ludicrous. The rest of the world gave their marriage fifteen minutes.

It has lasted fifteen years.

In midlife, when other voices from other rooms inside demand to be incorporated, we must loosen the imposed life structure. Often the process is begun by breaking out altogether and sailing off on a fantasy trip toward another extreme. The ballerina defies the discipline of forty years to enjoy being fat and lazy. Eventually, though, the new extreme will give evidence of its own limitations. Most of us will have to move back and forth between such extremes until a way is found to bring more of our important parts together in a new integration.

Irina could hardly have dreamed up a more romantic escape from the confinements of her former skin. Yet she would not have remained content forever stuffing herself and watching TV game shows until her husband came home. Her solution had to include her in the creative process. But it had to be in some way that would not disrupt the domestic harmony she now so highly valued. The narrowness of her former life worked in her favor. Having committed herself body and soul to attaining excellence with the gifts given her, she had no fight with herself about the decision to stop dancing. And it was her decision alone.

"I'd had my career, and I was very secure with that," as she says. "There was really no other achievement possible except the continuing of it. I had done all I set out to do."

She became her husband's assistant, creative mentor, spiritual mother—call it what you will, it is all those things. He launched a new career as a movie director, and she was there beside him, on location hunts, doing the casting and wardrobe, evaluating the rushes. From the start he relied on her in a hundred ways.

"If I'm dithering around, she always has a definite opinion," he says. "Irina has terrific taste. And she manages to keep everything in perspective for me. 'It's only a movie; there'll be another one next year.' I used to be very self-destructive. I would avoid waking up until afternoon. One of the best single qualities Irina has is she wakes up very early in the best mood." He grins. "It's not so good about five in the afternoon, but the mornings are wonderful." The idealization is not so total that he has to feel wholly dependent on her; maybe that is why he doesn't feel he has to get away. "We're never farther apart than yelling distance."

Irina affirms their extraordinary closeness. It is not hard to see where her generative instincts have been channeled. "We have no children. So we're really focused on one another, with no outside pulls."

Most of the time their special intimacy remains on an unspoken level. For just a moment the lively director's face rests in seriousness. He looks at his wife. "I don't think I've actually said it to you, but it's through you that I learned to realize whatever my potential is and fulfill whatever I'm able to do."

"He's the boss, and I'm the subordinate. It's fine."

"She just says that."

"But I couldn't begin to do all the things you do."

"That's different," he agrees. It's a fine ego save. And now their mood shifts easily back to the playful. "Let's put it this way. I do all the hard stuff, and she has the luxury of pissing off in the midst of the most abominable locations to go shopping."

"And then turning up for dailies and telling you it's lousy."

"Which only confirms what I already know but wouldn't face."

It is hard after a while to tell who is talking. That's how things are with this couple.

The Change-of-Life Affair

For every Irina, there must be a dozen amorous adventurers of a like age who have nothing so serious in mind. Many other purposes can be served by the change-of-life affair. It can be a display ("See, other men still find me desirable") or a weapon ("Younger women turn me on; they don't have your hang-ups") intended to force attentions from a listless spouse. Or the whole idea may be to leave behind a smoking gun, in hopes it will be discovered and blow the marriage wide open.

But the greatest temptation in the change-of-life affair is the fireworks of romantic love. What could be more splendidly therapeutic in dispelling middlescent gloom? While the blaze is high, it bathes us again in aureoles of beauty and strength, eclipses this dreary review of past and future, fixes time in the breathless present, or still better, delivers us back to the cheerful selfishness of adolescent infatuation. "I have to" is transformed into "I want to." This new love has no stake in holding us to a stale identity. The sky's the limit!

Months pass (six seems to be the magic number), and the blaze of romantic love dies down. This is hardly the first time; we should have anticipated it. But somehow we managed to forget that when the fire-works burn out, the embers cool down to the same old things: caring, commitment, trust.

If this natural progression finds the lovers ready to alter the conditions of their lives radically, they will be willing to go with it. But now they are wading into deep water. Certain illusions about this change-of-life affair will be dampened, and for a while it can feel very cold indeed.

A publisher I interviewed, who felt his boyishness had been released by a woman twenty years his junior, was 52 when we spoke. Their change-of-life affair had become a remarriage. A new crisis was in the making. This man of ideas and words and concepts was tongue-tied when the subject of Where I Am Right Now in My Marriage came up. The conflict concerned his young wife's wish for a child. He had already gone that circle several times in a former life. Could he bear to be made Number Two again? he wondered. How much does a man have in him for sustaining relation-ships under strain? There was more to his crisis. He was a man who had lived in his head, and now he wanted to be vulnerable.

"I get sensations these days of a real thickness in my head," he said, "like densely packed straw. I want some help."

The irony of it is, as a volunteer counselor, he has been helping other men to make midlife career transi-tions. I asked him if being 52 has made him more cautious in his marriage and other relationships.

"That's one of my great dilemmas. Which 'me' do you want to listen to? The one who helps other 52-year-old people to feel what they really are and are able to do? The one who shows off his blood pressure and wiry physique? Or the one who from time to time *feels* 52 and keeps looking and listening for the worst to happen?"

Shortly thereafter, his young wife left him.

Many more middlescent lovers never give com-mitment a thought. Intimacy is just what they are trying to escape. In the past this furlough from responsibilities has been thought of largely as a prerogative of men. Columnist Art Sidenbaum reminds us that

> the 50-year-old man creaking around with the 25-year-old girl is still a commonplace, leaving a large number of 45-year-old women with nothing to do. It remains a cruelty and perhaps a stupidity. But it remains a luxury of manhood because men can better afford to indulge themselves with sports cars, scarves, seaside motel rooms and the accessories of irresponsibility. Their ex-wives, generally, are still left at home with the kids and other visible proofs of adulthood.[1]

Not if she says, as she just might these days, "You take the kids."

There is another new dent in this age-old luxury of manhood. Once upon a time before the sexual revolution, a young woman turned more readily to the older man. He was like Daddy, experienced, protective. He could entertain her stylishly and would be glad of any small sexual favors.

Today the silvery-sideburned sexual hunter finds himself in competition with younger men who can pick up from one good porn film the technique it took their elders years to acquire. And among the current generation of young women, he is apt to find an aggressive bluntness that is positively shriveling in bed. Even if he does find his perfect girl and eventually pulls together a satisfactory performance, why is she in it? She wants his knowingness, a cram course on the world. But will she stay interested once he tells her what everything means? Or will he?

Nevertheless, the fantasy persists. *I can make a clean break. I don't need commitment. I'm flying beyond all that.* With a man as our guide who has pushed this fantasy to its limits, let's look at the gains and losses at the end of the flight.

Before I begin the story of Jay Parrish, I want to make clear the essential distinction between his solution and Irina's. The two biographies are certainly not meant to suggest that any woman who takes impetuous flight in midlife is going to find a rainbow at the end, and that a man who does the same will find something less. The difference between these tales has nothing to do with gender. The dancer is a person whose deep investment in the choices of her early life has made possible the enrichment of her middle years. She is living out her fantasy of love and maternalism with all the commitment she once brought to her career. The person we are about to meet, by contrast, has a history of limited emotional involvements and no clear occupation. Although he recoups a good deal of vitality by the course he takes in midlife, it can have only as much sustained meaning as he brings to it.

Busting Out

Things happen to Jay Parrish. He would not have thought of himself as a sexual pedagogue, for instance, had he not stopped by his daughter's apartment that night for a drink before catching the train. He went into the bedroom to call his wife. There were thick blinds at the window blotting all light from the room. When he stood up and turned around, a female form was there and her arms went around him and they kissed for a long time.

"Mr. P., I wonder if you'll do me a favor?"

He recognized the voice of his daughter's roommate. "Sure, what?" he said.

"Teach me to fuck."

Nothing quite like this had ever happened to him in 41 years. Speechless, he moved the girl back through the doorway and into the light, duly noting that she was beautiful. He also remembered she was 19. He told his daughter that he would have to hurry to catch the train.

Shortly thereafter Mr. P. did exactly what had been asked. This is when, he says, "a lot of changes began to happen to me. Not only was I introduced to directness, but this girl was deeply involved with

472

politics and SDS, very liberal thinking. All this was new to me. Just fantastic discussions. And I'd get little notes from her with beautiful thoughts. I remember one: 'Don't be a magician, be magic.' That kind of thinking I'd never been exposed to. So we had a glorious time together for two years."

If there was any sense of loss when the affair ended, Mr. P. does not remark on it.

He was beginning to be disillusioned with American business. As the vice-president of an advertising agency, he'd had a close look at certain trinkets enjoyed by the chief executives of major corporations that do not appear on annual reports to stockholders: a Gulfstream jet with a leather-bumpered bar to fly friends and sweethearts to Cape Cod, for example. The misuse of power, tax gimmicks, phonied expense accounts, the whole package of lies and vanity began to turn his stomach. When his wife grew bored with the dinner plates she replaced them. His children went to private schools. Whenever he returned to the city after a certain hour, a limousine would be waiting for him at the airport because he wasn't supposed to take a taxi. He was allowed to go first class only. He almost came to believe he was entitled to such privileges.

When he was 46, the company treasurer cornered him to talk about profit sharing. "Do you realize, Jay Parrish, that when you retire fifteen years from now, your stock will be worth at least half a million dollars?" the treasurer said.

That's it, that's the way they trap you, he thought during the commute to the house in the suburbs with seven bathrooms and six children. Or was it seven children and six bathrooms? He'd had too much to drink. The two teen-agers were with his former wife; his oldest daughter lived with the roommate, that's right, there were two boys left at home and a six-year-old girl. He decided he didn't need to buy another thing as long as he lived.

That night Jay Parrish told his wife, "Nan, I've got to get out of here. Because each year that $500,000 is going to look bigger and bigger until I get to the point where I say, 'God, I've only got a few years to go.' Like it or not, I'm going to be doing it all for the money, which I really don't need. What I really want to do is enjoy my life. Now. Not fifteen years from now. I don't even know if I'll be alive."

Nan scarcely said a word. This blast of rebelliousness was completely out of character for her husband. The conservative eastern suburb in which they lived had been her lifelong shelter. Her friends were here and all the relations from whom she stood to inherit a lot of money. She knew the pantsuit uniform and how to give the right parties. Theirs was a safe, polite, and utilitarian marriage, just as it was supposed to be. Wasn't it?

Well, that was the original idea, back when Parrish had just been made a vice-president. He was 35 and anxious to move up in the world. It didn't hurt to marry an attractive heiress. "We started off on what would have been a really beautiful marriage," Jay muses, "if I had been content to stay in that suburb." They never did have what you would call a torrid sex life. It wasn't to be expected from someone as restrained as the second Mrs. Parrish. He had selected her for the same purposes he chose the first Mrs. Parrish: to be a facilitator of his career. Nonetheless, to his bill of midlife grievances he now added a dull sex life.

He wanted to get moving. He bought a Volkswagen camper. He studied the map of California.

Nan stalled about putting the house on the market. She couldn't just turn the children's lives upside down, she said. And it was important that Victoria, their six-year-old, finish the year at her special school.

"They're all in such good shape; it isn't going to make a damn bit of difference in the long run," he said.

"But Victoria is retarded."

"Victoria'll have a ball. I'll take her down to Big Sur."

Overnight he decided the time was now. After breakfast he walked out to the camper and drove from sea to shining sea.

How to describe the way it was out there in the vortex of nowness? The beach life, the people who moved in and out, how it felt to doze with his groin against the warm bottom of a strange woman, their strengthless legs after love being painted by a sun perfectly made for nudists. She was an astrologer. Together they would hone down into the blissful meditative oneness, and later she would read the Tarots for him. It is true that Parrish was suspended in space much of the time, but by and by he would be at his easel. Everything was flowing. He decided he must write an article about it and send it back to *Advertising Age*. This is an excerpt from the unpublished article he wrote:

> If you think you want to live like I do, don't expect country clubs and carpeted homes and the easy expense account living you are used to. . . . This is a fantastically productive period for me. I've painted 26 canvases in the first three months out here, and have already had two shows.

There was no mention of what was in the paintings or what they meant to him. The article was straight ad copy. He was still on a production schedule.

When the astrologer took another lover he was relieved, another burden off his shoulders.

Nan kept writing and phoning to say she wanted to join him. He wrote back, "Are you sure you want to walk around without any clothes on and go camping and have two-hour massages in the sun with hot baths? Because these are things which are becoming an important part of my life."

Nan wrote back yes.

"From the moment I got here," Nan admitted timidly when I met her in California, "I didn't feel I was part of it. Westchester is a little stuffy, and I probably am, too. I thought I was pretty, well, 'with it,' back east. But out here I'm not. And I'd like to be accepted by people." She was like a silk lampshade with its protective covering ripped off, fragile, easily soiled, so patently absurd in this setting. Lost.

Her husband would lie nude a few yards away. She sat with her back to him in a doubleknit pantsuit, eating her lunch from a tray. He gave her a copy of *The Happy Hooker*. She made no comment.

To accommodate her and the children, Parrish bought a baby white elephant of a house. It served as a laboratory for his carpentry experiments. He was trying to hire himself out as a carpenter, at $50 a day. Once in a while he sold a painting. Monthly checks for $500 will continue to trickle in from his old company for another few years. "I would really like to get to the point," he said, "where I could exist without money."

The exterior change in Parrish was extraordinary. He brought out his old standard Bachrach business portrait. It showed a corpulent, jowly, dull-eyed man with an allover grayish glaze. The escapee who stood before me two years later was tan, vibrant, lean-cheeked, with a hawkish nose and burning blue eyes and a luxuriant head of hair. An altogether stunning physical specimen. The most curious part of it all was that Jay Parrish, like others who move deep into adult life without acknowledging their strong identification with a parent, was only now beginning to look like himself.

Parrish was 16 when his father died. Unable to get his bearings in the shock and confusion, unable to do any healing grieving, he fled to California. From the age of 16, with a tenth-grade education, he began making his own living. He was never a teen-ager.

The society divorcée he married in his twenties already had two little babies. From being an unresolved son, he graduated into being a clumsy stepparent. Altogether it was a stormy marriage right from the start, his wife's social credentials were helpful when he opened a fashionable restaurant back east. The prodigal son had returned to his hometown. Commercially, he prospered. He also put away a lot of tap beer while his wife played around. They had children. Nothing much seemed to take, and when he was 30 the marriage fell apart.

He did not do well over the Age 30 transition. Working as a middle-management beer salesman, he slipped one day on a saloon floor while drunk. He was in a cast when his mother died. It hardly bears repeating that the death of important people during sensitive passages has an enormous impact on our sense of safety. Parrish ran into his ex-wife at the funeral. He couldn't wait to remarry her.

With no other alteration in the life of his twenties then, except for an enlargement of his working territory, he moved to Manhattan at 32 and pushed into the middle-management pool of advertising. The reconstituted marriage started right where it had left off; with the drinking and fighting. They stuck it out for a few more years. Then, with few apparent ripples, he exchanged the first for the second Mrs. Parrish. By now he walked, talked, and behaved with such a rigid resemblance to his father, it was as though Jay Parrish had been inhabited by the dead man's ghost. Quite possibly, his father's premature death had knocked all developmental schedules askew.

What comes through in the way Jay Parrish now talks about himself is his feeling that he is a fraud. He assumes various stances, but they are not freely chosen. The fit between what he is doing in the world and who he is or what he wants internally is always a misfit. If one asks what Parrish is occupationally, his own sense of it is that he's nothing. He's not a restaurateur, not a beer salesman, not an advertising executive, not a painter or a carpenter, not even a husband or a father to any deep or sustaining degree. He is a man who continually changes situations at the level of action, plunging into something like a new job or a marriage or escaping out of it without doing any work on himself. Energy, yes, he finds that easy to invest. But very little of his own substance goes into any pursuit or person. Hence his losses are sloughed off rather easily. He is the very embodiment of the lifelong transient.

What then are the gains and losses of his midlife solution? It is clear even to Parrish that today, at 49, he is grabbing hungrily for the adolescence he never had. All of us have to come to terms in midlife with the fact that we are not 20, and most of us will have some leftover developmental work we didn't do earlier. But that is not the same thing as trying to be 20.

Nan has now asked for a divorce. Parrish wanders down to the hardware store. The cashier is a pretty 18-year-old girl. "I'm looking for a place to live," he mentions.

"I'm in the same boat," the cashier says. "My family's going back east. But I'm of age now, I can do what I want to do."

"What's your name?" he asks.

"Mickey."

"Maybe we can find a place together, Mickey."

Hunting across the soft blur where sea and sky meet, looking for a philosophical clue—he never tires of it. Mickey brings around her freshmen friends to the beach house. It's not much, a shack really, but the discussions are what fascinate him. He can get all worked up with the kids about what Kant said, about numerology and Sufism.

"I can't get that from my own group," Parrish says. "They're talking about the stock market. That's why I spend so much time with young people. It may have something to do with the fact I was never on a college campus. Mickey and I went into this house together knowing we weren't going to be serious about each other. I don't want it to last very long. She insisted on paying half the rent. And every hundred dollars counts to me these days. But in the meantime, she's teaching me to find the positive in everything. I'll say, 'Oh hell, the fog's rolling in.' Her face will light up and she'll say, 'Isn't that beautiful? The way the fog is rolling in?' "

Parrish still commutes every day from the beach to Nan's house. He does his carpentry work there until the children come home from school. They talk a few moments, and then his daughter says, "Bye, Dubby," and the boys say, "See you tomorrow, Dad," and he goes back to his 18-year-old girl friend.

"It's a weird arrangement," he will admit, "but Nan and I are getting along much better since the pressure is off. She's never said anything about the girl I'm living with. Recently, I suggested we all get together and have a picnic over on the beach by my house."

Nan is paralyzed. "Since our daughter was born—she's retarded—I just didn't think about the future. There was no way of saying, 'Well, in five years I'll be doing this or that,' because I don't know what her future is. I'd like to say that I have some talent, but I don't. I really should do more—" she halts. A shiver of helplessness goes down her face. "Something to do with either clothing or decorating. I don't know quite where to start really. I might move closer to San Francisco."

Parrish is against this. "It would be silly to move," he tells her. "Suppose you meet someone who wants you to live in Kansas and then you have to move again?" It's an effective campaign tactic because he knows Nan is just waiting for him to want her again.

But the real reason he wants to keep her here is to provide access to his children and a home where he can touch base now and then.

"The difficult thing for me to justify is leaving Nan high and dry because she hasn't done anything wrong. She's still in that other world where we were all brought up to live according to plans: ('Would you like to go out next Saturday night?' 'I'd like to be vice-president next year.') She still believes you develop relationships in that way. What I've learned from the younger people I've met out here is that there are no commitments. It's right now."

The gamble in Parrish's solution is obvious to him. He cannot find a way to live as an adult, doesn't want to, rejects commitment. He may have to go from adolescence to old age.

Late one night after driving me over to see Nan, he withdrew into the shadows of his camper. "The devil I have to wrestle with is, I could end up a very lonely, disappointed old man. If something happens and I can't work with my hands, I'm going to be a candidate for welfare. The odds are against me. There's really no way to exist in this society without making at least six or eight thousand a year, even to exist at poverty level."

He started the motor and hunched down to peer through the fog. "When I'm ten years older, I can't be living with 18-year-olds because they won't find me attractive. I'm flattered now because they accept me. But I wonder if I'm just kidding myself. Is it going to be 17-year-old girls and then 14-year-old girls? And how about 12-year-olds?"

That summer Parrish gave up the beach shack to save rent. He went to visit his eldest son in Colorado for the summer. It wasn't as if he could pick and choose where to live thereafter. Someone told him food was cheaper in Guatemala, that lettuce there was a penny a head. He was considering heading down to Guatemala in the fall with his truck.

"With or without Mickey. Or it may be somebody else by then."

Last I heard, Parrish had shoved off to Central America. He went with a 17-year-old girl.

24

LIVING OUT
THE
REALITY

No one knows why the master is afraid to close his eyes. Why at 43, he has trouble simply keeping his equilibrium. The supports of success are not holding.

The invitation from Paris came when Aaron was 40. The coup of coups. Here was the bastion of French design, asking for an exhibition of the upstart American's work. Aaron's exhibition changed the direction of design thinking in France. His show was treated as a major sociological event. Invitations began rolling in from all over the world. The show took off on an international tour, and Aaron and his wife traveled with it whenever they could.

For all the glory and flimflam that accompanied the tour, the fabulous Paris party, the silken reception in Tokyo, champagne in the courtyard in Milano, Aaron was pursued by a bittersweet sense of loss. At the highest pitch of the party in Paris, he was notified that a dear friend had been rushed to the hospital, near death. Again, a chill intruded on the champagne party in Italy: another call about a sudden death. Aaron began to brood on these events. A new conviction began taking shape in his mind: *You have to be ready to give it all up.*

"The most influential [designer] of our time," pronounced a leading critic in his field. He read the article. And then he closed his eyes and let it overtake him, a sense of internal collapse so powerful that he no longer wanted to resist it.

"I have always used my work as a substitute for solving problems in my life," he is now aware. "It began when I married. I packed my life with activity in order to avoid major personal decisions. What I do is *give up* autonomy by creating a high-demand situation,. so that I must always jump from project to project, never really allowing time to think about what I'm doing it all for. Since I turned 40, it's become clearer to me that the reason I do this"—he hesitates a beat—"is I really haven't wanted to scrutinize what my life is all about. Just the idea of stopping to investigate is an indication that something has changed."

The metropolis where he was born, in the back of a grocery store in a grimly poor section of the city, has been made gayer and more livable by his own hand. People can point to his work and say, "That's an Aaron Coleman Webb." By external measurements there is a strong continuity to Aaron's life. Many men spend years between two chairs, not quite sure if they are innovators or administrators, original researchers or teachers, lawyers or politicians, politicians or hacks. Aaron's career, however, is a clear center around which his life has been organized since the age of five.

Yet he is not locked in like Kilpatrick the citizen-soldier. Aaron has done some probing of his feelings with a guru of karma-yoga, although more of his explorative efforts have gone into finding unique design techniques to solve sophisticated artistic problems. "Another of Webb's uniquely American works," the critics may say. He will chuckle, knowing that he brings together information from all over the world, melds the experience of previous centuries into the style of the moment. He is completely permeable. As for the transient Jay Parrish, he and Aaron are poles apart. It is one thing to go from impulse to impulse, as Parrish does it, and quite a different thing when Aaron talks about wanting to enrich his experience by letting go of the old formulas. Aaron Coleman Webb is a bona fide wunderkind. One might think his would be an exempt status.

It only looks that way.

Aaron appears to go through life's growth processes as naturally as grass. I have known him for years. He spreads around his exuberance for rock stars and cheap Greek restaurants as easily as for high art. While others only watch, he learns from everything. There is no creative block whatsoever. If a design problem comes up at the studio, he breathes on it. It's gone. He wears jeans and fruit and vegetable ties, and there is always a big wet kiss forthcoming when one bumps into him.

His wife, Michele, in contrast, is ethereal as a fern. About displaying her own singular artistic imagination she has been very private—in fact, recessive. She cooks magnificently. Or did. Now he cooks. They migrate on weekends to an old-shoe country house. In place of children they have a worldwide network of friends and associates.

But closing his eyes, in the instant between realms when outer achievements must be let go, Aaron Coleman Webb is alone with that sense of internal collapse. "What I've discovered over the last year is how much of what is inadmissible to myself I have suppressed. Feelings that I've always refused to admit are surfacing in a way that *I am no longer willing to prevent*. I'm willing to accept the responsibility for what *I really feel*. I don't have to pretend those feelings don't exist in order to accommodate a model of what I should be. I'm really shocked now at the range and the quality of those feelings—feelings of fear, of envy, of greed, of competition. All these so-called bad feelings are really rising where I can see them and feel them. I'm amazed at the incredible energy we all spend suppressing them and not admitting pain."

Michele graduated from the same design school but was in every other respect, to his eyes, an exotic. He was as urban Jewish as an egg cream. She was white milk from a dairy farm. "In some way that I have yet to understand," he puzzles, "I was attracted not only by her beauty but by the fact that she had nothing to do with my beliefs or background."

Did Michele want to be a designer, too?

"There were no clues to the fact that that's what she wanted. She never said that, never demonstrated that."

In fact, after design school Michele had taken a job replacing Aaron Coleman Webb. He was away in Europe on a Fulbright. He wrote postcards to say hello to the "new girl." People told her how fast Aaron could do perspectives; she did them faster. Even before she had laid eyes on the man, she felt a great competition with him.

"The strange thing is, I was much better at the job than Aaron was," she had told me. "Then the ambivalence. I wanted the security of being married. But there was no way I could see that that wasn't the end of my creative life. I've fed an enormous amount of my hidden ambition and my need to express myself into Aaron. He had aspirations that I couldn't dare to have. And I loved his aspirations."

Aaron envisioned building his own firm and making it a true community. He and his partner began hiring young designers with their own ideas. Their conviction was that each man should identify his work personally. As a result, people became recognized, famous, left the firm, and new people came in. Aaron liked that in-and-out motion. He felt a paternalistic pride in developing a fine community of designers.

The home fires were tended exquisitely by Michele. She learned how to buy ten different salad greens and twirl them into Baggies, faster and faster, to arrange fresh flowers and put backups in the refrigerator beside the gourmet dishes so there would be no chance that her husband's last-minute dinner guests would get Hamburger Helper. Then she wouldn't have to feel guilty about curling up for the rest of the day with her books and her own imagination.

Aaron asked her at one point to set up a gallery and devise a show for the fine arts school where he taught. With her left hand, it seemed, Michele launched the concept of theme shows. It was her original idea to bring together many artists around a theme rather than bore the public with one-man shows. It set a trend that was quickly picked up along Madison Avenue's glamour gallery row. Michele worked hard and well at this job for five years. Then mysteriously, she stopped. It was back home to arrange flowers and fresh vegetable platters for Aaron's guests.

At an awards dinner some years later, Aaron took credit for the theme-show idea.

"She was supposed to be the perfect wife," Aaron says, "always supportive and understanding, the gracious hostess, agreeable, charming, acceptable. The central thing—I always wanted Michele to provide peace of mind." He is now able to dig beneath those idealizations to his own more raw motives. "This is the most difficult admission to make. I realize that I was really seeking a situation which would be free from intimacy in a deep way. Where I would never have to reveal myself. It's quite possible I may have chosen a woman from a very different background so that I could be resentful of her if she did not act out my dream. That would be just another mechanism for preventing intimacy."

During his late thirties, when the mortality issue would have been needling anyway, Aaron's mother fell ill and kept faltering. He was pursued by one thought and awoke every morning to its pitiless edict: *You are going to die.* Aaron fell into depression and eventually became ill with colitis. For so many years, his mother had been the sole figure who protected and endorsed his artistic dreams against his father's disapproval. Bearing such a strong identification with the inner custodian, it was easy to believe that his self would perish with her.

The day Aaron picked up the phone and was told his mother had died, his obsession with death vanished. "There was a shift then, and my goal became a very specific one—to move the firm to the position where it would be the best of its kind in the world." His capacity to take in other people's views or inspirations shrank abruptly. "And it had nothing to do with the validity of their information. I didn't want any other input regardless of whether it was effective or not." The relationship between Aaron and his partner became confining. "I really wanted to achieve a kind of professional mastery which would make me immune to anybody's control, to get into a leverage position of such dimension that no one would be able to criticize me. And to a large extent, I achieved that."

Had he talked to his wife about the death fears?

"A little bit."

"She gave you peace of mind?"

"I was hoping she would."

"But then she had her own emotional crisis?"

"Yes. Because in our relationship, one of the things Michele has counted on was my parental qualities, my support, my strength, the sense that I knew where I was going. Any manifestation of weakness on my part was very destructive in our relationship. If I was insecure or weak or fearful, then Michele's fear of being depended on by *me* would make her more panicky. That would mean, of course, my anxiety increased. This kind of knotting has been very dangerous for us. Weakness on my part would reinforce danger on Michele's part. It's a system that tends to destroy."

Where was Michele at 38? Alone in the country house reading *Zelda* and other books about men who used the ideas of women who loved them. *Why?* she tormented herself. *Where is it written that women are the only nurturers?* All at once she felt a desperate need to balance herself. She ran out to the yard and hoisted herself onto her head. Trembling there, in harmony for a moment with this upside-down universe, she felt a snap in her neck. Not even her body would work for her anymore. She decided this was the time to die. Foraging through the house for pills, all she could find was a bottle of vitamin E. The long-life vitamin. She had to laugh.

Once, in conversation, Michele's normally light voice had curdled and suddenly she was on the offensive.

"I made Aaron a better designer," she declared. "And I don't care if anybody, in this case you, finds that hard to believe."

I said I didn't find it hard, having seen evidence.

"But I've always made it clear to competitive people that I wasn't in the game with them," she went on. "Whether that put me out of the game and therefore the winner or out of the game and the loser, I couldn't tell the difference. Also, in Aaron's eyes, there was no possibility that I could be in the same field with him. It's just not the way he wanted things."

But the experience of launching the art gallery and innovating theme shows, why didn't she stick with it?

"I think it may have been a fear that if I really got into it, I would get in so heavily, I would be alone."

Autonomy equals aloneness. How relentlessly this idea pursues women! If it isn't put to the test earlier, the stark terror is there to face at the crossroads into midlife.

For Aaron, the French museum exhibition marked the official end of that part of his life. Just to hear himself believing it, he said to several people, "I have been formally told I am a good boy, I did good work. It means that I will have to invent something else to do."

Saying it was one thing. Wrestling with the panic was another. If he did not invent himself anew, he would go on repeating his old formulas, become his own stuffed-shirt archivist. No, he would have to dig down beneath all his prize-winning techniques and find out if the creative clay was still soft. But in the process, he would take the risk of failing at the top.

Toward the end of our first formal interview, Aaron spoke of trying to find a way to "phase out a little." At the same time, he slipped in the phrase, "hold on to a piece of control." His voice funneled down to a hush.

"I don't know what I want to do. What I really have to learn for myself are the feelings of passivity, dependence, weakness, frailty—all the things that are abhorrent to me on the intellectual level. As a counterweight to that, I must permit myself to acknowledge my own aggression, my punishing quality, all the rest of that. I can't pretend anymore that the duality of roles does not exist. It's a time of confusion for me, great personal confusion."

Michele. The amazing whiteness of her skin, so delicate it has gone grayish under the eyes like the center of dogwood blossoms, and her blazing dark eyes—Michele has always seemed to me concocted to fulfill other people's fantasies. Elusiveness is her central quality. Like all exquisite and fevered things, she cannot be captured nor made content by the rational world. Her life is filled with artistic visions, daydreams, restlessness, chain-smoking.

One never quite knows what she might do next. To watch this fragile woman with a fresh gardenia pinned to her bosom drag heavily on her Lucky Strikes and talk about the joys of being a street peddler— yes—in the midst of her husband's elaborate success, she took to selling objects of junk along with the old crones in a teeming section of town. It was something of her own, she said. The next time I saw her she had enrolled in a four-year degree program to study an esoteric philosophy.

We kept putting off our talk. A year passed.

I caught a glimpse of her with Aaron at a crowded election night celebration. She had tinted her hair a livid red and crimped it into hundreds of bouncing rubber band curls. Next to the whiteness of her skin and delicate features, the kinetics of her new design were slightly hysterical. Such an extreme style would have made most women her age a laughing stock. It only made Michele more infectious, more tantalizing.

No, I thought, Michele's beauty would not die. It would build first toward this phosphorescence and hover there—who knows how long?—on the edge of the grotesque.

The moment I called to set the date, she froze. A few days later Michele called back to cancel.

"I've been shaky ever since you called," she explained. "I'm tumbling around with so many thoughts, things coming up that I haven't paid attention to for a long time. I don't know, I guess I just haven't thought of myself before as being middle-aged. It frightens me to admit being frightened."

I told her she wasn't middle-aged. She was 42 and probably in the eye of midlife crisis. What she said next captured beautifully the mingling of dark and light that so many find hard to describe.

"It's very strange, but there's an underground of singing to myself."

A few hours later Michele phoned back to say that she wanted to contribute to the book now, in the honesty of her uncertainness, not wait until it was all composed. I thanked her.

We met at her favorite restaurant, where the pace is unhurried, unbusinesslike, and the rum drinks come floating with gardenias.

"It came up on Sunday with me, after we spoke," she said, "maybe later than it does with other people. I had the strong feeling about my talents, that if they're not acknowledged, they don't exist. That there might be, there might really be a possibility of dying before you ever do get to express them. This was the first time it hit me in full. Before, there was the importance of fighting with your husband about resenting his role in the relationship, blaming it on the outside, your mother, your father, the place that society put you in. Sunday was the first time I sat down and acknowledged my contribution to that, my hiding out in that. It was very clear."

I said it was a good sign.

"I don't know if it's a good sign, but it's a very shaky place."

She told me she would like to put an ad in the paper listing the whole grab bag of abilities she has acquired over the years. She wants urgently to let out her energy and share it with others. "I think it's the first time that any maternal wish has come out in me."

This matter of childlessness is pivotal. From the time she first learned where babies came from, there was a voice over her shoulder repeating the lament: "I wanted to be an artist, and I would have been a *great* artist, if I didn't have you." Had Michele's tubes been tied in knots, the restraint on her having children probably would have been no stronger than her mother's words.

"Girls usually look to their mothers as the guide to how they want to be. I dismissed that early in life. I didn't want to be like her because *she* didn't want to be like her." But as we talked back through Michele's warm memories of watching her mother draw night after night, not just sketching a horse but taking time to explain to the little girl every articulation in that horse's leg, something important about that old mother-daughter lock gave way.

"I've just realized—I *did* want to be like her!" Michele exclaimed. "That aspect of her. I wanted to be an artist more than I wanted to have children"— her voice is without regret—"and I'm absolutely certain it was to fulfill my mother's wishes."

The parental mix was curious in Michele's case. Her father, whose own hopes had been crushed, warned her, "Know your station in life. You're a modest child from a very modest family. Don't aim too high, Michele. You're only going to fail." As Michele says, "It somehow made reaching for anything quite forbidden, because you wouldn't get it." This combination of parental messages, it would seem, neutralized all action.

"At least now I still have my hopes—always,"

Michele added. "It's as if the unborn child in me is to fulfill what I can do."

She lifted the gardenia from her drink, breathed in the fragrance slowly, and as if revived, began to probe at her dark. "I've never been afraid of death. But I am afraid of getting old. When I was young I was very pretty. It's the fear that if I am abandoned—which is very much on my mind all of a sudden—I wouldn't have the young, fragile appearance that always made people want to take care of me. The last thing I ever thought I would have to do was to take care of myself."

A startled smile broke over her face. "But faced with that direct challenge, I see the reserves are there. That's what the singing underneath is about."

Aaron and I talked again after he had given up the studio entirely. He was in high gear.

"I don't want to give up my design activity," he said. "I just want to take it in other directions. I want to initiate the work, rather than accept commissions." He talked about environments he was designing and restaurants and fountain pens. Before my eyes rose the irrepressible thumb of Gulley Jimson, measuring out a battleship for one of his murals.

"And Michele?" I remembered the fervor with which his wife had told me, after several drinks: "I think the reason I'm so rocky now is to feel this re-emergence of competitiveness and not to know what to do with it."

Aaron feels it, too. "She really has to acknowledge her own feelings, her own reality and competition, and act them out in a way that's independent of my dream," he said. "That's what Michele is trying to do right now. I try to be supportive of her, but the issue of supportiveness becomes a very involved parental one."

For the moment, I shifted the emphasis away from Michele. I talked with Aaron about his range of feelings for the many young men he has mentored and dispatched from his firm to distant successes of their own. Was he always supportive as an artistic parent, or sometimes detached and dictatorial, depending on how much fealty a former student showed him?

"I do know that part of my parental quality can be punishing," he offered. "And for some people it has been, although for a long period in my life I wouldn't admit that. I would want to be the good father."

"Good, but with control?" I suggested.

"A lot of control and a lot of punishment. I was the guru. And the guru is a detached position, another way of preventing intimacy."

"Have you sometimes been a punishing parent with Michele?"

"Uh—" he hesitated, "I think so."

"Is withdrawal a form of punishment?"

"One form." He paused; this was a painful dredging operation. "Withdrawal and criticism. Whether I really want her dependent on me as a kind of—" he stopped short of the word *father* and substituted, "it's so complicated."

We jumped into a taxi. Aaron was on his way to cooking school. Michele would be at the university, learning above all to feel at home in her own universe. They are working at it. Aaron working at giving up the role he formerly enjoyed, that of Michele's surrogate father; Michele at relinquishing the dependency on him that she now so vividly resents. But in unbolting that door, she will lose all her illusions of absolute safety. And he will have the frightening opportunity to admit what he is now registering inside. It is a confession that goes to the heart of Aaron's image of himself, both as celebrated creator and strong husband: "It's very hard to give up your personality successes. The *manipulative* things that have worked for you. But they have to be given up if your sense of them has been false. I don't want to screen out the bad again so I can be a 'good' person." He was quiet for a time. His expression softened. "What I really want is a clear, unencumbered beginning."

If he were to invent his own concept of what love

should be in the middle years, I asked, what would it have in it?

He considered. "I think it would require an acknowledgment of my own dependencies. And from there, just possibly, we could move on to a sense of concern that has nothing to do with dependency. Where both people want to see one another grow and mature whether there's any advantage to themselves in it or not."

"Taking pleasure in freely watching each other live."

"Yes. It's something that occurs so much more often in deep friendships than in marriages." He seemed buoyed by his own insight. "There's something special about friendship."

The last time I was with the Webbs, they were surrounded by friends and admirers at a dance in Aaron's honor. Michele's hair was natural again. She looked relaxed. They are still in the midlife passage but no longer so afraid or confused.

"The last year has been the best one in our marriage," Michele said. "I thought I was the only one with fears and dependencies. What a great relief to find out they are reciprocal! It's so important for people to admit being interdependent, don't you think?"

"Yes, I do."

How many can look into their own dark? I thought. And those who do, and give themselves permission to let go? Who make this leap of bold faith toward a new beginning? Perhaps ideas of the opposite come together and lose their oppositeness, and a new writing begins. Perhaps at the farthest outpost of our explorations, we come back to knowing ourselves for the first time.

Part Seven

RENEWAL

So the riders of the darkness pass
On their circuits: the luminous island
Of the self trembles and waits,
Waits for us all, my friends,
Where the sea's big brush recolours
The dying lives, and the unborn smiles.

—LAWRENCE DURRELL

25

RENEWAL

Nevertheless, why growth? If we have been brave enough to confront each of life's passages, what do we have to look forward to?

Middle age is the time of maximum influence. Many people who are younger have power, but influence, which has broader implications, is generally wielded in politics, education, banking, and the community by those who are middle-aged. The average age of men in the upper echelons of business is 54. And although Americans aged 40 to 65 represent only about a quarter of the population, they earn more than half the nation's income.[1]

The chief virtue traditionally associated with middle age is experience, but that cuts two ways. The person who arrives at 50 having ignored the opportunities for reassessment in midlife passage may take the familiar, mulish stance of protector of the status quo. It is no mistake that such people are called "diehards." Another stock figure is the middle-aged kid who denies his age and therefore his experience: the producer with mutton chop whiskers who will be 26 until the fast fade to 60, the Mrs. Louds who wear yarn bows and ask their hubbies for Toyotas to play with, the professor who suspends the healthy skepticism of experience to embrace the evangelism of the young and the life-style of a Latin American revolutionary.

On the other hand, people who have seen, felt,

and incorporated their private truths during midlife passage no longer expect the impossible dream, nor do they have to protect an inflexible position. Having experimented with many techniques for facing problems and change, they will have modified many of the assumptions and illusions of youth. They are practiced. They know what works. They can make decisions with a welcome economy of action. A great deal of behavioral red tape can be cut through once people have developed judgment enriched by both inner and outer experience. It is this striking improvement in the exercise of judgment, Bernice Neugarten observes, that is one of the most reassuring aspects of being middle-aged.[2]

New Veins of Energy

Secondary interests that have been tapped earlier in life can in middle and old age blossom into a serious lifework. Each tap into a new vessel releases in the later years another reservoir of energy. An aspect of life that was dominant and satisfying earlier—the excitement of competing in business or taking care of children, for instance—should not be expected to be forever the mainstay or purpose of one's life.

But there are no golden years if there has been no anticipation in midlife of the need to cultivate parallel interests. A man retired at 65 doesn't suddenly pick up a camera and revive himself with a second career as a photographer. Whether one has a natural talent or not, any learning period requires the willingness to suffer uncertainty and embarrassment. Even in the fifties, one is apt to be too self-conscious to wait out such a period of trial.

An inspiring model is the doctor who took up photography in his thirties. For many years he struggled with this avocation, but he kept at it. At 45, his pictures were extraordinary. He had brought a new dimension to color photography; what had begun as an artistic hobby was ripe for conversion into a second career. Since then he has traveled the world, often with his wife, to photograph his most beloved landscapes. Today, well into his seventies, he is a man with the physical stamina and mental attitude of a person in the prime of life.

Men in the middle years take their age cues primarily from their career position and health changes; women tend to define their age status in terms of timing of family events. They are more concerned over the body-monitoring of their husbands than of themselves.[3] They are not so much imperiled by heart attacks as by widowhood, and they must rehearse for enduring alone. It is imperative that a woman find a sense of importance and a means of independent survival before the empty nest leaves her feeling superfluous. Otherwise, she may let her fears dictate the very future she most dreads: becoming helplessly reliant on the continued health and constancy of her husband and the largess of her grown children. Every woman fears becoming the proverbial widow who barges in on the family life of her married children, or who treads on the periphery, saying stoutly, "They have their own lives." Whether she has enough money to float around the world on cruise ships or has to sit feeding pigeons from a park bench, she is still a little old girl waiting to die.

Margaret Babcock, the mother of the Yale graduate we met early in the book, provides an example of a more enlivening alternative. At 35 she realized, "I had no way at all, emotionally or financially, of making any real change in my life. Something had to be done to take the pressure off the marriage. By now I wasn't sure it was going to work. I had a hurry-up feeling that I'd better find a way I could stand on my own."

With time pushing from behind, she slowly opened her mind to college. Philosophy, psychology, then art filled the old emptiness. The laundry room became her studio, a place to paint in until exhaustion overtook her and then to hasten back to, barefoot, in daylight, to see if the proof of her second genesis was still there. Beyond the exhilaration of it, she was working toward a goal that would someday be convertible into financial independence. But to juggle this goal with the responsibilities of family, to be home for her four children, she had to proceed slowly. Margaret took eight years to get her college degree.

Today, at 46, she is as eager as any graduate in his or her twenties, when for one untested and therefore unlimited, all the world seems within arm's length of mind and will. With a master's degree, a career as a psychiatric social worker, and a weekly paycheck, she is assured that she could leave home any time she wanted to. She doesn't want to. "It's amazing after all these years. I feel more than at any other time in my life there's really a chance for a good marriage."

People in corporate life have to work even harder to tap new sources of energy because they may not have much to say about the age at which they retire. Some corporations are already cutting off their managers at 60; others are discussing the cold-turkey approach for retiring their top executives at 55. The people who make such decisions would do well to consult the suicide statistics. The steep climb in suicide for men between the ages of 55 and 65 is potential evidence that many retirees feel junked. A far more humane approach is being tried in Sweden, where employees are being given the opportunity for a "phased retirement," a gradual reduction in working hours over the years between 60 and 70. But although we can all campaign for reforms, we cannot count on them.

Business executives complain jealously that civil service workers have the best deal. They can start accumulating their twenty years of service in time to retire on a sweet pension when they are about 40 and then easily launch into a second career or combine a remunerative hobby with loafing in Florida. A surprisingly large number of workers are choosing to accept early retirement, provided it will not mean a drastic drop in income.[4] All the more reason why nongovernment employees must draw upon their own resources and convert them to new uses before their former purpose is outlived. And the wise ones do. The history buff prepares for retirement by starting research on a book. For some it's as simple as extending an interest in carpentry into the pleasure of cabinet-making. For others who have read voraciously all their lives, the sense of value in later years comes from being an artful conversationalist.

A No-Panic Approach to Physical Aging

More than anything else, it is our own view of ourselves that determines the richness or paucity of the middle years. People who face up to their age won't expect their bodies to run smoothly after 40 without help, any more than one would expect to prize an antique car for its handsome patina without constant maintenance and frequent tune-ups. Performance levels in sports do correlate with the biological curve. But Frenkel-Brunswik observed that there are a number of functions influenced by one's inner life, such as knowledge and experience, that actually counteract the biological decline.[5]

The new middle-aged no longer think sick. Impressive changes have been noted in the symptoms described by middle-aged men and women seeking clinical counseling today as opposed to twenty years ago. White Institute analysts Lionells and Mann found in a comparative study that the psychosomatic complaints so characteristic of the middle-aged in the past—crucial personal problems that used to be expressed as "a vague, diffuse sense of fatigue and lethargy"—are now being faced for what they are: issues of self-realization and fulfillment.[6]

The "use it or lose it" concept popularized by sex researchers holds true in other areas as well, such as learning ability. The more we have worked our brain, the more it will continue to work for us. Highly educated people show little or no decline with age in test performance—indeed, accuracy generally improves over the years—up to the age of 50. After that, it is lack of speed, not accuracy, that accounts for decline, if there is any. Adult learning ability does not slack off in a generalized way; it is in the ability to absorb unfamiliar or inapplicable material that a loss is noticed later in life.[7]

Here I would like to put in a good word for the thrill of learning something new *after* 45. I have watched many middle-aged men and women hoist themselves on skis and veer down the slopes behind an instructor, positively giddy with the delight of being learners again. They're never going to do dazzling jet turns, but so what! The same holds true for menopausal women who have told me about taking up golf or hiking for the first time. One busy career woman who made time to start piano lessons enjoyed it so much that she has gone on to tap dancing. When undertaken in the right spirit, such activities have nothing to do with dilettantism. The point is to defeat the entropy that says slow down, give it up, watch TV, and to open up another pathway that can enliven all the senses, including the sense that one is not just an old dog.

The bonuses are considerable if one of the new pursuits chosen is an active one that can be done in fresh air. True, after 40 we may tire faster during exercise because we can't incur the same oxygen debt, which means we can't count on stored oxygen to keep us going for long after we run out of breath. Regular exercise, rather than sudden spurts, is best, but certainly there is nothing good to be said for physical inactivity. The brain needs oxygen, and the lungs need help in providing it because the natural chest expansion lessens as we get older. The heart muscle can use all the new and collateral pathways for blood circulation that can be opened up with regular physical activity. Well-chosen exercise can literally retard the aging process.

Those who settle back for a sedentary, indoor

middle age conspire with their backaches, hernias, broken hips, and heart attacks. A sluggish heart cannot be expected to meet sudden demands, any more than slackening muscles can be expected to provide the spine and vital organs with sufficient support. Once again, the more we use, the less we lose.

Taking up an active pursuit in midlife doesn't mean falling into the trap of physical competition with one's younger athletic self. The hard-won resources gained by half a lifetime of experience can be directed to other goals, other prizes. In parts of the Far East, for example, where the most highly valued occupations are those that take many years to prepare for (contemplation, meditation, poetry, and the arts), the 40-to-50 age group is thought of as relatively young. In our culture it is widely believed that in middle age colors appear less bright, tastes, smells, and sounds are less memorable than during the vivid days of youth. Such a stereotype finds little or no support among psychologists. The perceptions of middle age have their own luminosity.[8]

Redefined Attitudes toward Money, Religion, and Death

The "I should" of the twenties, which gives way to the "I want" of the thirties, becomes the "I must" of the forties. Some of the musts are all too real. Tuition payments for college-age children, for instance, often coincide with the need of aging parents for financial assistance. But a good deal of the "I must" attitude, particularly when it extends into the fifties, is colored by habit and the shaping experiences of the earlier years.

Today's late-middle-aged, being of the Depression generation, learned the hard way to worship at the altar of financial security. Long after the wolf had retreated from the door and prosperity had pacified them with credit cards and deluxe cars, the habit of caution remained.

Tyler is such a man. He went into the fledgling field of advertising as a young man because it looked like a promising place to make a buck. Writing, his secret aspiration, seemed to him utterly frivolous at the time. And although he came from a background of intense social involvement that he intended to duplicate, he found himself in midlife to be an administrator, not an artist; a romancer of clients, not a reformer; a good gray burgher with his own small agency and longings too insurrectionary to be acknowledged.

"I gave myself the justification of necessity. I looked at the agency as an opportunity to put together a bundle. All through my forties the dissatisfaction got worse. I bought a boat and went sailing a lot, but the boat wasn't the answer. I accused my wife of draining me for her stimulus, even though I was aware I had no right to blame her. I wanted to regain a sense of vigorous participation in life. I started the sex games, where I could play different roles with new women. Sometimes I played the captain of industry; sometimes it was the artist manqué, blunted but destined one day to spring forth phoenix-like. You get some stimulus from that kind of approval. Short run. These are all the wrong places to find the answers, but I didn't know that then. It's your own attitude that makes whatever you do a vigorous participation."

Tyler's midlife crisis mounted for fifteen years before he could allow himself to act on the real inner message. Quite unconsciously, however, he had begun taking preparatory steps long before. At 45 he took up stone carving. "It was a substitute for the writing I wasn't doing, and because it was a hobby, I didn't have to worry about other people's judgment." Another step was taking a studio in the city. He despised the suburbs, but his last child was still at home. Passing 50, Tyler reached a point when establishing security looked less important than living the time that was running out.

"I had to say to myself, 'So okay, you're not going

503

to have it all riveted with the Palm Beach hideaway and the coupons to clip. There are other values to be concerned with in one's life. How certain is certain, anyhow?' "

In his yearning for an absence of reins, Tyler's next step was moving back to a small apartment in the city. He felt a physical sense of lightening: "I'm no longer tied to an edifice and a mortgage." The last justification fell away when his wife went back to work after twenty-seven years at home. "It helped me to make the decision because now, if I failed, I might wind up a Bowery wino, but I wouldn't be punishing her."

The moment of greatest astonishment in his life was when he called together his associates and heard himself saying, "Look, I want out." Tyler left the business world at the age of 55 to be the writer of his boyhood dream. He still carries a tie around in his pocket, but he has stopped wearing it.

If an examination of attitudes toward money is the focal point of renewal for some, for others the turning point hinges on spiritual questions.

Margaret Babcock wonders today what would have happened if she had remained locked in to the "religious phase" of her thirties. "I'd gone through all the routine of being brought up an Episcopalian, but I didn't know if I believed in God or not. And I didn't start looking into it until I was kind of desperate in my personal life. For two or three years there I was terrible, very dogmatic."

Margaret's security blanket was torn off one middle of the night when she was 38 with her mother's call from Florida: "Daddy's not very well." She watched her father die abruptly of cancer of the esophagus, no holy spirit of contentment on his face, no legacy of father's magic.

"I went through a period of seeing myself dead, seeing myself in a coffin and the people at the funeral. I imagined it as clearly as one could, to the point where I was ready to go out and buy my burial outfit."

After this period of morbidity, Margaret mourned for her own loss of safety, for the buffers of God and father who had gone unchallenged as her higher authorities. The supreme test came in her early forties and concerned the tie to her mother. In order to deal with her grief, Margaret's widowed mother sentimentalized her forty-seven years of absorption in one man's future as a "blissful union," and her concepts of religion became rigid. She took scathing exception to the way Margaret was conducting her life, "running off to college, neglecting her husband and children, losing your faith."

Margaret could not say aloud what she saw in her mother: "a person with a very closed system." Any doubt raised about an afterlife struck at the very core of her mother's conviction that she would be reunited with her husband after death. Yet this was precisely the question Margaret was struggling with. "I had come around to doubting that there was such a thing as an afterlife. For this reason it became very important for me to do whatever I had to do and to make it good in this lifetime. As I became stronger and more differentiated, if that's the word, I began to realize that I could afford a break with my mother and not die from it."

It took some years after the break before Margaret, who had always meant to be as different from her mother as possible, discovered that in fact she was very much like her. Her choice of social work, her snobbish do-goodism disguised in sackcloth, her judgmentalism—all these were part of the hand-me-down costume she eventually recognized as coming from her mother. Only when such parts are dredged up in midlife and stripped of their archaic childhood identifications can they be fully worked on and remodeled into a more benign form.

At 46 Margaret can say, "Only in the last two years have I been able to look at aspects of my mother in myself that I can value. And I'm not so deeply involved in searching for the ultimate spiritual answers anymore. I accept the fact that there are many answers I'll never have. I find that now a very comfortable belief."

Companionship or a Zest for Aloneness

Studies record a dramatic climb in satisfaction with marriage in the mid-forties for those couples who have survived the passage into midlife together. What this finding reflects is not that our mate miraculously improves but that tolerance can become spontaneous once we stop displacing our inner contradictions on our spouse. The steep rise of contentment levels off after 50 at a higher plateau.[9]

Partners know each other pretty well by this time (although there is, and always should be, room for surprise). Middle age presents many couples with the opportunity for true companionship, for by now it is clear that shared interests and a healthy respect for privacy are not mutually exclusive. There is a good chance of having someone to grow old with, to share friends and memories and walks in the rain with, someone to absorb the hush of a household where children no longer reside and to make it resonate with the joys of recaptured time together.

First-time marriage among the middle-aged is a rarity. But many of those seasoned by a former match are ready and willing to make a new meld. Among those who remarry each year, one-quarter are middle-aged.[10]

As age increases, there is a decreasing tendency to compare oneself with others. People become more preoccupied with the inner life, benefiting them with two of the most salient characteristics of the mature years: insightfulness and philosophical concern.[11] In the process of moving toward this interiority, people find themselves beginning to enjoy a welcome detachment from others.[12]

Not only is one's mate seen more as a valuable source of companionship, rather than as a substitute parent, but it is usually a surprise to find that grown children can be delightful companions. Especially when they are no longer underfoot, sneering at their parents' set ways and leaving their cola cans all over the floor. That doesn't mean we lose interest in others as we get older. As writer Florida Scott-Maxwell attests from the vantage point of being 82: "No matter how old a mother is she watches her middle-aged children for signs of improvement."[13]

Middle life is definitely a time to have a healthy respect for eccentricity. This is only possible when we overcome the habit of trying to please everyone, which seems to be a late development for many women. Dr. Estelle Ramey, a robust physiologist nearing 60, with grown children and a longstanding marriage, is now in that frame of mind. "I find that I'm telling the truth more often. I didn't realize I was lying. I just thought I had good, ladylike manners. The one thing in the world I always wanted was to have everybody like me. Now I don't give a damn. I want *some* people to like me, and I'll settle."

People who are alone in middle age may be ready to accept that learning to live alone is not just transitionally good; it can also be essentially good. Especially if one's light has been eclipsed by a mate's dominant personality or if, having existed for many years as that corporate entity known as the couple, one has no idea if the resources are there to survive as an individual, it can be a self-affirming experience to discover that the answer is yes.

Several of the women interviewed spoke about the thrill of realizing: "I am wholly responsible for myself, and isn't that wonderful!" At a workshop where life stories were being traded, a delightfully honest woman of 52 began by saying, "I was dumped after thirty years of marriage." Before anyone had time to feel sorry for her, she ended by saying, "I hate a lot of being alone, but I want to stay single if I possibly can. It's the most exciting thing that's ever happened to me. And it's amazing how much more real I can be with my children, now that I'm not part of a couple. I don't want to be alone the rest of my life. But I don't want the full-time thing either. I think these new weekend relationships sound terrific."

One widower expressed a similar change of heart. Shortly after the death of his wife, uncertain about his ability to shepherd a heartbroken daughter through adolescence, he began a cheerless round of dating in search of a new wife. A year passed, then two; he was still single. But by then, having restructured his career to make room for companionship with his children, he felt confident as a single parent. And although he enjoyed friendships with several women, he treasured the newfound ability to cook for and entertain himself.

Perhaps the most vivid example of a public figure who discovered self-reliance in the middle years is Katherine Graham. Painfully shy and dependent while her dynamic husband was alive and directing all the operations of the *Washington Post*, Mrs. Graham resisted turning over the newspaper to other managers after her husband's suicide. Slowly, she gathered the force of her own dormant talents until, somewhat astonished, she emerged as one of the most powerful and respected chief executives in the nation.

But a change of such magnitude can easily take many years. For a lady I'll call Janet, it took ten. Poised at 44 for reentry to her field of social work, after a decade happily spent as the complete auxiliary to her scientist husband, Janet stood agape when he made his announcement. He would wait until their daughter came home from college in June, he said, and then he was going to leave.

He still hadn't written his book, and he accused Janet of being the reason. How could he write with all the responsibilities at home? In fact, Janet had not only carried the responsibilities of home and children, she had made an art of it to the exclusion of all else. Her husband, who considered himself a genius, was in the process of discarding his unrealized dream. And to ease his self-contempt, he seemed determined to discard every vestige that had been part of it.

"The agony of it was," says Janet, "I knew that was the mechanism. And after seeing it for what it was, my ego could even have ridden it out, except that I was sick. A hypothyroid condition I'd had as a girl flared up again as I went into menopause. Physically, I wasn't able to be the durable spirit I always had been when faced with any calamity. It was a disappointment to him that I couldn't be the strong one at that point. And I was still living totally in his world. I had no identity apart from him."

Janet found the strength to move south and take a job. She leaned on friends for a year until her physical stamina began to return. Little by little she edged back into academic life, although it always felt "unreal." And temporary. By her mid-fifties she had accomplished the feat of introducing a brand-new department into the medical school of the local university. Finding that she had generated from within a season of life altogether new and animating, she began waking up in the mornings without the ache of aloneness. She came out of celibacy and found that there were men who thought she was attractive and what's more, because most of them were burdened with alimony or child-support payments, that her self-sufficiency was an exceptional plus. She watched herself organizing conferences, giving dinner parties, writing papers, even enjoying a holiday in the South Seas alone, and she knew at last that she was home free. "There's a full me now, and that's thrilling—to know that ten years ago I had no identity at all."

Approval of Oneself at Last

One of the great rewards of moving through the disassembling period to renewal is coming to approve of oneself ethically and morally and quite independent of other people's standards and agenda. By giving up the wish that one's parents were different and by navigating through various life-styles to that point of dignity worth defending, one can achieve what Erikson calls *integrity*. By this he means arrival at that final stage of adult development, in which one can give a blessing to one's own life.

To accomplish such a step may mean breaking out of a life pattern that has been unsatisfactory. It certainly means becoming aware of one's own step-style so that one can play into it or work around it, but not be defeated by it.

Ken Babcock, much to his family's amazement, departed in midlife both from his pattern and his inhibiting step-style. Born of a father who drummed into him the necessity to strive and provide, he had passively accepted all the values of the corporate pecking order and locked in early. He had to become a company president. But all the while he was pursuing this laminated goal, trying to live up to his father's agenda, Ken was scared. His constant fear of failure was innocently disguised as fiscal conservatism. Hence, his step-style: In order to avoid taking any chances, Ken would deny anything negative—deny that he hated the job he held, deny that he couldn't afford the house he lived in, deny that it was his self-doubt that discouraged him from running for political office—until someone else pushed him out of that position.

At 43, Ken's dream went bust. Presidents, he discovered, do not automatically promote good boys to succeed them. When the recession hit his company, he was fired. Just like that. The irony did not escape him. Having for so long pursued safety through financial security, what did he have to show for his withered revolts, his limbless risks?

"It took me three months to make up my mind

to take a chance—the only real risk I had taken in my life. I felt it was an important time to see what I could do. Margaret felt I had been too conservative from day one; yet the most important thing to me is financial security."

He took the jump and bought a Wall Street brokerage firm that was on the verge of bankruptcy. Gritting his teeth, he sank his life savings into the gamble, along with most of his emotional capital and every waking moment for six months, even taking a room in town to be on all-night duty with the business he was nursing. This was a step that would really "mean something." It would mean that by breaking out, Kenneth Babcock might at last become his own man. This was a step completely out of his style. It failed.

What has become by now of the Babcocks' fine white Colonial picturebook house? Sold.

What does it mean, this small, one-floor dwelling pictured in the back of the Babcocks' album? Does it mean we shall mourn for the couple's laboriously gathered nest, now reduced to a few separate straws? Is this what is meant by an empty nest?

Late at night when Ken answers the phone, he says he will have to take a message for Margaret. "She's up to her elbows in dirt—out gardening by spotlight in her nightgown." One midnight they found a forgotten pack of zinnias. With a flashlight they went out to sow the seeds under their bedroom window. Together, they are building an addition to their new home.

It was Margaret who prodded Ken to get out from under the money pressures by selling the big house, which for two adults alone had also become embarrassing. But for Ken the house was a display of all that he had accomplished, the sum of his life's work. "It's really my only asset," he had said in resistance, "aside from my family." Ken today says, "Now that we're out, it's a relief. I don't miss the old house one bit."

Recovering from his business failure required a much harder look inside. Ken either had to ignore and repress the fact that his president dream had not worked out, or he had to make peace with his fallen illusions and go on from there to seek refreshment in less stereotyped ways.

"I made up my mind that I'd finally fallen victim to the Peter Principle. I had reached my peak of inefficiency, and I'd better get back into something I was a declared success in, which was running a branch brokerage office and being a salesman myself."

By changing his level of aspiration within the business that he was best suited to, rather than changing fields, as he had tried in the past, Ken was able to open up his own local office and be full captain of a smaller ship. This in itself was gratifying, but there was more. Another part of himself was allowed expression. In place of the driven man who had to hurl himself into Wall Street, there emerged a gentler self who thrived on combining his work with the peace of a country setting near to home. And outside the arena of international finance, he found that his dream could be realized on the local level again and again. "I find that every time I get on a board, I become president. I'd been running down like an old clock," he says, his eyes now dancing. "Once I gave up commuting, it was a joy."

The future is effervescent with plans. With two good incomes and minimum domestic duties, the Babcocks look forward to travel together and perhaps even an early retirement for Ken. He is hankering these days after the precarious pleasures of running for local political office.

The man who appeared on first meeting to be clearly not a winner, if measured only by the external yardstick of American business values, turns out to be a success in a deeper sense: a man who forced openings in himself that many others find too painful, who took the risk and surmounted a failure, and who in that hollow gathered together an integrity of self. A man replenished.

Would that there were an award for people who come to understand the concept of enough. Good enough. Successful enough. Thin enough. Rich enough. Socially responsible enough. When you have self-respect, you have enough; and when you have enough, you have self-respect. Fortunately, because there are always people and events to stretch us, none of us needs worry about falling into the self-satisfied sloughs of "absolute" maturity.

It would be surprising if we didn't experience some pain as we leave the familiarity of one adult stage for the uncertainty of the next. But the willingness to move through each passage is equivalent to the willingness to live abundantly. If we don't change, we don't grow. If we don't grow, we are not really living. Growth demands a temporary surrender of security. It may mean a giving up of familiar but limiting patterns, safe but unrewarding work, values no longer believed in, relationships that have lost their meaning. As Dostoevsky put it, "taking a new step, uttering a new word, is what people fear most." The real fear should be of the opposite course.

If physical strength and pleasures of the senses are held to be life's greatest values, then we deny ourselves anything beyond youth but a dull ebb of all experience. If we see nothing to rival the accumulation of goods and success, then we trap ourselves into a stale and repetitious middle age. Yet the delights of self-discovery are always available. Though loved ones move in and out of our lives, the capacity to love remains. And for the mind freed of the constant strivings of earlier years, there is time in the later years to ponder the mysteries of existence without interruption.

RENEWAL

The courage to take new steps allows us to let go of each stage with its satisfactions and to find the fresh responses that will release the richness of the next. The power to animate all of life's seasons is a power that resides within us.

NOTES
AND
SOURCES

For complete publishing information consult the Bibliography.

CHAPTER 1   MADNESS AND METHOD

Pages 2 through 28

1 Robert Coles gives a most convincing interpretation of life as a series of steps, and the mind as always in its essence developing, in his biography of *Eric H. Erikson: The Growth of His Work* (1970), pp. 132–139.

2 It is rather humbling to realize that such a view of life as a series of passages, in which former pleasures are outgrown and replaced by higher and more appropriate purposes, was set down in the second century A.D., and it is interesting to compare this ancient Indian concept with ideas about adult development only now evolving in the West. In the first stage described by Hindu scriptures, those gloriously suspended years between the age of 8 and the early twenties when one is a student, one's only obligation is to learn. The second stage, its beginning marked by marriage, is that of householder. The next twenty or thirty years are the time to satisfy the wants of man: pleasure, primarily through family; success through his vocation; and duty through citizenship. When time inevitably dims the pleasures of sex and the senses, when achieving success no longer yields novelty and discharging one's duty has become repetitious and stale, it is time to move on to a third stage: retirement. Anytime after the birth of the first grandchild, the individual should be free to begin his true education as an adult, to discover who he is and ponder life's meaning without interruption. Traditionally, people in this stage were encouraged to become pilgrims. Man and wife together, if

she wished to go, were to pull up stakes and plunge into the solitude of the forests on a journey to self-discovery. At last their responsibilities were only to themselves. The final stage, when the pilgrim reaches his goal, is the state of *sannyasin*. With no obligations, no belongings, no further expectations of the body, the *sannyasin* is free to wander and to beg at the back door of one over whom he was master. In the Hindu texts, the *sannyasin* "lives identified with the eternal Self and beholds nothing else."

This material is ably covered by Huston Smith in *The Religions of Man* (1958), pp. 51–66.

3 The original work of Else Frenkel-Brunswik was titled "Studies in Biographical Psychology" (1936) and currently appears under the title "Adjustments and Reorientations in the Course of the Life Span" in *Middle Age and Aging*, ed., Bernice L. Neugarten (1968), pp. 77–84. Frenkel-Brunswik acknowledges her debt to her teacher, Charlotte Bühler, one of the first in the field of developmental psychology, although Bühler's work was more concerned with the process of goal setting, and Frenkel-Brunswik later made a break from her in order to pursue the central layer of personality as expounded by psychoanalysis.

4 In presenting the stages of the life cycle in an epigenetic chart, Erikson lists a series of conflicts or crises. At each stage a gain can be made that adds a new ego quality and another dimension of personality strength. The first four stages occur during childhood: basic trust vs. mistrust; autonomy vs. shame and doubt; initiative vs. guilt; industry vs. inferiority. The fifth stage, identity vs. role diffusion, is tied to adolescence. This is followed by the three adult stages mentioned in the text and taken from Erik H. Erikson's *Childhood and Society* (1950), pp. 247–274.

5 The observations on Erikson's life were read between the lines of his autobiography, *Life History and the Historical Moment* (1975), by Marshall Berman in a book review for *The New York Times*, March 30, 1975.

6 Paul C. Glick and Arthur J. Norton in "Perspectives on the Recent Upturn in Divorce and Remarriage;" study done for Bureau of the Census, U.S. Dept. of Commerce (1972), p. 4.

7 Daniel J. Levinson is, officially, Professor of Psychology in the Department of Psychiatry at Yale University School of Medicine, but has evolved through his work into a hybrid psychologist-psychiatrist-sociologist. The collaborating mem-

bers of his study team are Charlotte N. Darrow, Edward B. Klein, Maria H. Levinson, and Braxton McKee. Apart from Dr. Levinson's general thesis, which was presented at the symposium sponsored by the Menninger Foundation, the references to his work and theories that appear in this book were taken from interviews. Dr. Levinson's long-awaited book is scheduled for publication in 1977, under the working title, *The Seasons of a Man's Life.*

8 Roger Gould reported his work in "The Phases of Adult Life: A Study in Developmental Psychology," *American Journal of Psychiatry* (1972), 129:5, pp. 521–531. Beginning with an observational study of all the psychiatric outpatients in group therapy at UCLA Psychiatric Clinic, he and his co-workers divided the patients into seven age groups and over the course of a year observed the most obvious and salient characteristics of each group. A questionnaire was prepared as a result of this effort and given to 524 nonpatients who were asked to rank order statements concerning their relationships to parents, friends, children, and spouses; their feelings about themselves, their jobs, time, and sex.

9 Study by Daniel Yankelovich, Inc. (1973), reported by *The New York Times* on May 22, 1974.

CHAPTER 2 PREDICTABLE CRISES OF ADULTHOOD

The theories and the developmental ladder presented in this chapter are a synthesis of the whole book and thus of all the sources and interviews upon which I drew.

Pages 29 through 46

1 "Marker event" is the term used by Daniel Levinson to define a particular occasion or extended period that brings about or signifies a notable change in the person's life, though a marker event is not always present to signal change.

2 Bernice L. Neugarten in her book on *Middle Age and Aging* establishes the concept of "age-role identity" and points out that: "The saliency of age norms in influencing the behavior of adults is no less than in influencing the behavior of children . . . social sanctions related to age-norms take on a psychological reality . . . ." (1968), p. 144.

3 The biography of a ballet dancer, sketched in Chapter 23, is exemplary of this principle.

4 It is important to note that people with a stable past are more likely to cope than those with backgrounds of poverty and emotional deprivation. For reference see Morton Beiser on "Poverty, Social Disintegration and Personality," *Journal of Social Issues* (1965), pp. 56–78.

5 The Feiffer cartoon appeared in *The Village Voice* on September 22 (copyright 1974).

6 A discussion and examples of *step-styles* are given in Chapter 7 of this book.

7 Interpreting the Eriksonian view that stages overlap and interpenetrate, Coles (1970) states it this way: "We do not acquire trust and forever rid ourselves of mistrust or 'achieve' autonomy and thus spare ourselves continuing doubts and hesitations." In Daniel Levinson's words, "The primary tasks of one period are never completely dealt with and cast aside when the period ends."

A demonstration that one does not automatically achieve autonomy appears in Chapter 20 of this book.

CHAPTER 3 BREAST TO BREAKAWAY

The basic source on concepts of self and object representations, from which my description of the "inner custodian" is derived, is Freud, particularly his paper, *On Narcissism: An Introduction* (1914), and *The Ego and the Id* (1923). Most helpful in understanding these concepts is Edith Jacobson's monograph, *The Self and the Object World* (1973), which was officially sponsored by the Journal of the American Psychoanalytic Association. Discussions with Roger Gould were provocative in applying the concepts to individual biographies.

The clearest explanation of the process of identification appears in Robert White's *The Enterprise of Living* (1972).

Pages 48 through 61

1 The individuation process, a major contribution to psychological theory by Carl Jung, is explained concisely by Jolande Jacobi in *The Psychology of C. G. Jung* (1973 edition), p. 107. "Taken as a whole, individuation is a spontaneous, natural process within the psyche; it is po-

tentially present in every man, although most men are unaware of it. Unless it is inhibited, obstructed, or distorted by some specific disturbance, it is a process of maturation or unfolding, the psychic parallel to the physical process of growth and aging."

2 It was Erikson who stated, "For the first component of a healthy personality, I nominate a sense of basic trust." *Psychological Issues* (1959), pp. 55–56. In a later essay, "The Golden Rule and the Cycle of Life" (1964), he wrote about mutuality, not as a separate phase, but as an ongoing process governed by the sense of basic trust established in early infancy. "The fact is that the mutuality of adult and baby is the original source of the basic ingredient of all effective as well as ethical human action: hope."

3 Mahler has proposed that for the first three months of life the infant has no awareness of self and other. As the infant becomes aware that its needs are met from without, the next phase—symbiosis—is entered, although the mother is still assumed to be part of the self. Somewhere around the age of 2 the child moves into the phase Mahler has termed separation-individuation, which allows the gradual building of an individual identity. See Mahler (1953 and 1963) and the discussion by Blanck and Blanck of Mahler's developmental scheme in *Marriage and Personal Development* (1968), p. 49.

Peter Blos proposes that the first stage of individuation is completed toward the end of the third year of life with the attainment of object constancy. He sees adolescence as the second stage of individuation: "Not until the termination of adolescence do self and object representations acquire stability and firm boundaries." *The Second Individuation Process of Adolescence* (1967), pp. 162–187.

4 Quote from Jacobson in *The Self and the Object World* (1964), p. 39.

John Bowlby, the distinguished British psychoanalyst whose lifework has been to examine effects on children of separation from parents, has now carried his thesis from infancy into adulthood. He argues in *Separation* (1973) that the child's emotional life is dominated by one theme—his need for closeness to the mother—and that all anxiety is basically a "realistic" fear of separation from the mother. In his third volume of the "Attachment and Loss" series, he hopes to demonstrate that the individual's ongoing need to defend against the threat of loss can explain most ramifications of personality.

5 Jacobson, Blos, and Roy Schafer (*Aspects of Internalization*, 1968) all posit that some mechanism of internalization or identification is at the center of psychological development.

6 After noting, in one life story after another, the dynamic interplay of forces I came to describe as the Seeker and Merger selves, I discovered that Abraham H. Maslow had also written about two competing forces in explaining his theory of growth. The reader should be aware that Maslow has talked about it, but in my opinion his formulation is too black and white. "Every human being has both sets of forces within him. One set clings to safety and defensiveness out of fear, tending to regress backward, hanging on to the past, *afraid* to grow away from the primitive communication with the mother's uterus and breast, *afraid* to take chances, *afraid* to jeopardize what he already has, *afraid* of independence, freedom and separateness. The other set of forces impels him forward toward wholeness of Self and uniqueness of Self, toward full functioning of all his capacities, toward confidence in the face of the external world at the same time that he can accept his deepest, real unconscious Self." Quote is from Maslow's *Toward a Psychology of Being* (1968), p. 45.

CHAPTER 4   PLAYING IT TO THE BUST

Pages 62 through 79

1 See White (1972) on parental expectations in *The Enterprise of Living*, p. 260.

2 Erikson writes (1968): "Youth after youth, bewildered by the incapacity to assume a role forced on him by the inexorable standardization of American adolescence, runs away in one form or another, dropping out of school, leaving jobs, staying out all night, or withdrawing into bizarre and inaccessible moods." From *Identity: Youth and Crisis* (1968), p. 132.

3 The study, done by Judith Bardwick, Professor of Psychology at the University of Michigan, is reported in the paper, "The Dynamics of Successful People," which appears in *New Research on Women* (1974), copyright by the University of Michigan. Dr. Bardwick writes: "A surprising number [of the 20 highly successful men she interviewed in depth] mentioned that they had stolen or had behaved

as truants when young; perhaps they were risk-takers even then."

4 Novelist Jerzy Kosinski tells the story of Lekh, a peasant who, for amusement, painted birds and then released them to be killed by their kin. *The Painted Bird* (1965), pp. 44–45.

CHAPTER 5 "IF I'M LATE, START THE CRISIS WITHOUT ME"

Pages 80 through 91

Excellent descriptions of the sense of identity are found in Greenacre (1958) and Mahler (1958). Erikson (1968) is unsurpassed in discussing the formation of ego identity in adolescence. Jacobson (1973) prefers to discuss the formation of personal identity as a process that continues through all stages of development and that builds up the ability to preserve the whole psychic organization. Another most important source is Peter Blos, *On Adolescence: A Psychoanalytic Interpretation* (1962).

1 See King on "Coping and Growth in Adolescence," *Seminars in Psychiatry* (November 1972), p. 355.

2 The J. E. Marcia paper defining the four types of identity status, "Development and Validation of Ego Identity Status," appeared in *Journal of Personality and Social Psychology* 3 (1966), pp. 551–559.

3 Conclusion about women college graduates was drawn by Anne Constantinople from her study, "An Eriksonian Measure of Personality Development in College Students," published in 1969 and discussed more fully in the footnotes for Chapter 6 of this book.

4 Harvard psychiatrist James M. Donovan discusses Marcia's distinctions in identity positions and adds to them from his own study of 22 liberal arts undergraduates in a large Midwestern public university. Donovan classified only two of his subjects "identity achieved," and they were both women over 35: "At twenty-one probably both these women were identity foreclosed [married and living according to their mother's model]. Both had apparently undergone change after they reached adulthood, which led them toward increased self-awareness and freedom within." Donovan's paper, "Identity Status and Interpersonal Style," was the basis for an article in the *Journal of Youth and Adolescence* 4:1 (1975), pp. 37–55.

5 King draws this conclusion. From a survey of studies on adolescence as well as his own study (1972), he distinguishes three common models among late adolescents: (1) seriously impaired: those who are antisocial and overcome by anxiety or depression; (2) normal and competent: those who are successful in coping, begin to develop a sense of identity, and show strong continuity with past experiences; (3) sensitive and vulnerable: those who have an active fantasy life, sudden and extensive swings of mood, painful questions about self-esteem, periods of strong depression, unrealistically high idealism, and active rebellion. Adolescents in this group, while not the common model, King asserts, in most cases become well-integrated and mature as adults.

6 Conclusion by Vaillant and McArthur, abstracting from the Grant Study of Adult Development at Harvard University, appears in *Seminars in Psychiatry* (November 1972), p. 420. A fuller description of this important study appears in Chapter 15 of this book.

7 The Yankelovich study, as reported by *The New York Times* on May 22, 1974, observed that: "Students of today are predisposed to reconcile themselves to society, feel less alienation and hope they will be able to function constructively within it."

8 The Sutherland and Cressey theory on criminal behavior is discussed by James Q. Wilson in "Crime and the Criminologists," *Commentary*, July 1974, pp. 47-53.

9 Percentage figures on radical youth are taken from *Generations Apart*, a study of the generation gap done by Daniel Yankelovich, Inc., for CBS News (1969).

10 Quote from Erikson (1968), p. 157.

11 Quote from White (1972), p. 413.

12 Quote from Erikson (1968), p. 158.

13 Quote from Wilson (1974), p. 49.

14 Quote delivered by the Reverend Moon during his Madison Square Garden appearance (1974).

CHAPTER 6   THE URGE TO MERGE

Pages 92 through 105

1 Maslow presented his theory of the hierarchical structure of needs in *Motivation and Personality* (1954).

2 "In general, it is the inability to settle on an occupational identity which most disturbs young people," Erikson has proposed (1968). Stating the case even more strongly, Burt Schacter insists that occupational experiences which confirm a person's competence are the most important, even more important than finding a group role, a sex role, or a world view. See "Identity Crisis and Occupational Processes," *Child Welfare* 47:1 (1968), pp. 26–37.

3 Taken from the Bardwick study (1974), p. 88.

4 Jessie Bernard discusses career planning in *The Future of Marriage* (1972), p. 165.

5 See Edward H. Pohlman's *Psychology of Birth Planning* (Schenkman, 1969) pp. 35–81, for a summary of reasons for wanting children.

6 In the year 1968, for example, HEW figures show that almost half (46 percent) of the married women ages 15 to 19 gave birth to a child, while only one-quarter of the married women aged 20 to 24—the group with the next highest birthrate—gave birth during that year. HEW also estimates that "somewhere in the neighborhood of 60 percent of the infants born to teenage mothers that year were conceived out of wedlock." From *Teenagers: Marriages, Divorces, Parenthood, and Mortality.* U.S. Department of Health, Education, and Welfare publication (August 1973), pp. 18–19.

7 Compulsory graffiti taken from U.S. census figures as reported in the Dept. of Labor's *Occupational Outlook Quarterly* (Spring 1973) by Gloria Stevenson. See also Paul Glick's updated report for U.S. Bureau of Census, "The Life Cycle of the Family" (in preparation at the time of writing).

8 Among nearly 5,000 high school graduates studied over a four-year period, those who "persisted in college were more likely to move toward an open-minded, flexible, and autonomous disposition [than] those who went to work or into full-time homemaking." This conclusion is from a study by Trent and Medsker in 1968 as reported by Stanley H. King (November 1972) in "Coping and Growth in Adolescence," *Seminars in Psychiatry*, p. 363.

9 Taken from the HEW report on *Teenagers: Marriages, Divorces, Parenthood, and Mortality* (1973).

10 Using 952 male and female subjects drawn from the four college classes, Anne Constantinople did a study entitled,

"An Eriksonian Measure of Personality Development in College Students," published in the *Journal of Developmental Psychology* 1:4 (1969), pp. 357–372.

CHAPTER 7   BEGINNINGS OF THE COUPLE PUZZLE

Pages 106 through 117

1 The step-style concept came out of an exchange of ideas between Dr. Roger Gould and me.

CHAPTER 8   GETTING OFF TO A RUNNING START

Pages 120 through 127

1 Quote taken from Block and Haan (1971) in *Lives Through Time.*

The end of this preparatory period comes at about the age of 28, and on that point observers remain in agreement with the original delineation of Else Frenkel-Brunswik. But since this scholar was writing from data collected in the 1930s, she placed the average initiation age at around 17. Since that time more and more deferments have been granted to the young, so that the first serious efforts to gain admission into the adult world are more likely to begin at about 22.

2 My data are consistent with Levinson's and Gould's on this point and correspond with the many statistical evidences of seven-year cycles.

3 Jung's explanation of the illusions that characterize marriage during the first half of life, and provide its "peculiar harmony," is based on his concept of archetypal images. While some would quarrel with the Jungian idea that these eternal images of the opposite sex are inborn—deposits of all ancestral experiences—few would dispute the notion that unconscious images of man and woman, whether inborn or acquired, infuse the romantic relationships of the twenties. And since these images are unconscious, as Jung says, they are unconsciously projected upon the person chosen for a mate. See *The Portable Jung* (1971), p. 173.

4 Erikson (1968) writes of the "double take" when, just about to gain our identity, we are startled to make its acquaintance.

5 Gould (1972), too, observed the "true course in life" attitude to be characteristic of the twenties age group.

CHAPTER 9   THE ONE TRUE COUPLE

Pages 128 through 144

1 Quote from Alvin Toffler, *Future Shock* (1971), p. 250.

2 See O. G. Brim's summary of a number of studies that find happiness is at a peak in the first year of marriage, decreases gradually for the next fifteen years, then rises again to level off at a higher plateau; summary titled "Adult Socialization" in *Socialization and Society*, J. A. Clausen (ed.), (1968), pp. 182–226. See also Roger Gould's marriage satisfaction curve in "The Phases of Adult Life" (1972); Neugarten (1968), pp. 93–98; and I Deutscher, *Married Life in the Middle Years* (1959), Kansas City Community Studies.

3 The youngest and best-educated women are also planning to have fewer children. In a survey of the projected decline in birthrates, the U.S. Census Bureau reported in 1974 that women in the 18-to-24 age group expect to have only 2.2 children, compared with 3.1 children for women now 35 to 39.

CHAPTER 10   WHY DO MEN MARRY?

Pages 145 through 154

1 Quote from Berkowitz and Newman, *How To Be Your Own Best Friend*, New York: Random House (1971).

2 Dr. Gould's formulation came out of one of our discussions.

3 Quote from Philip Slater's *Earthwalk* (1974).

4 Quote is from Lederer and Jackson, *The Mirages of Marriage* (1968), who explain their thesis on pp. 87-97: "According to the systems concept, a change occurs when related parts are rearranged—be they atoms or the behavior of closely associated human beings, such as two people who are married. . . . The systems concept makes it clear that a change in the behavior of one spouse is usually a reaction to changes in his partner's behavior, and in turn causes additional change in the partner's behavior. This action-reaction system operates in a *circular* fashion (sometimes vicious, sometimes positive)."

CHAPTER 11 WHY CAN'T A WOMAN BE MORE LIKE A MAN AND A MAN LESS LIKE A RACEHORSE?

Pages 155 through 168

1 Margaret Mead made a similar comparison back in 1935, in *The Forum*, p. 302.

2 Levinson presented his thesis at a symposium, "Normal Crises of the Middle Years," sponsored by the Menninger Foundation in New York in 1973.

3 Even Freud warned of this trap (though he repeatedly fell into it himself): ". . . though anatomy, it is true, can point out the characteristics of maleness and femaleness, psychology cannot," he wrote in 1930. "For psychology the contrast between the sexes fades away into one between activity and passivity, in which we far too readily identify activity with maleness and passivity with femaleness, a view which is by no means universally confirmed in the animal kingdom." Both sexes and every individual, Freud emphasized, show a combination of activity and passivity. Quote from *Civilization and Its Discontents*, J. Strachey (ed.), (1962), p. 53.

4 The findings of the Oakland Growth and Development Study were analyzed in 1969 in the book *Lives Through Time*, prepared by psychologists Jack Block and Norma Haan. Conclusions drawn from the book and listing the differing personality acquisitions of men and women can be found in a Norma Haan article, "Personality Development from Adolescence to Adulthood in the Oakland Growth and Guidance Studies," *Seminars in Psychiatry* 4:4 (November 1972), pp. 399–414.

There are important differences between longitudinal studies, such as this one, and cross-sectional studies, such as Constantinople's previously described comparison of male and female college students. Cross-sectional studies are conducted at a given time and in a given place and usually cut across age groups. Though informative, they do not take into account the fact that people differ according to the life stage they are in and the generational group to which they belong. In a longitudinal study, the members of a single generational group are studied, and data are collected on them at regular intervals over a period of many years. Because the design of such an extended study is a gamble at the start, and because the harvest may well not be realized in the lifetime of its originator, longitudinal studies are rare. The Institute of Human Development longitudinal study is unprecedented for its size and duration.

5 Quote from Juliet Mitchell in her essay, "On Freud and the Distinction Between the Sexes," appears in *Women and Analysis* (1974), p. 35.

6 Matina Horner's unpublished doctoral dissertation was titled, "Sex Differences in Achievement Motivation and Performance in Competitive and Non-Competitive Situations" (1968).

7 For further examination of sex differences, see *The Psychology of Sex Differences,* by Maccoby and Jacklin (1974), and *Man's Aggression, The Defense of the Self,* by Gregory Rochlin, M.D. (1973).

CHAPTER 12 SNEAK PREVIEW: MEN AND WOMEN GROWING UP

Pages 169 through 196

1 The clearest presentation of Jung's thinking in this area appears as the chapter, "Marriage as a Psychological Relationship," in *The Portable Jung* (1971), pp. 163–177. Original work was in *The Development of Personality. Collected Works,* vol. 17 (1925).

2 Taken from *The Psychology of C. G. Jung,* by Jolande Jacobi (1973 edition), pp. 122–123.

3 Levinson cited as one of the seven tasks of mid-life transition for a man: overcoming the "masculine-feminine polarity," acknowledging the feminine in himself, and seeing the loved woman as a true peer. Paper given at the Menninger Foundation symposium, "Normal Crises of the Middle Years" (1973).

4 Quote from Fellini appeared in *Time,* October 7, 1974, p. 11.

5 Taken from a study done by Career Design, a San Francisco firm that conducts seminars for adults who want to make career changes.

6 Margaret Hennig's doctoral dissertation is titled, "Career Development for Women Executives," Graduate School of Business Administration at Harvard University (1970).

7 Hennig (1970).

CHAPTER 13   CATCH-30

Pages 198 through 216

1 Quote from Blecher appears in *New American Review 14* (1972), p. 147.

2 Frenkel-Brunswik's description of this phase appears in *Middle Age and Aging* (1968) pp. 77–84.

3 Blecher (1972).

4 Bertrand Russell's account appears in *The Autobiography of Bertrand Russell* (1951), pp. 218–221.

5 Frenkel-Brunswik (1968) and Gould (1972).

6 Quotes from Russell (1951), p. 221.

7 Given the fact, previously noted (Glick and Norton, 1972), that the median duration of marriage before divorce has been about seven years for the last half century, and the fact that the average age of first marriage has not varied much in the last two decades between the ages of 20 to 21 for women and 22 to 23 for men, it is no surprise that researchers for the Bureau of Census of the U.S. Department of Commerce find the peak years for divorce to be 28 to 30.

8 Material on the closed dyad, taken from interviews with Ray L. Birdwhistell, appears at greater length in "Can Couples Survive?" by Gail Sheehy, *New York*, February 19, 1973.

9 Galbraith quote appeared in "How the Economy Hangs on Her Apron Strings," *Ms.* (May 1974), p. 75.

CHAPTER 14   THE COUPLE KNOT, THE SINGLE SPOT, THE REBOUND

Pages 217 through 247

1 For an example of a man who rebounds, see the biography of Jay Parrish in Chapter 23 of this book.

2 Jacobson (1964).

CHAPTER 15   MEN'S LIFE PATTERNS

Pages 253 through 292

1 Quote from Jerry Rubin past in *Do It, Scenarios of the Revolution* (1970). Quote from Jerry Rubin present in "From

the Streets to the Body," *Psychology Today* (September 1973), p. 71.

2 A full and illuminating case history of Shaw can be found in Erikson (1968), pp. 142–150.

3 Since 1970, there has been a continuous and significant increase in the proportion of men under 35 who are still single. Reported by Arthur Norton and Robert Grymes in "Marital Status and Living Arrangements" for the U.S. Dept. of Commerce (March 1973).

4 Quote is from Barbara Fried's *The Middle-Age Crisis* (1967—out of print).

5 The Vaillant and McArthur paper (November 1972), to which I referred in earlier chapter notes, presents an overview of the Grant Study, pp. 415–427.

6 Harriet Zuckerman's study of "Nobel Laureates in Science: Patterns of Productivity, Collaboration and Authorship," appeared in *American Sociological Review* 32 (1967), pp. 391–403.

7 Quote taken from the Bardwick study (1974), p. 93.

8 The book-length study of superachieving men is *Sex and the Significant Americans* (1965) by John F. Cuber and Peggy B. Harroff. For abundant case histories, see also *Victims of Success* by psychiatrist Benjamin B. Wolman.

9 Ten of the men I studied fit clearly into the wunderkind pattern. All of them suffered confusion and depression and some felt wrath at the world when, having worked so hard to bring their original dreams to fruition, they shook the golden bough expecting to be showered in personal gratification and heard the rattle of the gourd. Such a direct and painful confrontation with the darkness of the mid-life transition motivated some of them to move toward the more highly developed stage of renewal, which many people never reach. One man who admittedly denied himself a crisis grew narrower as he entered his fifties and is now contemptuous of his job, his family, and himself. The others are still in transition.

10 Shana Alexander's observation appeared in her article "Korff's Last Tape," *Newsweek*, September 30, 1974, p. 108.

11 Dr. Willard Gaylin's description of sociopathic and paranoid personalities extracted from his article "What's Normal?," *The New York Times Magazine* April 1, 1973.

12 Bardwick (1974), pp. 88–93.

13 Statistics provided by Arthur Norton at the U.S. Dept. of Commerce.

14 The comparison of mental health profiles for married men and married women, and for single women compared with wives, which appear in Dr. Bernard's book, *The Future of Marriage* (1972), are based on tables compiled by the National Center for Health Statistics in *Selected Symptoms of Psychological Distress*, U.S. Dept. of Health, Education, and Welfare (1970), table 17, pp. 30–31. See also Genevieve Knupfer, Walter Clark, and Robin Room, "The Mental Health of the Unmarried," *American Journal of Psychiatry* 122 (February 1966).

15 For the psychological comparisons between never-married men and never-married women, see *Americans View Their Mental Health* (1960) by Gerald Gurin, Joseph Veroff, and Shelia Feld, pp. 42, 72, 110, 190, 234–235. The socioeconomic comparisons are taken from U.S. census figures (1970) in *Marital Status*, tables 4, 5, and 6. The symptoms of distress are matched in mental health statistics compiled by HEW in *Selected Symptoms of Psychological Distress* (1970), table 17, pp. 30–31.

16 Robert E. Samples's work, described in "Learning with the Whole Brain," *Human Behavior* (February 1975), pp. 16–23, provided the basis for discussion of the two cerebral hemispheres.

17 Quote from Samples (February 1975).

CHAPTER 16 WOMEN'S LIFE PATTERNS

Pages 293 through 347

1 Virginia Slims commissioned The Roper Organization in 1974 to poll women's attitudes on love, marriage, divorce, sex roles and stereotypes, the working wife, etc. Available from Ruder and Finn, 110 E. 59 St., New York, N.Y.

2 Studies done by Social Research, Inc., from the 1940s to as late as 1965 showed that the life of the blue-collar wife "was captive to the triangle of husband, children and home." The sweeping changes in her attitude reflected in more recent studies were reported by Dr. Burleigh B. Gardner in "The Awakening of the Blue Collar Woman," which appeared in *Intellectual Digest* (March 1974), pp. 17–19.

3 Quotes from *The Total Woman* by Marabel Morgan (1973), pp. 61, 70, 87, 117, 127, 167.

4 Morgan (1973), pp. 24–25.

5 Twentieth Reunion Book is titled *Radcliffe 1954 in 1974.*

6 Betty Freidan made her admission in an article titled "Up from the Kitchen Floor" for *The New York Times Magazine,* March 4, 1973, p. 28.

7 From time to time, economists try to estimate the dollar value of a full-time wife's services. Inflation and new minimum-wage laws render the figures obsolete within a year. An estimate made by the Chase Manhattan Bank in 1972 placed the housewife's economic value at $257.53 a week or $13,391.56 a year. Those figures were quickly outmoded by the 6 percent annual increase in wages, but more importantly, the bank left out many of the jobs done by wives. In March 1974, *Potomac* magazine of *The Washington Post* asked housewives with two children—one in school and one pre-school—to figure out how they spend an average week. The jobs listed by the wives were food buyer, nurse, tutor, waitress, seamstress, maintenance worker, lover, nanny, cleaning woman, cook, housekeeper, laundress, chauffeur, gardener, psychological counselor, errand runner, bookkeeper, interior decorator, caterer, veterinarian. The editors priced the same services on the open market and arrived at a grand total of $793.60 a week.

Only 2 percent of widows collect a private pension, as reported by William V. Shannon in *The New York Times,* September 9, 1974.

8 Data collected by the U.S. Dept. of Health, Education, and Welfare appear in *Selected Symptoms of Psychological Distress* (1970).

9 For mothers born after 1930, the median age at which they have given birth to their last child is 30. See Arthur J. Norton's paper, "The Family Life Cycle Updated" for Bureau of the Census, U.S. Dept. of Commerce, which appears in *Selected Studies in Marriage and the Family* (March 1974), 9th edition.

10 Study done on women achievers selected at random from several editions of *Who's Who of American Women* was by Dr. M. Elizabeth Tidball, Professor of Physiology at George Washington Medical Center. Reported in *The Executive Woman* (February 1975).

11 The achieving woman who defers nurturing is a pattern championed by sociologist Jessie Bernard, who points to evidence that the marriage rate is lowest among young women with the better jobs and higher salaries. "These facts suggest to me that young women often marry as the only thing they feel they can do," writes Bernard in *The Future of Marriage* (1972).

12 Bureau of the Census provided me with the figures comparing women's earnings with earnings of the total population. From *Current Population Reports*, Series P-60, no. 97, table 64.

13 Survey was done by the New York consulting firm Spence Stuart and Assoc. and reported in *The Executive Woman* (January 1975).

14 Dr. Hennig's doctoral thesis is titled "Career Development for Women Executives" (1970).

15 Dr. Ramey, Professor of Physiology and Biophysics at Georgetown University School of Medicine, made this trenchant remark at the close of a paper, "A Feminist Talks to Men," which appeared in *Johns Hopkins Magazine* (September 1973).

16 This quote taken from *Blackberry Winter: My Earlier Years* by Margaret Mead, pp. 99–100. Except where noted, all the other quotes in this section are from personal interviews with Dr. Mead.

17 Mead (1972), p. 164.

18 Mead (1972), p. 240.

19 Mead (1972), p. 263.

20 This idea was expressed in an unpublished manuscript by Dr. Levinson, "Toward a Conception of Adult Development."

21 From an article on *The New York Times* Op Ed page by Consuelo Saer Bahr titled "Blondie, Dagwood, Jiggs, Maggie, and Us," August 24, 1974.

22 Repeat of studies cited in note 14 for Chapter 15.

23 From an introduction by Louise Bernikow to *The World Split Open: Four Centuries of Women Poets in England and America, 1552–1950* (1974), p. 14.

CHAPTER 17   SETTING OFF ON THE MIDLIFE PASSAGE

Most helpful to me in synthesizing the many aspects of the midlife period were personal interviews with research scientists Bernice L. Neugarten at the University of Chicago, Roger Gould at the University of California at Los Angeles, Daniel Levinson at Yale University, Marylou Lionells and Carola Mann at the William Alanson White Institute in New York, and writer Barbara Fried. A primary written source is Jung, the first important analytic thinker to conceptualize personality changes in the second half of life (and the only one who distinguishes between the age at their onset in men and women). References to the work of Elliott Jaques (an American psychoanalyst now practicing in London) throughout this and the next chapter are from his paper "Death and the Mid-Life Crisis." Jaques's analysis of creative genius and interpretation of midlife processes has become a classic in the field. Also useful are some of the findings in Kenneth Soddy's book, *Men in Middle Life.*

Pages 350 through 364

1 From an interview with Bernice Neugarten. Amplified in "The Awareness of Middle Age," *Middle Age and Aging* (1968), pp. 93–98.

2 Fried (1967).

3 Source is U.S. Public Health Service, table on Expectation of Life in America (based on 1968 data).

4 Quote from Terkel, *Working* (1972), p. xviii.

5 Jung, Jaques, and Levinson make the strongest case for the inevitability of personality change.

6 A 1973 report by the Dept. of Health, Education, and Welfare on "Work in America" indicates that some executives would suffer fatal consequences rather than face a reduced image of themselves: "A general feeling of obsolescence appears to overtake middle managers when they reach their late thirties. Their careers appear to have reached a plateau, and they realize that life from here on will be a long and inevitable decline. There is a marked increase in the death rate between the ages of 35 to 40 for employed men, apparently as a result of this 'midlife crisis'. . . ."

7 Psychiatrist Roger Gould was particularly helpful in formulating the ideas about subjective changes in self and object

representations during the midlife period. Psychoanalyst
Judd Marmor also describes midlife crisis as a developmental
stage, the central theme of which is a separation loss involving the giving up of fantasy hopes of youth and a
confrontation with personal mortality. In a paper read before
the annual meeting of the American Orthopsychiatric Association in March 1967, Marmor cited four modes of coping
with midlife crisis: denial by escape in frantic activity; denial by overcompensation (as in sexual escapades); de-
compensation, including anxiety, depression, and diffuse
rage; or integration at a higher level with less narcissistic
self-involvement.

8 Quote from *The Velveteen Rabbit* by Margery Williams,
Doubleday (1958).

9 Jaques (1965) discusses the "grief work" of midlife and the
return to the infantile depressive position. This mourning
for our lost illusions and innocence is what gives the crisis
of midlife its depressive quality.

10 From an interview with Dr. Levinson.

CHAPTER 18   YOU ARE IN GOOD COMPANY

Pages 365 through 375

1 I have drawn biographical details and some interpretation
of Dante's life partially from George P. Elliott's essay in
Brief Lives (1965), pp. 200–202.

2 This quote from Michael Harrington and those that follow
are from his article, "Notes on My Nervous Breakdown,"
adapted from his book, *Fragments of the Century*, for
New York, September 24, 1973, pp. 49–56.

3 All of the material from Jaques drawn from his paper
"Death and the Mid-Life Crisis" (1965).

4 Jaques (1965).

5 Jaques (1965) quoting Gitting's biography of Keats.

6 Fitzgerald (1945).

7 Jaques (1965).

8 Psychiatrists Marylou Lionells and Carola H. Mann pro-
filed junior and senior analysts in their paper on "Patterns
of Mid-Life in Transition." Their research raises the question of whether closer age matching of doctor and patient
might be a prerequisite for effective therapy at these life
stages.

NO.

NOTES AND SOURCES

9 Bernice Neugarten reported this class difference in perception of the life cycle in her paper on "The Middle Years" (March 1972), p. 3.
10 Quote from Neugarten (1968), p. 93.
11 The reason that most 40-year-olds are unwilling to identify themselves with middle age was suggested by Fried (1967).

CHAPTER 19 THE AGE 35 SURVEY

Pages 376 through 393

1 All quotes from Eleanor Roosevelt's diaries appear in *Eleanor and Franklin*, by Joseph P. Lash (1971).
2 See Sears and Feldman, *The Seven Ages of Man* (1973); Linda Wolfe, *Playing Around* (1975); Cuber and Harroff, *Sex and the Significant Americans* (1965); and Morton Hunt's survey for *Playboy* (1975).
3 U. S. census figures reported in the Dept. of Labor's *Occupational Quarterly* (Spring 1973) by Gloria Stevenson. In October 1972, for example, 51.3 percent of all women ages 35 to 39 were working or looking for jobs, as were 54.5 percent of women from 40 to 44, and 55.7 percent of women from 45 to 49.
4 Conclusion about women working to help make ends meet from a 1969 nationwide survey by the University of Michigan's Institute for Social Research.
5 The Bureau of the Census lists 250 different occupations, but half of all working women are employed in only 21 of them, usually the low-pay, low-responsibility jobs.
6 The fact that as of 1972, only 10 percent of women 30 to 44 years old had graduated from college is from a U.S. Dept. of Commerce paper by Larry E. Suter titled "Occupation, Employment, and Lifetime Work Experience of Women" (1973), p. 5. Younger women present a far-brighter educational picture. Eighteen percent of women 20 to 24 years old had completed some college in 1957, compared with 34 percent in 1972.
7 The fact that three-quarters of all the women who work either have no husband or one whose income falls below $7,000 a year was published in 1973 by the U.S. Census Bureau.
8 The blue-collar woman quoted is Barbara Mikulski, Baltimore city councilwoman, in her introduction to the excellent pamphlet by Nancy Seifer, "Absent from the Majority" (1973).

535

9 See "Occupation, Employment, and Lifetime Work Experience of Women" by Larry E. Suter for the U.S. Dept. of Commerce, based on the 1967 National Longitudinal Study of Women which measured the cumulative effects of discontinuous work experience on women 30 to 44 years old.
Statistics on the work reentry prospects for women over 30 are from a study by Ohio State University for the Labor Department's Manpower Administration (1973).

10 The average age at remarriage for women is drawn from statistics presented by Norton in "The Family Life Cycle Updated" (1974).

11 Irma Kurtz's account of her late love for motherhood appeared in *Nova* (April 1973), p. 49.

12 Extracted from Kurtz (April 1973).

13 From Novak's *Textbook of Gynecology* (1970), p. 397. Among other sources consulted for the section on childbearing after 35 were Dr. Kurt Hirschhorn, Director of the Division of Medical Genetics at Mount Sinai Hospital; Dr. Raymond L. Vande Wiele, Professor and Chairman of the Department of Obstetrics and Gynecology at Columbia Presbyterian Medical Center; Dr. Len Schoenberg, Medical Director for Planned Parenthood; an analysis of 3,100 infant deaths done by National Foundation March of Dimes in *Perinatal Health: Challenge to Medicine and Society;* "The Elderly Primigravida" by Ian Morrison, M.D. in *American Journal of Obstetrics and Gynecology* (March 1, 1975), pp. 465–469; and "Antenatal Diagnosis of Genetic Disease," by T. A. Doran in *American Journal of Obstetrics and Gynecology* (February 1, 1974), pp. 314–321.

CHAPTER 20   THE AGE 40 CRUCIBLE

Pages 394 through 412

1 See *The Portable Jung* (1971), pp. 12–13.

2 Quote from *Man and Superman*, Act IV, by George Bernard Shaw.

3 Survey by the American Management Association, "The Changing Success Ethic," was reported in "Why a Second Career?" by Richard J. Leider for *The Personnel Administrator* (March–April 1974).

CHAPTER 21   SWITCH-40S AND THE COUPLE

Pages 413 through 439

1 Quote from *The Psychology of C. G. Jung* (1973 edition) by Jacobi.

2 Quote from Fitzgerald (1945).

3 Quote from William Gibson's *A Season in Heaven* (1974).

4 According to Margaret Mead, and based on unpublished case material collected with Geoffrey Gore, there is often a spurt of creativity when a woman knows she won't have children (whether because of an untimely hysterectomy or because she has deliberately had her tubes tied or because of natural menopause).

In a study of the "Transition to the Empty Nest: Crisis, Challenge, or Relief?" (1972), Lowenthal and Chiriboga examined intensively a sample of 54 middle- and lower-middle-class men and women whose youngest child was about to leave home. Contrary to the stereotype, the researchers concluded that both the men and women "look forward to establishing a somewhat less complex life-style, and the anticipatory relaxing or re-orienting of child-rearing goals affects their morale only favorably."

5 See Jung (1973), Marmor (1967), and Gould (1972).

6 Dr. Paul Glick of the Bureau of the Census, Dept. of Commerce, confirmed in an interview that there does not seem to be a bump in the divorce rate during the midlife period. It continues a steady decline from the peak in the late twenties and early thirties.

CHAPTER 22   THE SEXUAL DIAMOND

Pages 440 through 464

1 Quote is from *Human Sexual Inadequacy* (1970). I have used this Masters and Johnson volume as one of the basic resources for the chapter. Other important sources consulted were: *Fundamentals of Human Sexuality* by Katchadourian and Lunde (1972); *The Nature and Evolution of Female Sexuality* by Dr. Mary Jane Sherfey (1972); *The Male Climacteric* by Ruebsaat and Hull (1975); *The Psychology of Sex Differences* by Maccoby and Jacklin (1974); *An Analysis of Human Sexual Response* by Ruth and Ed-

ward Brecher (1966); *Sex in Later Life* by Dr. Ivor Felstein (1970); and "Human Sexual Behavior" from the *Encyclopaedia Britannica* (1974).

Most helpful to me both in interpreting printed material and in developing my ideas were Dr. Estelle Ramey, physiologist at Georgetown University School of Medicine; Dr. Ray Birdwhistell, anthropologist and Professor of Communications at the Annenberg School of the University of Pennsylvania; and Dr. David Marcotte of the Kinsey Institute.

2 Facts cited from Masters and Johnson (1970) and the *Encyclopaedia Britannica* (1974).

3 Masters and Johnson (1970).

4 Although little noted by biologists, as Dr. Sherfey points out, the "innate femaleness of mammalian embryos [was] a startling discovery [firmly established by 1958] which overturns centuries of mythology and years of scientific theory." From *The Nature and Evolution of Female Sexuality* (1972), pp. 37–53. In the 1974 edition of the *Britannica* the explanation is as follows: "If the embryo has a Y-chromosome, the gonads become testicles; otherwise, they become ovaries. The testicles of the fetus produce androgens and these cause the fetus to develop male anatomy. Animal experiments show that, if the testicles of a male fetus are removed, the individual will develop into what seems a female (although lacking ovaries). Consequently, it has been said that humans are basically female," p. 595.

5 Sixty-seven percent of all births are in the twenties; 17 percent at ages 15 to 19; 10 percent at ages 30 to 34; and 6 percent over age 35. From my reading of the 1970 birthrate statistics, National Center for Health Statistics: *Monthly Vital Statistics Report* (March 1974).

6 Quote from Katchadourian (1972), p. 183.

7 See Sherfey (1972), pp. 133–134.

8 From an interview with Dr. Birdwhistell.

9 The newborn in 1971 had a life expectancy for males of 67.4 and for females of 74.8. At age 1 this becomes 68.9 for males and 76.1 for females. With each year survived, there is some increment in life expectancy. For instance, in 1971 a man aged 40 might expect to live into his 72d year; a woman the same age could add 6 years to that. This

holds true for ages 34 through 41. By age 42 the man might expect to complete his 72d year, and at 43 the woman her 78th year. *Life Tables*, vol. 2, section 5, National Center for Health Statistics (1971).

10 Quote from "What Is the New Impotence, and Who's Got It?" by Philip Nobile, *Esquire* (October 1974), pp. 95–98.

11 Quote from Kinsey (1948).

12 See Katchadourian (1972), p. 183.

13 Some of the studies by Dr. Rose were reported in "I.S. Plasma Testosterone Levels in the Male Rhesus: Influences of Sexual and Social Stimuli." *Science* (1972), by Rose, Holaday, and Bernstein.

14 Quote from an interview with Dr. Ramey.

15 Quote from Katchadourian and Lunde (1972).

16 Jakobovits reported the average age of 53.7 years from a study done by Heller and Myers (1944); and two by Werner (1945, 1946). For details, see Dr. Jakobovits's article for *Fertility and Sterility* (January 1970) on "The Treatment of Impotence with Methyltestosterone Thyroid," pp. 32–35.

17 Ruebsaat and Hull (1975) in *The Male Climacteric*. The symptoms described in the text are compiled from this book and the Jakobovits paper (1970).

18 Quote from Hull's introduction to *The Male Climacteric* (1975).

19 Quote from Ruebsaat (1975).

20 From "Letters" column in *The New York Times Magazine*, January 28, 1973.

21 From Jakobovits (1970).

22 From a talk given by Masters and Johnson at Harvard Business School (May 1974).

23 See Lionells and Mann (1974) and Katchadourian and Lunde (1972). The actual term "postmenopausal zest" is Margaret Mead's.

CHAPTER 23   LIVING OUT THE FANTASY

Pages 465 through 481

1 Quote from Art Sidenbaum's column in the *Los Angeles Times*, September 26, 1973.

Pages 496 through 514

1 Estimate from "Generation in the Middle," Report by Blue Cross, vol. 23, no. 1 (1970), p. 11.

2 From an investigation by Neugarten of 100 men and women (1968), p. 97.

3 In 1850, the American man and woman both had a life expectancy of 40. By the year 1900, she had for the first time exceeded the life expectancy for the American man and lived an average of 2 years longer, 48 to his 46. Women today live an average of 6 years longer than men, and one out of every six women in this country over the age of 21 is a widow. While more than seven-tenths of the men over 65 are married, only three-tenths of the women that age have husbands. They are alone. (If present trends continue, there may be 40 percent more women than men in the United States by the year 2000.) Women's concern over the body-monitoring of their husbands is well-founded in the statistics.

The distinctions between age cues taken by men and women in the middle years are from Neugarten (1968), p. 96.

4 From a report by the Committee on Work and Personality in the Course of the Life Span" (1968), pp. 74–84.

5 From Frenkel-Brunswik in "Adjustments and Reorientations in the Course of the Life Span" (1968), pp. 74–84.

6 From the Lionells and Mann paper (1974).

7 Discussed in Soddy's *Men in Middle Life* (1967), p. 84.

8 From Soddy (1967).

9 See Brim's summary of studies (1968), Roger Gould (1972), Neugarten (1968), and Deutscher (1959).

10 Source is the U.S. Public Health Service: Only 1 percent of all initial marriages in the nation involve middle-aged people, but 26 percent of those who remarry are middle-aged.

11 The salient characteristics of the middle years were reported by Norma Haan from the Berkeley Growth and Development Studies (November 1972). See also Neugarten's paper in *Journal of Geriatric Psychology* (1970) and the Lionells and Mann paper (1974).

12 Quote from Florida Scott-Maxwell's *The Measure of My Days* (1968).

BIBLIOGRAPHY

BARDWICK, JUDITH. 1974. "The Dynamics of Successful People," *New Research on Women*. Ann Arbor; University of Michigan.

BEISER, MORTON. 1965. "Poverty, Social Disintegration and Personality." *Journal of Social Issues* 21(1).

BERNARD, JESSIE. 1972. *The Sex Game*. New York: Atheneum.
———. 1972. *The Future of Marriage*. New York: Bantam edition 1973.

BERNIKOW, LOUISE (ed.). 1974. *The World Split Open: Four Centuries of Women Poets in England and America, 1552–1952*. New York: Vintage Books.

BETTELHEIM, BRUNO. 1943. "Individual and Mass Behavior in Extreme Situations." *Journal of Abnormal and Social Psychology*.

BLANCK, RUBIN AND GERTRUDE. 1968. *Marriage and Personal Development*. New York: Columbia University Press.

BLECHER, GEORGE. 1972. "The Death of the Russian Novel." *New American Review 14*. New York: Simon & Schuster.

BLOCK, JACK, AND HAAN, NORMA. 1971. *Lives Through Time*. Berkeley, Calif.: Bancroft Books.

BLOS, PETER. 1962. *On Adolescence: A Psychoanalytic Interpretation*. New York: The Free Press.
———. 1967. "The Second Individuation Process of Adolescence." From *Psychoanalytic Study of the Child*.

BOWLBY, JOHN. 1973. *Separation*. New York: Basic Books.

BRECHER, RUTH AND EDWARD. 1966. *An Analysis of Human Sexual Response*. New York: New American Library, a Signet book.

BRIM, O. G., JR. 1968. "Adult Socialization." In *Socialization and Society*. J. A. Clausen (ed.). Boston: Little, Brown.

BUHLER, CHARLOTTE, AND MASSARIK, FRED (eds.). 1968. *The Course of Human Life*. New York: Springer.

CARO, ROBERT A. 1974. *The Power Broker*. New York: Alfred A. Knopf.

COLES, ROBERT. 1970. *Erik H. Erikson: The Growth of His Work*. Boston: Little, Brown.

BIBLIOGRAPHY

COMMITTEE ON WORK AND PERSONALITY IN THE MIDDLE YEARS. June 1973. New York: Social Science Research Council. Mimeograph.

CONSTANTINOPLE, ANNE. 1969. "An Eriksonian Measure of Personality Development in College Students." *Developmental Psychology* 1(4).

CUBER, JOHN F., AND HARROFF, PEGGY B. 1965. *Sex and the Significant Americans.* Pelican Book.

DANTE ALIGHIERI. Circa 1300. *Divine Comedy.* Translated by John Aitken Carlyle. New York: *The Temple Classics.*

DEUTSCHER, I. 1959. *Married Life in the Middle Years.* Kansas City: Community Studies.

DONOVAN, JAMES M. 1975. "Identity Status and Interpersonal Style and Object Relatedness." Basis for article in *The Journal of Youth and Adolescence.*

EPSTEIN, JOSEPH. 1974. *Divorced in America.* New York: E. P. Dutton.

ERIKSON, ERIK H. 1950. *Childhood and Society.* New York: W. W. Norton.

———. 1964. *Insight and Responsibility.* New York: W. W. Norton.

———. 1964. "The Golden Rule and the Cycle of Life." A George W. Gay Lecture, Harvard Medical School, May 4, 1962. Erikson's lecture was published as an essay in *The Study of Lives.* Robert W. White (ed.). New York: Atherton Press.

———. 1968. *Identity, Youth and Crisis.* New York: W. W. Norton.

———. 1974. "Once More the Inner Space: Letter to a Former Student." *Women & Analysis.* New York: Grossman.

———. 1975. *Life History and the Historical Moment.* New York: W. W. Norton.

FELSTEIN, IVOR. 1970. *Sex in Later Life.* Baltimore: Penguin Books.

FERGUSON, MARY ANNE. 1973. *Images of Women in Literature.* Boston: Houghton Mifflin.

FITZGERALD, F. SCOTT. 1945. *The Crackup.* New York: J. Laughlin.

FRENKEL-BRUNSWIK, ELSE. 1968. "Adjustments and Reorientations in the Course of the Life Span." In *Middle Age and Aging.* Bernice Neugarten (ed.). Chicago: University of Chicago Press.

———. 1974. *Frenkel-Brunswik, Else: Selected Papers.* Nanette Heiman and Joan Grant (eds.). New York: International

Universities Press. (Published as Monograph 31 for *Psychological Issues*.)

FREUD, S. 1955. Case Studies (1893, 1895), in *Complete Psychological Works*, Standard ed., vol. 2. James Strachey (ed.). London: Hogarth Press.

————. 1962. (originally published in 1930). *Civilization and Its Discontents*. James Strachey (ed.). New York: W. W. Norton.

FRIED, BARBARA. 1967. *The Middle-Age Crisis*. New York: Harper & Row.

FRIEDAN, BETTY. 1962. *The Feminine Mystique*. New York: Dell.

————. March 4, 1973. "Up from the Kitchen Floor." *The New York Times Magazine*.

GARDNER, BURLEIGH B. March 1974. "The Awakening of the Blue Collar Woman." *Intellectual Digest*.

GAYLIN, WILLARD. April 1, 1973. "What's Normal?" *The New York Times Magazine*.

GESELL INSTITUTE OF CHILD DEVELOPMENT. 1955. *Child Behavior*. Ilg, Francis L., and Ames, Louise Bates. New York: Dell.

GLICK, PAUL, AND NORTON, ARTHUR. 1972. "Perspectives on the Recent Upturn in Divorce and Remarriage." Bureau of the Census, U.S. Dept. of Commerce.

GLICK, PAUL C. "The Life Cycle of the Family." U.S. Bureau of the Census. (Updated report in preparation at time of writing.)

GOULD, ROGER. November 1972. "The Phases of Adult Life: A Study in Developmental Psychology." *American Journal of Psychiatry*.

GURIN, GERALD; VEROFF, JOSEPH; FELD, SHEILA. 1960. *Americans View Their Mental Health*. New York: Basic Books.

HAAN, NORMA. November 1972. "Personality Development from Adolescence to Adulthood in the Oakland Growth and Guidance Studies." *Seminars in Psychiatry* 4(4).

HARRINGTON, MICHAEL. 1973. *Fragments of the Century*. New York: Saturday Review Press.

HELLER, JOSEPH. 1974. *Something Happened*. New York: Alfred A. Knopf.

HELLMAN, LOUIS M., AND PRITCHARD, JACK A. 1971. *Williams Obstetrics*. New York: Appleton-Century-Crofts.

HENNIG, MARGARET. 1970. "Career Development for Women Executives." Doctoral dissertation for Graduate School of Business Administration, at Harvard University. Basis for 1977. Women & Management, coauthor Anne Jardim. New York: Doubleday.

HORNER, MATINA. 1968. "Sex Differences in Achievement Motivation and Performance in Competitive and Non-Competitive Situations." Unpublished doctoral dissertation for the University of Minnesota.

HORNEY, KAREN. 1974. "The Flight from Womanhood: The Masculinity Complex in Women as Viewed by Men and by Women (1926)." In *Women & Analysis*. Jean Strouse (ed.). New York: Grossman.

HUBER, JOAN (ed.). 1973. *Changing Women in a Changing Society*. Chicago: University of Chicago.

JACOBSON, EDITH. 1964. *The Self and the Object World*. Journal of the American Psychoanalytic Association, Monograph Series Number Two. New York: International Universities Press.

JACOBI, JOLANDE. 1973 edition. *The Psychology of C. G. Jung*. New Haven: Yale University Press.

JANEWAY, ELIZABETH, 1971. *Man's World, Woman's Place*. New York: Delta.

———. 1975. *Between Myth and Morning: Women Awakening*. New York: William Morrow.

JAQUES, ELLIOTT. 1965. "Death and the Mid-Life Crisis." *International Journal of Psychoanalysis* 46.

———. 1965. "Is There a Male Menopause?" *The New York Times Magazine*.

JUNG, C. G. 1957. *The Undiscovered Self*. New York: Mentor Books.

———. 1963. *Memories, Dreams, Reflections*. (autobiography) New York: Pantheon.

———. 1971. *The Portable Jung*. Joseph Campbell (ed.). R. F. C. Hull (tr.). New York: Viking Press.

KATCHADOURIAN, HERANT; AND LUNDE. 1972. *Fundamentals of Human Sexuality*. New York: Holt, Rinehart and Winston.

KEATS, JOHN. 1970. *You Might as Well Live: The Life and Times of Dorothy Parker*. New York: Simon & Schuster.

KING, STANLEY, H. November 1972. "Coping and Growth in Adolescence." *Seminars in Psychiatry* 4(4).

KINSEY, A. C.; POMEROY, W. B.; AND MARTIN, C. E. 1948. *Sexual Behavior in the Human Male*. Philadelphia: W. B. Saunders.

KNUPFER, GENEVIEVE; CLARK, WALTER; AND ROOM, ROBIN. February 1966. "The Mental Health of the Unmarried." *American Journal of Psychiatry*.

KOMAROVSKY, MIRRA. 1962. *Blue-Collar Marriage*. New York: Vintage Books edition, February 1967.

————. 1973. "Cultural Contradictions and Sex Roles: The Masculine Case." In *Changing Women in a Changing Society*. Chicago: University of Chicago.

KOSINSKI, JERZY. 1965. *The Painted Bird*. Boston. Houghton Mifflin.

KRONENBERGER, LOUIS (ed.). 1965. *Brief Lives*. Boston: Atlantic Monthly Press.

LASH, JOSEPH P. 1971. *Eleanor and Franklin*. New York: W. W. Norton.

LEDERER, WILLIAM J., AND JACKSON, DR. DON D. 1968. *The Mirages of Marriage*. New York: W. W. Norton.

LE SHAN, EDA. 1973. *The Wonderful Crisis of Middle Age*. New York: David McKay.

LEVINSON, DANIEL J., CHARLOTTE M. DARROW, EDWARD B. KLEIN, MARIA H. LEVINSON, AND BRAXTON MCKEE. 1974. In *Life History Research in Psychopathology*, Volume 3, edited by David F. Ricks, Alexander Thomas, and Merrill Roff. Minneapolis: University of Minnesota Press.

————. 1973. "Toward a Conception of Adult Development." In Progress.

LIONELLS, MARYLOU, AND MANN, CAROLA H. 1974. "Patterns of Mid-Life in Transition." New York: 26-page monograph from William Alanson White Institute.

LOWENTHAL, MARJORIE FISKE, AND CHIRIBOGA, DAVID. January 1972. "Transition to the Empty Nest." *Archives of General Psychiatry 26*.

MACCOBY, E. E., AND JACKLIN, C. N. 1974. *The Psychology of Sex Differences*. Stanford, Calif.: Stanford University Press.

MAHLER, M. S. 1953. "On the Significance of the Normal Separation-Individuation Phase." In *Drives, Affects and Behavior*, II. M. Schur (ed.) New York: International Universities Press.

————. 1963. "Certain Aspects of the Separation Individuation Phase," *Psychoanalytic Quarterly 32*.

MARCIA, J. E. 1966. "Development and Validations of Ego-Identity Status." *Journal of Personality and Social Psychology*.

MARMOR, JUDD. 1974. *Psychiatry in Transition*. New York: Bruner/Mazel.

MASLOW, ABRAHAM H. 1954. *Motivation and Personality*, 2d ed. New York: Harper & Row.

————. 1968. *Toward A Psychology of Being*. New York: D. Van Nostrand.

MASTERS, WILLIAM H., AND JOHNSON, VIRGINIA E. 1970. *Human Sexual Inadequacy*. Boston: Little, Brown.

MEAD, MARGARET. 1972. *Blackberry Winter: My Earlier Years*. New York: William Morrow.

————. 1974. "On Freud's View of Female Psychology." In *Women & Analysis*. Jean Strouse (ed.). New York: Grossman.

MILLETT, KATE. 1974. *Flying*. New York: Alfred A. Knopf.

MITCHELL, JULIET. 1974. *Psychoanalysis and Feminism*. New York: Pantheon Books.

————. 1974. "On Freud and the Distinction Between the Sexes." In *Women and Analysis*. Jean Strouse (ed.). New York: Grossman.

MORGAN, MARABEL. 1973. *The Total Woman*. Old Tappan, N.J.: Fleming H. Revell.

NEUGARTEN, BERNICE L. (ed.). 1968. *Middle Age and Aging*. Chicago: University of Chicago Press.

————. 1970. "Dynamics of Transition of Middle Age to Old Age." *Journal of Geriatric Psychiatry* 4(1).

NEUGARTEN, B. L., AND DOWTY, N. (S. Arieti, ed.) March 1972. "The Middle Years." *American Handbook of Psychiatry* 1, pt. 3.

NORTON, ARTHUR. March 1973. "Marital Status and Living Arrangements." Washington, D.C.: U.S. Government Printing Office, U.S. Dept. of Commerce.

————. 1974. "The Family Life Cycle Updated." *Selected Studies in Marriage and the Family*, 9th ed. Robert F. Winch and Graham B. Spanier (eds.). New York: Holt, Rinehart and Winston.

PARKER, RICHARD. 1972. *The Myth of The Middle Class*. New York: Liveright.

PASCAL, JOHN AND FRANCINE. 1974. *The Strange Case of Patty Hearst*. New York: New American Library.

PRESSEY, SIDNEY L., AND KUHLEN, RAYMOND G. 1957. *Psychological Development Through the Life Span*. New York: Harper & Row.

PYNCHON, THOMAS. 1974. *Gravity's Rainbow*. New York: Bantam.

RAMEY, ESTELLE. September 1973. "A Feminist Talks to Men." *Johns Hopkins Magazine*.

RIESMAN, DAVID. 1950. *The Lonely Crowd*. New York: Doubleday Anchor 1955 edition (by arrangement with Yale University Press).

ROCHLIN, GREGORY. 1973. *Man's Aggression*. Boston: Gambit.

ROTHSTEIN, STANLEY H. 1967. "Aging Awareness and Personalization of Death in the Young and Middle Adult Years." Unpublished doctoral dissertation for the University of Chicago.

RUEBSAAT, HELMUT J., AND HULL, RAYMOND. 1975. *The Male Climacteric*. New York: Hawthorn Books.

RUSSELL, BERTRAND. 1951. *The Autobiography of Bertrand Russell.* Boston: Little, Brown in association with the Atlantic Monthly Press.

SAMPLES, ROBERT. February 1975. "Learning with the Whole Brain." *Human Behavior.*

SAXE, LOUIS P., AND GERSON, NOEL. 1964. *Sex and the Mature Man.* New York: Pocket Books.

SCARPITTI, FRANK R. 1974. *Social Problems.* New York: Holt, Rinehart and Winston.

SCHACTER, BURT. 1968. "Identity Crisis and Occupational Processes: An Intensive Exploratory Study of Emotionally Disturbed Male Adolescents." *Child Welfare* 47 (1).

SCHAFER, ROY. 1968. *Aspects of Internalization.* New York: International Universities Press.

SCHEINGOLD, LEE D., AND WAGNER, NATHANIEL N. 1974. *Sex and the Aging Heart.* New York: Pyramid, 1975 edition.

SCOTT-MAXWELL, FLORIDA. 1968. *The Measure of My Days.* New York: Alfred A. Knopf.

SEARS, ROBERT R., AND FELDMAN, S. SHIRLEY (eds.). 1973. *The Seven Ages of Man.* Los Altos, Calif.: William Kaufman.

SEIFER, NANCY. 1973. "Absent from the Majority." New York: National Project on Ethnic America of the American Jewish Committee.

SHEEHY, GAIL. February 19, 1973. "Can Couples Survive?" *New York* magazine.

————. February 18, 1974. "Catch-30 and Other Predictable Crises of Growing Up Adult." *New York* magazine.

————. April 29, 1974. "Mid-Life Crisis: Best Chance for Couples to Grow Up." *New York* magazine.

————. January 26, 1976. "The Sexual Diamond: Facing the Facts of the Male and Female Sexual Life Cycles." *New York* magazine.

SHERFEY, MARY JANE. 1972. *The Nature and Evolution of Female Sexuality.* New York: Random House.

SLATER, PHILIP. 1970. *The Pursuit of Loneliness.* Boston: Beacon Press.

————. 1974. *Earthwalk.* Garden City, N.Y.: Anchor Press/Doubleday.

SMITH, HUSTON. 1958. *The Religions of Man.* New York: Harper & Row.

SODDY, KENNETH, WITH KIDSON, MARY C. 1967. *Men in Middle Life.* Philadelphia: J. B. Lippincott.

STERN, RICHARD. 1973. *Other Men's Daughters.* New York: E. P. Dutton.

STROUSE, JEAN (ed.). 1974. *Women & Analysis.* New York: Grossman.

TERKEL, STUDS. 1972. *Working: People Talk About What They Do All Day and How They Feel About What They Do.* New York: Pantheon Books.

TOFFLER, ALVIN. 1971. *Future Shock.* New York: Bantam.

U.S. BUREAU OF THE CENSUS. 1972. *Current Population Reports,* Series P-20, no. 239, "Marriage, Divorce, and Remarriage by Year of Birth: June 1971," Washington, D.C.: U.S. Government Printing Office.

U.S. DEPT. OF COMMERCE, BUREAU OF THE CENSUS. 1973. "Age at First Marriage and Children Ever Born, for the United States: 1970."

———. 1973. "Occupation, Employment, and Lifetime Work Experience of Women." Paper by Larry E. Suter.

U.S. DEPT. OF HEALTH, EDUCATION, AND WELFARE. 1969. "Marriage Statistics, 1969" and "Births, Marriages, Divorces, and Deaths for 1973." *Vital Statistics Report.*

———. 1970. "Selected Symptoms of Psychological Distress." National Center for Health Statistics, Series 11, no. 37. Rockville, Md.

———. 1971. *Life Tables.* vol. 2, sec. 5. National Center for Health Statistics. Rockville, Md.

———. August 1973. "Teenagers: Marriages, Divorces, Parenthood, and Mortality." HEW Publication no. (HRA) 74-1901. Rockville, Md.

———. December 1973. "100 Years of Marriage and Divorce Statistics, United States, 1867–1967." HEW Publication no. (HRA) 74-1902. Rockville, Md.

———. 1973. "Work in America." National Center for Health Statistics. Rockville, Md.

VAILLANT, GEORGE E., AND MC ARTHUR, CHARLES C., November 1972. "Natural History of Male Psychologic Health. I. The Adult Life Cycle From 18–50." *Seminars in Psychiatry* 4(4).

WHITE, ROBERT W. 1972. *The Enterprise of Living.* New York: Holt, Rinehart and Winston.

WILLS, GARY. March 1974. "What? What? Are Young Americans Afraid to Have Kids?" *Esquire.*

WILSON, JAMES Q. July 1974. "Crime and the Criminologists." *Commentary.*

WOLFE, LINDA. 1975. *Playing Around.* New York: William Morrow.

WOLMAN, BENJAMIN B. 1973. *Victims of Success.* New York: Quadrangle/The New York Times Book Co.

ZUCKERMAN, HARRIET. 1957. "Nobel Laureates in Science: Patterns of Productivity, Collaboration, and Authorship." *American Sociological Review* 32.

INDEX

A

abortion, 102, 448–49
achievers who defer nurturing, 296, 321–28
Adams, Mrs. Henry, 376–77
Addams, Jane, 344
adolescence, studies of, 14, 159–60
adolescent crisis, identity and, 48–49
age range, of interviewees, 24, 145
age-role identity, 31–32
age 35, for women, 324–25, 377–78
age 40, for men, 45, 394–412, 419
aging:
    anticipation and fears of, 44–45, 155–56, 350–52, 355–57, 375, 455–56
    no-panic approach to, 500–1
Alcott, Louisa May, 343
Alexander, Shana, 276–77, 328
Alexander the Great, 273
alimony, 295, 313
aliveness, sense of, 30–31, 200–1, 253–54, 417–18
aloneness, 44, 488, 506–8
Amarcord, 172
American Graffiti, 94–95

American Management Association, middle manager survey of, 409
anonymity, of interviewees, 24–26
As You Like It, 18
athletes, wunderkinder as, 272–73
Austen, Jane, 343
authenticity, 192–93, 357–60
    meaning of, 48–49
    see also identity
authenticity crisis, 43–44, 350–52, 375
autonomy, 36–37, 48–49, 130
    aloneness and, 341–42

B

bad mother role, 238
Bahr, Consuelo Saer, 341
Bardwick, Judith, 278, 323
Bateson, Catherine, 336
Bateson, Gregory, 335–38, 338
Berkowitz, Bernard, 148
Bernard, Jessie, 286
Bernikow, Louise, 343
biographical method, 20–28, 251–52
Birdwhistell, Ray L., 212, 451, 453
bisexuality, 90, 99

ABOUT THE AUTHOR

Educated at the University of Vermont and Columbia University, GAIL SHEEHY received an Alicia Patterson Foundation Fellowship to study adult development. Her books (*Hustling*, *Panthermania*, etc.) and magazine articles for *New York*, *McCall's*, *The New York Times Magazine* have won major national awards, including the 1975 University of Missouri Magazine Award for articles developed from this book.

Bantam
On Psychology

☐	20138	**PASSAGES: Predictable Crises of Adult Life,** Gail Sheehy	$3.95
☐	20336	**PEACE FROM NERVOUS SUFFERING,** Claire Weekes	$2.75
☐	20540	**THE GESTALT APPROACH & EYE WITNESS TO THERAPY,** Fritz Perls	$3.50
☐	20220	**THE BOOK OF HOPE,** DeRosis & Pellegrino	$3.95
☐	20315	**THE PSYCHOLOGY OF SELF-ESTEEM: A New** Concept of Man's Psychological Nature, Nathaniel Branden	$3.50
☐	14936	**WHAT DO YOU SAY AFTER YOU SAY HELLO?** Eric Berne, M.D.	$3.50
☐	14201	**GESTALT THERAPY VERBATIM,** Fritz Perls	$2.75
☐	14480	**PSYCHO-CYBERNETICS AND SELF-FULFILLMENT,** Maxwell Maltz, M.D.	$2.75
☐	13518	**THE FIFTY-MINUTE HOUR,** Robert Lindner	$2.25
☐	14827	**THE DISOWNED SELF,** Nathaniel Branden	$2.95
☐	14940	**CUTTING LOOSE: An Adult Guide for Coming** to Terms With Your Parents, Howard Halpern	$2.75
☐	14372	**BEYOND FREEDOM AND DIGNITY,** B. F. Skinner	$3.50
☐	20066	**WHEN I SAY NO, I FEEL GUILTY,** Manuel Smith	$3.50
☐	20253	**IN AND OUT THE GARBAGE PAIL,** Fritz Perls	$2.95